FEAR OF SEEING

GLOBAL CHINESE CULTURE

GLOBAL CHINESE CULTURE

David Der-wei Wang, Editor

Robin Visser, *Questioning Borders: Eco-Literatures of China and Taiwan*

Cheow Thia Chan, *Malaysian Crossings: Place and Language in the Worlding of Modern Chinese Literature*

Michael Berry, ed., *The Musha Incident: A Reader on the Indigenous Uprising in Colonial Taiwan*

A-Chin Hsiau, *Politics and Cultural Nativism in 1970s Taiwan: Youth, Narrative, Nationalism*

Calvin Hui, *The Art of Useless: Fashion, Media, and Consumer Culture in Contemporary China*

Shengqing Wu, *Photo Poetics: Chinese Lyricism and Modern Media*

Sebastian Veg, *Minjian: The Rise of China's Grassroots Intellectuals*

Lily Wong, *Transpacific Attachments: Sex Work, Media Networks, and Affective Histories of Chineseness*

Michel Hockx, *Internet Literature in China*

Jie Li, *Shanghai Homes: Palimpsests of Private Life*

Andrea Bachner, *Beyond Sinology: Chinese Writing and the Scripts of Culture*

Shu-mei Shih, Chien-hsin Tsai, and Brian Bernards, editors, *Sinophone Studies: A Critical Reader*

Alexa Huang, *Chinese Shakespeares: A Century of Cultural Exchange*

Michael Berry, *A History of Pain: Literary and Cinematic Mappings of Violence in Modern China*

Sylvia Li-chun Lin, *Representing Atrocity in Taiwan: The 2/28 Incident and White Terror in Fiction and Film*

Michael Berry, *Speaking in Images: Interviews with Contemporary Chinese Filmmakers*

FEAR OF SEEING

A POETICS OF CHINESE
SCIENCE FICTION

MINGWEI SONG

Columbia University Press
New York

Columbia University Press wishes to express its appreciation for assistance given by the Chiang Ching-kuo Foundation for International Scholarly Exchange and the Council for Cultural Affairs in the publication of this series.

Columbia University Press
Publishers Since 1893
New York   Chichester, West Sussex
cup.columbia.edu
Copyright © 2023 Columbia University Press
All rights reserved

Library of Congress Cataloging-in-Publication Data
Names: Song, Mingwei, author.
Title: Fear of seeing : a poetics of Chinese science fiction / Mingwei Song.
Description: New York : Columbia University Press, 2023. | Series: Global Chinese culture | Includes bibliographical references and index.
Identifiers: LCCN 2023005191 (print) | LCCN 2023005192 (ebook) | ISBN 9780231204422 (hardback) | ISBN 9780231204439 (trade paperback) | ISBN 9780231555531 (ebook)
Subjects: LCSH: Science fiction, Chinese—History and criticism. | Chinese fiction—21st century—History and criticism. | Invisibility in literature. | LCGFT: Literary criticism.
Classification: LCC PL2419.S34 S66 2023 (print) | LCC PL2419.S34 (ebook) | DDC 895.13/087620906--dc23/eng/20230411
LC record available at https://lccn.loc.gov/2023005191
LC ebook record available at https://lccn.loc.gov/2023005192

Cover design: Chang Jae Lee
Cover image: © Jung Jihyun, *Construction Site 04*, 2012

CONTENTS

Acknowledgments vii

PROLOGUE: A LONELY HIDDEN ARMY, 2010   1

1. POETICS OF THE INVISIBLE:
INTRODUCING THE NEW WAVE   14

2. SCIENCE FICTION AS METHOD:
WORLDING THE GENRE   43

3. CAN WE READ "A MADMAN'S DIARY" AS SCIENCE
FICTION? REWRITING LITERARY HISTORY   75

EXCURSUS I: LOOKING BACKWARD: 2010–1900   105

4. A POETIC HEART IN THE DARK FOREST:
LIU CIXIN'S THREE-BODY UNIVERSE   116

5. THE POWER OF DARKNESS IN HAN SONG:
MYTHOLOGY OF THE CHTHONIC   160

6. VARIATIONS ON UTOPIA:
SPECTERS AND MYTHS 201

7. A TOPOLOGY OF HOPE:
SINOTOPIA AND HETEROTOPIA 225

8. CHINESE NEW WAVE GOES GLOBAL:
THE POSTHUMAN TURN 252

EXCURSUS II: THE RISE OF SHE-SF: 2010–2022 276

9. NEW WONDERS OF A NONBINARY UNIVERSE:
OPENING OF THE NEO-BAROQUE 280

EPILOGUE: *THE WANDERING EARTH*, 2019 305

Notes 313
Bibliography 339
Index 357

ACKNOWLEDGMENTS

There are so many people to thank: those who enchanted me with their wondrous imagination, those who shared their knowledge and wisdom, those who opened their hearts and worlds to me, those who inspired and guided me through the process of writing this book, and particularly those who supported me at challenging and difficult times. There are so many of them that these pages may not be enough to list every one. It took me nearly a decade to complete this book, longer than originally planned. Here I will keep my "thank you" notes short, but deep in my heart I am grateful to all of you.

I am most grateful to Yan Feng, my longtime friend, who first shared with me the manuscript of a novel titled *Santi*. Through Yan Feng, I got in touch with many science fiction writers who trusted me with their work and never failed to amaze me with their new writings. Han Song and Fei Dao, the two writers I first met in 2010, ushered me into the science fiction community. I have always felt awed when in company with Liu Cixin, whom I have met twice in person (in Sydney and Shanghai). Both Han Song and Liu Cixin have often candidly exchanged their ideas with me by e-mail. I also thank Wang Jinkang, Ling Chen, Jiang Bo, Zhao Haihong, Chen Qiufan, Bao Shu, Xia Jia, Cheng Jingbo, Chi Hui, Tang Fei, Gu Shi, Liu Yang, A Que, Wang Kanyu, Shuangshimu (Feng Yuan), Peng Simeng, Muming, Duan Ziqi, and Wang Nuonuo for their generosity, trust, and kindness. I cherish the friendship with Chi Ta-wei, Chan Koonchung, Lo Yi-chin, Dung Kai-cheung, and Egoyan, who expanded my vision of science fiction beyond genre conventions.

David Der-wei Wang, my former advisor, has been the most important person in the little history of this book. It was he who first showed faith in this project, kept encouraging me to think out of the box, read my drafts numerous times, and offered concrete advice on how to sharpen the theoretical edges. I am indebted to Carlos Rojas, Hua Li, Nathanial Isaacson, Jing Jiang, Astrid Møller-Olsen, Erik Mo Welin, and Jannis Jizhou Chen, who have read parts or the entirety of my manuscript and offered unreserved constructive feedback. I would also like to thank the three anonymous readers of my manuscript; their reports guided me to clarify my major arguments. I have learned from other scholars in the field of science fiction studies: Wu Yan, Veronica Hollinger, Istvan Csicsery-Ronay Jr., Seo-Young Chu, Zhan Ling, Li Guangyi, Ren Dongmei, Yang Qiong, Cara Healey, Yingying Huang, and Frederick Schneider-Vielsäcker. Special thanks go to Yao Haijun and San Feng, who could always find for me the materials I needed.

I thank those who invited me to work on projects on science fiction or give talks on the topic in their institutions: Theodore Huters, Rüdiger Zill, Dale Knickerbocker, Andrew Jones, Thomas Moran, Han Li, Shellen Xiao Wu, Michael Berry, Christopher Rea, Jing Tsu, Ao Wang, Qian Ying, Yang Zhiyi, Felix Meyer zu Venne, Olga Lomová, Lena Rydholm, Marco Fumin, Claudia Pozzana, Pamela Hunt, Yingjin Zhang, and many other colleagues in mainland China, Hong Kong, and Taiwan. I particularly appreciate the tremendous support from Jianmei Liu and Shengqing Wu, who offered me the opportunity to organize the international conference "Science Fiction and Its Variations in the Sinophone Literary World" at the Hong Kong University of Science and Technology in 2018. I also appreciate Fudan University's generous support for my international symposium on science fiction in 2016. I am most grateful to the Institute for Advanced Study (Princeton) for an Elizabeth and J. Richardson Dilworth Fellowship, which enabled me to launch this project in the spring semester of 2016. I am also grateful to the Ching Chiang-kuo Foundation for International Scholarly Exchange for a publication grant for this book, which was awarded in 2022.

To my home institution, Wellesley College, I am thankful for a variety of institutional and intellectual support. Sabbatical leaves in 2015–16 and 2019 gave me enough time to draft the manuscript. Several faculty awards provided resources for me to gather materials and reach locations to gain first-hand knowledge about the subject. I am deeply grateful to the Provost's Office for awarding me a special publication subvention in February 2023 to help fund the publication of this volume. I found intellectual support in many colleagues who share interest in science fiction, particularly Jens Kruse, Larry Rosenwald, Marylin Sides, Wesley Watters, Orit Shaer, and Y. Tak Matsusaka. The three directors of the Newhouse Center over the past fourteen years, Carol Dougherty, Anjali Prabhu, and Eve Zimmerman, have all supported my numerous science fiction events held on campus. Carol Dougherty particularly gave me full support to host my first international symposium, "Global Science Fiction," in 2013. At the Department of East Asian Languages and Cultures, I am particularly thankful to my mentor, Ellen Widmer, and in the larger academic community of Wellesley, I appreciate the friendship and collegiality of Shiao-Wei Tham, Sarah M. Allen, Robert Goree, Heng Du, Sun-Hee Lee, Pat Giersch, Jim Kodera, Yong Sun Lee, Yu Jin Ko, Wini Wood, David Teng-Olson, Adam Weiner, Koichi Hagimoto, David Ward, Sergio Parussa, Elena Creef, and Maurizio Viano. I feel extremely supported by my friends at Wellesley, Dai Chen, Qingmin Meng, Sun Ming, and Heping Liu. In the greater Boston area, I treasure the friendship with Ha Jin, Wang Pu, John Plotz, Jie Li, Junot Diaz, and Ken Liu.

I could not have possibly written a second book without emotional and intellectual support from many of my friends—Shengqing Wu, Eric Nelson, Michael Berry, Michael G. Hill, Carlos Rojas, Jianmei Chen, Nicolai Volland, Jiwei Xiao, Ji Jin, Zhang Huiwen, Li Fengqun, Jingling Chen, Ying Lei, Dylan Suher, Yan Feng, Wang Hongtu, Song Binghui, Zhang Xinying, Duan Huaiqing, and Zhang Yesong. I still remember the first questions asked about this project by the late Professor C. T. Hsia and feel grateful to my other former teachers, David Damrosch, Chen Sihe, and David Der-wei Wang, who have always been ready to offer advice and encouragement.

I thank my students who took my science fiction seminar, so far taught three times at Wellesley. Among those dozens of students who took the seminar, I want to particularly thank Emily Jin, Lizao Wang, Lilian Sall, Ella Apostoaie, Kelly Song, Kexin Zhao, and Kiara Liu, who have embarked on their own academic journeys to explore science fiction and other literary wonders. Kexin also assisted me in compiling the index to this book.

I am extremely grateful to my editors at Columbia University Press, Christine Dunbar, Leslie Kriesel, and Christian Winting. I deeply appreciate the support of Jennifer Crewe. Earlier drafts of chapters of this book have appeared in journals such as *Science Fiction Studies*, *China Perspectives*, *ACTA Universitatis Carolinae Philologica*, and volumes such as *The Oxford Handbook of Modern Chinese Literature*, *Lingua Cosmica*, *The Making of Chinese-Sinophone Literatures as World Literature*, *The Making of* The Wandering Earth, and *Out of This World*. Chinese essays that I wrote on the topic have been published in journals such as *Twenty-First-Century Bimonthly*, *Dushu*, *Shanghai Culture*, *Shanghai Literature*, *Chinese Comparative Literature*, and *Modern Chinese Literature*. I am grateful to all my editors and have revised the previously published parts thoroughly when integrating them into this book. Some of these previously published articles have been translated into German, French, Spanish, Russian, Italian, and Japanese. I am grateful to my translators, Gwennaël Gaffric, Chiara Cigarini, Anne Vonderstein, Kristof Kurz, and Céline Letemplé, among others.

My words of gratitude cannot make up for the three long years when I could not go to China to see my parents in person or visit my friends. It was during the time of the pandemic that I finalized this manuscript. My parents and my wife, Qiuyan, have always trusted that I am doing the right thing—writing this book and expressing my opinions with honesty and integrity. Qiuyan has witnessed my metamorphosis from a plain humanist into a "posthuman monster" obsessed with the invisible and accepted it. She shared with me this odyssey all along.

FEAR OF SEEING

PROLOGUE

A Lonely Hidden Army, 2010

About a decade ago, I witnessed a new wave of Chinese science fiction (SF) coming to the center stage of contemporary Chinese literature. A landmark event occurred at a conference at Fudan University in Shanghai, which intended to celebrate the achievements of twenty-first-century Chinese literature while its first decade was coming to an end.[1] Very few writers and scholars arriving at Fudan's campus on a summer day in July 2010 knew that Chinese SF had undergone a recent revival, bloomed and flourished since the very beginning of the new century, and a new wave of SF had achieved far more than usually expected for genre fiction. Few were aware that this new wave SF had created an exuberant and profuse new literary universe distinguished by its own poetics.

The first day, July 11, was entirely devoted to panel discussions about Mo Yan 莫言 (b. 1955), who was to win the Nobel Prize in Literature in two years. But Mo Yan was not the thunderbolt that shook up the conference. After all, like many other writers present, he had already been long established in the literary field. What was new in contemporary Chinese literature? Had anything different arrived with the new century that redefined contemporaneousness? These were big questions for the conference participants. Mo Yan and his generation had dominated contemporary Chinese literature for three decades. A phenomenon tagged as the "midlife crisis"[2] in Chinese literature received heated discussion.

There was a general worry about the decline of literature: its detachment from immediate reality; a lacuna in the "contemporary" as a new history in the making; the lack of proper successors to carry on the cultural zeitgeist that originated in the Reform Era of the 1980s. The prevailing frustrations that writers experienced were profound and unspeakable, including political taboos and censorship/self-censorship that increasingly regulated literary writing, the decay of the avant-garde cultural spirit, and the loss of the vivacity and relevance of literary realism, together with those established realist writers' evasion of China's formidable and opaque contemporary reality.

On the last day of the Fudan conference, July 13, two SF writers, Han Song 韓松 (b. 1965) and Fei Dao 飛氘 (b. 1983), were given ten minutes each to introduce their genre at a late afternoon roundtable. Throughout the previous three days, they had appeared like two awkward outsiders among a large cast of literary celebrities—Mo Yan, Wang Anyi 王安憶 (b. 1954), Yu Hua 余華 (b. 1960), and Su Tong 蘇童 (b. 1963), and other famous writers and literary critics, scholars, editors, publishers, and journalists. Han Song and Fei Dao were invisible in the crowd, conscious of their unimportant, if not completely obscure status. But when I later read Han Song's account of his experience at the conference, I realized that they had taken it as a once-in-a-lifetime occasion to present Chinese SF to the literary field. When they left Beijing to come to Shanghai, their comrades—fellow authors and sci-fi fans—bid them farewell as solemnly as if they were warriors tasked with a mission of paramount importance;[3] as a matter of fact, Han Song and Fei Dao spoke at the conference of warriors and even referred to a lonely hidden army ready to change the world. Nobody had expected that the black horse of the Fudan conference would be SF, and that SF would be one of the most dynamic and driving new forces to reshape "what was contemporary" in twenty-first-century Chinese literature.

THE FIRST ENCOUNTER OF A PERSONAL KIND

Before I present a critical evaluation of this SF new wave, a personal account of my first encounter with the genre is in order, to demonstrate how SF can inform our sense of ourselves and the changing world. I first came across a manuscript written by a then obscure author, Liu Cixin 劉慈欣 (b. 1963), in 2007, which Yan Feng 嚴鋒 (b. 1964), a professor teaching at Fudan, had e-mailed me. Today Liu has become a household name in China, and his "Three-Body" trilogy has been translated into nearly thirty languages. Back then his name was totally unknown to me, a literary scholar supposed to be paying attention to contemporary Chinese literature. But this manuscript, titled *The Three-Body Problem* 三體 (2007), threw me into a totally new world.

At the beginning of the novel, in an absurd, unsettling situation, a scientist, who has just been informed of a secret truth concerning an invasion of aliens from deep space, looks beyond a briefing room filled with military staff, fixing his eyes on the normal life scenes outside the window and wondering: *Which is more real? The world inside or outside these walls?*[4] The invisible unreal, coming from the darkness of the universe, invades reality. I felt like that scientist, stepping into an estranging world filled with invisible wonders, fearful but more truthful than the apparent reality I faced in daily life. I read *The Three-Body Problem* to the last page and realized that an epic story had just begun. I waited and got to read its sequel, *The Dark Forest* 黑暗森林 (2008), the next summer, and had to wait for two years to read the third and last volume, *Death's End* 死神永生 (2010). During those two years, I couldn't get the Three-Body universe out of my mind. If what Constance Penley says about SF studies—"there is no better critic than a fan"[5]—is correct, I indeed became a fan first. I read Liu Cixin's two novels many times to comprehend his clues and try to guess what was to come, long before I knew that I would one day do research on Chinese SF and write this book.

The encounter with Liu Cixin created a unique point, a singularity, in my academic life. The Three-Body universe mesmerized me to such an extent that I felt drowned in an enormous unknown and an infinity of wonders. I lost myself in a perpetual uncertainty beyond the reach of my academic training in modern Chinese literature. Through Yan Feng's introduction, I got in touch with Liu Cixin and sent him a fan e-mail. A modest and polite person, Liu Cixin told me that he was only an amateur author. Knowing that I was by profession a literary scholar, he advised me to pay more attention to a fellow SF writer instead. That was the first time I heard of Han Song. Liu Cixin believed that Han Song's stories and novels could be more meaningful to me than his own; he argued that if his own works were two-dimensional, Han Song's would be three-dimensional.[6] "Han Song is an avant-gardist; he has more literary experiments in his SF," Liu Cixin he told me in an e-mail. Following Liu's advice, I read Han Song's dark, grotesque, chthonic stories and particularly his poignant and provocative novel *Mars Over America* 火星照耀美國 (2000). If Liu Cixin mainly wrote SF as genre fiction, Han Song turned SF into an avant-garde literary form. I began to give Chinese SF new consideration: it posited a serious challenge to the literary conventions of the day, a subversion in both message and form. Han Song's abysmal darkness and Liu Cixin's sublime wonders were as audacious and affronting as works by Mo Yan or Yu Hua, but with an astonishing newness in their spectacular and otherworldly representations beyond the predictions for knowable literary experimentalism.

While waiting for the grand finale of the Three-Body saga, I tried to collect and read every piece of Chinese SF published between 1999 and 2010. In addition to Han Song and Liu Cixin, I found a handful of other writers, including Wang Jinkang 王晉康 (b. 1948), Xing He 星河 (b. 1967), Liu Wenyang 柳文揚 (1970–2007), Ling Chen 凌晨 (b. 1971), He Xi 何夕 (b. 1971), Pan Haitian 潘海天 (b. 1975), Jiang Bo 江波 (b. 1978), Zhao Haihong 趙海虹 (b. 1977), Qian Lifang 錢莉芳 (b. 1978), and Ma Boyong 馬伯庸 (b. 1980). I also got to read fresh pieces coming from an emerging generation of much younger authors still in their twenties at the time, such as Fei Dao, Xia Jia 夏笳 (b. 1984), Chi Hui 遲卉 (b. 1984), Chang Jia 長鋏 (b. 1984), Hao Jingfang 郝景芳 (b. 1984), Chen Xi 陳茜 (b. 1986), Qi Yue 七月 (b. 1983), Cheng Jingbo 程婧波 (b. 1983), Bao Shu 寶樹 (b. 1980), Zhang Ran 張冉 (b. 1981), and Chen Qiufan 陳楸帆 (b. 1981). Through joining online fan sites, I got access to unpublished writings, fanzines, and personal memories of the genre's history. I gradually pieced together a history of the hidden genesis of the genre's most recent revival, locating its inception in those dark long nights of the late 1980s. I read the annual anthologies edited by Han Song and Wu Yan 吳岩 (b. 1962), which began to be published in 2000. After that year, the genre expanded with accelerating momentum; it burst like a fire running underground, stirring in the deep and coming to the surface just when I looked for it. It was already an ebullient literary universe of its own kind.

In 2010, Yan Feng tried to invite Liu Cixin to the Shanghai conference. But Liu turned it down; he was staying home in Shanxi Province, preoccupied with completing the last volume of his trilogy. Liu had a day job as a computer engineer, and his workplace was a power plant near Niangziguan 娘子關, a mountain pass on the Great Wall, the former northern frontier of the Middle Kingdom. He composed nearly all his major stories and novels at Niangziguan. He didn't want others, particularly his superiors and co-workers, to know that he was squandering time on dreaming and depicting speculative wonders in an estranging universe.[7] When he published the first two volumes of his space saga, it quietly attracted some young adult readers but caused very little attention in domestic or international media. So, even two years after the releases of the first two volumes of the "Three-Body" trilogy, Liu Cixin was still an unknown author in the mainstream literary world.

When I was sitting among the audience at the Fudan conference, I felt as if I were holding a big secret—as if living in a SF story, I anticipated the big bang, a moment of singularity, the birth of a new parallel universe in Chinese literature. I was nervously watching Han Song and Fei Dao, who were nervously sitting down on the stage. . . .

UNPACKING CHINESE SCIENCE FICTION

The microphone was finally handed to Han Song. It was 4:00 p.m., near the end of the conference. Han Song opened with a confession that he could not share the other writers' feelings about the midlife crisis of literature, because SF had long been categorized as children's literature, a lower and insignificant caste in China's literary hierarchy. He self-deprecatingly said that speaking after those renowned writers, he represented a genre that was barely recognized as literature and depicted nonexistent unreal worlds. He also spelled out the question that the audience might have wanted to ask: Is there such a thing as Chinese SF with literary values? Han Song quoted an unnamed cultural cadre's questions: How could you possibly write SF in China? For example, how would you describe the Communist Party's dealing with the invading aliens?[8] These words threw the audience into fits of laughter. Indeed, this

Communist cadre's questions pointed to China's overall hostile environment to the otherworldly science fantasy that implies uncertainties and may elicit alternatives to existing discourses on the political and cultural orders associated with the Party-dictated worldview. The remarks recalled the 1983 nationwide criticism of SF when both the scientific and literary communities attacked the genre as "spiritual pollution" 精神污染 in a campaign that caused the genre to vanish from the Chinese literary field for nearly two decades.[9] That disgraceful episode was probably the last time most of the scholars and writers present had heard about the genre in a domestic context. Since then, the general impression of SF had been that it was nothing more than nonsensical fantasy and vulgar escapism.

Han Song's and Fe Dao's carefully prepared presentations rehabilitated the genre through a strategic connection between contemporary Chinese SF and Lu Xun's 鲁迅 (1881–1936) literary legacy. Lu Xun is widely adored as the founding father of modern Chinese literature. His experiments with fictional realism laid the foundation for modern China's mainstream literary tradition. But as Han Song and Fei Dao claimed, Lu Xun was also the spiritual father of Chinese SF. His early passion for the genre was exemplified by his translations of Western SF novels, including two by Jules Verne. In a later chapter, I will reevaluate the genre's potential links to Lu Xun's literary vision, including his invention of a certain truth-claiming mode of representation that can be interpreted as SF as well. To say the least, realism and SF crossed paths in Lu Xun, which created the point and counterpoint to form a dialogue and validate each other. In contemporary Chinese SF, Han Song, Liu Cixin, Fei Dao, and other writers consciously appropriated famous metaphors drawn from Lu Xun's writings, which were actualized as plot designs and literalized as world-building: representing the new age transportation as technologized "iron houses," delineating postapocalyptic human (d)evolution to cannibalism, and displaying bioengineered mutant images of the diseased nation and deranged individuals.[10] The allusion to Lu Xun recast SF with a seriousness that fastened the genre to social criticism. The new wave authors learned from Lu Xun how to reinvent the genre as a truth-telling method that went against the grain: instead of conforming to social norms, it engaged social problems through a technologized "seeing," unfolding concealed truths and shedding light on the invisible depth of contemporary

Chinese reality. As Han Song said at the conference: "SF writers had a strong desire to represent the fears when confronting the absurdity of life."[11]

Han Song revoked the audience's outdated impression of Chinese SF and announced the genre's revival: in the first decade of the new century, a surge of SF writings, publications, and activities formed its own literary universe in parallel to the mainstream literary field. The genre had attracted millions of readers, both children and adults; prosperous sci-fi communities were founded around the country, and sci-fi fans and writers organized festivals, created awards, and even raised funds to make independent films. Han Song celebrated all these vigorous activities as well as the achievements of writers like Liu Cixin and Wang Jinkang, who were all "amateur" authors deeply devoted to their beloved genre without calculating economic gains and cultural esteem. Han Song emphasized that what truly mattered was the astonishing imagination that SF had liberated. These writers presented an infinite variety of possibilities for imagining the future and gave China, a country deprived of liberal imagination, a multitude of new dreams.

When it was Fei Dao's turn to speak, he described the entire new generation of SF writers as a "lonely hidden army" 寂寞的伏兵. To use his own words, they "lie low in the wilderness where nobody cares to look. One day, when the opportunity is ripe, some valiant generals and warriors will rush out and change the heaven and earth. But it is also possible that they will remain forever hidden and unknown, without anyone listening to them, and they will just perish without ever seeing daylight." Then in the future, "people will excavate some mysterious weapons from where the army was once hidden, but they will have no clue who invented the weapons or used them."[12] Incarnating SF as a "lonely hidden army" is a revealing way to characterize the genre's invisibility in the literary field, and I found Fei Dao's imagined story of SF itself a SF allegory.

I take from this allegory three implied meanings that are applicable to studies in Chinese SF, particularly regarding the representation of the invisible, a central theme of this book. These meanings are not necessarily all Fei Dao's intended messages, but more based on my strategic (over-) interpretations of his allegory with reference to my own understanding of the genre in terms of historical context, cultural politics, and suggestions of a unique poetics of the invisible. The first meaning refers to

Chinese SF's position in literary history, which was Fei Dao's original message. Despite a promising beginning during the final decade of the Qing Dynasty, the genre remained mostly obscure throughout the twentieth century, except for a few short-lived booms that took place in Hong Kong's Cold War years, Taiwan's 1970s and 1980s, and China's early Reform Era. It was not until the beginning of the twenty-first century that SF underwent a new surge, which, however, had largely been kept to its own circle. At the time of the Fudan conference, this new wave was not yet known, thus still "invisible," in the literary field.

Fei Dao's allegory can also be interpreted as speaking to the unique position of SF in the entire literary field. It is portrayed as an army that has maneuvered to a place in the wilderness from which to launch an ambush, suggesting a potential conflict with the "visible," or the "mainstream" literary establishment. If unleashed into combat, this lonely army would be not merely a marginalized genre but a literary force to oppose or contend with the "center." The new wave of Chinese SF, like its Anglo-American counterpart, represents a courageous attempt to "find a language and a social perspective for science fiction that is as adventurous and progressive as its technological visions."[13] The new wave reinvented the genre with a new literary self-consciousness and a new social awareness. Its strength came from its alternative worldviews and subversive textuality, which oriented the genre toward a confrontation with the established paradigm of literary representation.

Concerning the poetics of the invisible, there can be a more intricate "hidden" meaning in Fei Dao's words. Imagining SF as a set of mysterious weapons to be excavated as ancient artifacts that will awe future generations but are invisible in our own time contains a self-reflective image illuminating the genre's poetic nature. The archaeology and futurology that the excavation alludes to suggest that the genre's beauty and strength are only visible in some "other" time and space—heterotopia, heterochronia, or simply an unreal or virtual world—all of which are proper themes for SF. Fei Dao's allegory implies that SF itself, like what it depicts, is the wonder invisible now and here, staying outside the continuum of the perceivable reality. SF itself is the "novum" for Chinese literature.[14] Its invisibility defines its nature, including both its form and its content, which are no longer binarily differentiated. The invisible wonder of SF requires an extraordinary, counterintuitive cognitive adjustment, an alternative critical position, and a technologized new method to see, understand, and unfold it into a new world image. Fei Dao's allegorical characterization of the genre's magic invisibility also invites us to speculate whether there is an invisible component of China's contemporary reality, or an alternative version of it, that can only be represented in SF. The way he told the story about Chinese SF, like a metafiction, changed how the relationship between representation and reality could be rewritten in or as SF.

CHINA IN AND AS SCIENCE FICTION

To speak in hindsight, the 2010 conference was a historical turning point. It ushered an entire new generation of SF writers into a larger world, when their various voices, inventive narratives, and ethical and aesthetic strengths began to attract attention from literary scholars and a wider audience both domestically and globally. It officially marked the surfacing of the new wave of Chinese SF, and it also marked the beginning of this book that studies the poetics, texts, and history of this new wave.

The new wave had multiple origins. The conference in 2010 was only a symbolic one, which indicated its acceptance by the literary mainstream. Another origin can be traced to at least ten years before, when three prominent SF writers, Liu Cixin, Han Song, and Wang Jinkang, all made their breakthroughs. Most scholars researching Chinese SF agree that the turn of the twenty-first century marked the beginning of the genre's revival. My own argument is that the new wave had yet another hidden origin that occurred even earlier—as early as the late 1980s, when Han Song and Liu Cixin experimented with a new style that challenged genre conventions in their earliest writings. The genre's later "underground" development as a "lonely hidden army" should be understood in the post-1989 social and cultural contexts: the abrupt end of the 1980s democratic movement, China's rapid marketization, the boom of new sciences and technologies, the rise of the internet, the maturing markets for genre fiction, and the flourishing of the netizen communities from where new wave SF lifted off.

Soon after the Fudan conference, Liu Cixin published the last volume of his "Three-Body" trilogy: *Death's End*. I was among the first readers before it reached the market and became a national best-seller. Han Song published *Subway* 地鐵 (2010), one of his most notable and darkest novels, around the same time. Extensive Chinese media coverage on SF began near the end of 2010. Professor David Der-wei Wang 王德威 (b. 1954) lifted SF studies to the top level of academic research through delivering a widely influential keynote speech, "From Lu Xun to Liu Cixin" 從魯迅到劉慈欣, at Peking University in May 2011.[15] Academic journals solicited research articles and reviews about Liu Cixin, Han Song, and other SF writers. Mainstream literary journals began to print SF, including *People's Literature* 人民文學, which reprinted four stories by Liu Cixin in 2012. In 2015, Ken Liu's English translation of *The Three-Body Problem* won the Hugo Award, gaining for Liu Cixin worldwide recognition and bringing Chinese SF into the spotlight in both China and the United States. This rapid rise posited challenges to the genre itself as well as to the larger literary field. It raised questions about science fiction's "definition," whether its strength exclusively came from its uniqueness as a genre of "cognitive estrangement,"[16] and whether it arrived at a pivotal point in a new cultural phase and came to represent a newness far more prevalent and significant than the genre itself. New scientific visions and technologies are changing our everyday life with artificial intelligence, big data, mobile internet access, virtual reality, and most recently the metaverse, as if we could now be living in a SF novel.

The genre's surfacing was an event, or an *événement*,[17] which would mark an ongoing change and differentiate a completely new sense of becoming "contemporary" in terms of vocabulary, narratology, technology, and epistemology. The surfacing is a process of coming to light, but the significance of the *event* is even more closely relevant to the coming to light of the invisibility that holds irregularities, revolts, horrors, unrealities, and unfolding new worlds. Through representing the invisible, new wave SF has invented a provocative "newness" in contemporary Chinese literature, which should no longer be just grounded in a tangible Chinese reality according to the long-standing conventions of mimetic realism. Literature should incite a daring spirit to "perceive not its light, but rather its darkness,"[18] a fearless truth-seeking gaze into the unknown abysmal deep beneath the accustomed, familiar surface reality. Unfolding the hidden dimensions of China's reality unleashes a subversive force that characterizes the new wave. New wave SF shatters the mainstream thought systems and inspires a departure from the stabilizing norms of knowledge and thinking..

The title of this book, *Fear of Seeing*, was inspired by Han Song, whose writings opened our eyes to see the darker sides of society and seek the deeper truth beneath the surface. A senior journalist working for China's Xinhua News Agency, Han Song knows too well what is *invisible*, which matters even more than the *visible* in China's broad daylight; as a disciple of Lu Xun, he is drawn to the power of darkness, and Lu Xunsque phantoms and paradoxical metaphors permeate Han Song's chthonic literary visions. Han Song has suggested that "China's reality has now become more science fictional than science fiction."[19] If China's formidable and forbidden, amorphous and alienated, uncertain and unpredictable reality is difficult or impossible to describe in traditional literary discourse based on the principle of mimesis, it comes to light in speculative fictional storytelling. SF, this marginalized, insignificant genre, has achieved a meaningful status as a unique literary form to represent the unsettling, abstruse, clandestine images coming from the terra incognita bordering China's proper "reality" and outside its ordinary literary landscape. In an allegorical sense, SF is a proper form to represent the uncertain and unfathomable reality of China. In other words, an invisible China that incites "fear of seeing" can be best represented in SF and as SF.

To a writer like Han Song, China—with its terrifying invisible truth—itself has become a SF story. In Chinese new wave SF writings emerges a "Sinotopia" 中托邦,[20] a virtual form of China, a fictive unreality that speaks acutely to the country's undefined, unclear transforming realities, where imagination rewrites what is real into a monstrous conglomerate, like a chimera, of dreams and nightmares, ideas and ruins, memories and regrets. SF depicting the hideous, disastrous, apocalyptic side to the story of modernity casts shadows of uncertainty over many domains of contemporary China's national program for reform, enlightenment, revolution, and rejuvenation; and even mundane life scenes depicted in SF can become paradoxical and phantasmagorical, when reality loses its meanings and purposes in estranging new experiences that may never settle in a singular form of truth.

The new wave of contemporary Chinese SF has been like a triumphant army and reached a breaking point to mark a larger paradigm shift for literary representation. In terms of poetics, new wave SF has pioneered in creating new patterns for literary representation in the twenty-first century. In a more provocative sense, these experiments create a subversion not only of the genre conventions but also of the authorities of a system that requires certainty and absolutism. However, the international success of the genre has attracted the government's attention as well. National leaders and cultural authorities have seen SF's potential in association with the promotion of scientific advancement. Chinese authorities have since tried to domesticate and appropriate the new wave, making it a "soft power" serving the national interests,[21] but as far as I have observed, nothing has been able to stop the flow of the free imagination that the genre has liberated.

I feel fortunate to have witnessed the rise of new wave Chinese SF. While writing and revising this book through the three years of the pandemic, I have also encountered the newest generation of women and nonbinary authors, who are decades younger than Liu Cixin and Han Song. Their visions of the "Möbius" time-space without beginning or end and their identifications with the "chimera" as a monstrous self-other combination[22] create new breakthroughs for the new wave's posthuman turn that began with Liu Cixin, Chen Qiufan, and Han Song, who resorted to posthumanism as a critique of China's prevailing inhuman conditions. These new writers of the younger generation embrace the posthuman identities and truly make kinship in a nonbinary posthuman universe, with more radical notions about sex, gender, class, cyborgian constructions, trans-species lives, symbiosis, and sympoiesis. This younger generation comprises Tang Fei 糖匪 (b. 1983), Wang Kanyu 王侃瑜 (b. 1990), Peng Simeng 彭思萌 (b. 1990), Shuangchimu 双翅目 (b. 1987), Gu Shi 顾适 (b. 1985), Mu Ming 慕明 (b. 1988), Duan Ziqi 段子期 (b. 1992), A Que 阿缺 (b. 1990), and Liu Yang 劉洋 (b. 1986).

The evolving new wave has kept generating new modes of literary representation that transcend categories and dichotomies, dissolving such a variety of borders that Chinese SF can be viewed as an enormous "spaceship" holding all sorts and species together to lift off from the grounded reality of certainty. The Chinese SF literary universe has widened to include a whole range of new concepts and new sensations: ecological and environmental themes, the Anthropocene and its challengers, the Chthulucene and trans-species kinship, algorithm and poesis, etc. The impact of the new wave has reached beyond the People's Republic and inspired writers who were not originally SF authors, such as Lo Yi-chin 駱以軍 (b. 1967) and Dung Kai-cheung 董啟章 (b. 1967), two experimental novelists living in Taipei and Hong Kong, respectively. In the Sinophone literary world, writers have been engaged in daring storytelling in the forms of SF, dystopian fiction, and posthuman narrative since before the rise of the Chinese new wave. These writers respond to the cultural, political, epistemological, ethical and aesthetic questions about our contemporary world in their own distinctive voices—such as Chan Koonchung 陳冠中 (b. 1952), Ho Ching-pin 賀景濱 (b. 1958), Chi Ta-wei 紀大偉 (b. 1972), Hung Ling 洪凌 (b. 1971), Egoyan Zheng 伊格言 (b. 1977), and Wu Ming-yi 吳明益 (b. 1971). *Fear of Seeing* is only the first step in my exploration of the larger, more inclusive world of Chinese SF and its impact on the changing literary paradigm in twenty-first-century Sinophone contexts.

Looking backward from this moment to ten or twenty years ago, this book traces new wave Chinese SF's journey from its invisible origins to center stage to experimentalist variations, investigating its strengths and limits, together with its contention with mimetic realism, sublime and chthonic aesthetics, heterotopian imagination, posthuman subversion, and in particular, its unique poetics—the representation of the invisible that changes how we view literature, China, and humanity.

This book elucidates the aesthetics and ethics of contemporary Chinese SF with a focus on the poetics of the invisible that characterizes its new wave inventiveness. It does not aim at an exhaustive study of the genre and its multitude of authors; nor does it just tell a success story of the genre. This study is only the starting point of a longer journey to comprehend the changing epistemology and aesthetics of twenty-first-century literature, and it begins with an appreciation of new wave SF's revelatory power as a new form of storytelling that provides readers with an otherworldly portal to comprehend the invisible and witness its unfolding into worlds of wonders.

1

POETICS OF THE INVISIBLE

Introducing the New Wave

The rise of a new wave of science fiction has been a momentous literary phenomenon in contemporary China. Since the turn of the twenty-first century, the genre has reemerged and gradually achieved wide popularity both domestically and globally. This has happened at a time when China is aiming at a new stage of national rejuvenation and mapping out various political, economic, and scientific projects to achieve a "Chinese dream." Yet, for the country concurrently embracing technological renovations and sparing no effort to secure its status quo, the shape of things to come remains far from certain. A form of speculative literature, SF speaks to both China's rapidly shifting reality and its formless future, voicing the anticipation and anxieties of a new epoch filled with accelerating alterations and increasing uncertainty. The genre unfolds invisible and hidden dimensions of and beyond China's reality and weaves together new trends in sciences and ethics, technologies and aesthetics, politics and the unconscious, and cybernetics and everyday life.

In a peculiar way, Chinese SF has simultaneously arrived at its Golden Age and generated its own subversion. Subversive elements in worldview, epistemology, and poetics filled in this new trend, which eventually convinced me that its most radical front should be properly dubbed a "new wave" 新浪潮.[1] "New wave" as a specific term underscores contemporary Chinese SF's cutting-edge literary experimentation and avant-gardism in aesthetics and politics, analogous to what the term implies in the Anglo-American SF tradition.[2] But in the Chinese context, "new wave" is more than a reconfiguration of genre conventions; I have also appropriated the insurgent meaning of this term, as it has been interpreted in cinema studies according to its etymology in the French "nouvelle vague,"[3] to project a cultural earthquake that could shatter the mainstream paradigm of contemporary Chinese literature. I have thus recognized the entire new trend of SF as an emerging *new wave* in relation to the entire Chinese literary field.

Though considered genre fiction, new wave SF challenges the distinctions between "popular" and "serious" literatures and engages with experiments altering our perceptions of what is literature, what is contemporary, what is real, and what is human. Its proliferation destabilizes the power structure in the field of literary production, and its adventurous experiments in thought and style push toward a paradigm shift while bringing new meanings to the political, ethical, and epistemological connotations of the literary imagination. To say the least, the Chinese new wave has grown out of continuous contestations with the conventions of both genre fiction and Chinese literature in general; and its most valorous visions give rise to a new mode of literariness that I propose to define as "a poetics of the invisible."

My main argument is that the unique strength of the Chinese new wave SF lies in its illumination of the "invisible." The invisible is a key element in the poetics of the new wave. As a symbolic trope, it points to realms beyond what we can ordinarily perceive, allows for the representations of fears and dreams, and challenges moral conventions and political doctrines. It is a category that includes those unknowable and inexplicable phenomena that bring into question the validity of our knowledge and belief systems, makes our sense of reality uncertain, and most importantly, presents possibilities for building alternative images of the world. In the context of contemporary China, the invisible also includes all that is not available for conventional representations due to artistic constraints or political prohibitions.

The representation of both the epistemologically and politically invisible functions as the center of gravity in the new wave world-building is exemplified by the two most remarkable cases that this book will explore: Liu Cixin's extravagantly blinding sublime visions of cosmic terror in the

"Three-Body" trilogy—the "dark forest" on the astronomical scale, the hyperdimensional universe in dazzling detail, and the unfathomable alternations of physical rules by superintelligence (chapter 4); and Han Song's fearless gaze into the abysmal deep, the gleams of darkness in the chthonic and posthuman lives, and his protagonists' confrontation with the unembodied, demonic algorithms exerting total control over the (post-)human world in the "Hospital" trilogy (chapter 5). In contemporary Chinese SF, seeing the invisible is never a simple and easy thing. It evokes fear of seeing, a formidable feeling of confronting the forbidden truth, the opaque mystique, and the unsettling uncertainty of realities, which converge in the SF textuality as terrifying and apocalyptic revelations.

Fear of Seeing constitutes the culmination of my reflections on the master plot of Chinese new wave SF. Daring to see the invisible registers the courage to take on an exigent mission to seek the deeper, hidden, cryptic truth. Catching a glimpse of what has been, or been deliberately made, "invisible" may lead to gutsy discoveries at odds with the fabricated smooth surface of "reality" represented in common knowledge, mass media, state propaganda, and "normative" human consciousness. By transcending that reality, new wave SF dismantles commonly accepted notions about the political, artistic, scientific, and technological permissible and probable and rewrites what is *real* after all.

The design of the SF plots is therefore closely intertwined with the ethics of storytelling—that is to say, the moral question of seeing or not seeing drives the narrative toward a moment of truth-claiming enlightenment. The plot of truth seeking penetrates the conventionally knowable reality and adventures into the dark, unseen, and intricately folded dimensions of the world. SF with a self-conscious intellectual tendency taps into deep discords with old-fashioned mimetic realism regarding what is reality. For the new wave authors, fictional representation is not bound by the phenomenal world and conventional social constructs but accentuates a variety of alternative ways of disputing what is real and contravening the rationales of mimetic realism.

In this and the next chapter, I will introduce my main argument concerning the poetics of the invisible, while charting the process of the new wave's metamorphosis from latency to unfolding into profusely outlandish world images. I will situate my inquiries in four case studies. The first three cases concerning Han Song and Liu Cixin will be presented in this chapter, which will, in turn, evoke a dark consciousness from deep space, enter a cybernetic phantom into historical uncertainty, and kindle the fear of seeing in a divergence with the government-endorsed comforting image of China's reality. The fourth and last case will be presented in the next chapter. It concerns a much younger writer who caught my attention during the pandemic, and her story opens new wonders of a Neo-Baroque nonbinary universe. These four are the "invisible" landmarks often overlooked in studies of contemporary Chinese SF, but their implications are revelatory about how the new wave was initiated, emerged, flourished, and transformed.

REPRESENTATION OF THE INVISIBLE

The invisible matters. In cosmology, scientists have come to realize that the invisible, such as the dark matters and dark energies, matters and, more than the luminary celestial bodies, reveals the truth of the universe.[4] In nearly all fields of modern science, scientists are reorienting their methodologies toward invisible matters for a comprehensive appreciation of the world—including, most prominently, genetics, quantum physics, and computer science, which together are remaking the "fabric of reality."[5]

Recognizing the invisible changes our perceptions of a wide range of matters in both the human world and the larger universe, and structural insight into the invisible depths beneath surface reality reshapes our comprehension of the apparent everyday reality as well as the cyber and virtual realities. Acknowledging the invisible is also a gesture of the posthuman turn in philosophical thinking, for it shows the limitations of human perception and rationality, destabilizing our accustomed sense of human-centered reality. Within a cultural context, crediting the invisible, conceding that there are certain things unseen, hidden, or erased in our social reality, brings into question the validity of beliefs and representations.

In a philosophical sense, the invisible can be a latent status of the Real that Jacques Lacan (1901–1981) defines, such as the invisible letter in the case of the "purloined letter."[6] This Real is a deeper form of the observable real. It is perennial but deliberately muted or misconstrued in the representations of a certain reality to create a deception or an ideological illusion. To Lacan, the detective or storyteller is ultimately a philosopher who needs to dissect the observable real and captures the ultimate, invisible Real that reveals the truth. Maurice Merleau-Ponty (1908–1961), in his posthumous treatise *The Visible and the Invisible*, illustrates "invisibility" as this world's "own and interior possibility."[7] "To see is as a matter of principle to see further than one sees, to reach a being in latency."[8] The entire methodology known as phenomenology, first coming from Edmund Husserl (1859–1938), converges in a "phenomenological seeing,"[9] which, to use Merleau-Ponty's terms, concerns how the invisible becomes visible. Merleau-Ponty locates this event at a "chiasm," the intertwining of different dimensions of the world, through which the invisible can be outlined, illuminated, and imaged to the world itself. It is a manifestation that Merleau-Ponty specifies as the "flesh." In a less phenomenological but more Proustian sense, the chiasm makes possible "abandoning the flesh of the body for that of the language"—"as Valéry said, the language is everything . . . it is the very voice of the things."[10] This echoes what Martin Heidegger (1889–1976) claims: "Language is the house of Being."[11] The phenomenological seeing that illuminates the invisible, to use Martin Heidegger's words, can be referred to as the opening up of a world from concealment; the *"world worlds"*—the Heideggerian worlding is a constant process of unfolding and becoming, which makes dwelling for humans in the world a poetic (or literary) form of being.[12]

In relation to the topic of this book, I borrow Merleau-Ponty's concept of the "chiasm" as intertwining different dimensions of the world. I use it to refer not to a "phenomenological seeing" but simply to a linguistic deviance that edges into a variety of the unknown. In SF, the use of the scientific, or speculatively scientific, discourse on the invisible disturbs the stabilizing "reality" and operates contrary to the conventionally affirmative depiction of the phenomenal reality in literary realism. On a more concrete level, the chiasm can be an unrepresentative representation of the invisible wonders of the world: aliens, posthuman phantoms, the hidden dimensions of reality, and what is yet to occur in the future.

I borrow from Heidegger the concept of worlding to refer to the unfolding of the invisible as the SF world-building out of speculations about the truth of the world. The worlding, particularly when it becomes specifically SF world-building, takes place in a poetic way. Even more profoundly, it changes the grammar of literary representation. When the invisible unfolds in the SF worlding, it brings about a baroque proliferation of marvels that require a language that approximates to infinity. In a futuristic and otherworldly sense, SF is an excessive mode of narrative and an extravagant discursive practice about the unseen and invisible—imaginary and nonexistent wonders and all the spectacles of speculative worlds that transform from an idea, a utopian pulse, or a scientific hypothesis into outlandish detailed depictions of the estranging and the unknown. This is a new universe with infinitely folded dimensions; it can be the quantum universe, the multiverse, or even the metaverse that has an unsettling interactive nature, including our own shape-shifting avatars—all refusing a singular, definitive form, constantly in the making.

Michel Foucault's (1926–1984) notion about the "invisible visibility" is even more relevant to my argument about "fear of seeing," in both technological and political senses. In his archaeological study of clinical observations during the eighteenth and nineteenth centuries, Foucault offers an epistemological interpretation of the relations between the visible and invisible through a technological analysis of the medical gaze: "The structure, at once perceptual and epistemological, that demands clinical anatomy, and all medicine that derives from it, is that of *invisible visibility*."[13] Foucault's studies, which take a multitude of forms of archaeologies of different things and ideas, present "gaze" as a technology, a method, a power; a doctor's gaze, the sovereign resumption of the anatomic gaze, is directed upon the fundamental visibility of things. In Foucauldian terms, seeing, as a sovereign power, can map all across the thresholds of the visible and invisible. However, Foucault also unveils the mechanism of knowledge production as an intricate process of folding and enfolding: "Knowledge *develops* in accordance with a whole interplay of *envelopes*; the hidden element takes on the form and rhythm of the hidden content, which means that, like a *veil*, it is *transparent*."[14] Nothing is invisible to the gaze of the power, and yet, there is the necessity of invisibility. The interchangeability of the visible and invisible is the key to power structures, knowledge production, and epistemic perspectives.

Foucault inspires a new way of understanding the invisible as a technological and political construct, and seeing, if positioned from the opposite of the power, forms a resistance to a certain opaque reality as a deliberate veiling of truth. The invisible in contemporary Chinese SF reverses the Foucauldian structure of seeing and power. In new wave SF, seeing is to return the gaze into the invisible darkness of the power. Already an established device in theology, fantasy, and SF, invisibility implies a certain extraordinary agency—a magic power, a forbidden ability, or a nefarious scientific method as practiced by H. G. Wells's (1866–1946) invisible man. In a mystical and transcendental way, the invisible "points to realms beyond our senses, serves as a receptacle for fears and dreams, hints at worlds where other rules apply and challenge our moral responsibility."[15] When historicized, however, the invisibles are not just phantoms and magic wonderlands, but as Foucault's studies have unveiled, they are also the epistemologically and politically enfolded and enveloped knowledge; the habitually ignored social injustice; the haunting absences stereotyped in the domains of sex, class, and race; and above all, the "heart of darkness" in both imperialist and socialist orders. Modern SF, since Wells, has never stopped alluding to the invisible dystopian nature of a present-day dictatorship or capitalist system.

Representing the invisible unchains and unpacks the literary imagination, breaks down conventions and doctrines, and creates images of alternative worlds that enlighten us as to the nature of our own, converging in "seeing" beyond a certain reality that we are accustomed to, which is "visible" but deliberately polished, glossed, or veiled by ideological illusions. The alternative visions arising from the astonishing wonders of the unseen and unreal challenge customary social codes and political doctrines that are dictated by the power. The poetics of the invisible prompts an insurgent imagination that makes our "disciplined" sense of reality uncertain and brings into question the validity of our "dictated" knowledge and belief systems. Seeing the truthfulness in the invisible also means that the perceivable reality is not always "real," and the "legitimate" worldview often falsely claims a singular "truth."

Today, what has been "invisible" for an ordinary Chinese citizen may just be the other side of a guarded high wall, quarantined districts, or the web page of HTTP 404;[16] in the purview of the entire nation, what is invisible in China today can be an entire world hidden so intricately that its truth has become inexplicably misty or forever lost. SF plots unfold as a process of "truth investigation," an action that Han Song literally refers to in his novels.[17] The choice of seeing the invisible decides the self-reflective nature of the new wave. With a gaze toward the unsettling, darker world, SF transforms its own storytelling into a virtual looking glass created on paper that helps readers overcome the fear of seeing and resort to scientific methods to behold a speculative world of truthfulness.

In a certain sense, new wave SF represents more than what China's conventional realism depicts in a literary text; it represents both the visible appearance and invisible depths of reality, both phenomena and noumena. Two outstanding characteristics surpass traditional realism to represent the truthfulness of our changing world in its *visible invisibility*. One lies in SF's genetic affinity to the advanced modern sciences that have long departed from the nineteenth-century epistemology corresponding to mimetic realism; the other is SF's generic affinity to utopianism that has varied, darkened, turned into its antithesis, or mutated into the other space (heterotopia) in responses to the drastic changes and catastrophes of modern times.

Han Song, Liu Cixin, and their peers' literary experiments have bid farewell to the long-standing tradition of mimetic realism, epitomized by assuring and persuading verisimilitude, the cultural equivalent to the stabilizing Newtonian universe founded on well-regulated physical laws. A SF way of spelling out the wonder of new wave SF is that it has achieved a "quantum revolution" in literary representation, which shatters the order of things in the contemporary Chinese literary and cultural establishment. The utopian, dystopian, and heterotopian variations of new wave SF have opened a new literary space—an uncharted, undifferentiated, nonhierarchical, and nonbinary universe that may have nothing solid to hold on to, that exists in eternal fluidity and fluctuation.

First, in a seemingly contradictory way, it is the scientific discourse that has made the new wave both "popular" and "subversive." The "popular" part can be categorical; as a matter of fact, Chinese SF is still categorized officially as a literature of "popular science," tasked with the mission to popularize scientific knowledge and promote technological savviness.[18] The new wave takes a complicated view of the cult of technology that prevails when our contemporary life—from social behavior to personal expression—has been technologized and continuously "upgraded" by all sorts of new gadgets as well as systematic changes in bioengineering, cybernetics, robotics, big data analytics, and social networking services. SF is the de facto popular literary form to illustrate these new changes effectively before they have arrived. To rephrase William Gibson's (b. 1948) prophetic proverb, "The future is already here—it's just not evenly distributed,"[19] SF popularizes the future of technology as a sign for the unseen changes that are bound to come, and for the uncertain and unpredictable transfigurations of all possible futures.

New sciences and technologies, ranging from quantum computing to artificial intelligence, from virtual reality to the superstring multiverse, function as the driving forces in contemporary SF imaginations. These theories have opened horizons toward new speculative wonders: subatomic folded dimensions, invisible dark matters, and quantum uncertainty; it is not an exaggeration to say that the new physics makes the world we know appear to lose its solid materiality and tangible realness. As a liberating force, the new revolution in sciences constitutes the nexus of assorted kaleidoscopic approaches and branches of new knowledges and judgments, and it forms the epistemological foundation for a breakthrough in literature, a new framework of imagination combined with a new relativity of perceptions.

As long as it is a theory, science *is* fiction; new scientific theories are as speculative and counterintuitive as fictional representations of the invisible. Every revolutionary new scientific theory sounds like a fictionization of reality contrary to our intuition: just imagine how you would, based on your instinct, respond to the heliocentric theory that Copernicus (1473–1543) advocated if Galileo (1564–1642) had never invented the telescope to detect the irregular movements of Jupiter's moons; not to mention what modern scientists—including Albert Einstein (1879–1955), Werner Heisenberg (1901–1976), Alan Turing (1912–1954), Stephen Hawking (1942–2018), and Roger Penrose (b. 1931)—have theorized, all impossible to think about based on observations by the naked human eye. SF typifies the most "contemporary" form of literature with its entanglement of science and fiction. The genre creates a literary space to allow speculative sciences and thought experiments to crystalize into narratives and world-buildings that edge out of our familiar reality and expand to include an infinitude of possible worlds. The wondrous marvels in SF can be based upon speculations that are as specific as changing basic physical rules, a strategy that Liu Cixin favors and often uses to create awe-inspiring spectacles;[20] or as grandiose as alterations of the entire human moral system and planetary ecosystems, such as Hao Jingfang's heterotopian vision of a Martian ecology and sociology, a mirror image to our own world or a soft version of the hidden 1984 scenario in our own society;[21] or as grotesque as the posthuman medical technologies that create narratives blurring reality and illusion, exemplified by Han Song's almighty algorithm named "Life Control," who assumes the personification of a delusional, suicidal behavior artist.[22] All these represent new wave SF's vigorous engagement with both contemporary sciences and society, pointing to alterity, defiance, and transgression in both domains.

Second, utopianism and its variations in new wave SF have strengthened the genre's political resonance in contemporary China. In the early twentieth century, SF was combined with utopian fiction as one genre dreaming of a better new China. The more recent dystopian turn in SF exhibits a different utopian impulse that takes the form of sharpened social criticism. The dystopian gaze also brings out a dark consciousness that can be manifested as vigilance before any menacing threats arise, or a self-conscious gaze into what is terrifyingly invisible and yet to emerge out of the nebulous future, or a post-anthropocentric attitude toward the apocalypse of the human-dominated world and a posthuman position to stay with trouble, making kin with all surviving species on a decaying, ruined planet.[23]

Utopian variation, including dystopia, always denotes a revolt against the apparent reality or a rejection of the status quo. But the most relevant variation of utopia in relation to the invisible is heterotopia, which can also be a nonbinary concept. The idea of heterotopia escapes the utopian/dystopian dichotomy and a totalistic certainty.[24] A medical term first appropriated by Michel Foucault to refer to the other space excluded or hidden from the normative society, heterotopia emphasizes the visible invisibility. Compared with utopia and dystopia, heterotopia is less based on an idealistic principle of hope but more dicentric and diverse, open to more practical possibilities without being limited to one singular form of dream.[25] It resides within the apparent reality but is invisible by design, traditionally enfolded into forbidden, separate spaces that serve as clinics, hospitals, prisons, etc. If utopia and dystopia are two sides of one singular coin, representing two opposing approaches to inspiring the same hope for a totalistic change, heterotopia is a multilayered and multifaceted version of hope, and when unfolding into a literary vision, it creates "a (textual, virtual, or actual) space of otherness. Its spatiality contains more layers of meaning or relationships to other places than immediately meet the eye."[26]

Utopian, dystopian, or heterotopian, the SF visions engage imaginary worlds disjointed from but also entangled with the immediate reality. In general, even in pure "soft" escapism, otherworldly speculation on the invisible can potentially instigate alternative thinking in the face of the "hard" reality. Grounded in a subversion of the familiar "reality" through imagining the "novum" in scientific, technological, and potentially political terms, new wave SF brings out a queer newness that lays the foundations for prodigious world-buildings that present anomalous senses of what is real and unreal, both reflecting our lack of vision and illuminating what is invisible in and beyond our sight.

IN TOMBS BEGINS A NEW LITERATURE, 1988/1925

Han Song's career as a SF author started far before he wrote *Mars Over America* in 2000. More than a decade earlier, he wrote "Tombs of the Universe" 宇宙墓碑. It was not only his own but also the entire new wave's first major story, a hidden origin long before its overt rise. In July 1988, Han Song, just graduated from college, wrote it over a stretch of three days while still on campus.[27] He sent the manuscript to *Science Fiction World* 科幻世界 (*SFW*), which first rejected it but later requested that Han Song resubmit it for publication, after it won a big prize in Taiwan in 1991. This story almost edged into oblivion and only surfaced through a roundabout detour. Now a classic, "Tombs of the Universe" was officially published in China four years after its composition, in May 1992, a new age that drastically differed from the 1980s, a decade of hope that had reached a dead end with the Tiananmen Incident.

If "Tombs of the Universe" is an invisible origin of the new wave, invisibility also sets the keynote of the narrative and defines the dark tone of its textuality. The story unfolds around the mystery of massive, monumental tombs disappearing into the darkness of the universe. At an uncertain point in the future, humans begin the journey into outer space, confronting various unpredictable fatal threats; tombs are built everywhere in space to commemorate those enormous sacrifices. Tomb building in deep space becomes a trade, an art, a ritual, and a culture flourishing in the vast inhuman emptiness. It creates a historical period named the "Grave Burial Era." But one day, those "vast clusters of tombs disappeared, as if they evaporated from time and space. This was an unbelievable phenomenon, and the truth has always been concealed."[28]

The narrative consists of two parts. The first part is set in a further distant future, when those tombs have been long gone, with only a few surviving clusters in remote, desolate areas in humans' home system: the solar system. The narrator catches an initial glimpse of the space graveyard on Mars in his boyhood and instantly succumbs to the grandeur and mystique of the tombs. He set his heart on becoming an archaeologist to investigate the history of this ancient ritual of tomb building. But he does not find the truth behind this opaque puzzle until he is 100 years old, when his son informs him of a new trend of grave digging. The narrator's wife, Ayu 阿羽, never happy with his research on the tombs, now relapses into a mysterious illness that seems to be triggered by this news. While attending to his wife, the narrator cannot help thinking about one specific tomb discovered on a planetoid orbiting Cygnus A. His research has concluded that it should be the last tomb built at the very end of the Grave Burial Era. In contrast to those imposing vast graveyards with compulsory magnificence, taking full advantage of the light from shining stars and gigantic planets, highly symbolic of the heroism of space exploration, this almost unobservable tiny tomb is built on the least noticeable small planetoid that travels in the longest possible protracted darkness, from where, despite rotation and orbit, the brighter, larger planets of the star system cannot be seen.

The second part is narrated by a person who informs us that he is the maker of that small unique tomb. He tells his life story, of his education as a tomb builder, his long career in outer space. The first tomb he builds is a giant cube; its magnificent shape "gave the feeling of the quiet and stillness of time and space, suggesting an eternal stance." The burial ceremony is a solemn expression of majesty and grandeur. At the time, however, he feels something eerie and uncanny. Very soon after, he learns that the tomb is empty. Nobody is in it. Then, what is the purpose of the tomb? Just a lie? After this, the narrator's belief in and perception of the world are changed. Disillusioned, he keeps building tombs without thinking, tombs without bodies inside. The entire team of tomb builders, who know the truth but never leak it, are mired in a cloud of uncertainty, which drives some to suicide. Even though romantic relationships are strictly forbidden in space because people believe they bring bad luck, the narrator meets a petite young woman named Ayu 阿羽, and likes her. Ayu dies in an accident two months after their first encounter. The narrator asks a friend to make a tomb for her on a desolate planet. Years later, the narrator finally musters his courage to visit Ayu's tomb, but by this time, all tombs in the universe have mysteriously disappeared. The narrator, now aged and delusional, believes that the universe is the *real* tomb. He sees Ayu's ghost, talks to her, and builds the last tomb for himself, one that is simple and obscure, floating in the eternal darkness like a blasphemy to his own death. At the end of his life, he comes to see the intention of the universe: "The kind, old, universe wants us to walk with it and rest in peace with it as one, but how could humankind, with their naivety and self-loathing, believe this!"[29] Finally he lies down in his tiny grave, waiting for "the endless darkness" to take him.

The tomb is the first image that connects new wave Chinese SF to Lu Xun. Sixty-three years before Han Song wrote "Tombs of the Universe," Lu Xun wrote a prose poem titled "Inscriptions on the Tomb" 墓碣文 (1925). The poem describes an eerie, uncanny dream, in which the lyrical narrator faces a stone tablet of a tomb, trying to read the inscriptions: "I see the abyss in the heavens. I see the nothingness in all eyes." The narrator walks around to the back of the tomb and finds it wide open, the dead a dismembered corpse, without heart and liver. The dead person is supposed to be the poet who writes the inscriptions. In doubt and dread, the narrator reads more words inscribed on the back of the tomb: "I tore out my heart to eat it, wanting to know its true taste. But the pain was so agonizing, how could I tell its taste?" The narrator hurries away, fearing to see the dead following him.[30]

It is not certain if Han Song borrowed the image of the tomb directly from Lu Xun, but it is clear that the tomb is the central image that connects the texts. The verbal intensity of Lu Xun's poem and the acute perplexity of its opaque implications are matched by Han Song's abstruse narrative and its semantic uncertainty. In both cases, the tomb, appearing together with the words of the dead, is the unsettling manifestation of something that would be better kept invisible. The tomb functions as the chiasm between the living and the dead, the apparent and the abysmal, and the visible and the invisible. The invisibility of what is inside conceals the "true event," a horror, a catastrophe, an apocalypse. Revealing or unconcealing the "invisible" not only evokes a profound fear but also marks an anachronism that comes in the form of either apparition or aporia. Something from the deep oblivion of a destructive past, or from a presaged future predicament echoing the historical contingency of the cosmic mystique, pervades the contemporary timeline. Catching a glimpse of the atrocious invisible leads to the agonizing confrontation with an inexplicable and unfathomable truth (or "death") beyond the reach of reason and human understanding. That the pitch-dark universe is the *real* tomb (of the universe itself?) in Han Song's story perpetuates an eternal mystery that overpowers human intelligence. Correspondingly, Lu Xun's corpse cannibalistically devouring its heart no doubt alludes to Lu Xun's own relentless self-doubt, which can never settle on a sound, valid, certain, or logical answer. In both cases, the "heart" of the matter is ultimately *absent*, and it is invisibility that entombs the foundation of an estranging literary world.

About a year after Lu Xun wrote this poem, he edited the first volume of his essays and titled it *The Grave* 墳 (1926). The tomb, again. To Lu Xun, "*The Grave* is a past life brought together in writing."[31] Here, the grave, or tomb, paradoxically gains two entangled significances. The tomb buries the dead and leaves traces of a past life. It signifies both the quietus and the testimonial of a life lived and ended. Yet Lu Xun uses this image to characterize his own literary writing, which, like the grave, both conceals the *enclosed* past and testifies to its *manifest* vibrance. In a miraculous way, literary writing both affirms the invisibility of an impenetrable world and unfolds it profusely and abundantly into words. In tombs begins a literary world that entangles the visible and the invisible.

Among all contemporary Chinese SF writers, Han Song is perhaps the most devoted disciple of Lu Xun. For him, tombs of the universe exemplify an even more paradoxical significance about life and death. A tomb begins with the intention to cover the dead, but when a tomb is found empty, what is covered is nobody, nothingness, a void. This emptiness is marked with a majestic and monumental shape representing the glory of humanity as a legacy for the future. This irony is quietly muted in the text, which turns cynicism into genuine sadness when all tombs, concealing nothingness, disappear into darkness. The story offers no explanation for this mystery. One can read it as a testimonial to the posthuman transcendence of human-centric arrogance[32] or a critique of deathly technologism. When connected to Han Song's later long novel cycles about the total population of human beings whose life and death are manipulated by algorithms, the inhuman conditions in tombs may elicit perorations of that necropolitics, a critique of our contemporary world as a "death-world" plagued by inequality, enmity, and terror, while humanness is already dead.[33]

In Foucault's study of the visible invisibility in relation to the birth of the clinic, he suggests that there may be an exception, a singularity that exists in "the forbidden, imminent secret: the knowledge of the individual"[34]—though transparent to doctors, death is one's incommunicable secret. In the case of tuberculosis for the nineteenth-century men of letters, "Death left its old tragic heaven and became the lyrical core of man: his invisible truth, his visible secret."[35] This last sentence may enable us to appreciate both Lu Xun's and Han Song's obsession with death and tombs. Death is ultimately individual and invisible, forming the hidden gravitational pull in the fabric of a literary cosmos.

Strategically, I propose to recognize this story as one of two cornerstones for the new wave. It is built upon Han Song's inheritance of Lu Xun's spectral picturing of the innermost darkness, a dark consciousness from the depth of history. This dark consciousness overshadows the entire oeuvre of Han Song. In "Tombs of the Universe," darkness is the eternal color of the universe, which not only incites fear but also embodies a profound sadness, combining both personal grief and historical melancholia. When the second narrator is genuinely mourning the death of his beloved woman at the very end of his life, the pitch-dark universe comes to him, as if it feels and answers the dark in his heart. Compared with the glowing light cast upon the monumental but empty tombs, the tenebrosity of his little tomb is a tiny counterpoint to the immeasurable dark of the universe. Holding a loving heart in the dark, this tiny spot in the almighty, all-embracing cosmic darkness also provides a counterbalance to Lu Xun's broken tomb that manifests, through inscriptions, the agonizing pains of the imperceptible internal conflict occurring in the void bosom of the dead, the depleted poet.

Both authors' obsession with the dark can be interpreted according to Chang Hao's 張灝 (1937–2022) notion of "dark consciousness": "an attention to and critical reflection on the inherent dark side of humanity as well as the dark forces deeply rooted in human society."[36] As further explained by David Der-wei Wang, "dark consciousness" is not just an ontological or historical notion of the "degeneracy of moral, religious or ideological schemata," it is a "fictional power that facilitates the diacritical thrust of *aporia* from within, and beyond, the establishments of human values and beliefs where disturbance is least expected." In other words, "dark consciousness" is an "abysmal force that voids established values."[37] It registers an anticipation of both fear and aspiration, in opposition to various forms of optimism that serve as foundations for various ideologies. From this dark consciousness arises the unorthodox and groundbreaking new wave.

The courageous, self-aware choice to see into the darkness gives new wave SF an ethical awareness of the agency of literary imagination. For example, Han Song's sober confrontation with the dark side of China's reality, combined with a strong sense of melancholia, opens his eyes to see deeper into the abysmal depth of contemporary reality. Han Song carries over Lu Xun's suspicion toward hope. His stories are based on an impenetrable despair that pulverizes hope, tearing apart the Panglossian faith in what is the best of all possible worlds. Lu Xun's ultimate recognition of the world as "nothingness," a profound void (无物之阵),[38] is another important spiritual inheritance that Han Song carries over. In his science fictional worlds, the future history that features a variety of advanced inhuman technologies as well as everlasting pains and sorrows imposed upon all humans culminates in a recognition that the splendid prosperity and great achievements of civilization are nothing but thinly veiled waste and ruin. After an exhaustive search for meaning in the universe, Han Song ends up, as Lu Xun's poem does, "seeing the abyss in the heavens; seeing nothingness in all eyes."[39]

If the sublime images in China's Panglossian dream are blinding, the new wave is the opposite. It turns to the dark and beholds the invisible gleams of the darkness, as Han Song says in a style reminiscent of Lu Xun: "Only by stepping into the darkest place can one see the strongest light. Only by falling into the deepest despair can one find the most promising hope."[40] Back in the late 1980s, Han Song secretly started to build in the darkness of the tombs a new literary universe that glows—invisibly.

LOST ORIGINS OF A POSTHUMAN UPRISING, 1989/2185

One year after Han Song wrote "Tombs of the Universe," Liu Cixin composed his first SF novel: *China 2185* 中國2185. Although it was never published, this novel formed another hidden origin of the new wave. Han Song and Liu Cixin did not know each other at the time, yet their respective visions function like parallel universes offering multiple entrances into the latent literary world of the new wave. The appearance of these two works, then invisible to all but their authors, marked a new paradigm of literary imagination that began to emerge and enliven the genre's cultural dynamics.

At twenty-six, Liu Cixin drafted *China 2185* in February 1989.[41] The importance of that year was highlighted by Liu himself in an essay that describes how he came to Beijing for a computer science conference that spring and got stuck in a small hotel because of the student protest in Tiananmen Square. On June 3, 1989, the fateful night of the protest's tragic end as Liberation Army soldiers marched toward the square, Liu was left alone in the hotel room. In his account of how he began to write SF, he mentions a nightmare he had on that restless night, featuring bayonets, troops, children, war, the dying sun, and an explosive supernova.[42] The nightmare evolved into an idea for a novel titled *Supernova Era* 超新星紀元. This novel and *China 2185* were the first two that Liu Cixin completed in his career as a SF writer. *China 2185*, still unpublished today, dramatizes a cybernetic uprising in which Mao is resurrected, and *Supernova Era* presents an anarchic future ruled by children playing a war game. Throughout the 1990s, Liu Cixin kept writing and rewriting the two novels until *Supernova Era* became his first published book in 2003.

Both novels feature themes and conflicts that reappear in Liu Cixin's later, more mature works, such as the changing of fundamental physical laws of our world, which correspondingly motivates the changing of social rules and moral codes; apocalyptical threats to human survival; negotiation between human conscience and posthuman uncertainty; contention between democracy and centralist leadership; and conflict between the limits of resources and the urge for development. Both novels already foreshadowed his aesthetics of the sublime and sober alertness to the invisible darkness within humans and the cosmos. *Supernova Era* bases its imaginary world system on the speculated catastrophic effect of an exploding supernova, which leaves only children alive on Earth. This brave new world populated by children is a wild experiment with uncontrolled social behavior and childish war games. But just as numerous revisions tamed Liu's text, the children in the novel learn to behave and administer the future world with adult wisdom.[43]

In comparison, *China 2185* depicts a future even closer to the 1980s and much wilder.[44] Without any direct reference to the student movement, the novel begins with a scene in Tiananmen Square: a young computer science student crosses the deserted square on a dark night and approaches the Mao Mausoleum, still standing in 2185 but invisible to the public, because the square, covered by abundant vegetation, has been long deserted. The student manages to scan Mao's dead brain cells, digitizing his consciousness and giving rise to the great man's cybernetic existence. Combining political fantasy with SF, *China 2185* describes the resurrection of Mao. After his digital specter is uploaded into cyberspace, a cybernetic uprising is triggered and paralyzes the authorities in the real world. But it turns out that Mao's cyber ghost is not, as one would have expected, the cause of the revolution, which was actually launched by an ordinary old man's cyberized consciousness. This unhappy, lonely old man, who has endless complaints about a fully rejuvenated China that adores youths more than elders, replicates his digital phantoms millions of times and quickly builds a virtual dynasty that lasts six hundred years—in virtual reality, which is equivalent to only two hours in reality.

This virtual world, called Huaxia Republic 華夏共和國, is the first cognitively estranging world that Liu Cixin contributed to Chinese SF and laid the foundation for nearly all his world-building in his future works. It is depicted as a universe of its own kind, which begins as a hyperdimensional paradise, a completely new realm born in cyberspace. Cybernetic subjectivities coming to life in this world experience boundless time and space all at once, a prototype of the hyperdimensional universe in the Three-Body novels. But almost immediately, this pastoral, idyllic world becomes a "dark forest" when awareness of the limitation of resources motivates competition and mutual attacks. Huaxia (the ancient name for China), like China, has to go through centuries of war and peace to find a better form of government, which is not a democracy like the "real-time" China in 2185. Rather, it is a restoration of the older patriarchal regime that places the elders at the top of the social hierarchy. The scholar Hua Li compares this mentality to the gerontocracy in Chinese politics during the 1980s, when conservatives staged two campaigns to attack the reformers; this is reflected in an attempted coup d'état that aims to force the real-time government of China in 2185, now administered by young people, to restore tradition.[45]

The government in 2185 is a fully realized democracy with a directly elected president, who is a young woman. Facing this aggressive cybernetic uprising, she has no way out but shutting down the entire internet, and the virtual Huaxia Republic is wiped out. When all the outcries for restoration in cyberspace stop, the novel ends with a conversation between Mao's digital specter and the young leader of the Chinese government. Mao's ghost honestly tells his future successor that "immortality is mortality" and what is dead, even though it is viewed as "immortal," is dead after all; he appears to be at ease with the young generation's eventual farewell to his own revolution.[46]

This novel is filled with the prevailing discourses on reform and democracy during the 1980s, but even so, Liu Cixin does not simply discredit Mao's political legacy. Instead, he concentrates on creating a strong sense of uncertainty in both historical and technological terms. His vision focuses on experiments of conceiving "alterity" for the "post-Mao" and "posthuman" new ages, even though there was no such term as "posthuman" when Liu wrote the novel. The future China he depicts seems to be an optimistic vision in the long line of Chinese utopian fiction about the future of New China, which started with the late Qing reformer Liang Qichao 梁啟超 (1873–1929), who first chose youth as a sign of the new age and invented the political utopian fiction tradition by composing *Future of New China* 新中國未來記 (1902).[47] Liu Cixin's future China also has a youthful face—restless, amorphous, impulsive, and constantly changing. This new China is a total rejection of historical determinism. At the same time, technological progress in this new world brings even more uncertainties, including Mao's second coming, a Maoist revolution, and uncontrollable interactions between the virtual and real-time realities.

China 2185 certainly displays a utopian hope: democracy will work in a future world where the young leader is passionately engaged in the free exchange of ideas through an online forum, simultaneously talking to millions of citizens sitting at their individual terminals. The novel sees the great potential for democracy in the development of an all-embracing internet. Compared with our current reality, Liu's version is primitive, not accessible through touchscreens or mobile devices. But its direct line of communication between users facilitates the extension of humanism into the human-to-artificial-intelligence relationships depicted in the later part of the novel. These communications are by nature democratic, recognizing equal rights between men and women and between humans and "posthumans." The virtual lives embodying the consciousness of elders who made revolution are known as "electronic pulsing men." Despite being purely digital and having no bodies, they are eventually considered to have equal rights like the humans. Thus, the democracy in *China 2185* not only is based on the humanist ideals of the 1980s but also evokes the trans-anthropocentric posthumanism of the twenty-first century.

Even with revisions made throughout the 1990s, *China 2185* is still primarily a work concerning China's experience in the 1980s, a decade of high idealism and optimism. If read as a political allegory, the novel offers a post-Mao alternative history about China's younger generation's pursuit of political reforms and their decisive battle with elders in a virtual space. *China 2185* seems to recognize in Mao's heritage a forward-looking utopian urge, which works well with the future government's youthful mindset, while Mao's specter, as a remainder of the past, is no longer part of this utopian dream, so the story ends with his exit from history. But in an uncanny way, it also presages a situation of uncertainty that has only become meaningful in our contemporary reality, the real future to the novel's age of composition.

The posthuman estrangement in this novel is a rather sophisticated world-building that gives virtual forms of cybernetic life a certain subjectivity, the foundation of political consciousness in the "unreal" digital world. However, cyber politics is radically different from what the pro-democracy reformers have envisioned. Online politics does not follow the rules of two-way negotiation, and information sharing is unpredictable, not at all the constructive communication required for a democratic political culture. The posthuman uprising in 2185 is made possible by an anonymous multitude of the phantom "mass," who are all mobilized in a Maoist strategy of a "human sea attack." Such attacks have become everyday life in China's cyberspace in the 2020s.

The virtual Huaxia Republic's invasion in the future "real" China is based on the changing science regarding the interface between reality and cyberspace. In 1989, when Liu envisioned the future, there was still a clear division between social reality and cyberspace. In *China 2185*, the virtual is still conceptual. Liu Cixin is, of course, not a prophet, and the novel is not a direct or intentional prophecy of what is happening now. However, reading *China 2185* three decades later, we may find that the interface between reality and the virtual world has become blurred, with the internet now under nearly total control by the state. In the future that has *actually* arrived, technological progress certainly does not translate into democracy in contemporary China. The state has taken advantage of cyberspace to construct "big data" and execute "deep surveillance." A virtual China, safeguarded or isolated by the Great Firewall, governs and mobilizes the anonymous virtual mass in an authoritarian national dream. The democracy compatible with cybernetics portrayed so optimistically in *China 2185* seems a lost illusion. What has become real is Liu's imagined world of technological progress, and decades after the novel was composed, China's prosperous cyberspace, indeed haunted by Mao's phantoms, is the opposite of a democracy. The specter of Mao has come back in Chinese political culture and taken digital and virtual forms, this time refusing to bid farewell to revolution and stirring up outcries for strongman politics. Mao's final gesture of farewell in *China 2185* fit well in the political culture of the 1980s, but it now reads like a poignantly faded daydream of democracy that missed its only opportunity in 1989. Reading this now "invisible" novel thirty-three years later, we may find its anachronism acutely poignant.

But in the history of Chinese SF, *China 2185*, as the hidden origin of Liu Cixin's SF universe, silently signaled the arrival of a new type of SF that combines political consciousness with scientific imagination. Although largely unknown until Liu Cixin became a best-selling author, it predicted a radically different roadmap for Chinese SF to break out from its original domain as a branch of children's literature. A SF novel like this had never appeared in China before, a work so sophisticated, reflective, and subversive in its mixed representations of hope and despair, utopianism and its dystopian potential, and democratic cybernetics alongside cybernetic totalitarianism. It may be a stretch to describe the work as political cyberpunk, but that impulse is unmistakable in the way it entangles science and politics in an almost quantum uncertainty, which continues and evolves to larger world-buildings in Liu Cixin's Three-Body novels, unfolding both the most sublime and the darkest visions in Chinese SF.

TECHNOLOGIES OF DREAMING, 2002/2012

Both Liu Cixin and Han Song made breakthroughs at the beginning of the twenty-first century. The new wave began to emerge in the SF circle, largely unknown to general readers. In 2002, Han Song wrote two stories that serve as the main inspirations for me to conceptualize the poetics of the invisible. The title of this book, "Fear of Seeing" (看的恐惧), is borrowed from one of the stories.

In Han Song's "Fear of Seeing," a baby is born with ten eyes in its forehead. The parents are worried, but also curious about what the baby sees, how it perceives the world, and how it dreams.[48] A computer scientist helps connect the infant's brain to a device that projects its visual perception onto a screen. What the parents see on the screen, however, is not the familiar scene of the bedroom where the baby is, but instead "some contiguous gray foggy mass."[49] After a long period of troubling research, the scientist comes to the conclusion that the baby, with its special vision, actually sees the "truth" of the world: "The true appearance of the world was something like that thick fog, chaotic and primordial, without form or flavor," and "the world as sensed by us so-called normal people is an illusion, it doesn't exist—*this* is actual reality."[50] This discovery throws the parents into a panic: when they take another look at their daily reality—the recently bought apartment, the expensive furniture and electronics, their jobs, their shared life—there is a creepy unrealness in everything. Are they all fabricated illusions? Then who engineers the ordinary sight we take for granted as reality? The story suggests a conspiracy involving national security, but before any clear answer is found, the ten-eyed infants—yes, there are many of them—have cut out the eyes of their parents. Here the story betrays an uneasy relationship between reality and representation: Do we all need ten eyes in our forehead to see through the falsity of the "reality"? Or do we all need a science fictional wonder to illuminate what is the invisible real? What is the cost of seeing the fearful truth?

This story by Han Song, deceptively simple but acutely uncanny, can serve as a metatext that conceives a self-reflective speculation on SF as a form of truth-claiming storytelling. SF opens our eyes to the fearful invisible, and the inexplicable and unaccustomed sensations that it generates through a scientific abstraction of the world's estranging appearance unsettle the comforting definition of reality. "Fear of Seeing" may appear to be detached from politics and more metaphysical, but new wave SF, as a literary experiment, has achieved about the same effect, seeing through a Chinese reality that has been fabricated in mass media and state propaganda and shaped by mainstream values and cultural habitus. By the time Han Song wrote this story, he had become a journalist. In China's current social milieu, investigative journalism—Han Song's official profession—has been strictly obstructed by state apparatuses; what happens in broad daylight but must be kept invisible turns into the creative motor of Han Song's science fictional storytelling, for him always a nocturnal, Kafkaesque activity, approaching the fundamental question of what is *true* of this world. His characters, who are often disguised, failed, or metaphysical "investigative journalists," take on treacherous, chthonian journeys to seek truth in the dark, in the deep, in abysmal outer space—truth beyond manifestations of knowable reality.

In the same year he published "Fear of Seeing," Han Song wrote "My Fatherland Does Not Dream" (我的祖國不做夢, 2002), one of his many stories that have never been published in China.[51] The latter presents another surreal image of China's invisible reality, a hideous story about the nightmarish side of the country's economic boom: the entire population of an unnamed capital city is "sleepwalking," unconsciously participating in the creation of the country's economic miracle and realizing the nation's dream of wealth and power. The word Han Song uses for "sleepwalk" is *mengyou* (夢遊), which literally means "dream walking," but he emphasizes that those who *mengyou* do not remember their dreams when they wake up in the morning. They do not "see" or even "envision" their dreams, and the entire sleepwalking population roams the land blindly and purposelessly.

Their nocturnal activities, however, make everyone feel so tired that they have to take medicine called "efficacious sleep repellents" (去睏靈), manufactured by a state-owned arsenal (once used to manufacture tanks and cannons!), in order to stay awake during the day. A young Chinese investigative journalist, Xiao Ji 小紀, is puzzled by the prevailing daytime exhaustion. He meets an American who offers him a special medical device that prevents him from falling asleep at night, whereas the China-made "sleep repellents" only work during the day.

Thus, Xiao Ji discovers the secret of the city's sleepwalking phenomenon. He witnesses his wife, neighbors, and everyone else residing in the community walking like zombies in the streets and boarding buses that transport them to factories, companies, arsenals, research laboratories, and shopping malls, where they work, research, and consume mindlessly. Sleepwalking teachers teach sleepwalking students, sleepwalking cadres talk to sleepwalking audiences, and sleepwalking policemen chase sleepwalking criminals.

Xiao Ji also discovers that every night his wife is transported to a hotel room to provide special sexual service to an old man, who is actually not sleepwalking. Xiao Ji confronts the old man, whom he recognizes as a national leader. The old man eloquently lectures Xiao Ji about why it is important to keep sleepwalking a national policy. The Chinese government has invented a marvelous technology for manipulating people's sleep through secretly sending "communal microwaves" (社區微波). Sleepwalking proves to be an efficient way of sustaining China's rapid economic development. It enables the sleeping people to be better organized to work, consume, and socialize harmoniously, creating a new nation of disciplined and devoted citizens. The old man proudly tells Xiao Ji, "Because of sleepwalking, over one billion Chinese people have awakened," which sounds like a reprise of Lu Xun and his generation's famous call for enlightenment but ironically betrays the self-contradiction in the current political discourse. Awaking only results in sleepwalking, which is perhaps even worse than sleeping. The entire population is fully manipulated to achieve one goal—the goal of the nation; they are deprived of the right to see the truth of reality and to dream an alternative dream.

Han Song's story was written ten years before the Chinese government began to promote the "Chinese dream" (2012)—a collective dream for the entire nation. In the story, sleepwalkers act out the uncanny unconscious of the Chinese dream dictated by the very few "sleepless" national leaders on a "Darkness Committee" (黑暗委員會). The sleepwalking population turns the Chinese dream into an (un)reality they do not see and live in a dream that is not theirs. But Han Song's protagonist chooses to see the fearful invisible, and like Lu Xun's protagonists—those who are enlightened living among the unconscious cannibals—Xiao Ji becomes the only sober observer of a chilling darkness. The invisible operations of the Darkness Committee exert total control, yielding success that relies on its own invisibility and thus manipulating the minds of the entire population.

Han Song's more famous novel *Subway* uses the same word, "sleepwalking," to refer to the madness of the Cultural Revolution. In *Subway*, the old passenger riding the train remembers the Red Guards as green creatures possessed by demonic spirits, putting long nails into the foreheads of the elders;[52] the mysterious paranormal events happening in the Beijing subway system motivate a younger passenger to become a truth investigator, who begins to perceive sleepwalking as part of a "cosmopolitan" conspiracy that manipulates the entire world. If usage of the word "sleepwalking" for the former time period indicates a historical precedent, its usage in the contemporary setting seems to imply a lack of change or an endless loop, in which time's moving forward is an illusion. If the Red Guards sleepwalked in a great leader's dream of superhuman/inhuman madness, what are the contemporary Chinese people sleepwalking for?

Both "Fear of Seeing" and "My Fatherland Does Not Dream" showcase the distinctive poetics of the new wave in relation to the representation of an invisible contemporary China. On one hand, they point to the technological mechanism of the power governing and administrating the ordinary life of the Chinese people and their sense of reality, which renders SF itself an allegory that illuminates the deeper truth of China's contemporary reality. The fear of seeing, the invisibility of a terrifying truth, and the clandestine technologies of dreaming can all be metaphorically interpreted with apparent references to China's current political culture. On the other hand, each story's narrative uses a self-reflective strategy of displaying its own technologies of dreaming—reflecting both the hidden political mechanism of mind control and an interpretative approach to making this invisible mechanism representable in dreamlike SF textuality.

In this way, Han Song's SF storytelling is self-consciously becoming a de facto Chinese method, with its text and its implied message combined in the Chinese technologies of dreaming . . . about the invisible (un)reality of China. SF becomes a Klein bottle, a topology of imagination in which there is no difference between the interior and exterior, the message and the medium, the content and the form. With "Fear of Seeing" and "My Fatherland Does Not Dream," Han Song's SF becomes a metatext that manifests the poetics of the invisible.

SINOTOPIA: CHINA'S SCIENCE FICTIONAL SUBCONSCIOUS DREAMLAND

As new wave SF gained wider recognition, Han Song speculated on the intertwined fates of the nation and the genre: "China has become the world's second largest economy in 2011, but that's largely based on cheap labor. We do not have Stephen Hawking or Steve Jobs. Is it related to [the lack of] SF?"[53] He laments general readers' lack of interest in SF, which speaks to a lack of imagination. Han Song sees a magical power that could inspire a nation: "SF is unpredictable, so its newness in literature is particularly precious. SF is a sort of literature that dreams, and it is itself a utopia. It is not wild conjecture, but an imagination based on a certain reality.... It is so fortunate that I encountered SF in such a special epoch because I can therefore dream of more worlds."[54]

Han Song's emphasis on the relation between contemporary China and SF implies that the former needs the latter to become whole. Without SF, the representation of China is only a superficial surface covering what is unseen but unfathomably true. For Han Song, SF has the magic power of illuminating the unseen part of China, as if putting the missing piece in a puzzle. In his stories and novels, the nightmarish dreamscape reveals reality's abysmal depth, breaking apart the popular imagination that has been labeled, defined, and contained by the only "legitimate" dream, that of the state. Han Song's SF lays bare the nature of "observable" reality as fabricated with technologies of dreaming. "My Fatherland Does Not Dream" presents the starkest illustration of this point, itself both an evocation and a subversion of the official discourse on the "Chinese dream," laying bare its hidden mechanism through both the message and the form of storytelling. It depicts the Chinese dream as a sleepwalking spectacle even prior to the emergence of the actual concept. Han Song's Sinotopia speaks to China's reality that cannot be spoken about in "reality."

Nearly all of Han Song's stories and novels allude to the invisible mechanism of a technologized totalitarian government, either blatantly or suggestively related to the technology of power in contemporary China. In addition to depicting the country's human leadership as the Darkness Committee in "My Fatherland Does Not Dream," he creates various forms of posthuman beings—artificial intelligence, dream networks, algorithms—that administer and manipulate society in a posthuman future. All characterize the state apparatus executing total control over society and serving a certain ideological purpose, invisible to ordinary sight but integral to the overall structure of feeling in ordinary life. Han Song's storytelling turns into a "technologized" manifestation that makes hidden power visible in a SF reconfiguration of the real, dismantling the ideological surface of the country and reaching its subconscious dreamland.

Han Song's audacity exemplifies the new wave's entanglement with China's current politics. This new wave either evades or challenges the official and familiar version of the China image, which is the product of a certain utopianism, an ideology based on determinist teleology and evolutionary thinking that have been underlying China's pursuit of wealth and power for over a century. The representation of the Chinese dream's nightmarish subconscious leads to serious reflections on enlightenment ideals and revolutionary teleology. In depicting the looming, menacing future, SF casts shadows upon some of the key notions of Chinese modernity, such as progress, development, nationalism, scientism, and humanism.

The new wave complicates visions of the nation's future, introducing a strong discord into the triumphant rhetoric of historical determinism and tempering political consciousness with scientific discourse on uncertainty. Its acute awareness of both the potential and the menace of technological revolution sharpens social criticism and invites rethinking of the fate of individuals and nations in an age of relentless, ever accelerating technologization. The poetics and politics of the new wave are particularly timely and relevant as the Chinese government works to engineer the "Chinese dream." As neonationalism and neoauthoritarianism are on the rise with inventive technological supports ranging from cyber surveillance to big data to total control, SF has increasingly zeroed in on the implications of living within a dream, a malicious dystopian one. Speaking to what is happening invisibly as well as what is unfolding from latency, SF catalyzes a cognitive transformation that can be the harbinger of Leviathan changes. Laying bare the technologies of dreaming, new wave SF unpacks the Chinese dream together with its invisible subconscious, redefining what is contemporary reality, sweeping through an invisible terra incognita that we can now recognize as China's subconscious dream, a SF shadow image.

A NEW LITERARY UNIVERSE

Just as Liu Cixin speaks against people's neglect of the enthralling starry sky above,[55] SF represents outlandish wonders and spectacles, the infinite diversification of futures. The poetics of the invisible has made SF a distinctive literary genre that cuts sharply into the popular imagination and intellectual thinking of those who are even faintly aware of alterity. Through representing the invisible, the new wave energizes the genre by opening new possibilities for imagining different worlds, inspiring new ways of telling stories about China and the world.

It has begun to make a wider impact on contemporary Chinese literature, prompting experiments that commandeer new wave motifs and methods with or without acknowledgment. A wide range of moments representing SF's influences in literary texts can be found in works as diverse as novels by the master realist Wang Anyi, such as references to the evolution of species and zooming out to the viewpoint of outer space in her 2016 novel *Anonymity* 匿名,[56] and Li Hongwei's 李宏偉 (b. 1978) novel *The King and Lyric Poetry* 國王與抒情詩 (2017). Such elements have also surfaced in poetry by Zhai Yongming 翟永明 (b. 1955), Ouyang Jianghe 欧阳江河 (b. 1956), Liao Weitang 廖偉棠 (b. 1975), and Wang Ao 王敖 (b. 1978), and short stories by Wang Weilian 王威廉 (b. 1982) and Chen Chuncheng 陳春成 (b. 1990), not to mention SF's impact on writers residing in Hong Kong and Taiwan, particularly the experimentalist novelists Lo Yi-chin and Dung Kai-cheung. SF has increasingly become a new mode of literary thinking that inspires more creative, unconventional literary practice.

In a larger sense, contemporary literature dealing with themes of change motivated by technology and mutations of (post)human social conditions has increasingly been related to "science fictionality," which Istvan Csicsery-Ronay Jr. defines as a prevailing "science fictional habit of mind . . . a mode of response that frames and tests experiences as if they were aspects of a work of science fiction."[57] Science fictionality is not limited to the nature of the genre but alludes to a new structure of feeling based on the configuration of a technologized new world in the making. It can refer to a broad range of aesthetic sensibilities responding to the transformations occurring or about to occur in our world and everyday life. A rather audacious way of redefining what is contemporary is to recognize that the contemporary world has become increasingly science fictional. Science fictionality has played an increasingly important role in emerging patterns of fictional narrative within and outside the genre, which implies an overall reconfiguration of literary representation.

Ultimately, this study of the poetics of the invisible in Chinese SF should be situated in larger inquiries about what is contemporary literature and specifically, what the twenty-first century has informed, incited, and invoked in literature: an emerging new literary world; the decay of the long-standing tradition of mimesis; the wobbling, ossifying, or antinomies of classical literary realism; and the muting of "objective reality." An emerging new epistemology includes the burning out of external materiality and the infinitude of interior involutions; the decentering of the human on the cultural, ecological, and planetary levels; and the rise of new kinships across forms and formats, species and kinds, identities and differences. The new wave's fracturing, fragmenting, and fluidifying of narrative disturbs the "defining" images of China as it metamorphizes into a world power or unfolds into a *world of power*, in which the "power" itself disperses and mutates, technologically and literarily.

Now it is time for us to return to the foundation. What is science fiction? How does it relate to reality? Assumed to be the opposite of realism, new wave Chinese SF nevertheless drills deeper into reality; with a truth-claiming discourse, it operates as if in a parallel universe to mimetic realism. But the two are intertwined at the chiasm of the new wave representation of the invisible. What can we say about the new wave within the existing and current theoretical framework of SF studies in relation to realism? Can we render the Chinese new wave into a method, a precursor of a new literature emerging in the twenty-first century? From here, let us reexamine some basic theoretical conceptions about SF.

2

SCIENCE FICTION AS METHOD

Worlding the Genre

Liu Cixin's novella "Mountain" 山 (2006),[1] published just a few months before *The Three-Body Problem* began serialization in *SFW*, depicts a metallic intelligent species evolving into a civilization, but completely stuck in a bubble world hidden at the center of a rocky planet. Their world is a rather limited, enclosed dark space. They have no such concept as an "outside world," and the universe beyond the planet's solid rocky mantle is completely unknown to them. In other words, the reality they know is not *truthful*. Their intuitive perception of the apparent, observable appearance of the real is exactly the contrary of the truth, or *our* truth based on observations of the larger world beyond their bubble. In fact, the universe is invisible to them. Liu's narrative outlines this "bubble" civilization's epic journey of speculating and exploring an alternative world that is contrary to their intuitive knowledge. Liu borrows landmark events from human history to describe how these intelligent metallic creatures make their own geographical discovery and scientific revolution: their "Columbus" and "Copernicus" use theory and evidence to discredit their civilization's intuitive conceptualization of the visible reality as the only valid one. They dispute their conventional worldviews based on "a Solid Universe Theory" that "the bubble is absolutely the center of the universe" and "infinite layers of rocks encircle the bubble world." It takes extraordinary effort for the brave ones among them to invent scientific tools to test the gravitational pull as well as to build special vessels to travel through layers after layers of rocks to the surface of their planet, where they finally see, for the first time, a much larger world beyond their own dark reality, a glorious, splendid night sky full of shining stars. That moment simultaneously signifies two events: the invisible truth of the universe is now unfolding in front of their own eyes; and their unseen civilization is now part of that universe, at the expense of losing their own familiar sense of reality that is now becoming absurdly estranging.

Liu Cixin's method of writing SF is rooted in speculations on altering physical laws and concretizing the consequences of such changes in the natural and human worlds. Speculation on a different world in scientific and aesthetic terms, technically called "world-building,"[2] is essential to science fictional narrative. Ultimately, world-building in SF is a thought experiment. It creates a world different from the familiar, knowable reality, but it has a truth-claiming purpose beyond understanding the surface. The way SF presents the truth is counterintuitive, like most of the modern scientific theories are, and accepting that truth requires extraordinary self-reflective thoughts on the relationship between what the story presents and what we take for granted as our ordinary reality. Both the unfolding of the world-building (from the author's position) and the reception of those speculative worlds (from the reader's point of view) create a "fold" in a cognitive sense—a fold that is thinking, a fold that makes thinking.[3] In this sense, SF carries a self-reflection that other fantasy genres, such as Chinese martial arts or Western medieval romance, do not have. SF does not just present otherworldly wonders but also claims a deeper truth that, though invisible in everyday reality, matters as if it were the essence of the entire world: AI programming in the *Matrix* films (1999–2022); robotic and genetic reengineering in the TV show *Westworld* (2016–); and the dark forest scenario in Liu Cixin's vision of the entire cosmos in the "Three-Body" trilogy. And only through SF speculation can storytelling unfold this invisible truth into a terrifying world image. Such a truth evokes fear of seeing. Representing the "invisible" truth, SF can clash with the equally truth-claiming literature of realism, prevalent in modern culture for at least two centuries. Realism, based on mimesis, depicts the world as it appears. But SF, based on speculation (world-building), discredits the belief in surface reality and inspires different thinking about what is *true* of this world—or of many different, divergent worlds.

"Mountain" can be recognized a "megatext," because it conceives an entire world system. But it can also be read as a "metatext" of the SF genre. Almost any SF story that develops around a self-reflective plot design concerning world-building can be such a SF story about SF. To borrow the words of Robert Scholes, a SF story represents a structural fabulation, permeated by "an awareness of the nature of the universe as a system of systems, a structure of structures."[4] Liu's concise, economical novella belongs to the same line of literary works that features Jorge Luis Borges's (1899–1986) "The Library of Babel" (1941), Isaac Asimov's (1920–1992) "The Last Question" (1956), Arthur C. Clarke's (1917–2008) "The Star" (1955), and Ted Chiang's (b. 1967) "Story of Your Life" (1998). Each presents a unique contradiction of our conventional belief in the truth of the world, inventing or reinventing "science fiction" as a new form of storytelling that estranges familiar knowledge while opening to the unorthodox (Clarke's Jesuit astronaut's discovery of "the star of Bethlehem" to be a supernova eliminating a splendid advanced civilization),[5] the unimaginable (Chiang's heptapods' experience of all events at once and their philosophy of time reflected in their nonlinear language and writing system),[6] the unfathomable (Asimov's ultimate question about the universe leading to the evolution of artificial intelligence to reach a singularity),[7] and the undefinable (Borges's infinite unfolding of a Baroque universe that consists of endless folds secretly shuffling differences, a universe without certainty, beginning, or end, completely nonhierarchical and nonbinary.[8]

Like these stories, "Mountain" can be read as both a megatext and a metatext of Chinese new wave SF, which epitomizes the master plot of SF: the encounter with the unknown, together with a self-conscious effort of resorting to scientific methods to comprehend such an encounter. The unsentimental, technically concrete, literal discourse the story uses to depict the "mountain" world makes the text almost like a scientific report, alluding to the very process of collecting and interpreting the counterintuitive new knowledge, which creates a newness, the "novum" as a plot device, that drives the narrative. In a larger sense, "Mountain" echoes the provocative, sublime grand design of the "Three-Body" trilogy's world-building, which culminates in the confrontation with the immense and infinite unknown of the universe. The will to knowledge leads the postapocalyptic diaspora of humans farther into the dark core of the immoral, inhuman universe. Different from the techno-optimism cherished in "Mountain," the contact with higher intelligences battling in outer space in the "Three-Body" trilogy presents "the worst of all possible universes,"[9] but it does not discourage the exploratory spirit that shines in Liu's magnum opus. For the humans, the eager exploration of what lies beyond the visible, the unfolding of a terrifying but "truthful" dark world, and their self-reflective repositioning in the atlas of stars happen simultaneously. Just like the metallic creatures in "Mountain," the human race in the Three-Body novels has to step out of their "bubble" illusion. They have to step into alien space, entering physical rule-changing interstellar wars, and in the sublime, awe-inspiring hyperdimensional universe, the world unfolds into a compound, intricate, tangled, fiddly Baroque image, where "a bottomless abyss exists in every inch."[10] The truthful image of the universe Liu depicts in *Death's End* is so complex that it transcends human epistemology, goes beyond human comprehension, and opens an enigmatic and fathomless Neo-Baroque literary world distinguished with a quantum aesthetics that subverts the long-standing tradition of mimetic realism based on the knowability and certainty of reality.

From a theoretical point of view, this chapter suggests considering SF a method instead of merely a genre. SF such as "Mountain," as both a megatext and a metatext, has a built-in method serving the purpose of world-building within the context of SF storytelling, but it is also a method of entangling reality and representation in a way drastically different from realism. When new wave SF began to make an impact on the literary field, SF as a method gained significance in the larger context of the paradigm shifts in not only contemporary Chinese literature but also world literature. Through discussing Liu's "Mountain," I situate the Chinese new wave in the ongoing negotiation of the genre's definition in relation to other literary forms, presents some of the most pertinent theoretical discussions on the genre's conventions and characteristics, reevaluates SF's contestation with literary realism, and proposes to consider SF *the* method to understand what is contemporary in twenty-first-century literature.

Beginning with this chapter, this book also proposes a new speculation concerning genre and gender, with a view toward recognizing a nonbinary vision of the Neo-Baroque wonders that have emerged in Chinese SF, particularly in the post-new wave She-SF. There are two provocative questions, which do not need definitive answers: Can we read Lu Xun's "A Madman's Diary" 狂人日記 (1918) as science fiction? (chapter 3) and Can we read Liu Cixin's text as nonbinary? (chapter 9). Both aim to shatter the fixations of definition and certainty usually associated with genre and gender. By asking these two questions, I aim to open a portal to enter an estranging and exhilarating Baroque galaxy that is alien to determinism and dichotomy, sterile to hierarchy and coercion, and never home to police and control.

SCIENCE FICTION: A GENRE IN NEGOTIATION

A common belief is that SF is a modern genre that, strictly speaking, has a very short history; it began to be known as "scientific romance" in Victorian England, gained its catchier proper name in the United States—"science fiction," a term coined by Hugo Gernsback (1884–1967) in 1929, and has since remained a mainstay in American popular culture—and part of the globalization with the worldwide successes of sci-fi films such as *2001: A Space Odyssey* (1968), *Star Wars* (1977), *E.T.* (1982), and *Jurassic Park* (1993).[11] However, contemporary scholars who study SF also tend to identify the genre's prehistories: Paul K. Alkon locates its origin in Mary Shelley (1797–1851) *Frankenstein* (1818), adding one hundred years to the genre's (pre-)history[12]; Adam Roberts drastically rewrites the history of SF beginning with the early novels by Roman authors writing in Attic Greek,[13] including the famous biographer Plutarch (c. 45–c. 125 CE), who penned a scientific story about the moon (80), as well as Lucian of Samosata (c. 120–190), the Syrian satirist whose humorous depiction of a space odyssey, "A True History" (c. 170), was first translated into Chinese by Lu Xun's younger brother Zhou Zuoren 周作人 (1885–1967).[14] What is so remarkable about Lucian's narrative is that it deliberately disputes what is truth, as the narrator eloquently argues with his contemporary authors who claim to write true histories:

> When I encountered all these tall tales, I did not much blame these writers for lying, since I observed that fiction is an ingrained habit even among those who profess to be philosophers. But what amazed me most

was that these writers believed that no one would realize that they were writing fictions and lies . . . I had nothing true to relate . . . I make this sole claim on the truth: I am lying. I think that by this confession I will be acquitted of the charge leveled against other writers who are made vulnerable by the very fact that *I* confess that nothing I say is true. And so, I am writing about things that I never saw myself nor actually experienced nor learned from others; things that, moreover, are not real at all nor can, fundamentally, be real. For this reason, those who open this book should believe nothing it says. (Omissions mine)[15]

A satirist, Lucian claims truthfulness through confessing that his stories are pure fiction. "A True History" is a lie. The story he tells is a fantasy parody, filled with stereotyped images in Homeric epics and Roman adventures, including exotic locations and bizarre creatures. But the purpose of his narrative is not to achieve a "make believe" effect; instead, it challenges beliefs in established knowledge and narratives that prevailed in his time, the heyday of the Roman Empire. If we agree with Adam Roberts that Lucian is the "father of SF," his practice of this primitive SF narrative challenges his contemporary "serious" authors about truth-claiming. His method is to invert the order of things and discredit the authenticity of mimesis, and his writing creates a fold in the speculation about the truth of the world. For Lucian, the world does not exist, for his representation of "reality" does not have a corresponding reality. In this intricate and hilarious text, there is no claim to a reliable foundation for mimetic representation, and the only truth that the narrative claims is the speculative nature of the narrative. The truth about fiction folds itself into its own method of storytelling. Obviously, Lucian's "A True Story" is also a metatext that self-reflectively works on world-building that aims to subvert the officially dictated reality.

Written nearly two thousand years ago, the story is as imaginative as Liu Cixin's "Mountain" and Han Song's "Tombs of the Universe," and also as subversive as Lu Xun's "A Madman's Diary" and Han Song's "My Fatherland Does Not Dream," laying bare the falsity, hypocrisy, and unreliability of the truth-claiming representation of reality and stirring up an unsettling dark consciousness of the unknown and uncertain invisible.

This second opinion that identifies Lucian as the first SF writer suggests that the genre is more than a modern genre, or even more provocatively, that SF is more than a *genre*. Lucian's literary power has always puzzled theorists, and he created an alternative mode of literary representation outside the tradition of mimesis, the dominant mode of literature founded upon imitation of the knowable reality and certainty about the knowability of reality. Mimesis is the golden rule of literature, as defined by Aristotle (384–322 BC). Lucian's alternative mode has long been considered nonsensical and obscure, but it interested two great twentieth-century literary theorists: Mikhail Bakhtin (1895–1975) and Northrop Frye (1912–1991). According to Bakhtin, Lucian's satires can be categorized as an independent genre, "Menippean satires," and he emphasizes the centrality of the thought experiment: "the creation of *extraordinary situations* for the provoking and testing of a philosophical idea, a discourse, a truth . . . the fantastic here serves not for the positive *embodiment* of truth, but as a mode for search after truth, provoking it, and most important, *testing* it"[16] (italics in original). Without alluding to SF, Frye identifies "scientific speculation" in Menippean satires, what he calls "the mythos of winter": "an expression of the hypothetical form of art . . . In the warfare of science against superstition, the satirists have done famously. Satire itself appears to have begun with the Greek *silloi* which were pro-scientific attacks on superstition."[17] Frye's examples range from Lucian's satires to Thomas More's (1478–1535) *Utopia* (1516), to Jonathan Swift's (1667–1745) *Gulliver's Travels* (1726), and all the way to Aldous Huxley's (1894–1863) *Brave New World* (1932) and George Orwell's (1903–1950) *Nineteen Eighty-Four* (1948). The two twentieth-century novels, known as dystopian fiction in contemporary context, rely on SF world-building to contest and subvert the mainstream ideologies. Both Bakhtin and Frye clearly emphasize the intellectual quality of this alternative mode of representation traceable to Lucian, which dismantles the systems and institutions of knowledge (ideologies, religions, superstitions, and popular beliefs) and divulges the uncertainty and unpredictability of reality.

THE AGE OF BAROQUE

Including Lucian in the history of SF expands the genre's scope to include a variety of Baroque and classical literary writings such as Cyrano de Bergerac's (1619–1655) *Voyage dans la lune* (1657), Swift's *Gulliver's Travels*, and Voltaire's (1694–1778) *Micromégas* (1750), all satires that use speculative narratives to pervert normative perceptions and invalidate popular "fallacies." In the style of unveiling the Baconian idols or false images, these satires all proffer reflections on the social, cultural, and epistemological fashions of the day, opening to wondrous, thought-provoking world-building.

Coming from the same tradition is utopian fiction, the closest kin to SF or its direct precedent before its rise in the modern centuries. More's *Utopia* was a product of the Age of Discovery, a historical period that began with Christopher Columbus's (1451–1506) landing on a new continent, which destabilized the ancient world system. The world suddenly opened up, became a wonder, motivating many authors to write fantastic stories about the "New World,"[18] adding a myriad of paradise-like isles and continents to the expanding atlas of the planet. To writers in the sixteenth century, the world was unfurling into an image of excessive complexity and outlandish irregularity. The New World was Baroque, and the Baroque made the expanding world itself a new wonder.[19]

The unfolding of a Baroque image happened on the celestial atlas too, when Galileo Galilei first used telescopes to detect the "totally invisible" (Galileo's own words)[20] moons of Jupiter, which led to discrediting Ptolemaic geocentrism and verifying Copernicus's earlier speculative heliocentrism. Galileo's observation and Isaac Newton's (1642–1726) theorization of the laws of universal gravitation completed the Copernican Revolution, the most important paradigm shift in science before the twentieth century, which for the first time presented a truth about the universe aversive to our intuition. The truth that came with the Copernican Revolution is like a Baroque irregularity, invisible in an orderly regulated realm of surface appearance and reality that folds only in speculation; it is a counterintuitive hypothesis, a thought experiment, or an unorthodox theory that does not correspond to solid realness unless validated by scientific experiments or observations. Without a telescope, even today, our observation of the movement of celestial bodies still confirms the Ptolemaic system. It was the new scientific narratives, theorized by Copernicus and affirmed by Galileo's scientific observations, that turned the seemingly unreal speculation into widely accepted truth. This process unfolded just like in "Mountain" with the metallic intelligent species' discovery of the gravitational pull, a truth hidden to them if they had stayed stuck in the enclosed "bubble" of their planet.

From around 1600 to 1750, Baroque as a style flourished in architecture, art, music, theater, poetry, and the novel. But its epistemology was deeply related to the scientific revolution that began with Copernicus's thought experiment. The new science of the Baroque, such as what Galileo and Newton eventually theorized, also conceived a new form of storytelling. What Copernicus first speculated was no doubt a new fiction that subverted the common belief about humans' fixed place in the cosmos and the well-regulated movement of celestial bodies. Mimetic literature can depict that the sun rises and the sun goes down; but if Copernicus had been a SF writer, he would have created a transhuman point of view, ideally in outer space, to present a totally outlandish wonder to readers who would find it estranging—contrary to our instinctual experience, we are traveling on a round planet that orbits the glaring sun.

In Murray Roston's *Milton and the Baroque*, the author makes an apology for Baroque art, because in the 1970s it was still considered a degeneration of the Renaissance style. Roston mentions Galileo's discovery of Jupiter's moons and the Copernican cosmology's impact on the order of things during the Baroque age, exemplified by John Donne's (1572–1631) famous long poem "An Anatomy of the World":

> For his course is not round, nor can the sun
> Perfect a circle, or maintain his way
> . . . . . .
> So of the stars which boast that they do run
> In circle still, none ends where he begun.
> All their proportion's lame, it sinks, it swells . . . (Omission mine)[21]

Roston recognizes the Baroque artists' welcoming a new world of estranging splendor, which has shifted from circle to eclipse, from perfection to irregularity, from stillness to motion.[22] The Age of Discovery and the Age of the Baroque laid the foundation for our modern world. It was an epoch of uncertainty, speculation, and wonder—the world as people had known it no longer existed; it seemed to have suddenly increased its dimensions, and from all the previously hidden folds were flowering dazzling details of a fresh new world that kept outgrowing its own concepts and regulations. The names Columbus and Copernicus are used in Liu Cixin's "Mountain" to refer to the unconventional adventurers and thinkers who combat the intuitive but false "solid universe worldview" that prevails among the metallic creatures living in that bubble world. What Columbus and Copernicus did in our time was the same: they combatted the intuitive but false knowledge of a stable humancentric world order. Inverting the ossified and outdated order of things that created fallacies is the key to cognitively reconfiguring what is truthful.

Adam Roberts suggested that the Copernican cosmology was particularly meaningful to SF for two reasons: it conceived "the dangerous notion of an infinity of worlds," and it created the "sense of wonder," or the sublime, an aesthetic experience "provoked by the gigantic scale, enormous devices or very long stretches of time."[23] It is equally meaningful to connect the history of SF to the age of the Baroque, which covers the scientific revolution and its counterpart in the humanities and arts. Here I use the term "Baroque" to refer not simply to the historical period but to a style, a method, and a worldview that subverts the order with irregular motions, unsettling changes, and infinite possibilities. The Baroque showed the estranging new phenomena of the cosmos, revealed the unknown territory that travelers explored without knowledge of its whole, disturbed existing physical and artistic regulations through "irregular, bizarre, or unequal"[24] forms, and as a Catholic and mythological extravagance, created a counterpoint to the Protestant simplicity and austerity that had become the traits of power and authority with the rise of modern kingdoms and nation-states. The Baroque, in a literary sense, is also the counterpoint to realism. It resists the tyranny of mimesis, transgressing the regulations of imitation and limitation. The Baroque is an art of wonder, an irregular form of both the sublime and the chthonic, and an endless unfolding of the excessive and exuberant. SF, which sharpens the thought experiments traceable to the Menippean satires, began to emerge on the horizon of the Baroque new world; unfolding wonders out of unconventional speculations, SF can be viewed as the (post)modern manifestation of the Baroque.

SCIENCE FICTION: A TRUE HISTORY

The above can serve as a prehistory of SF, which was not yet a genre in the age of antiquity and the Baroque. SF as a modern genre was born in the nineteenth-century industrial revolution and gained recognition in the twentieth century. Different from the Scientific Revolution during the Age of the Baroque, which was mainly a revolution in thought and epistemology known to a small circle of scholars, the industrial revolution, together with waves of political revolutions occurring on various continents over the past two centuries, made real changes in everyday reality. The verisimilitude of literary realism maturing in the nineteenth century corresponded to the vicissitudes of the sea-changing social reality. SF emerged and matured almost simultaneously but received little attention before the late twentieth century.

The first landmark novel that exemplifies the genre is no doubt Mary Shelley's *Frankenstein*. Shelley did not know that she had invented a genre (I will have more to say about *Frankenstein* when examining the posthuman image and genders in negotiation in chapters 8 and 9). She wrote a second SF novel, an apocalyptic narrative about a twenty-first-century pandemic that drives the human race into extinction, *The Last Man* (1826). After Shelley came two great SF writers of the nineteenth century: Jules Verne (1828–1905) and H. G. Wells. These three writers modernized the genre as a mode of fiction: Shelley wrote into it the distorted nightmarish aftermath of the Enlightenment and Great Revolution under the moonlight of romantic irrationality; Verne rebuilt the myth of science and technology through ebulliently showcasing the "Extraordinary Voyages" in the expanding landscapes of global empires that began to universalize the modern world; Wells, who wrote both realistic novels and scientific romances at the fin de siècle, envisioned the fin du monde and the twilight of empires, the apocalyptic war of the worlds, and the menacing future of the human civilization that lost its own purpose by abusing science and technologies. But although these three writers are usually counted as SF authors, they were not aware of the genre's boundaries (or even definitions) in their own explorations of literary possibilities. For them, SF was literature, not a genre.

Their heirs in the twentieth century were Karel Čapek (1880–1938), Yvegeny Zamyatin (1884–1937), Aldous Huxley, George Orwell, Jorge Luis Borges, Abe Kōbō (1924–1993), Stanisław Lem (1921–2006), Thomas Pynchon (b. 1937), and Margaret Atwood (b. 1939), among others who certainly wrote SF but were not categorized or refused to be identified as the same as popular SF authors like Isaac Asimov, Ray Bradbury (1920–2012),

Arthur C. Clarke, Philip K. Dick (1928–1982), Robert A. Heinlein (1907–1988), Frank Herbert (1920–1986), and William Gibson—grandmasters dominating the (Anglo) world SF. One may wonder about the bifurcation behind the above name-dropping: Even for SF, is there a distinction between the highbrow and lowbrow? Or is there a divide between pulp SF and literary SF, between professional SF authors who turn out popular stories and amateur SF writers who experiment with the genre, who are actually "serious" modernists—literary experimentalists? Actually, it was the first group of modernist writers who carried on the spirit of the Menippean satires and self-consciously utilized the genre to create a counterpoint to challenge the mainstream realism. For this reason, they were indeed avant-garde. The second group of writers, inheritors of the same spirit, blended in modern mythologies of science and technology, which also created a counterpoint to the mainstream realism but kept distance from it as if SF and realism were parallel universes that never crossed paths.

The truly popular SF, or what is popularly called "sci-fi," has prevailed in the United States since the end of World War II, creating its Golden Age peak moment and spurring its new wave subversion. American SF has become an industry, generated its own formulas and stereotypes, which nurtured and fed mass entertainment in various forms from pulp fiction to film to TV drama to game and VR experience. Sci-fi classics such as *Foundation* (1951), *Dune* (1965), the *Star Trek* series (1966–), and the *Star Wars* film franchise (1977–) contributed to the mainstream narrative of American modernity and postmodernity, creating the United States' otherworldly empire self-image, fantasy of space missions beyond our solar system, self-identity as messiah, and a new-age American mythology. America became its own fiction, a science fiction, in the late twentieth century.[25] What American SF achieved in that century has become the goal for Chinese SF, as if two rivals entered a virtual arena in two separate time periods, but the competition only mattered to the newcomer, who aimed to win.

Western SF's new wave experiments, which originated in the United Kingdom, revolted against stereotypes and conventions and also in their own ways disseminated the science fictional elements to the soils of Anglo-American literature in general, influencing avant-garde and experimental metafiction authors ranging from Pynchon and Kurt Vonnegut Jr.

(1920–2007) to Atwood and Ian McEwan (b. 1948) to embrace SF as either speculative fiction or metafiction. The genre "resists easy definition,"[26] particularly when we take into consideration such a large cast of authors belonging to different time periods and practicing different ways of literary writing, not to mention the proliferation of the genre in diverse literary traditions outside the Anglo-American realm. All these are reshaping contemporary SF in a postimperial, postcolonial, and posthuman new world. Defining SF can be a thought experiment itself; now let us begin to look at some of the current SF theories.

COGNITIVE ESTRANGEMENT: A DEFINITION IN NEGOTIATION

Earlier scholarly efforts to define and interpret SF heavily leaned toward the methods of formalism. Darko Suvin's definition of SF as a form of "cognitive estrangement," the most venerated of all existing statements about the genre, allows it "both relevance to our world *and* the position to challenge the ordinary."[27] Suvin borrows the concept "estrangement" from the Russian school of formalism as well as from Bertolt Brecht (1898–1956), but departs from the latter's "still dominantly 'realistic' context" and develops a new framework to elucidate the poetics of SF, in which "the look of estrangement is both cognitive and creative."[28] For Suvin, cognitive estrangement decides SF's nature as a creative process "analogous to modern polycentric cosmology, uniting time and space in Einsteinian worlds with different but covariant dimensions and time scales," and from there "*a cognitive—in most cases strictly scientific—element becomes a measure of aesthetic quality.*"[29]

Interestingly, Suvin, who takes the widest possible view of the genre's genealogy and prehistory, uses the word "Baroque" on the first page of his landmark book *The Metamorphosis of Science Fiction*, referring to "the Renaissance and Baroque 'utopia' and 'planetary novel'"[30] as one of the earlier literary subgenres, a literature of wonder that has close kinship with SF, but he does not say more about the Baroque wonder and SF.

With emphasis on cognitive estrangement, Suvin creates a dynamic interaction between SF and realism, with the former opening up to the imaginary unknown in scientific terms, the newness known as the novum, and the latter concentrating on familiar human affairs. Other scholars have since proposed revisions to Suvin's concept, such as Robert Scholes's structuralist interpretation of SF as "structural fabulation,"[31] Damien Broderick's replacement of "cognitive estrangement" with a postindustrial, postmodern cultural description of the genre's relation to reality marked by "metaphoric strategies and metonymic tactics,"[32] and Carl Freedman's theoretically strengthened Suvinian reflections on the structural affinities between SF and critical theories.[33] All these theoretical interventions form a collective effort to highlight SF's agency in creating an imaginative, poetic, speculative newness that exists in a productive tension with the realistic mode of representation.

In recent years, scholars have come up with groundbreaking ideas that deviate from Suvin's genre definition and applied the theories concerning SF to much larger contexts. Istvan Csicsery-Ronay Jr. believes that SF, instead of being just a genre, "can be treated as a particular, recognizable mode of thought and art." He emphasizes the anticipatory agency of SF, or science fictionality, in confronting a rapidly and radically transforming world, from where he reshuffles the relations between science fictional imagination and reality: "It is from sf's thesaurus of images that we draw many of our metaphors and models for understanding our technologized world, and it is as sf that many of our impressions of technology-aided desire and technology-driven anxiety are processed back into works of the imagination."[34] Csicsery-Ronay Jr. presents seven formative elements that are essential to SF, which he calls the "seven beauties," rendering it as an aesthetic form imagining new horizons. His most radical thought is the possibility of having an anticipatory cognitive and aesthetic experience that precedes its actualization in reality but has already generated its virtual existence in fictional textuality.

Among various contemporary theories about SF, Seo-Young Chu's provocative reconceptualization of a science fictional theory of representation suggests that "the objects of science-fictional representation, while impossible to represent in a straightforward manner, are absolutely real."[35] Chu redefines the Suvinian concept of "cognitive estrangement" to propose two assumptions: "all representation is to some degree science fictional because all reality is to some degree cognitively estranging"; and "conversely, what most people call 'science fiction' is actually a high-intensity variety of realism, one that requires astronomical levels of energy to accomplish its representational task insofar as its referents (e.g., cyberspace) elaborately defy straightforward representation."[36] Chu significantly changes the relationship between realism and SF by dismantling the dichotomy between them and offers a mutually inclusive interpretation: "'realism' designates low-intensity mimesis, while 'science fiction' designates high-intensity mimesis."[37] Her theoretical inquiries recognize SF as a mode of representation that achieves a status equal to realism, not as its inferior or opponent but as a representational home for referents that are not susceptible to representation in conventional realism.

Certainly, the typical science fictional referents, like aliens and super A.I., extrasolar civilizations and future technologies, do not exist in daily reality but have been represented in SF. But only saying this is not enough, forming a loop of self-referentiality. What Chu means by naming SF "high-intensity mimesis" implies something more than the obviously science fictional. As Chu argues, "SF is distinguished by its capacity to perform the massively complex representational and epistemological work necessary to render cognitively estranging referents available both for representation and understanding."[38] Here, her revision of the Suvinian concept "cognitive estrangement" does away with the binary differentiation between the cognitive (reality) and the estranging (novum): the estranging is now not just the novum but can also be anything whose representation requires "high-intensity mimesis": in other words, a representation that cannot be achieved straightforwardly but requires a cognitive reconfiguration through thinking complexly, alternatively, reflectively. What appears to be truly amazing in this redefinition is that "cognitive estrangement" can now be applied to literally everything, from the unfathomable immensity of the cosmos to such a small, simple, and mundane thing as a pencil that seems easy to represent in flat description with alacrity, but as Chu suggests, can actually become so estranging that it is absolutely impossible to represent as a thing in itself, "in all its unmediated pencilness."[39] Yes, even a pencil can become a science fictional novum if SF no longer is just a fixed set of genre conventions in opposition to realism but can actually execute its agency as a method to estrange, destabilize, and transform "reality," and from there SF can perform a cognitive reconfiguration to represent the estranging, infinitely complex, and transformative "reality" in a profoundly alterative way.

The above-mentioned theories, particularly Chu's nonbinary theory about SF and realism, have inspired me to ask questions concerning new wave Chinese SF and its impacts on contemporary Chinese fiction in general. Thinking about SF not only as a genre but also as a method posits challenges to the current scholarship in Chinese literary studies, which has not yet formed an alternative interpretation of SF outside the established theoretical system of literary realism and mimetic representation—as evidenced by Chinese SF writers and scholars' tendency to view SF as a variant of realism. A most acute question, then, is: How are we to make sense of SF's complicated relationship with both reality and realism in a Chinese context? If it operates in a newness that differs from the principle of mimesis, what is it? Or what is it becoming?

SCIENCE FICTION AND REALISM

While it may be commonplace to say that SF is not realism, as Suvin says, there have been strong voices among both Chinese SF authors and critics arguing that contemporary Chinese SF is actually a variant of critical realism, and thus its proper definition should be "science fictional realism" 科幻現實主義. Zheng Wenguang 鄭文光 (1929–2003), a SF writer active in the 1950s–1980s, first coined this term in 1981;[40] it conveys his belief that SF is a part of the modern Chinese literary mainstream, and therefore, it carries on the May Fourth literary tradition and exemplifies the doctrines of a serious literature devoted to the representation of real life. In Zheng's words, SF also reflects reality. His notion of "reflection" indicates "a reflection of real life," but he also adds that SF, as an imaginative literature, is not "a plane mirror, but a refracting mirror."[41] Thus science fictional representation is like "refracting" that twists and displaces the images of reality but still engages with actual social reality. Zheng's theorization represents this earlier generation of Chinese SF writers' strong wish to give the genre legitimacy based on the rules of China's cultural establishment, which prioritized realism within the literary hierarchy.

Indeed, realism has long been enshrined as the crowning representational mode in modern Chinese fiction, generating the largest body of literature in the twentieth century. Mao Dun 茅盾 (1896–1981), China's foremost master of literary realism, emphasized a naturalistic-realistic literary paradigm that he considered the most scientific method for modern novels, though his didactic advocacy and moral mandate behind this mode of representation, particularly his exclusive claim to the truth of reality through a Marxist brand of realism, have been disputed by scholars like Marston Anderson and David Der-wei Wang.[42] When Chinese literature began its post-Cultural Revolution revival, Zheng Wenguang's brand of "SF realism" resonated with the thematic concerns and aesthetic pursuits frequently encountered in the new realistic schools, such as "scar literature" 傷痕文學 and "contemplative literature" 反思文學.[43] If realism is the most truthful and scientific literary form, SF plus realism must heighten the scientific truthfulness to safeguard its legitimacy; this sets a high bar for the genre largely within the limited framework of realistic literature—tempering SF into a realistic narrative form tasked with spreading scientific knowledge. However, Zheng's version of SF realism met with relentless criticism from the scientific community, who claimed that Chinese SF was not scientific but completely imaginary. The famous physicist Qian Xuesen 錢學森 (1911–2009) dismissed it as pure senseless literary fantasy. At the same time, the literary establishment refused to verify SF's claim to realism. The tragic failure of Zheng Wenguang poignantly pointed to SF's embarrassing position, stuck between the truth-claiming scientific discourses and the truth-claiming literary realism, eager to embrace both but belonging to neither.[44]

Now, decades after Zheng Wenguang made his argument, "SF realism" has gained currency again among the new wave authors. This new conceptualization, promoted by Han Song first and then further explained by Chen Qiufan, has implied equivocal connotations and apparent diversions from the orthodox framework of literary realism.[45] If SF still implies some level of realism, it is no longer considered a reflection or refraction of reality in the traditional sense, but a transgressive notion of reality that does not equal being completely real and observable. This new wave version of SF realism suggests a cognitive inversion of the order of representation and reality; it claims the truthfulness of its representation through literary discourse that is legitimized by its self-proclaimed scientific or logic coherence but does not need to be faithful to the observable, or visible, reality. In other words, SF speaks with its own grammar and obeys its own rules of representation in articulating the alternative to what can be said about the observable surface reality.

More recently, Chen Qiufan has suggested characterizing SF as a sort of "hyperrealism," based upon an extended interpretation of Jean Baudrillard's notion of "hyperreality" in the digital age.[46] Hyperreality is a representation without the original referent, and as Chen Qiufan suggests, the "reality" that SF represents is no longer a reality that we can invoke as original or organic. Instead it can be an invented "reality," a virtual, simulated, digital mixture of images and information, or even an unreality produced by algorithm, which requires the invention of a new method of literary writing.[47] Hyperrealism, when applied to the nonexistent "reality" or a new reality in transforming, unfolding, and becoming, can be more evocative (liquid) than descriptive (solid), more metonymic (fragmented) than metaphorical (totalistic), and more memetic (folded) than mimetic (figurative).

Han Song, Chen Qiufan, and other new wave authors' literary visions regarding SF realism bring home Istvan Csicsery-Ronay Jr.'s theory about the science fictionality of the contemporary world. Hyperrealism also resonates with Seo-Young Chu's argument that "science fiction designates high-intensity mimesis."[48] Such radical redefinitions of the genre outdate the doctrine of conventional realism that captures the observable reality largely in a mimetic style. If SF realism can still be considered realism, it represents a very different reality that runs the gamut from the invisible, the spectral, to the deeply hidden and structurally absent. SF realism can be understood as a self-reflective mode of metafiction. It creates a textual space serving as a heterotopia in relation to the experiential reality; it is a virtual space not conceivable merely through postulations and imitations of everyday experience and knowable reality. On the contrary, this SF reality, or a verbal heterotopia, is constructed by signs and symbols, words and images that have severed direct connections to reality, and the world images that it conceives are estranged and surreal but logically plausible, more fabulous than factual, invisible but inherent to understanding what is real.

Such extraordinary science fictional "realities" can be built upon speculated changes to the laws of physics, such as Liu Cixin's Three-Body universe, or futuristic technological revolution, such as Chen Qiufan's AI-managed worlds in 2041,[49] or the deeper, darker posthuman existential status of the everyman in China now, such as Han Song's various versions of "Sinotopia"—the hospital world, the chthonic underground in *Subway*, and the cannibalistic aquatic (post)human hunting ground in *Red Ocean* 紅色海洋 (2004). These heterotopian constructs of estranging wonders feel more "truthful" than the perceivable reality that can be talked about in everyday speech, as if the SF truthfulness speaks to the quantum reality, a deeper reality of the world involving its fundamental structure and potential movement rather than its thickly decorated surface appearance.

Compared with conventional realism, SF realism is more revelatory than mimetic. When these intense negotiations with realism are localized in the metamorphosis of contemporary Chinese literature, the representation of science fictionality or the so-called "SF reality" gains its unique aesthetic, ethical, and political significance. Restyling the representational mode into a new method of writing and gesturing toward larger changes in the scientific and cognitive paradigms, the new wave has both exhausted and eclipsed the existing methods of mimetic realism. Perhaps we do not need the term "realism" to validate SF's relevance to our new reality. SF has become a new method to create a new literariness.

THE REAL, THE LITERAL, AND THE TRUTHFUL

What differentiates SF and literary realism in terms of the literary discourse is related to a key element in the former, which is the scientific discourse. But here I do not take scientific discourse as merely rhetoric or a localized device in the text of SF, but instead consider it the general foundation of science fictional textuality. What matters is not the validity of the scientific discourse but its function in the construction of the SF worlds. Even when the scientific ideas represented in SF are imagined rather than factual, the discourse of science must function logically, consistently, and most importantly, literally. Compared with realism, which tends to use figurative, metaphorical language, SF often flattens literary metaphors, in such famous cases as "His world exploded" and "He was absorbed by the landscape,"[50] which both turn ordinary scenes, if read as metaphors, into wonders through collapsing the figurative literary language into literal technical language. Understanding these sentences literally gives us astonishing SF narratives; this is the strategy that Liu Cixin employs to create wonders in the Three-Body novels. Liu uses a fairy tale to predict the endgame for humans. In the tale, the New Royal Painter,

Needle-Eye 針眼畫師, can make a person disappear by painting him or her in a portrait. For humans who do not know its literal meaning, this sounds like an allegory. In the context of the plot, the message indeed is not understood by those trying to interpret fairy tales for information related to the life-and-death fate of humankind. But its meaning is actually literal. Only a long time later do the humans realize that what Needle-Eye did literally means "lowering the dimensions," a strategy that the most powerful intelligent creatures in the universe frequently use to wipe out potential enemies—lowering the dimensions so that those living in the hyperdimensional universe will disappear into a two-dimensional flat world.[51]

Han Song describes this scene in *Hospital* 醫院 (2016):

> This was clearly not the world I had once known.... The illuminated names of this army of hospitals lit up the night sky: SONY TREATMENT CENTER, MICROSOFT EMERGENCY CENTER, GOOGLE COMMUNITY HOSPITAL, HUAWEI SPECIAL TREATMENT WARD, ALIBABA HEALTH CLUB, SINOPEC HEALTH CENTER, INDUSTRIAL AND COMMERCIAL BANK OF CHINA SURGERY CLUB ... the names were endless.... Across the street, some fast-food restaurants and specialty stores had been remodeled as twenty-four-hour FastMed clinics, extremely convenient for emergency patients who lived in the neighborhood. The hotel where I had been staying also had a massive red cross erected on its rooftop.
>
> The entire city was one enormous hospital.[52]

The protagonist is told: "You are not hallucinating. This is the true face of the world."[53] When reading this novel in 2016 upon its publication, a reader's reaction to this statement might have been a bewildering epiphany, taking it as a Lu Xunsque metaphor: China—or the so-called C City—is a hospital! But Han Song's SF text does not unfold only as a metaphor. The entire trilogy creates a labyrinth of signs and symbols that convey a message, through various levels of storytelling, systematically, over and over again—a message articulated in a literal and technical discourse that flattens the metaphor: China or C City *is* a hospital! Of course, the hospital is more than that: it is the system that reforms people, makes new people, and recycles the political dramas of life. However, reading this paragraph again in May 2022, after Shanghai was under lockdown for nearly two months, would perhaps have sent chills down a reader's spine. Without giving Han Song credit as a prophet, which he is not, one may still wonder how literal this statement has become. For now, nothing can be more truthful than Han Song's astonishing vision of the entire nation's transfiguration into an almighty hospital executing total control over the mind and body of the entire Chinese population.

Interestingly, the semantic literalness in SF estranges the conventional sense of reality and creates a counterintuitive scientific sense of the unreal, as if we were seeing something astronomically larger or quantumly tinier than what is perceivable in daily experience, or simply something that is uneasy, uncomfortable, and unsettling. Scientific discourse in SF enables the concretization of augmented reality, hyperreality, virtual reality, and unreality to convey some truths outside the context of mundane reality. The principle of literalness establishes the truthfulness in SF on the level of grammar, and from there, SF as a language unfolds into estranging worlds that are truthful in logic, consistent in systematic style, and technically literal in depictions of the details of the worlds. Such fictional worlds, like new scientific theories, present a cognitively estranging alternative to the prosaic reality that we take for granted. However, the inconvenient "truth" is arguably more truthful than the surface real we perceive. In a seemingly contradictory way, the literal discourse makes SF obviously unreal but counterintuitively truthful.

What can we talk about when we talk about what is going on in Chinese reality? Is there a direct way to confront it that assures any certainty and comprehensiveness? This is like asking how we can talk about a black hole: we have to resort to the scientific discourse that presents a difficult, provocative truth about what it is, instead of depicting it in a metaphorical way. To talk about a black hole as a metaphor is not to talk about it. The black hole, as an invisible phenomenon, is mute in metaphor, and it has to be literally proven to be the end of all light. In this same sense, Han Song's way of talking about China as a hospital is not to reaffirm a national allegory that metaphorizes Chinese reality but to reveal a deeper truth beneath all the illusions, an unfathomable but more truthful reality that people tend to ignore. The hospital is a heterotopia in Chinese reality. It is always there, the field of life and death, the system of total control, and the very form of effective administration. Has China always been a hospital? To think this way certainly evokes the fear of seeing. Even for those living in the hospital and seeing only the surface of its interior, it can be the Foucauldian invisible visibility.

If we consider SF a truth-claiming literary genre, its representational mode is entangled with mimetic realism, which also claims to be truthful. They may operate as parallel universes, each claiming truth in its own way. But intertwining the two points to a divergence between two different modes of representation. At the cost of oversimplification, I offer a rather succinct way of differentiating them, which can be summed up in the following descriptions. Mimetic realism relies on an effective literary discourse operating upon a foundational faith that there is a factual reality, such as a literary metaphor of a *thing* that evokes a realness through a discursive feedback loop connecting representation and reality. But SF is not about the "fact" or "faith" that there is reality. Its world-building unfolds with a technologically literal and plausible discourse operating upon speculations about what is not "reality" but can be treated as "real" through counterintuitive thinking or cognitive reconfiguration. I mean to define realism as not a fixed target or a stereotyped mode, but rather a well-established system that underlines representations of the knowable reality. If SF remains a marginal genre, an escapism of no significance to Chinese literature, its spectacular and wondrous representation of the invisible (un)realities may never matter. But when the new wave rises and its challenge concerns a recognition of what is invisible in China's reality, SF previses a new literary universe that is reshaping the relationship between reality and representation.

In *The Antinomies of Realism*, Fredric Jameson situates the decline of classical realism in the confrontation with new realities that require stylistic plurality as exemplified by David Mitchell's (b. 1974) *Cloud Atlas* (2004), a science fiction novel:

> I am tempted to see this as a serious defamiliarization of the whole ideological thematics of information and communication which has become omnipresent today and a virtually official philosophy of the postmodern. This intrusion of technological consciousness into the reading process at once demotes that official philosophy to a conceptual reflex of the mode of production and in its own way rewrites the history of the alleged "break" of the newer technologies with the older modern ones. It is in

any case significant that *Cloud Atlas* overleaps the moment of computers and the Internet in its temporally ambitious chronology, and stages our own present as historical by diminishing it to a passing stage between nostalgia-pasts and a Science-Fictional far future.[54]

In chapter 8, I will talk about *Cloud Atlas* in the posthuman and Neo-Baroque contexts, which are shared by the Chinese new wave authors; Jameson does not really confront those contexts when he talks about this novel. What concerns him is rather the inadequacies of realism that such a text, "this immense glissando," can show through slaughtering the Hegelian totality and teleology. Jameson does not like *Cloud Atlas*, treating it as if it were a terminator to realism, but he has to admit that Mitchell's novel better captures what the present is, what is contemporary—it "stages our own present as historical."

Jameson's admission of the antinomies of realism are probably shared by a large number of contemporary realists. Yan Lianke 閻連科 (b. 1958), famous for revealing the darkest Chinese reality, coined a new term to give realism a new life: "mythorealism" 神實主義, which does not cling to the objective reality but rather portrays a mythological or spiritual reality. His definition sounds very similar to how I have so far described Chinese new wave SF: "it can be said that mythorealism is a creative process that rejects the superficial logical relations that exist in real life to explore a kind of invisible and 'nonexistent' truth—a truth that is obscured by truth itself."[55] Yan Lianke's brand of mythorealism is as speculative as SF, and this case demonstrates that SF and many other experimental forms are all part of a larger paradigm shift that redefines what is contemporary in terms of literary representation. This new literary universe is certainly no longer centered on mimetic realism.

THE NEO-BAROQUE: A HYPOTHESIS IN NEGOTIATION

It requires another book to fully address this hypothesis, which I intend to write in the near future. Here I present my speculation in a simple statement: I consider contemporary SF, particularly its new wave, a manifestation of a paradigm shift in literature and culture that corresponds to what happens in contemporary sciences and technologies, an earthquake-like new event equivalent to the irregular, destabilizing epistemological shift that occurred in the past, four hundred years ago—the Age of Baroque. SF as method opened a Neo-Baroque world.

This term, "Neo-Baroque," has appeared in many areas—architecture and fine art, but also cinema—such as Raúl Ruiz's (1941–2011) "dark and oceanic" Neo-Baroque poetics of film;[56] philosophy—such as Gilles Deleuze's (1925–1995) elucidations of the Leibnizian (and Foucauldian) fold in science, epistemology, and aesthetics;[57] and culture in general—such as Omar Calabrese's (1949–2012) interpretation of the Neo-Baroque as a sign of the instability, virtuosity, changeability, and polydimensionality of the entire contemporary culture.[58] Even though named "Neo-Baroque," it does not signify a simple return to the Baroque. Resonating with the Baroque, it suggests a restlessness that takes many forms in scientific and cultural changes in the twentieth and twenty-first centuries, pushing toward a new departure from all that has been solid, established, and essentialized over the past three centuries defined by the Newtonian physical laws, Cartesian ontology, Hegelian teleology, and the political topology contrasting the (inferior, adverse) other and the (imperial, triumphant) subjectivity.

Both Deleuze and Calabrese have used the term to characterize not only one form of representation, but the fundamental shape of the contemporary world in all its representations, both scientific and cultural, at a threshold moment before the unfolding of the future. Unlike the popular term "postmodern," "Neo-Baroque" gives up the linear image of time, instead suggesting a curve, a labyrinth, and a fold in space, movement, and time, which cannot be straightened or abstracted, the opposite to the totalistic tendency of understanding the world with an assumed theory of everything. The Neo-Baroque does not have an actual beginning, nor is it an actual event; it unfolds everywhere in the structure of feeling, the way of seeing, and the method of knowing. Deleuze says: "The Baroque refers not to an essence but rather to an operative function, to a trait. It endlessly produces folds. . . . Yet, the Baroque trait twists and turns its folds, pushing them to infinity, fold over fold, one upon the other. The Baroque fold unfurls all the way to infinity."[59] Calabrese considers the Neo-Baroque "a spirit of age" "that pervades many of today's cultural phenomena in all fields of knowledge," which he uses to "associate certain current scientific theories (catastrophe, fractals, dissipative structures, theories of chaos and complexity, and so on) with certain forms of art, literature, philosophy, and even cultural consumption."[60] I do not intend to oversimplify both philosophers' complicated methods and theorizations; but we can agree that Deleuze and Calabrese, together with Ruiz, have approached the Neo-Baroque as a motion that never stops in its fluidity and infinity.

My hypothesis situates SF in a longer history that connects this modern genre to the Baroque age, breaking down a linear narrative largely dominated by the rule of mimesis and entangling SF with realism in a way that transcends the prevailing binary structures in literary and epistemological categories. This hypothesis also positions SF at the entrance to a Neo-Baroque literary universe, viewing it as more than a genre, an almost scientific method of thinking alternatively and counterintuitively, a revolutionary way of conjuring up insurgent visions that destabilize and subvert the well-regulated administration of power and order, and an unsettling structure of feeling that remakes what is human and rewrites what is real. SF as the method of opening the Neo-Baroque points to a planetary consciousness that transcends any singular utopian or dystopian view on humans and any dichotomies between genders, classes, races, species, and identities. What makes our time a brave new world has simultaneously beckoned the science fictional egress from mimetic realism and the advent of a Neo-Baroque aesthetics that manifests an infinitude of folds and holes punctuating the fabric of time and space, piercing and perforating the smooth and neat constitutions of nationhood, state ideology, the monumentality of history and war, and the global behemoth of transnational capitalism.

In a nutshell, I consider the new wave an audacious experiment with novelty, which entangles quantum poetics with the Neo-Baroque infinity. The new wave rises with a curiosity about the unknown, uncertain, and unpredictable, a gesture of transgression across borders between the familiar and nonexistent, an act of dreaming about the alternative and beyond. I contend that at its most radical, the new wave has been thriving on an avant-garde cultural spirit that calls into question commonly accepted ideas and observed rules regarding morals, ideologies, and knowledge about the self and the world, humans and the universe. It generates new modes of literary discourse that estrange what we take for granted, open our eyes to insurgent knowledge and subversive images, and evoke an array of (un)real or virtual sensations ranging from chthonic to sublime, uncanny to spectacular, inebriate to exuberant, transcendental to apocalyptical, human to posthuman, and so on. The harbinger of a larger epistemological shift, the new wave breaks apart the binary correspondence between reality and representation. Looking both outward and inward, the new wave brings out unorthodox nonbinary forms such as cyborg, chimera, heterotopia, hyperdimensionality, multiverse, sympoiesis, and metaverse, which transgress the borderline between reality and representation and dismantle exclusive identities and dichotomies across categories such as gender, class, race, hierarchy, and ideology, recasting the human self in or as the posthuman other—so that "I" can have or be an invisible "monster" residing in a nonbinary universe that shines with a Neo-Baroque splendor, which illuminates infinite possibilities and may never settle in a singular form of a *certain* reality.

Here I will discuss the fourth case announced in chapter 1 as an example to illuminate the Neo-Baroque that has surfaced in contemporary SF. This case shows the futility of binary thinking in a Neo-Baroque universe.

THE BIRTH OF A NONBINARY UNIVERSE, 2020/200,000 YEARS LATER

"Men, lions, eagles and partridges, horned deer, geese, spiders, silent fish that dwell in the water, starfishes and creatures which cannot be seen by eyes—all living things, all living things, all living things, having completed their cycle of sorrow, are extinct.... For thousands of years the earth has borne no living creature on its surface, and this poor moon lights its lamp in vain. It is cold, empty, dreadful. The bodies of living creatures have vanished into dust, and eternal matter has transformed into rocks, into water, into clouds, while the souls of all have melted into one. That world-soul I am—I.... In me the consciousness of men is blended with the instincts of the animals, and I remember all, all, all! And I live through every life over again in myself!"[61]

. . . .

They were born in the north. The long summer days are warming up Lake Baikal. Fully equipped, they dive to explore the bottom of the lake. The underwater forest has scarce vegetation. They believe they have reached the end of the universe. In winter, they run in the cold of 40 Fahrenheit degrees below zero and can see the Milky Way in the sky on a sunny day. By the end of the spring, trees are still sprouting, and they are watching the opening to the ancient tunnel built in the twentieth century, with their four legs dangling in rhythmic and cheerful ways. One is watching the zigzag tracks far away, spotting the train that enters the tunnel. The other is listening to the sound of the train, closer and closer. They seize the opportunity, jump into the ancient train. Following the tracks, they come from the far eastern backwater all the way to the south.

The earth has never abandoned its past, even after humans began their evolutions. Thousands of years of human expeditions feed back into the earth, making it a living fossil that keeps growing, giving birth to layers of layers of tree rings that record its own growth. That planet is indeed an ecological museum of human civilization, populated by both the premodern tribes and the nonhuman beings of the twenty-ninth century. They hide themselves in the third-class train's third-class carriages, mingling with people and things that they have never seen. They manage to survive, completing a microhistory of evolution equivalent to an entire millennium for human beings. When the train reach the edge of the Indian Ocean, she has learned how to process all the quantum images and how to record all the quantum sounds. They have become the senior engineers who adventure into the new frontiers of the universe. Everyone wants to have them, recruiting them to join their crew. They choose a monster named Leviathan, which takes them to the limits of the human world with the maximum speed. The entire route is more challenging than imagined. They have turned from the camouflaged hidden in the trains into the predators in space. They have learned to live in a narrow space and die in the cosmos of enormous magnitude. They have overcome all kinds of uncertainties in life and reached the end of the cosmos. There seems to be a cliff in the void. Standing on the edge of the cliff, they simultaneously catch sight of the birth and death of stars. Farther away, they see the unknown desolate. Humans have not found a way to make a first step into the void.[62]

These resplendent, ornate words, glowing with Neo-Baroque splendor, are from a writer named Shuangchimu, which means "diptera." The diptera, a kind of insect, is so far removed from humans in terms of classification of species that we have no way of determining its gender. With poetic language, this story, "The Solar Studio: Seagull" 太阳系片场：海鸥 (2020), depicts an artificial solar system that is the set of Chekhov's (1860–1904) famous play *The Seagull* (1896). Like Nina criticizing Treplev in the play, and like the "anticlimactic" effect that Chekhov himself pursues, this story lacks action and is full of speech. It does not rely on the "wonder" of action, but rather crams "wonder" into its dense language. The text strives to depict a radiant new universe, creating a labyrinthine heterotopia in a textual space bordering both SF and mainstream literature. Reading even just the three paragraphs above, requires the reader to break down many dichotomous prejudices; it almost demands as much imagination from the readers as from the author.

Shuangchimu is the pen name of Feng Yuan 馮原, a writer with a Ph.D. in aesthetics belonging to a new generation of women and nonbinary writers who dare to challenge gender and genre conventions in a way that far surpasses what Han Song and Liu Cixin have done. This story was published in 2020, ten years after the new wave began to make an impact on contemporary Chinese literature. It is one of the thousands of SF stories written in the so-called post-"Three-Body" epoch, which has seen the coronation of SF as the new favorite among all genres in Chinese literature but has not yet seen another earth-shattering breakthrough like Liu Cixin and Han Song made in the past. The year 2020 was also the beginning of the pandemic that brought out a new normal defined by fear of contagion, which envelopes both the world and its literature. Quarantine and lockdown have deprived the world of its mobility; literature faces "the danger of a single story,"[63] as Chimamanda Adichie (b. 1977) has warned us, more than ever. Separationism and isolationism have nourished neonationalism, extremism, and fascism, while the common ground in public opinion has disappeared. Perhaps this is the moment when we need a literary text that can best represent the nonbinary, in terms of both gender and genre, feeling and thinking, more than ever.

I encountered this story by Shuangchimu in the first summer of the pandemic. I began to realize its significance as the precursor of an emerging newer wave of Chinese SF in the third summer—in 2022, after witnessing the rise of She-SF, when a generation of younger female authors (and some hidden nonbinary authors) made their voices collectively heard. If SF was a marginal genre before 2010, SF stories like Shuangchimu's are still located almost outside the margin of the now much enlarged atlas of the genre, which has been conventionally gendered as male. But again, the margin resettles the gravitational field of contemporary Chinese literature. Shuangchimu ushered us into a new world, a Neo-Baroque nonbinary universe.

This text itself is nonbinary in many ways. Even if the title of the story reveals that it is a SF retelling of Chekhov's *The Seagull*, readers need to be careful to determine which sentences in the text belong to Chekhov and which are intentionally subtle imitations of the sentences in Chekhov's play-within-a-play. The first scene in the play is about Treplev, who is deeply in love with Nina, asking her to appear in his own play, which depicts a world 200,000 years from now, when humans are extinct and the souls of all humans and creatures (including both Napoleon and the last leech in the world) are gathered into one, which is Nina. But who is she, a goddess, a cyborg, a chimera? In the play, she appears as a soul rising from a lake, waiting for Satan and ready to fight him to death. Whether this plot hides a parody of H. G. Wells's *The Time Machine* (1895), published a year earlier, we do not know. But reading Shuangchimu's story reveals that its textuality conceals more than what meets our eyes. Almost all of what we thought were Chekhov's original lines, those ingenious Chinese translations by Jiao Juyin 焦菊隱 (1905–1975), have been modified or misplaced, like the following sentence: "Spirit itself may be a combination of material atoms,[64] but we have never achieved the freedom of the universe." This is a chimeric sentence, half quoted from the bookish village schoolteacher in Chekhov's original play, half unattributed and added from nowhere. Most importantly, there is no identifiable narrator, and soon readers realize that there are no definite characters either throughout the entire text.

The most important protagonist in the story appears to be a young stage crew member who is asked to play Trigorin, a misanthropic playwright who abducts Nina after the show on the lake in Chekhov's play. The main character of the original play, Treplev (the young man who takes a shotgun to the stage and shoots himself to death at the end) is played by the director of the play in Shuangchimu's story. Of the two female characters, the first is Nina, who is initially Treplev's lover, performing in his plotless impressionistic play, but later elopes with Trigorin, causing Treplev to take his own life after he finally realizes that she never loved him. The second is Arkadina, who is both Treplev's mother and Trigorin's lover. In Shuangchimu's story, the two characters are played by a pair of identical twins. They seem to be shaped by the characters they play, thus appearing to the stage crew member, or the observer in the story, as two Russian girls from the far north. The stage crew member envisions their northern experience in the second and third paragraphs quoted above. But they are actually nonhuman beings whom the text introduces this way: "One of them is responsible for processing the images of the universe, the other the sounds of the universe. One responsible for the particles of everything, the other the waves. . . . The quantum ocean is enormous, and you can never tell the difference between particles and waves. They have been using their resources in technology to create the entanglement with each other. People are often confused by the two of them, exactly like they are never certain about whether the universe exits as particles or waves."[65]

Wave-particle duality is a nonbinary phenomenon presented in the fundamental principles of quantum mechanics; Heisenberg's uncertainty and Schrödinger's cat are both famous cases interpreting this phenomenon. The uncertainty in the wave-particle duality also affects the way we understand the world: whether the world as we perceive it with human eyes truly exists. Shuangchimu's story asks this question while staging the Chekhov play against an enormous backdrop on an astronomical scale. The fate of the universe is indeed also the theme of Chekhov's play-within-a-play, and the text unfolds its invisible truth, the nonbinary wave-particle duality, into extravagant and splendid images depicted in the very poetic, dazzlingly ornamental language.

The question concerning the truth of the universe also involves the fundamental question concerning representation and performance: How can the universe be represented or narrated? How can the universe be presented through performance? Even if the universe is real, how can it be realistically written and authentically performed? The story, at least, tells us in the beginning that the solar system on the set is not real; it is artificially programmed by the stage crew member. In the deep future when this play is staged in this artificial studio of the solar system, the real earth and solar system have long been submerged in the depths of space-time. The text offers a virtual embodiment of the unreal, a romance of information flow, and a dense narrative filled with folded details flowering exuberantly.

On this virtual set, the artificial solar system, also exist the laws of astrophysics. As the play progresses, it is no longer a Chekhovian human comedy but unfolds as a worlding of an invisible physics experiment. The staging of *The Seagull* in deep space ends with the bursting of a black hole created by the director and the wave-particle twins. All exists, all is nothing. In fact, the stage crew member has long been expecting this to happen:

> It is rumored that the solar studio's Green Room can adjust the mind and soul of humans to the simultaneous movements of the quantum ocean, which is unbound and unknowable. Crew members call it the subconscious of the universe. In it, everything is connected, mingled, and everyone will become the characters in the play, without showing a trace of performance. Directors tend to understand it from another perspective: every character exists in the torrents of the quantum ocean, which can flow into everyone's mind, a shared force, the force of the universe's subconscious. Humans do not live for themselves. They live for the subconscious of the universe.[66]

"The Solar Studio: Seagull" truly crosses many categories: gender and genre, realness and falsity, the wave-particle duality, and the dichotomies of all, including the human and animal (Napoleon and the leech, not to mention the seagull); even further, this story disintegrates the correspondences between representation and reality, dissolving the line between truth and illusion and canceling the representational purpose of the text. On the concrete level of the literary discourse, it fuses lyrical and scientific styles into a megatextual chimera. The story has no proper ending, or its ending marks a new beginning. After the stage crew member lives the double lives of the twin girls, or the divine wave-particle entanglement, he sees the director kiss the seagull with a sorrowful look before raising the gun, killing both himself and the seagull. Afterward, the black hole devours all. The twin girls never reappear in the universe. Stricken by melancholia, the young stage crew member rebuilds his own set, a new solar system. The moment he steps on his earth, he starts to cry. His tears are real.

In Shuangchimu's "The Solar Studio: Seagull," the original and the duplicate become one; translation and creation merge into one; science and poetry merge into one; SF and Chekhovian realism merge into one; the representation of the invisible and the performance of the outlandish become one; the virtual presence of a truth of the world and the truth's eternal escape from notice are one; the science content of SF and the literariness of its style are one. And with this story, a newer wave has risen, broken gender and genre stereotypes, and begun to form a nonbinary literary universe of abundance, baroque, complexity, diversity, and extravagance.

"The Solar Studio: Seagull" is an echo of the earth-shattering of the momentous world-buildings in Liu Cixin's sublime, awe-inspiring "Three-Body" trilogy and Han Song's chthonic, subversive "Hospital" trilogy. It also directly speaks back to "Mountain," with an outlandish display of the new wonders bursting out of a universe entrapped in a nutshell; this worlding of new wonders, by referring to the poetics of the invisible, also creates a hyperdimensional literary space where "a bottomless abyss exists in every inch." But in an ultimate way, SF as a method for thinking is like baroque, a curve instead of a straight line, and thus reveals the invisible depth in the fold of the fabric of reality. This revelation first came from the courage to overcome the fear of seeing, as Lu Xun first showed us one hundred years ago.

3

CAN WE READ "A MADMAN'S DIARY" AS SCIENCE FICTION?

Rewriting Literary History

Lu Xun's groundbreaking modern story "A Madman's Diary" 狂人日記 (1918) offers a fearful account of a man's delusion—or enlightenment, depending on the reader's perspective regarding a cultural conflict between tradition and revolution. In Lu Xun's narrative, this man discovers a truth that has been deliberately made invisible to people for thousands of years: people are eating people; cannibalism prevails in the society. History is filled with moral teaching that thinly veils anthropophagic urges. As if living in the middle of a conspiracy, the man suspects that his own family members have eaten their siblings, and he is sure that he is one of them, a cannibal. He is caught in the fear of seeing: "my heart pounded with fear . . . There is darkness all around me. I cannot tell day from night."[1]

The first-time reader, if not aided by any knowledge about the intellectual history of modern China, may wonder about the genre of this story. In the context of this book's topic, Lu Xun's madman easily reminds us of Han Song's characters, the so-called truth investigators, who have overcome the fear of seeing to unearth the terrifying truth about the world. It was of course Han Song who learned from Lu Xun, but reading Lu Xun's story in light of the poetics of the invisible today can help us recapture the fresh shock that such a subversive text caused upon its first publication.

There is no doubt that Lu Xun made considerable impact on new wave SF, and he looms large in the genre. He even appears as a character in some SF stories written by new wave authors. For example, Fei Dao appropriates Lu Xun's own strategy in "Old Chinese Tales Retold" 故事新編 as a narrative device in the making of the so-called "Chinese sci-fi blockbusters" 中國科幻大片. One such narrative delivers Lu Xun into the surreal virtual reality of *Cube* (1997). Lu Xun appears as Zhou Shuren 周樹人 (his name used when enrolled in a naval academy; often considered his original name but not his birth name), a young physician who uses his blood to create some red pills. He feeds the pills to sleeping young people, awakening them to a terrifying reality—the Cube world plagued by cannibals, zombies, and all sorts of demons. Though he tries very hard to lead those enlightened few to escape the Cube, it is a hopeless battle. Zhou Shuren knows that it is a predesigned game: this reality is only virtual, and the game designer did not create any exit.[2]

Fei Dao's story playfully showcases Lu Xun's bewildering position in China's modernity project: though a leading intellectual, he never stopped doubting the result of the Chinese enlightenment. Fei Dao's narrative also sheds light on the entanglement between Lu Xun's role as China's prominent modern writer and his devotion to science studies and SF in his earlier years, when he trained to become a physician. In Fei Dao's depiction, Lu Xun's fight and despair, his gaze into demons and darkness, his epiphany that this is a hopeless game, and his self-conscious "role play" have all heightened the affinity between SF and Lu Xun's literary writings.

Back in 1903, when Lu Xun was still studying Japanese in Tokyo and planning to get into medical school, he published a translation of Jules Verne's *From the Earth to the Moon* 月界旅行, based on a secondhand Japanese translation that was based on an English translation.[3] This was one of the earliest Chinese translations of Western SF novels. Through the same detour, Lu Xun also translated Verne's *A Journey to the Center of the Earth* 地底旅行, the first two chapters of which were published in 1903 in a magazine edited by Chinese students in Japan, *Tides of Zhejiang* 浙江潮. The entire book of this second translation was printed in Nanjing in 1906 and signed with the pen name Zhijiang Suozi 之江索子, the second part of which Lu Xun used as the pen name for "The Art of Creating Humanity" 造人術, his third extant translation of SF.[4] This third translation provides some clues that have long been overlooked but can be very useful for understanding Lu Xun's first modern story from a new perspective. When it was written, "A Madman's Diary" was an audacious, genreless experiment never tried before in Chinese literature. Only later did scholars define it as "realism," interpreting its estrangements as rich symbolic references to China's ruthless inhuman reality. For a long time, scholars have focused solely on the story's cultural symbolism but may have missed its experimentalism in terms of genre making. This chapter reexamines the tensions between Lu Xun's devotion to translating SF and the origins of Chinese literary modernity by asking a rather audacious question.

Can we read "A Madman's Diary" as SF? This is the first provocative question I ask in this book. It does not yield an easy or certain answer. Rather, it aims to inspire a new understanding of the relationship between SF and the modern Chinese literary tradition, both of which Lu Xun helped create. I ask this question purposefully to shatter any certainties that are written into the hierarchical and orthodox narrative of modern Chinese literary history, which almost always favors realism but rarely mentions SF. My aim is to create a nonbinary method to understand the entanglement of SF and realism in Lu Xun's "A Madman's Diary." This story has long been venerated as the foundational text of Chinese literary realism. My argument is that it should also be viewed as a pioneering experiment—before all the acclaim deified (or ossified) it as part of a modern canon. "A Madman's Diary" was born out of an avant-garde spirit of cutting into the chiasm between the visible and invisible, and the story inspires a perpetual resistance to constraining conventions in all forms of literature. In this book, I consider "A Madman's Diary" a major inspiration for the subversive new wave in twenty-first-century Chinese SF.[5]

My efforts to explore the connections between Lu Xun and the new wave have led me to investigate the epistemological, ethical, and cultural turns that shaped both the earlier New Culture movement (1915–19) and Chinese new wave SF. I consider the new wave a literary experiment heavily indebted to Lu Xun rather than to earlier SF. My purpose is not just to claim the genre's legitimacy as an integral part of modern Chinese literature but also to open up at least one hidden dimension of Chinese literary modernity. David Der-wei Wang has revealed the diversity and dynamism of the repressed modernities in late Qing science fantasy and other genres,[6] and my question about "A Madman's Diary" and SF further probes whether the May Fourth literature is truly a monolithic "modernity." The way I ask the question can also be viewed as a practice in "rewriting literary history,"[7] with the awareness that "rewriting" should not be done to replace one narrative with another, but with a hope that "rewriting" will lead to a more diverse, inclusive, and democratic way of elucidating Chinese literary modernity. This is also a way of illuminating invisible paths in literary history, which allows us to recollect, for example, how Lu Xun's largely overlooked earlier dedication to science and SF contributed to his later literary ideas, aesthetic style, and cultural vision, key to Chinese literary modernity.

Reading "A Madman's Diary" as SF requires repositioning Lu Xun's early engagements with SF within his lifelong career as a modern writer. His practice as a translator of Western SF and his devotion to Western sciences can be linked to the inception of his literary vision. How does "A Madman's Diary," which contains an epistemological paradigm shift that attempts to discredit the Confucian hermeneutics regarding reality, create an alternative vision of the real? How is it related to Lu Xun's knowledge of modern sciences, which brought out the larger epistemological shift worldwide in the early twentieth century? In this chapter, my inquiry centers on the following three topics: Lu Xun's translations of SF during his youth, his appropriations of new scientific views for cultural purposes, and the science fictionality in "A Madman's Diary." My discussion begins with the late Qing, when Lu Xun was a student of medical science and a devoted translator of Western SF, and then looks at Lu Xun's role as a translator, a science student, and a literary "madman."

THE TRANSLATOR

The background for Lu Xun's translations of SF was the 1902 "Revolution in Fiction," launched by Liang Qichao, who believed that fiction had an immensely magical power to enlighten common readers.[8] Five years before, an even earlier project to reform Chinese fiction was the 1897 joint statement by Yan Fu 嚴復 (1854–1921) and Xia Zengyou 夏曾佑 (1863–1924) about printing translated novels through Commercial Press 商務印書館.

Yan and Xia believed that fiction was an effective means to change the mind of a nation because of its popularity among the masses—vendors, footmen, and women all read novels, so they argued that translated novels from advanced Western countries, if also popular with Chinese readers, could enlighten them to modern thought.[9] Scholars like Patrick Hanan noted that even before Yan and Xia, Western missionaries such as John Fryer (1839–1928) had already made efforts to induce literary intellectuals to write novels criticizing the social ills in the early 1890s.[10] It seemed that the late Qing saw a consensus among progressive intellectuals regarding the use of literature for reform. After the 1898 "Hundred Days' Reform" failed, Liang Qichao was exiled to Japan, where he revived these earlier projects to launch a revolution in fiction. SF was one of the most important new genres that he promoted.

Lu Xun undertook his translations of SF under Liang Qichao's influence. He wrote a concise, persuasive preface to his first translation of Verne, depicting how people overcame obstacles to communicate with each other across mountains and oceans, and how humans, with a hope for progress and evolution, will eventually have interplanetary travel. He makes clear that his mission is to promote modern science in order to reform China, and because science writings are not appealing to common readers, he resorts to the genre of SF to encourage people to learn about science. Lu Xun concludes: "If we are to guide the Chinese people to progress, we must begin with writing SF."[11] He followed Liang Qichao's new style, using vernacular Chinese to translate the two Verne novels, his earliest literary practice in the vernacular.

As Lu Xun later confessed in a letter, he would rather characterize his early translations as rewritings 改作, which was not unusual at the time when Lin Shu's 林紓 (1952–1924) unfaithfully "creative" but effectively "enhanced" translations of classic Western novels were making a deep impact on Chinese intellectual readers.[12] Lu Xun domesticated his translations of Verne with both Taoist and Buddhist terminology, bringing the estranging world images home. What stands out in his unfaithful translations is a sweeping optimism that certainly originated in Verne's novels, but Lu Xun's contemporary authors also applied the utopian vision of the nineteenth-century industrial revolution to an imaginary vision of China's future, fully reformed and technologized, which was the main theme of late Qing Chinese original SF.

Yet Lu Xun's translations of Western SF are not limited to the abovementioned two novels. In the 1930s, Lu Xun noted his early passion for translating SF: "Because I studied science, I also favored SF. When I was a youth, I was ambitious and arrogant, so I was never a faithful translator, and now it is too late for regrets."[13] He then said that he had translated altogether four SF novels and stories, including a third piece titled "Adventures at the North Pole" 北極探險記 whose author is still a mystery. Lu Xun's translation of this story was lost after being turned down by the Commercial Press. But he did not mention the title of the fourth piece.

This fourth work was not known to Lu Xun scholars until the 1960s. Lu Xun translated it into classical literary Chinese and published it in 1905. Titled "The Art of Creating Humanity" 造人術, it is a translation of a short story by the American writer Louise Jackson Strong (1849–1929).[14] The original, "An Unscientific Story," was published in *The Cosmopolitan* in February 1903.[15] Lu Xun's translation, signed with the pen name Suozi 索子, was discovered in 1962 alongside his brother Zhou Zuoren's commentary, both originally published in a double issue of the Shanghai magazine *Women's World* 女子世界 in 1905 (though the actual publication date was 1906). In 1962, Zhou Zuoren verified that this was indeed Lu Xun's work.[16] Scholars have confirmed that Lu Xun's translation, much shorter than the original story and with important modifications, was actually based on a Japanese translation by Hara Hôitsu-an 原抱一庵 (1866–1904), published in June and July 1903, just one year after the original story's publication. Hara's Japanese translation was serialized in a Japanese magazine, but only the first part was included in an anthology of Western fiction published in September 1903. It appears that Lu Xun only saw the anthologized part, so he translated only the first part of Hara's translation, thus creating a text that is only about one-seventh of the original length of Strong's story. However, Lu Xun's Chinese translation is largely faithful to Hara's Japanese translation.[17]

Like the majority of SF and popular writings about science of the late Qing, this translation is marked by optimism: it depicts a scientist experimenting with creating life. The 1,000-word translation by Lu Xun is filled with excitement about the art of creating humanity. The scientist successfully creates "sprouts of humanity" 人芽, which makes him feel like a god:

Hooray! Have I not succeeded in unlocking the world's secrets? Have I not succeeded in explaining humanity's mysteries? If the world has a primal creator, then am I not the second? I can create life! I can create worlds! If I am not the creator of everything under the sun, then who is? I beget all, peopling the peopled people. I rule over all, as the king of the king of kings. What a wondrous thing it is for a mortal to become a creator![18]

The translation ends with tears of gratitude rolling down the cheeks of this new creator. Compare to Strong's original text that sticks to third-person narrative: "Life! Life, so long the mystery and despair of man, had come at his bidding. He alone of all humanity held the secret in the hollow of his hand. He plunged about the room in a blind ecstasy of triumph. Tears ran unknown and unheeded down his cheeks. He tossed his arms aloft wildly, as if challenging Omnipotence itself. At this moment, he felt a very god! He could create worlds, and people them!"[19] Lu Xun's translation resonates with his belief in science. When he translated this story, he was still a science student obsessed with new theories, in particular, evolutionary thinking. Scientific optimism deified a scientist as a god, the maker of life, which Lu Xun celebrated wholeheartedly.

Translating SF synchronized Lu Xun's interests in literature and science while strengthening his belief that through literary representation, science could motivate larger social progress. Carlos Rojas points to Lu Xun's "using literature to reflect on some of the implications of those same scientific aspirations."[20] Jing Jiang's analysis of Lu Xun's translations of SF confirms that "Chinese men of letters pinned their hopes for a strengthened nation on a brand-new species of man that had no ties whatsoever to the Chinese people's biogenetic past. In Lu Xun's imagination, this new species of man boasted of a new man-made body, a new physiology."[21] This belief in the making of the new man, body and soul, continued in Lu Xun's later reflections on reforming the national characteristics, a cultural motif that repeatedly reemerged in the mainstream of modern Chinese literature throughout the twentieth century.[22]

But what makes this minor translation by Lu Xun uniquely interesting is that it is not as simple as it appears to be. When the story was published in *Women's World*, it was followed by two commentaries, one by Zhou Zuoren (under the pen name Lady Pingyun 萍雲女士) and the other by the editor, Chuwo 初我 (Ding Zuyin 丁祖蔭 1871–1930). Both commentaries derive a pessimistic message from Lu Xun's story and condemn it as being "mythical" or evil fallacy. The critics denounce this art of creating humanity as inhuman behavior, claiming that the true creators of life are women, or the nation's mothers. Chuwo states that the art of creating humans actually "disseminates evil causes and spreads deviants seeds, which is scary."[23] Yoojin Soh proposes, through a contrast between the commentaries and the text, that "Lu Xun's translation does not showcase the omnipotence of science but motivates pessimistic interpretations; carrying out reforms through scientific means does have great potential, but it is also likely that this will further worsen the problems with the national character."[24]

Here, our plot thickens. Translation, if representing the translated modernity tasked with spreading scientific views and reforming the minds of the Chinese people, met resistance. The way that the story and the commentaries were presented in the magazine simultaneously created the thesis of scientific modernity and its antithesis. We have no clue whether this arrangement involved a real debate between Lu Xun and his younger brother. It is quite clear that the commentaries view science, or scientism, as counternatural and unethical, which forms a tension between the text and the commentaries, predicting the later debate on science and metaphysics 科學與人生觀 (1923–24) on a much larger scale, dividing China's cultural elites and prompting a counteraction to a totalistic belief in scientism. If Lu Xun was on the same page with the two commentators, this translation actually could be viewed as an ironic portrait of the mad scientist, who is no longer a god but an evil being pretending to be a god, a violator of the natural order, and an enemy to the organic human society. In terms of biopolitics, the intertextuality created by the two commentaries shows a clear tendency toward treating life as organic rather than a product of technology. In other words, the commentaries amount to a disbelief in science, contrary to the story's advocacy for scientific progress. The scientific story creates a "myth" of science, and when the commentaries turn back to "reality," they discredit this scientific mythology for its ethical ambiguity.

What is really uncanny is that the untranslated part of Louise J. Strong's "An Unscientific Story" exactly contains the antiscientific message that Chubo implies in his commentary. Lydia Liu questions how the editors "could have correctly predicted the dystopia of Louise Strong's original on the basis of partial knowledge."[25] It is just so obvious because Strong's story is titled "An Unscientific Story," and its second half far outweighs its first half. Lu Xun's translation ends with the scientist's creation of lives in the laboratory. But in the rest of the story that Lu Xun did not translate, those beings quickly mutate into cannibals, and the glory of scientific creation quickly darkens into an apocalyptic vision. Strong may have followed Mary Shelley in depicting the Frankenstein-like scientist, or "mad scientist," whose disastrous experiments give rise to a skeptical attitude about science. This doubt, rooted in Romanticism, is presented to counter "Baconian optimism and Enlightenment confidence that everything can ultimately be known and that such knowledge will inevitably be for the good."[26] Strong's story, written after H. G. Wells, is even more sharply critical of the belief in scientific progress represented by Jules Verne. The living creatures that the scientist creates are more hideous than Frankenstein's monster. They are not romantic and sensitive; they are cannibals with the lowest animal ferocity. The creation of life turns into a detriment to science. The scientist has no choice but to lock all the devilish creatures in the laboratory to destroy, but before he does so, the creatures destroy themselves. The scientist tells his wife that he now belongs to her and their children, indicating his intention to return to the normative organic society.[27]

The self-contradictory title "An Unscientific Story" almost lays bare that this tale could be read as a parody of a "scientific story." Its deeply dystopian suspicion of the benefits of science for humanity continues a sentiment that H. G. Wells expressed in *The Time Machine*, *The Invisible Man* (1896), and particularly *The Island of Dr. Moreau* (1897). The bright progressive worlds built by Jules Verne give way to a darker world of shadowy phantoms—alienated mutants, half-humans, man-made monsters, zombies, and cyborgs that have populated world SF since H. G. Wells. Strong's text epitomizes the questioning of science in both natural and ethical terms, a perpetual motif that defines SF as a genre that engages with science in both its positive and negative aspects.

In the first decade of the twentieth century, Chinese SF was almost completely defined by a rejuvenated Confucian utopianism mingled with Western scientific advancement. All three translations by Lu Xun are no exception. However, the commentaries voice a discontent with scientific optimism. There is no evidence to prove whether Lu Xun later read Strong's original story or a complete, faithful Japanese translation published in 1912.[28] It remains uncertain whether Lu Xun intended to express wholehearted praise for science in his translation or, like the commentators, was aware of the mythical or evil fallacy of science, which his younger brother's commentary highlighted.

"A Madman's Diary" was written twelve years after Lu Xun published "The Art of Creating Humanity." He never mentioned this translation again in any writing or recorded conversation. However, "A Madman's Diary" shares four crucial elements with "An Unscientific Story," particularly the second half that Lu Xun did not translate. Because he may not have read the second half at all, the four elements discussed here are not proof of Louise J. Strong's influence, but rather manifestations of the potential for a shared complicated manifestation of science fictionality in both texts. The first element is cannibalism, which is the most obvious. With a plotline showing that technology creates cannibalism, "An Unscientific Story" registers a warning that science can be a vicious threat to humanity. "A Madman's Diary" registers a similar warning, but it comes from a look beneath the surface reality, the madman's discovery of the long-standing tradition of cannibalism as the core of Chinese civilization. While cannibalism can be read as a cultural metaphor that constitutes an allegory about the national character,[29] in the text it creates a truthful discourse supported by a reconfiguration of scientific knowledge and epistemological paradigm. "A Madman's Diary" can be read as "an unscientific story" full of delusional moments about "eating people" and fear that dismantles the orderly structure of everyday life. But it can also be read as a "scientific story," which presents a scientific method to form a fold in thinking, going counterintuitively to apprehend and interpret the most fearful social ill, which has been hidden in traditional Chinese culture. By making "cannibalism" visible in Chinese society, Lu Xun's story is equivalent to a scientific diagnosis of the disease in body, mind, and culture of the Chinese people.

The second motif shared by both stories is the danger of hope. In Strong's story, it is the hope to use science to create humans; and in Lu Xun's case, it is the hope to use enlightenment ideas to create new humans, or real humans. "An Unscientific Story" begins with this hopeful intention, but the hope collapses as the plot evolves—the scientist's ecstasy soon turns into agony when he tries to imprison the cannibals in the laboratory. "A Madman's Diary" also ends with the collapse of hope. Lu Xun, a pessimistic loner among the New Culturalists, had a profound suspicion about the enlightenment project. When Qian Xuantong 錢玄同 (1887–1939) invited him to contribute "something" to the progressive magazine *New Youth* 新青年, Lu Xun told Qian a story about an iron house in which people were confined and about to suffocate to death. In Fei Dao's story mentioned earlier, Lu Xun's iron house has evolved into the virtual Cube world. Lu Xun argues: "Is it right to cry out, to rouse the light sleepers among them, causing them inconsolable agony before they die?"[30] The iron house where the people are imprisoned, if they are cannibals as described in "A Madman's Diary," bears some resemblance to the locked laboratory in Strong's story. The two stories diverge with regard to whether the intention is to sympathize with or condemn them. Either way, waking people up from the iron house can be a dangerous mission, which easily turns into a nightmare if there is no exit. Thus, the second shared element between the two stories has turned into a vicious pitfall: both present the good intention to make new humans, but both end with a catastrophic moment—the emergence of cannibalism. Both the laboratory in Strong's story and the iron house in Lu Xun's metaphor opens the gate of darkness and leads to a desert of humanism, where hope dries up.

The third element shared by both stories is the fearful confrontation with the menacing truth of the world. "An Unscientific Story" shows the failure of science straightforwardly. "A Madman's Diary" is much more sophisticated and ambivalent regarding the truth and its hideous effects. Lu Xun's story consists of a preface and thirteen diary entries. The preface, written in classical literary Chinese, and the following diary entries, written in vernacular Chinese, each represent a claim to truthfulness. While the madman's discovery of the cannibalism in Confucian society can be understood as a truth-claiming moment, the madman's pathological status both endangers and limits the power of this truth, depending on how much credit the reader gives to the assumed orthodoxy and truthfulness in the preface. Nevertheless, the deeper truth that the preface tries to cover but the madman has glimpsed evokes the fear of seeing. In the first diary entry, the madman reaches enlightenment. His immediate thought is, "I have reason to be afraid." The fear may indicate a realization of the iron house situation, where there is no exit. Compared with those suffocated to death, those who awake and see the truth of the world have a torturing fate. The enlightened are soon to become the disillusioned driven to despair. The fear also comes from the madman's awareness that he is not only surrounded by the cannibals but also one of them: "With the weight of four thousand years of cannibalism bearing down upon me, even if once I was innocent, how can I now face real humans?"[31]

Who are the real humans? "A Madman's Diary" ends with a famous quote: "Save the children." It echoes the scientist's last words to his wife in Strong's story when he turns to his children. This moment marks another shared element between the two stories: children, innocent and immune to old evils, must be saved. Lu Xun's profound self-reflection leads to a deep suspicion of the enlightened subjectivity in his own generation, who insert themselves as self-sacrificing pioneers. He is in deep denial that his generation, poisoned by tradition through and through, do not belong to the future. Thus, he later offered the famous metaphor of the gate of darkness: "Let the awakened man burden himself with the weight of tradition and shoulder up the gate of darkness. Let him give unimpeded passage to the children so that they may rush to the bright, wide-open space and lead happy lives henceforward as rational human beings."[32] Lu Xun believed that there is no hope here and now; "saving the children" from becoming cannibals represents the last and only hope.

The richness of Lu Xun's textual techniques and implications makes "A Madman's Diary" far superior to the straightforward narrative in "An Unscientific Story" in terms of literary quality. But reading "A Madman's Diary" alongside "An Unscientific Story" helps illuminate Lu Xun's doubt about scientific progressivism in the larger context of twentieth-century world literature. Furthermore, "An Unscientific Story" helps us connect Lu Xun's earlier views on science and SF to his later literary practice, particularly in "A Madman's Diary." SF can serve as one of the many gates through which to enter Lu Xun's literary world.

THE SCIENTIST

Lu Xun did not become a physician, based on his original plan of studying abroad in Japan. Instead he became a man of letters. His later reputation as a great writer has obscured his early education in sciences. Interestingly, after the rise of the New Culture that the magazine *New Youth* promoted, SF was no longer popular, and Lu Xun was mainly reviewed as a literary realist. Reestablishing his connection to science can help us at least reconsider his writings in the context of the worldwide scientific revolution that shaped the twentieth century. How much did he know about the newest theories indicating a paradigm shift in physics and mathematics that began in around 1900? How did new sciences impact his literary writings?

In the following pages, I propose a new understanding of Lu Xun as an intellectual author writing in a new epoch that was well informed by modern sciences. The first set of scientific knowledge that Lu Xun accepted can be epitomized by Darwinism. The second set of knowledge is much more complicated, with roots in the new physics, such as quantum theory and the theory of relativity, which emerged at the beginning of the twentieth century and posed great challenges to not only the well-regulated Newtonian universe but also the corresponding worldviews—including imperialism, industrialism, and humanism—based on the knowability, certainty, and visibility of the world as a stable reality. Darwinism revealed to Lu Xun the heart of darkness in the ruthless struggles for national survival; the new physics shattered worldviews based on certainties, which prompted Lu Xun to reflect on the power of imagination and the agency of speculation.

The modern idea of science was new to Lu Xun's generation, living in the last days of Imperial China. Science was first of all considered a Western idea. The entire nation was hungry for scientific knowledge imported from the West, which was deemed the correct path to modernity. While the Anglo-American missionaries, in collaborations with local literati, used modern printing technologies to produce new books on the so-called "Western learning," which opened a wealth of advanced scientific knowledge to Chinese readers during the second half of the nineteenth century, they deliberately kept one important scientific theory secret: the theory of evolution. Eventually, the Chinese intellectual Yan Fu composed *Tianyanlun* 天演論 (1898) in elegant archaic prose, a landmark translation that introduced Darwinism as the most important scientific thinking of the century.

Yan Fu's version of evolutionary thinking was largely based on Thomas Huxley's (1825–1895) *Evolution and Ethics*, and he also accepted Herbert

Spencer's (1820–1903) social Darwinism. As Benjamin Schwartz summarizes, this new system invented by Yan Fu, treating biological knowledge, human history, and the histories of nations "as an integrated whole is overwhelmingly attractive," a system that "explains all the phenomena of reality."[33] This laid the foundation for a scientific realism rooted in a universally valid theory, applicable to a whole range of subjects. Evolutionism became a default mode of thinking for anyone who sought a scientific view of the world, an approach that "offered Chinese readers and writers not only new terminology, but a new *narrative mode*, a way of telling stories."[34] The most profound revelation for the Chinese intellectuals after learning about this theory was a ruthless political reality: facing a world populated by countries competing for limited resources, they had to follow the law of natural selection, which means the inevitable life-and-death struggle among nations and the survival of the fittest.

Missionaries' deliberate avoidance due to their religious concerns created a delay in the Chinese acceptance of Darwinism, but this enabled it to spread widely in China because it arrived at the right time, immediately after China lost the war with Japan. The 1894 defeat was a decisive inspiration for the former naval officer Yan Fu to introduce Darwinism to China: it was meant as a wake-up call. China must join this dark jungle of international competitions and grow into a strong nation. Darwinism was considered the most relevant, profound scientific validation of China's flaws and inadequacies in dealing with other modernized nations. Quickly, evolutionary thinking became the very principle underlying the entire new system of modern Chinese thought: it "reframed national history in terms of natural history, casting China as an actor in the unfolding of a vast and tumultuous world-historical drama, one in which species, races, and nations alike were caught up in a relentless struggle for survival."[35] The nearly blind faith in Western science, a kind of scientism,[36] emerged after Yan Fu's *Tianyanlun* had made a deep impact on educated Chinese readers. Science was considered essential for China to survive and prosper as a sovereign nation on planet Earth.

A century later, Liu Cixin depicts in his space saga the "worst possible universe," in which only the fittest species survive. His vision resonates with late Qing social Darwinism. A key moment in his "Three-Body" trilogy projects China's 1894 defeat by Japan into a space war on astronomical scale. Just as the Chinese northern naval fleet was wiped out by the

Japanese navy in a single day, Earth's combined defensive force is wiped out in a few seconds by a simple droplet, a hitherto unseen, unimaginably but extremely advanced weapon. Liu Cixin is less optimistic than Yan Fu, for the wake-up call is useless. Liu depicts the interstellar Darwinist universe: "The universe is a dark forest."[37] His saga leaves no hope for human survival but reveals the foundational truth of the universe as determined by the ultimate dark force that motivates all civilizations' deathly struggles, pushing social Darwinism to its extreme—any other civilization is viewed as a rival and thus to be preemptively extinguished.

Lu Xun describes his first contact with Darwinism as a wondrous experience.[38] But he also describes the family elders' attitude: Yan Fu's book was "not right." However, what attracted Lu Xun was exactly the subversive nature of *Tianyanlun* in defying the orthodox Confucian moral and philosophical doctrines. Yan Fu's translation opened the young Lu Xun's eyes to a new world, different from the "correct" version of a stable world based on the Confucian norms. Modern science functioned as a new method to investigate and understand the heart of the matter. But Lu Xun soon began to use this method in a different context.

In 1902 Lu Xun went to Japan. Two years later, he began to study at Sendai Medical Academy. In an essay in memory of his professor of anatomy, Mr. Fujino 藤野先生, Lu Xun presents a paradoxical narrative about an important lesson for him as a medical student. Mr. Fujino explains to him:

"Look, you have moved this blood vessel slightly out of place. It certainly looks more elegant when you do this, but a dissection-based diagram is not fine art. If this is what the real thing looks like, there is no way we can change it...."

Yet I was not going to be persuaded by him. Though agreeing out loud, I thought to myself: "I did a pretty good job drawing those diagrams. As for the actual state of things, of course I remember how these things look."[39]

This moment shows the artist Lu Xun clashing with the scientist Lu Xun. In the name of science, he should be completely faithful to the observed facts. However, he was not satisfied with the scientific realism Mr. Fujino taught him. Reality can be improved upon. Lu Xun didn't become a scientist or a physician; he took up a different kind of realism, questioning the appearance of reality, just as he had done in the anatomy class. For the rest of his life, he carried his respect for Mr. Fujino's scientific realism, but he betrayed his teacher with a purposeful application of science to viewing reality differently, which goes beyond what appears to be real and reaches the imaginary, the mythological, and the poetic.

After Lu Xun quit medical school, he produced a series of treatises, beginning with "The History of Man" 人之歷史 (1907) and "Lessons from the History of Science" 科學史教篇 (1908). Both promote evolutionary thinking. The former presents a historical account of the emergence and development of the theory of evolution in Europe; the latter is a more sophisticated reflection on the history of science, ending with a doubt: "If knowledge were exalted as the only virtue, humanity would surely regress to a haggard and lonely state, and if this were to continue the sense of beauty would drift away, and acuity of thought would be lost; what we call science would also tend towards extinction." For Lu Xun, Newton, Kant, and Darwin should be venerated side by side with Shakespeare, Raphael, and Beethoven.[40] From here, Lu Xun continued to argue for the necessity of art and literature, promoting the power of imagination and poetry, particularly in three long treatises on culture and poetry he completed in the same time period.

Throughout his life, Lu Xun kept the touchstone of evolutionary thinking. In "A Madman's Diary," the madman describes to his elder brother the theory of evolution, warning with a twisted interpretation of devolution: "Primitive men probably did eat human flesh. But their thinking changed, developed over time, and some of them stopped—they were determined to become human, genuinely human. Those who wouldn't give it up remained reptiles, some of them changing into fish, birds or monkeys, then finally men. But they remain reptiles at heart—even today."[41] These seemingly illogical words are far from an accurate Darwinian narrative. Here the madman is that young student criticized by Mr. Fujino for mingling imagination with science; knowing "what the real thing looks like," he aims to create a powerful aesthetic and ethical effect. On the surface, all appear to be human, but at heart they are reptiles, less than human, and cannibals.

The madman's way of perceiving the world dismantles the appearance of reality. The madman is like a scientist, who has to form a narrative using a seemingly scientific discourse, but this can be less realistic than revelatory about a truth that is hidden, buried beneath its deceptive surface. The truth cannot be articulated in everyday speech, only communicated in an unnatural scientific discourse; in this estranging literary text, the madman's description of the scientific theory of evolution turns into a thicket filled with estranging metaphors.

David Der-wei Wang has pointed to Lu Xun's doubt about the efficacy of positivist modern science even during his youth and preference for the "divine thought" 神思, a euphemism for imagination, arising from ancient mythological visions and "best manifested in the form of literature."[42] Lu Xun applauds the demonic power of romantic poetry as a "new school of divine thought" in his treatise "On the Power of Mara Poetry" (摩羅詩力說, 1908),[43] criticizing those who consider science the only approach to understanding the world and restoring myth as equally a source of truth.[44] In this line of thinking, Lu Xun combines science and imagination, investing the magic power of literary imagination in scientific speculation as well as evoking a truth-claiming scientific spirit from the poetic voice of the heart.

In a larger context that sees a fusion of science and imagination, we must understand that Lu Xun's early treatises on science and culture, his translations of Western SF, and his literary experiment in "A Madman's Diary" all echoed, even without his knowing it, a great earthquake happening in Western sciences and aesthetics at about the same historical period. From 1900 on, a series of scientific discoveries, experiments, theorizations, and arguments leading to the Bohr-Einstein debate that erupted at the 1927 Solvay Conference questioned the tenets of the Newtonian universe: the theory of relativity changed the way we see the world, and the quantum revolution declared that the world as it appears does not exist.[45] Newtonian mechanics, the pride of the British scientific community, met ruthless challenges from Prussian physicists, which paralleled a political challenge to the British order of the world as well as a cultural avant-gardism that revamped the entire artistic world.

The Newtonian principles had long been taken for granted as universal truth, compatible with the visible world in almost all aspects. The same orderly principles underlined the political and cultural pinnacles of the British Empire, which expanded to almost the entire planet during the nineteenth century. But the twentieth century dawned with Max Planck's

(1858–1947) discovery of the "quantum" through his study of black-body radiation, which quickly led to the postulation of the principle of elementary disorder.[46] The invisible quantum shattered the edifice of Newtonian mechanics and ushered in a new epoch characterized by the principle of uncertainty. The visible Newtonian universe was unsettled by the invisible phantom particles. The same process happened in other branches of science and various forms of literature and art. Quantum physics, a new worldview that sounds like mystical speculation to laymen, was the driving force of the twentieth century that soon subverted traditions in all ways—from manufacturing to warfare to daily life. We became modern through performing the invisible quantum jumps.

Planck, Einstein, Niels Bohr (1885–1962), and Heisenberg fundamentally reshaped the scientific view of reality in the first half of the twentieth century, an earth-shattering revolution parallel to what happened in literature and art during the same time period. Lu Xun's contemporaries, Pablo Picasso (1881–1973), Igor Stravinsky (1882–1971), Isadora Duncan (1877–1927), W. B. Yeats (1865–1939), Marcel Proust (1871–1922), Virginia Woolf (1882–1941), James Joyce (1882–1941), and Franz Kafka (1883–1924), were dreamers, experimentalists, lawbreakers, and the creators of new forms in their areas of creativity. Chinese writers were dealing with the collapse of their own world in thought and practice, politics and economy, literature and language, simultaneously in truly all areas. The questioning of the fundamental laws in science, art, and thought pushed the Chinese intellectuals to seek new rules for observing and comprehending reality, not merely on physical terms but also on cultural and political terms. Lu Xun's madman stands at the center of this vortex of flushing down everything old and creating new worlds from foams and fragments of old and new ideas. The madman eventually penetrates the millennia of China's ossified past and breaks down the hierarchical structure of cultural spheres like a phantom quantum. He brings uncertainty and disorder to Confucian China, and his diaries estrange the reality to such an extent that Confucianism horridly morphs into cannibalism.

Earlier scholarship on Lu Xun has primarily focused on his acceptance of Darwin's theory of evolution.[47] But there have also been sporadic studies on Lu Xun's relationship to twentieth-century modern physics, such as Liu Na's efforts to connect Lu Xun's early thought to the new physics, which she traces to his treatise "On Radium" 說鉬 (1903).[48] This article, one of the first Lu Xun published, explains what was happening in the fields of chemistry and physics, introducing new knowledge about radioactivity and electromagnetism, which paved the way for the rise of quantum physics. I have no evidence to prove that Lu Xun knew quantum physics; the best I can do is to find traces of these new scientific knowledge within Lu Xun's circle of friends—his fellow New Culturalists.

Max Planck had a Chinese student as early as 1909. This person was Xia Yuanli 夏元瑮 (1884–1944), the son of Xia Zengyou, the literatus who first promoted fiction together with Yan Fu in 1897. Xia Zengyou came from the same province as Lu Xun. The two were not only acquaintances but also colleagues working at the Ministry of Education in Peking after the Republic was founded. Xia Yuanli, the first Chinese scientist who learned quantum physics firsthand, was invited by his father's friend Yan Fu, then president of Peking University, to teach there upon his return to China in 1913. Later, under the presidency of Cai Yuanpei 蔡元培 (1868–1940), Xia Yuanli was appointed dean of sciences, equivalent to Chen Duxiu 陳獨秀 (1879–1942), the dean of arts, who was the main advocate for the New Culture. Xia Yuanli also contributed to the movement. In 1918, he created a curriculum containing brand new courses such as "Theory of Relativity" 相對論 and "Quantum Theory" 原量論 at Peking University, and he published the first Chinese translation of Einstein's original papers.[49]

Xia Yuanli's reform of the science curriculum was just the beginning of the history of quantum physics in China. A decade later, Wu Ta-You 吳大猷 (1907–2000) became the first Chinese scientist to make important contributions to theoretical physics. During the Second Sino-Japanese War, Wu mentored two students in China's hinterland at the Associated Southwestern University 西南聯合大學, Chen-Ning Yang 楊振寧 (b. 1922) and Tsung-Dao Lee 李政道 (b. 1926), who later, in 1957, became the first two Chinese Nobel Prize laureates in physics for "important discoveries regarding the elementary particles."[50] The new physics was put into practice when Mao sought nuclear power, but this was not known to common readers until the Reform Era. Physicists such as Fang Lizhi 方勵之 (1936–2012) popularized quantum physics during the 1980s, which deeply influenced the generation of Liu Cixin and Han Song.

However, Lu Xun, confronting the edifice of the Confucian order in the first two decades of the twentieth century, saw in the darkness a shapeless revelation combining scientific speculations and poetic visions, mythology and skepticism, cannibals and new humans. He had already performed a quantum leap in the making of an elementary disorder, which became a literary revolution. Lu Xun's madman is that quantum of action shattering the universe of Chinese tradition. The force comes from both the new science and new literature.

THE MADMAN

Lu Xun quit medical school and started a crusade for cultural reform. But his idealism soon faded in disappointment at the lack of response to his call to arms. He felt the chilling loneliness, and for more than ten years, he lived like his madman, knowing the terrifying truth but unable to communicate it to others. He had to wait until his old friend Qian Xuantong invited him to write for *New Youth* in April 1918. At the age of thirty-seven, Lu Xun, though doubtful of the mission of the New Culture, responded by producing a completely "new" piece of writing in a completely "new" literary form, including using "new" punctuation and "new" grammar. "A Madman's Diary" was a surprising wonder upon its publication. It was an estranging story written in an estranging way that Chinese readers had never seen before: thirteen diary entries, inconsistently and incoherently organized in the form of a "short story."

Ironically, it was printed side by side with Dr. Hu Shi's 胡適 (1891–1962) essay "Short Story" 短篇小說 in *New Youth*. Dr. Hu presents a definition of the short story as a modern literary form, alluding to two examples by nineteenth-century French writers, Alphonse Daudet (1840–1897) and Guy de Maupassant (1850–1893). According to Dr. Hu, a modern short story should show "a slice of life." It is a literary form that represents reality with the greatest clarity and economy in words.[51] In contrast, Lu Xun's story defied not only the conventions of traditional Chinese fiction but also Hu Shi's new doctrines that correspond to the canonical mimetic realism. Shunning realistic details and failing to provide satisfying clarity, the diary entries are the very embodiment of confusion, insanity, and chaos. Even the language of the madman represents an estrangement as a new literary discourse. Lu Xun used a sort of vernacular

Chinese that was twisted and tweaked to the extent that it read more like a foreign language, with broken sentences, fragmented phrases, words and paragraphs disorganized; the Western punctuation that he used had never appeared in print before in China. Lu Xun's "A Madman's Diary" almost seemed to be an avant-garde revolt against Dr. Hu Shi's classical standards of nineteenth-century realism.

If we return to the text of "A Madman's Diary," the madman's horror, confusion about what is real, and shocking discovery of cannibalism as a hidden truth can be theorized as cultural criticism, a revolutionary outcry, or the voice of enlightenment, but these do not naturally exist in the text. The modern truth-claiming discourse of literary realism is supposed to have originated in "A Madman's Diary," but in the text, it is, first of all, a subversive claim. In the history of modern Chinese fiction, "A Madman's Diary" was the first work to create a narrative strategy that subverts the then conventional knowledge about social and moral norms through presenting its own storytelling as an alternative, insurgent truth-claiming practice. The text creates a counterintuitive literalness when it spells out the astonishing "scientific" truth about cannibalism, an alternative truth against the common sense of everyday reality. The shock that this story caused comes from the novum of both the estranging vernacular language and its semantic literalness that forces readers to accept a seemingly unreal but "true" wonder: the Chinese are all man-eaters.

By the logic asserted by the narrative of "A Madman's Diary," the truth is found through an inversion of the usual order: madness is sanity, benevolence is a lie, the surreal is real. The reader is left in a labyrinth of signs and senses, with no ready answer to the question which is real: the counterintuitive nightmare of cannibalism or the conventional family harmony of Confucianism? Here, I suggest that the conception of the real in the eyes of the madman has become so uncertain that it could be characterized as "an unavoidable element of unpredictability or randomness,"[52] much like Heisenberg's discovery. In "A Madman's Diary," surface reality has been washed off. The real has become abysmal and uncertain.

What I propose to do is to treat "A Madman's Diary" as an open text that has not yet stabilized. This may actually have been Lu Xun's deliberate design. It is not a simple imitation of Western realism, nor a manifesto with a certain purpose. The text itself is more than meets the eye, like a nightmare. Before readers hear the voice of the madman, an authorial voice is first presented in a preface written in elegant literary Chinese. The archaic style gives the preface a sense of authority—with all the rules in place, social hierarchy untouched, and moral universe intact—very familiar to educated Chinese readers at the time. The "narrator" of the preface indicates that he has "extracted occasional flashes of coherence, in the hope they may be of use to medical research" and "[has] not altered a single one of the author's errors."[53] Zhou Shuren, though a failed medical student, may still be able to produce a scientific case study of the psychology of a delusional Chinese gentleman. Literally, a reader can take it easy and believe this authorial voice, and thus dismiss the diary entries as nonsense.

However, the very first diary entry contradicts the impression that the preface tries to establish. The madman speaks his mind directly, without any conventional formality or cultured manners:

> The moon is bright tonight.
>
> I had not seen it for thirty years; the sight of it today was extraordinarily refreshing. Tonight, I realized I have spent the past thirty years or more in a state of dream; but I must still be careful.[54]

The moment marks the madman's sudden enlightenment. Contrary to the preface's claim, he asserts his sobriety: after many years of perceiving the world as an illusion, he has just begun to see the truth. The moonstruck moment, called "lunacy," insanity, and madness, transforms him into a truth seeker. The following entries further develop a truth-claiming discourse that drives the "madman" to speak about the world from a fresh perspective. As he says to himself, *everything requires careful consideration if one is to understand it.* The madman positions himself as if he were a scientist using the Baconian investigative method. In the traditional Chinese context, what he does is exactly the neo-Confucian way of "the investigation of things and the extension of knowledge" 格物致知.[55] In early modern China, the neo-Confucian term *gewu* was used to stand for "science" before the Japanese loanword *kexue* came into use.

Thus, the diary entries also present a scientific view, which conflicts with the comforting explanation in the preface. Technically, "A Madman's Diary" offers readers two options, both scientifically plausible, but they create an ethical question. We the readers meet a pivotal moment of choice: to see or not to see. Accepting the narrative presented in the preface written in literary Chinese discredits the madman's enlightenment, reducing his words to crazy speech that can be only treated as a scientific report about schizophrenia, which normalizes the insurgent vernacular textuality and explains away its subversive significance. The more challenging choice is believe the madman, which takes the courage of a committed "truth investigator" who bears witness to the brutality hidden in Chinese reality, the pervasive but invisible horror, the heart of darkness. If we believe the diary entries, we become the madman's accomplice, and the task is to unearth the concealed "truth" that has been covered by all the traditional untruths. The madman's experiment begins with a new study, which is exactly "looking closely." He finds in the space between the lofty words "benevolence, righteousness, morality" two other words hidden everywhere: "Eat people."[56] This horrifying, counterintuitive discovery is the most important event in the intellectual history of modern China.

It is easy to take this notion as a metaphor: cannibalism stands for the oppressive patriarchal system. However, the madman in the text does not think metaphorically. He begins to view Chinese history as a chronicle of cannibalism in the literal sense: people ate each other in ancient times; orthodox Confucian commentaries on one of the earliest historical classics, *Spring and Autumn*, record the gentlemen's exchange of sons to eat; the traditional Chinese classic of herbs and medicines declares that boiled human flesh is edible; and during the recent uprisings that led to the Republican Revolution, a revolutionary's heart was eaten by the Imperial soldiers.[57] The madman's careful observations discover more and more evidence for the unpalatable truth: China is a country of cannibals. Within the story, cannibalism is literal, not metaphor or allegory, and regarding his discovery in that light, the madman transforms into a mad scientist, the only one aware of the world's darkest secret that is beyond mundane comprehension.

To publish this story, Zhou Shuren used the pen name Lu Xun, the first time that this name appeared in print. The author Lu Xun was born together with his first unconventional literary experiment. Subsequently, the magazine published reviews written by radical intellectuals, who had now found the most powerful metaphor to condemn Chinese tradition: Confucian teaching creates inhumane cannibals. Exactly one year after the publication of "A Madman's Diary," college students in Beijing staged the unprecedented May Fourth Movement (1919), which shook the entire country and led to the politicization of the Chinese progressive intellectuals, including Chen Duxiu, who founded the Chinese Communist Party soon after. In the meantime, "A Madman's Diary" created a new paradigm in Chinese literature. Following in the footsteps of Lu Xun, a new generation of Chinese writers began to use an estranged vernacular literary discourse, imitating his style, to betray the estranging reality of the old China. Younger writers discovered an array of terrifying truths: the family is the slaughterhouse, parents kill their children, and the entire society is a cannibalistic banquet—such as what Ba Jin 巴金 (1904–2005) described in his popular novel *Family* 家 (1931). From their point of view, China's new literature began with "A Madman's Diary," and Lu Xun shaped China's literary modernity with this single piece. The story rewrote China's national image and created China's national allegory.

Beginning with the New Cultural radicals, progressive educated readers agreed to a singular interpretation of Lu Xun's notion of cannibalism as a cultural metaphor that demonized tradition. This is an efficient way to tidy the chaotic and subversive textuality of "A Madman's Diary." Lu Xun's madman created a new imperative for Chinese literature: "telling the truth." So the short story that broke laws thus created a new law. This marked the beginning of the mainstream of Chinese literary realism, even though its printed form so violently contrasted with Dr. Hu Shi's textbook definition. Nearly twenty years later, Lu Xun described his early stories, together with those imitating his, as "a literature for life,"[58] echoing his younger brother Zhou Zuoren's call for "humane literature."[59] Realism, in this sense, is accordance with the advancement of modern scientific views. The will to truth flows in both literature and science. This all makes sense when considering that Lu Xun was a student of medical sciences during his youth, and he saw in literature a scientific study of life. As a truth-claiming prophet speaking through the madman's mouth, Lu Xun thus became both a beacon of the New Culture movement and a national physician tasked with diagnosing the spiritual disease that plagued China.

During the rest of the twentieth century, Lu Xun's strategy was integrated into the dominant mode of cultural representation in line with the communist revolution and gradually lost its cutting-edge social critique to the ossified doctrines and regulations of socialist realism. Scholars specializing in Lu Xun spent decades taming the text. After over a hundred years of interpretations and overinterpretations, "A Madman's Diary" has been framed in a well-regulated system of signs and symbols. It no longer provokes a sense of wonder; its estrangement becomes invisible, sinking into readers' subconscious. Either the estrangement, like the wonder, has long been tamed, so that the unsettling uncertainty in Lu Xun's text has been made less dangerous through well-rounded cultural explanations; or the potential danger of the text is no longer perceivable, just like cannibalism has become an invisible part of the cultural symbolism. But if we turn back, refuse this process of refamiliarization, and retrace our steps to the moment when the wonder of the world is still portrayed by Lu Xun as unbearably estranging, too scary to see, can we overcome our fear of seeing and recognize the social ills in our own time?

Asking if "A Madman's Diary" is SF is more unsettling than recognizing it as SF. The question is unfathomable, impossible to answer with certainty. It exiles the text into terra incognita. But this estrangement is compatible with the mazelike, nightmarish textual world that the story presents. Later interpretations through many decades of canonization refamiliarize the estrangement in the original story, solidly planting its cultural significance in known ideological soil. But when it was produced during that long night in April 1918 and printed for the first time in *New Youth*, it was a world-shattering, estranging, grotesque literary text.

"A Madman's Diary" presents a contrasting vision to the canonical realism. It converges in a textual poetics that disputes what is real, creates ruptures in its representation of reality, so that the real is no longer what it appears to be and the fragmented, the speculative, and the surreal appear more truthful than what cultural conventions dictate to be real. Whether "A Madman's Diary" can be read as SF is meaningful as a question rather than a decoy to induce a definitive answer. The question itself contains a subversion of the knowledge system marked by inevitability and certainty. To borrow the words of the quantum physicist Werner Heisenberg, whose theory of the uncertainty principle was published in the 1920s, shortly after the publication of "A Madman's Diary," the question regarding Lu Xun's story points to a state of uncertainty in terms of epistemology: it is impossible not to disturb the object's momentum when measuring its location. Asking if "A Madman's Diary" is SF makes its position "uncertain" in relation to both literary realism and SF. It inspires a wide range of questions about literary history, literary genres, and knowledge systems related to constructs of the cultural and educational mechanisms that dictate our sense of reality. If our trust in that system is broken, how can we judge? Without the conventions, can we still relate our understanding of the text to reality? Or is it possible for us to come up with a singular correct answer about what is true, what is reality?

Now let's just hypothesize that Lu Xun wrote "A Madman's Diary" as a SF story. The madman sees the abysmal darkness in the familiar comforting scenes. He does not submit to the fear of seeing and chooses to open his eyes. When he salvages the truth hidden at the center of this inhuman maze, the dreamscape is collapsing. By this time, the madman realizes that he has also been part of the game, and he has no way out. He can only pretend that there is still hope for the future generations. The madman resorts to cognitive choices against his instinctive sense of reality and turns his everyday experience into a world-changing SF textuality. He uses scientific methods to estrange the familiar. With this newly gained vision, he arrives at a new understanding that the world is not what it appears to be. With cognitive speculation and imaginative vision, he sees through this unfathomably dark, treacherous, inhuman world.

SF textuality is not subject to rules of mimetic realism but sticks to the principle of literalness, coherence according to logic rather than real experience. Even if the literalness is abstract, surreal, subversive, and contrary to reality, as long as it can be validated by logical coherence, it still lends authenticity to SF world-building. This notion can be applied to "A Madman's Diary," which interprets cannibalism literally within the text and bases its entire world-building on this literal meaning. The madman studies history. He looks at events that happened far and near and comes to a logical conclusion within this framework. This counterintuitive, completely estranging world is convincing because the text replaces a familiar reality with a truth-claiming speculation. SF requires readers to make a choice whether to commit to this speculative, estranging world or step back into the comfort zone of the familiar reality. Choosing the former is difficult, demanding a devotion to imagination that makes the speculative a true event. The madman chooses this challenging route; reading between the lines to capture the invisible truth and observing reality through the lens of estrangement, he replaces normalcy with abnormal sensations. The horrifying discovery of cannibalism in both his family and his own self drives him crazy. He loses the path back into reality. In his understanding, the surreal is true, and the reality is only a cover to hide the truth. This decides his choice to reside in the truthful limbo where certainty is lost.

It is not my purpose to argue that Lu Xun's story is certainly SF. I'd rather imagine how first-time readers respond to this text before any interpretation is certain. My own speculation is that "A Madman's Diary" can be read, out of its specific context, as a horror story, as it was first read in Korea.[60] It can also be read as SF, or psychoanalytic fiction, speculative fiction, and certainly, a work of critical realism. And it can be designed as a zombie game or a virtual reality experience. Making these hypothetical readings is meant to discard the established reading habits within the framework of modern Chinese literary criticism. I contend that Lu Xun's "A Madman's Diary" served as a precedent for both twentieth-century literary realism and twenty-first-century new wave SF in a nonbinary way, dismantling the genre conventions. Rewriting a literary history connecting Lu Xun and the new wave authors completes a timeline that does not make SF and realism exclusive to each other. Their entanglement in Lu Xun led to multiple trajectories in the unfolding of Chinese literary modernity.

CODA: BACK TO THE FUTURE

"A Madman's Diary" is a literary text that resists definition and releases phantoms and strange images that will haunt Chinese literature forever. It caused an earthquake in the literary field of modern China, and the aftershocks are still felt today. This story is a work difficult to imitate, and even impossible to be repeated by Lu Xun himself—the closest work he produced later is the prose poetry collection *Wild Grass* 野草 (1927). An entire year after "A Madman's Diary," Lu Xun published his second short story, "Kong Yiji" 孔乙己, a reminiscent narrative of childhood and hometown, "a slice of life," which is much easier to emulate, and modern Chinese fiction that came into being mainly under its influence inally lived up to Dr. Hu Shi's standards. "Kong Yiji" rather than "A Madman's Diary" confirmed Lu Xun's position as the master of literary realism. But clearly, it is the quantum chaos of "A Madman's Diary" that defines Lu Xun's artistic strength—a power of darkness.

Lu Xun's literary talent went far beyond writing a national allegory and social criticism. He later wrote more personal, lyrical stories about childhood, his hometown, nostalgia, disillusionment, despair, regret, self-deception, and self-questioning. Lu Xun was a writer with a profound self-consciousness. He remained soberly reflective about romanticism and various new trends of thought and lifestyles that he helped create. He questioned the notion of progress and doubted the utility and validity of his own writing together with its "poisonous" effects in enlightening youths but driving them to a spiritual limbo with no way out. In his 1924 short story "New Year's Sacrifice" 祝福 he questions himself (as the narrator) relentlessly. He asks if he is responsible for the suicide of a poor peasant woman, Xianglin's Wife 祥林嫂, who asked a question about the afterlife that he failed to answer clearly.[61] This literary piece is not a simple act of mimesis, a faithfully realistic representation of social ills, or a transparent direct manifestation of the author's mind; its literary discourse has been marked by a poetic ambiguity and a lyrical uncertainty.

Many decades later, Lu Xun's darker, cannibalistic, morally ambivalent literary vision was echoed in Liu Cixin's *The Three-Body Problem*, which, together with its two sequels, depicts the epic journey of humans into deep space where they see the dark truth of the universe, swirling above the tombs of perished civilizations. It is a truth based in chaos and amorality: the universe, once a hyperdimensional paradise, has been ruthlessly reduced by competing intelligent species to three-dimensional ruins, and further to a two-dimensional flat world, and ultimately to nothingness. The universe has been consumed by its populations, which cannibalized one another. Written a century after Lu Xun learned about Western sciences, Liu Cixin's novel understandably bases its world-building on concepts and theories drawn from the newest quantum theories.[62] When the new wave of Chinese SF began to emerge, all the new physics had become popular among the Chinese scientific community. The virtual reality game featured in *The Three-Body Problem* renders the physicists into game players to explore the chaotic, lawless universe of the Trisolarans, though their speculations about that invisible world are not related to how the world appears to be; like the madman, they look through the appearance to capture the hidden truth beneath.

Cannibalism also returned as a salient motif. Liu Cixin's "Three-Body" trilogy depicts cannibalism as a reasonable means by which the survivors of space wars continue to live in the isolated Starship Earth; Han Song's many stories and novels depict cannibalism prevailing in all sorts of worlds—the red ocean, the underground, airplanes, islands, and hospitals. If Liu Cixin tries to use SF speculation to justify cannibalism as a necessity for survival, Han Song continues Lu Xun's method to create a truth-claiming literary discourse that goes beneath the surface reality, illuminating the invisible darkness where dream is sleepwalking, utopia is dystopian, life is illusion, human is posthuman. Contemporary Chinese SF, outside the mainstream paradigm of Chinese literature, reveals a hyperrealist effort to capture the truth about China's invisible reality. In this sense, the nightmarish, the cannibalistic, and the surreal all answer to Lu Xun's first outcry in "A Madman's Diary," a story that has become like Planck's constant, moving through all variations of its own positions or states and still there, invisible, uncertain, inexplicable—whether you believe it or not.

Ultimately, the aesthetics of the new wave offer us a new interpretation of "A Madman's Diary." The madman overcomes the fear of seeing and observes the invisible, deep structure of reality that is too evasive and elusive to fit into conventional views. Such an unusual question as "Is it right to eat people?"[63] leads to a revolt in linguistic certainty, logical inference, narrative orientation, and the structure of feeling, and projects a revelation about the dark and invisible depths in humanity beyond the accustomed social behaviors. If we read "A Madman's Diary" as SF, it estranges the familiar reality and inspires an insurgence in our knowledge about what is real. Its alternative, disruptive truth-claiming discourse resonates with new wave SF's challenge to the fixed cultural values and ethical notions of contemporary China.

In the present day, Chinese new wave SF writers like Han Song have truly revived Lu Xun's madman, seeking the deeper truth and delving into the world's conspiracy-like invisibility. Inspired by Han Song, I have connected the science fictional epiphany about the truth hidden beneath the world's surface reality to Lu Xun's early practice in science and SF, which preceded and prepared for his truth-claiming strategy that was later associated with both literary realism and new wave SF. I contend that there is a profound interaction between SF and Lu Xun's audacious experiment with the literary form. Just like the madman makes his discovery through thinking against the grain but in line with scientific hermeneutics, new wave SF presents estranging images about China's reality through scientific discourse and methods. This chapter does not end with any certain answer to the question asked at the beginning. But Lu Xun's, Han Song's, and Liu Cixin's texts all point to a deeper reconfiguration of the text that disputes certainty. What is real? What is truth? Lu Xun conjures up unsettling speculations to subvert our reality. One hundred years later, new wave SF does the same.

In January 2020, before the Chinese New Year, Bao Shu wrote a story, "Blessings of the Time" 時光的祝福, in which Lu Xun, coming back to his hometown to celebrate the Chinese New Year in 1920, encounters his fictional characters—Xianglin's Wife and Lü Weifu 呂緯甫, who originally appear in two stories Lu Xun wrote back to back in February 1924. The former commits suicide, as depicted in "New Year's Sacrifice," but the latter is not the same cynical disillusioned intellectual, as Lu Xun's alter ego in his short story "Upstairs in the Tavern" 在酒樓上. In Bao Shu's new narrative, Weifu has returned from the United Kingdom, bringing home H. G. Wells's Time Machine. The two soon learn about Xianglin's wife's suicide. They decide to team up to experiment with time traveling into the woman's past, to save her from reaching this tragic end. Time travel works, they go back in time several times, but they cannot save Xianglin's wife, no matter what they do. They go back farther and farther into the past, but things only get worse and worse. Finally, both Weifu and Xun come to a sad realization that China's past has ossified to such an extent that it won't change at all. "It is an unbreakable iron house." Desperately, Weifu bids farewell to Xun and travels in the other direction. He disappears into 2020, which he believes to be a bright future.[64] Even the author did not know when writing the story that the pandemic was about to begin. If Fei Dao's story recasting Lu Xun in *Cube* unfolds a technologized iron house in cyberspace, Bao Shu's story situates it in time. Back to the future, there is no escape—even in 2020.

EXCURSUS I

LOOKING BACKWARD

2010–1900

Liang Qingsan 梁清散 (b. 1982), by training a scholar of early Chinese SF, published two Chinese "steampunk" novels, titled *From The New Daily News: Mechanical Wonders* 新新日報館：機械崛起 (2017) and *From The New New News: Metropolitan Phantoms* 新新新日報館：魔都暗影 (2021), which take readers time traveling back to Shanghai in 1905–1908, an important time period in both the Chinese revolution and the history of SF. These two novels deliver a vivid picture of late Qing Shanghai, where crisis and hope coexisted as the nation's predicament came to a pivotal moment. Liang's novels are populated by an array of strange figures related to Chinese SF. The protagonist is Liang Qi 梁啟, a journalist whose name is just one character shorter than that of Liang Qichao. Liang Qi has a friend, Tan Si 譚四, an unconventional scientist and underground revolutionary, whose name recalls Liang Qichao's martyred comrade Tan Sitong 譚嗣同 (1865–1898). The latter, an unorthodox Confucian philosopher, attempted a synthesis of scientific materiality and moral courage through a revisionist definition of the Confucian notion of *ren* 仁 (benevolence), which underlay the late Qing political philosophy and SF visions of Confucian utopias.[1] Liang Qingsan's novels also present a fictional version of an idiosyncratic anonymous writer who published under the pen name The Lone Fisherman on a Cold River 荒江釣叟, or Huangjiang Diaosou, and wrote the earliest extant Chinese SF novel, *Tales of the Moon Colony* (月球殖民地小說1905).[2] In Liang's novels, Huangjiang is a young lady studying at Shanghai's St. John's College. The novels not only present an anachronistic theme that speaks to the hope and crisis of contemporary China through alluding to an earlier critical historical juncture; their wondrous textuality also resonates with the late Qing orogeny of tremendous social and cultural changes that motivated the birth of Chinese SF. In this excursus, I will present a brief history of Chinese SF. It began in 1900.

THE LATE QING

As a modern genre, SF was imported from abroad. Its world building represented an otherworldly imagination from its beginning as a translated genre,[3] unfolding visions of modern settings shaped by the flourishing new technologies. Its inception is traceable to the turn of the twentieth century, when Xue Shaohui 薛紹徽 (1866–1911) collaborated with her husband, Chen Shoupeng 陳壽彭 (1855–?), fluent in French, to produce a largely faithful translation of Jules Verne's *Around the World in 80 Days*.[4] Around the same time, Liang Qichao and his colleagues translated into Chinese other novels by Verne. Liang called for a revolution in fiction in 1902 and named SF as one of the new genres that could help cultivate new citizens of a young China. The term that he used is *kexue xiaoshuo* 科學小說 (literally "scientific fiction"), borrowed from his Japanese mentors, including Yukio Ozaki 尾崎行雄 (1858–1954) and Kato Hiroyuki 加藤弘之 (1836–1916), who were both advocates for SF in the Meiji period of Japan.[5] Liang's "new fiction" project created the first literary reform movement in modern China. During the last decade of the late Qing (1902–1911), SF gained legitimacy and popularity as a serious genre and reached its first "Golden Age." From the last generation of late Qing intellectuals came numerous novels and short stories that combined science fantasy, political utopianism, and technological optimism.[6] Through the efforts of Liang Qichao and his contemporaries such as Wu Jianren 吳趼人 (1866–1910) and Xu Nianci 徐念慈 (1875–1908), together with Huangjiang Diaosou and a few other obscure authors about whom we know very little, the genre was instituted as mainly a utopian narrative that projected the political desire for China's reform into an idealized, technologically more advanced country, exemplified by the wondrous Civilized Realm (文明境界) portrayed in Wu Jianren's *New Story of the Stone* 新石頭記 (1908).

Early Chinese SF manifested the cultural hybridity resulting from a combination of translated modernity and self-conscious yearning for the rejuvenation of the Chinese tradition. Most SF novels by late Qing writers were under the obvious influence of Western authors, particularly Verne, at least ten of whose novels were translated during the late Qing. The scientific "nova" foregrounded in his narratives was a major "point of difference" that has been recapitulated by Chinese authors in their depictions of the Confucian versions of a "brave new world."[7] For example, in *New Story of the Stone*, many new things such as submarine adventures and airborne safaris are clearly modeled upon similar images in Verne's novels, but the Civilized Realm that the protagonist Jia Baoyu 賈寶玉 visits is unveiled as a utopian version of a revitalized Confucian world, with all its scientific inventions grounded in Chinese tradition and the merits of its political system deeply rooted in Confucianism. While Baoyu is impressed by what he sees, his tour guide, Lao Shaonian 老少年, never fails to point out the "Chinese" qualities in these spectacular scientific inventions: the flying car and other modern mechanical engineering products are inspired by Chinese mythology; Chinese medical science is proven superior to Western medicine; the most efficient and benevolent political system is completely based on Confucian morals. Baoyu's experiences consistently verify the traditional Chinese epistemology: his aerial safari in Africa brings him to see the real Peng 鵬, the mythical bird depicted in the Daoist classic *Zhuangzi* 莊子;[8] during a voyage to the South Pole, Baoyu sees the fantastic creatures and scenery described in the ancient book *Shanhaijing* 山海經.[9] Transplanted from the West, SF took a domestic turn. The earliest SF world buildings in a Chinese context were born out of the authors' negotiations between Western modernity and Chinese tradition—showcasing both the genre's global vision and its localized utopian variety.

The late Qing was an age defined by China's national predicament, and yet it saw emerging new cultural and epistemological paradigms that opened up many possibilities for the nation's political and cultural transformation while sustaining confidence in tradition. The boom in SF was a key moment in the coming together of the new mediasphere, scientific education, literary revolution, political reform, and utopian thinking that bridged the old and new, a preeminent phenomenon defining the epoch's cultural exuberance, comparable only to the current new wave in the genre's history. The two time periods of the genre's impact on the intellectual outlook, the late Qing and the contemporary, were characterized by heightened aspiration for change and deep anxieties about China's future. While a comparative reading of SF stories from the beginnings of the two centuries can certainly shed light on their common themes, such as China's rise on the global stage and the expanding of its global vision, recapitulations of the earlier stage's literary motifs, as this current study shows, lead to self-reflective variations that point to the latter period's uniqueness in forming vanguard positions in both scientific outlook and the poetics of experimentality.[10]

MODERN TIMES

Despite such a promising beginning, the history of Chinese SF has never been continuous. It is full of gaps and interruptions caused by politics or changes in cultural paradigms. Following the first Golden Age of late Qing SF, only a few short booms can be identified—the reemergence of the genre as children's literature in the 1950s–60s under the socialist regime, the flourishing of more popular versions in Hong Kong during the Cold War, the comeback in Taiwan and mainland China during the 1970s-1980s—none of which gained enough momentum to prevail and continue. This situation did not change until the rise of the new wave at the turn of the twenty-first century. The booms alternated with dormant periods that lasted long enough for later writers to be little influenced by their predecessors. Each time the genre was revived, the new generation of writers had to invent their own tradition, thus giving Chinese SF multiple points of origin. Also, each time the genre was influenced by a foreign source, such as Japan for the late Qing, Russia for the socialist period, America for Taiwan and Hong Kong, and the worldwide new wave as well as global SF for the Chinese new wave. Each generation had to find their own ways to integrate foreign influences into domestic SF forms and conventions to represent new modes of political ethos, intellectual visions, and epistemological paradigms.

During the three decades following the foundation of the Republic of China in 1912, the genre lost momentum while the mainstream of modern Chinese literature was conceptualized almost completely in terms of realism. However, the literary discourse invented by Lu Xun, who himself had been a translator of SF, differs from the later period's realism epitomized by Mao Dun's epic novels. With an aspiration to reveal the deeper truth beneath the surface reality, the Lu Xunsque truth-claiming discourse is a subversion of the conventional, normative perceptions, a contention with the mainstream epistemological paradigm. But Lu Xun's impact on SF did not happen until the rise of the new wave, and for a long time, literary realism, as exemplified by Mao Dun's naturalistic realism and later the socialist realism under Mao's regime, eclipsed SF as an obscure genre that was not taken seriously for most of the twentieth century.

SF nearly disappeared for several decades, with only a small number of works emerging between the late Qing and the 1950s, including Gu Junzheng's 顧均正 (1902–1980) espionage SF thrillers and Lao She's dystopian novel *Cat Country* (1932). Gu Junzheng was a relatively less known writer whose short fictions, including "A Dream of Peace" 和平的夢 (1940) and "Under the North Pole" 北極底下 (1940),[11] present the latest technological advances as a central motif pertaining to international conspiracies and competition for military success. Both stories can be read as wartime literature. Lao She's *Cat Country* was also written against the backdrop of the war. Lao She began this dystopian story about China's prevailing corruption and total lack of individual integrity after the Japanese attack on Shanghai in February 1932. Recent research shows that this novel was written after the author read about Aldous Huxley's *Brave New World*, published in January 1932, and this puts Lao She's story in the global atlas of dystopia.[12] The Martian Cat Country's uncanny resemblance to the Middle Kingdom points to the latter's "backward" national character and a suffocating hopelessness. The novel carries over Lu Xun's criticism of traditional Chinese culture and can be read as an antidote to the didactic "realism" and patriotic propaganda that prevailed throughout the war years. Because of its undisguised contempt for communism, *Cat Country* became completely invisible when the People's Republic of China was founded in 1949, and Lao She died seventeen years later as one of the first victims of Mao's Cultural Revolution.

Outside mainland China, Hong Kong writer Ni Kuang 倪匡 (1935–2022) wrote nearly 150 SF novels and stories, all centering on an adventurous superhero, Wei Sili 衛斯理. Ni's stories began to capture readers' attention in the early 1960s, and Wei Sili became an established figure in Hong Kong's popular culture. Recently scholars have unearthed some obscure SF stories and novels from China, Singapore, Hong Kong, and Taiwan during the 1950s–1970s. But these newly reemerged works have not changed the overall structure of the literary field of the time period, which largely marginalized SF on the map of Chinese literature.

By the late 1950s, under the socialist regime, SF was reinstated as a subgenre of children's literature in imitation of the Soviet literary system. Its generic name was changed to *kexue huanxiang xiaoshuo* 科學幻想小說, a translation of the Russian equivalent.[13] Political teleology and determinism did not leave much room for visions beyond the known, the familiar, and the purely scientific, which discounted the genre's dynamism as an imaginative genre and its embrace of the unknown and uncertain. The function of SF during Mao's Great Leap Forward movement (1958) was elevated, as demonstrated by the increasing number of SF works produced in the late 1950s. The image of China's rapid march—the great leap—toward industrialization and collectivization became itself a SF theme, exemplified by the fantastic vision of an idealized communist society in a documentary film about the construction of a reservoir near Beijing, *Rhapsody of the Ming Tombs Reservoir* 十三陵水庫暢想曲 (1958). It shows a thoroughly modernized China at the end of the twentieth century when all goals that Mao's ambitious project set in 1958 have been achieved.

Important SF writers of this time period include Zheng Wenguang, Tong Enzheng 童恩正 (1935–1997), and Ye Yonglie 叶永烈 (1940–2020). Mainly serving young readers, they made the best of the genre as an almost transparent vehicle for propagating correct political worldviews and scientific knowledge. Most of their stories feature children who are as much adventurous as determined about their goal in exploring exotic and extraterrestrial space, which should be in line with the Party's teaching. Their world building is limited by narrowly defined political correctness, and any vision of unknown and future worlds was not allowed to introduce a truly alien difference but had to replicate the predetermined "unaccustomed lands" and future scenarios underscored by the state ideology. This situation lasted until the beginning of the Reform Era. In the context of the Party's new policy calling for scientific and technological modernization, the SF imagination was again crystallized in the figure of a young character, this time created by Ye Yonglie in his best-selling novel *Little Smartie Travels to the Future* 小靈通漫遊未來 (1978).[14] During the early Reform Era, Little Smartie became the best-known figure in young adult SF, which predicts a bright future without any uncertainty, filled with optimism about technological and ideological progress combined in one march toward a definitive end of human history.

But by this time, writers in Taiwan had begun to reanimate the genre by incorporating dystopian visions and social criticism into world buildings, which reflect an array of unconventional themes such as historical trauma, the ethical results of scientific and technological innovations, and diaspora in extraterrestrial space that remotely echoes the national pathos about the 1949 divide. In the early 1980s, the most famous SF writer from Taiwan, S. K. Chang (張系國, b. 1944), became familiar to PRC readers when his novella "Biography of a Superman" 超人列傳 (1968), much darker than *Little Smartie*, was reprinted in 1983. Influence from Taiwan came together with sudden exposure to American popular culture when China's reform began. The influence of Hollywood films was obvious in Tong Enzheng's widely acclaimed story "Death Ray on a Coral Island" (珊瑚島上的死光 1978), in which readers can detect prominent tropes of American sci-fi movies like laser weapons, mad scientists, mysterious islands, apocalyptic events, and transnational conspiracies. All these were eventually translated back into cinematic images when a film based on Tong Enzheng's story was produced in 1980, generating even wider interest in SF in the PRC.[15]

Other major SF writers of this period include Zheng Wenguang, Xiao Jianheng (肖建亨, b. 1930), and Liu Xingshi (劉興詩, b. 1931), whose careers all crossed different historical eras, starting during the socialist campaigns of the 1950s–60s and adapting to the Reform Era in the 1970s–80s. Not until 1980 did some writers, such as Zheng Wenguang, Jiang Yunsheng (姜云生, b. 1944), and Wei Yahua (魏雅華, b. 1949), begin to consciously experiment with the genre conventions. Their stories were no longer completely tasked with spreading scientific knowledge and correct ideology and could include political reflections and social criticism, which at the time was still in accordance with the Party's new policy on reexamining the historical mistakes made by Mao and the Party during the Cultural

Revolution. During this short-lived period of "liberation in thought" (思想解放) or thaw, the genre established its reputation as a serious literary effort, or as Rudolf Wagner calls it, a "lobby literature" that differs from propaganda literature but supports the nation's reform agenda with subtly expressed yearning for changes.[16]

Several famous works, such as Zheng Wenguang's "The Mirror Image of the Earth"地球的鏡像 (1980) and Wei Yahua's "Conjugal Happiness in the Arms of Morpheus" 溫柔之鄉的夢 (1981), attained national recognition as part of the new literary front line. These stories demonstrated the genre's success as a literature of intervention to reflect on historical trauma ("The Mirror Image of the Earth") and social problems ("Conjugal Happiness in the Arms of Morpheus").[17]

This generation soon met with harsh criticism in the Party-led campaign against spiritual pollution. During this setback from the reform, the genre's short-lived boom came to an abrupt halt when the scientific community and the Party's propaganda organs both named SF as one of the sources of "spiritual pollution" in 1983. An entire generation of Chinese SF writers was silenced by political criticism; all the SF magazines that had been launched during the early Reform Era ceased publication, with the sole exception of the Chengdu-based *Science Literature* (科學文藝), later renamed *SFW*. Under this new name, it sustained the survival of the genre and became the base for its latest revival since the 1990s.

But even when the major authors stopped writing, a culture of SF still existed and developed because of the unprecedented scope of the importation of Japanese and American popular culture, which brought such iconic figures and stories as Atom Boy and *Star Wars* to China. A large number of major works by contemporary SF writers, including Arthur C. Clarke, Isaac Asimov, and Sakyo Komatsu 小松左京 (1931–2011), were translated into Chinese during the 1980s. Between the middle of the 1980s and the late 1990s, *SFW* kept publishing SF stories featuring foreign names and international settings, as a way of keeping a safe distance from the Chinese reality. Liu Cixin, Han Song, Wu Yan (吳岩, b. 1962), Ling Chen, Bao Shu, Chen Qiufan, and many other new wave authors grew up reading translated SF works that brought splendid alien universes, apocalyptical scenarios, and estranged, uncertain future histories to an entire new generation and sustained China's sci-fi fandom. The seed was buried and waited for the right time to sprout.

THE NEW WAVE

The game-changing new wave was conceived in the 1980s, when futurology, cybernetics and informatics, quantum physics, chaos theory, new methods in scientific and humanistic research, and various experiments in literature and art collectively challenged the monolithic ideological discourse with an emerging, diversified space for a multiplicative structure tolerant of different kinds of knowledge and ideas.[18] The decade also saw China's widening reform and a young generation's struggle for democracy, which ended abruptly when the 1989 nationwide student protest came to a tragic conclusion in Tiananmen Square. As mentioned in the introduction, Liu Cixin and Han Song both started writing SF around the end of the 1980s, and their first stories and novels contained reflections on the failed idealism and China's lost opportunity to become a democracy. Their efforts, together with the growth of the sci-fi fandom and online communities, prepared for the genre's revival exactly one hundred years after the late Qing "Golden Age." Some contemporary factors appear similar to conditions in the late Qing, such as the rapidly changing mediasphere, technological advances, and anxious expectations concerning China's future changes. In particular, the free platform for new authors to publish on the internet and a "perfect vacuum" for fantasy when mainstream realism lost its appeal to younger readers contributed to a profound change in the field of literary production, which helped create the cultural conditions for the rise of a new wave of Chinese SF.

The term "new wave" refers to this recent trend as a new force emerging in the Chinese literary scene, though it also specifically implies a new wave literary experiment. The term and its meanings have caused controversy among SF scholars and writers in China. The emphasis on the subversive force of SF was questioned by those with more faith in China's contemporary pursuit of wealth and power. They preferred the more straightforwardly celebratory term "Golden Age" (borrowed from the American Golden Age) to the subversive, cutting-edge "new wave" that suggests a representation of the invisible, darker aspects in world building. That said, it is commonly agreed that at least part of contemporary SF is decidedly a new wave variation, particularly represented by Han Song, Fei Dao, and Chen Qiufan, among others. And above all, contemporary SF writers have reenergized the genre by consolidating and reinventing a variety of generic conventions, cultural elements, and political visions—from space opera to cyberpunk fiction, from utopianism to posthumanism, and from parodied visions of China's rise to a deconstruction of the myth of national development. Even Liu Cixin, who resists the "new wave" label while sticking to the technologically defined "hard SF," has integrated new wave elements into his space saga, such as multilayered narratives, sophisticated metaphors, uncertainties of interpretation, and a poetic form of imagination of the sublime, uncertain, and unknowable.

The earlier attack on Chinese SF as "spiritual pollution" opened a fissure in the genre's relationship with the state ideology. When the genre revived at the beginning of the twenty-first century, it kept a distance from the tensions between literature and ideology without seeking recognition from the state. This new wave emerged on the margins of Chinese literature as well as the margins of China's geopolitical map. The Chengdu-based *SFW*, which is distanced from the major metropolitan centers on China's east coast, has been the center of this new SF boom, and several major authors such as Liu Cixin, Wang Jinkang, and He Xi reside in the so-called third-tier or even fourth-tier cities. None started as a professional writer, and a certain amateurism kept them out of the literary establishment, which enabled them to dream of imaginary realms freely and independently.

The new wave of Chinese SF has radically revolutionized the mode of fictional representation. With the underlying philosophical theorems and cognitive models substantially rewritten and restructured, the genre outgrows the earlier innocent optimism represented by Little Smartie, leaning toward more ambiguous, darker visions about the future and other worlds. Over the past three decades, orthodox Marxist materialism and historical determinism faced a number of challenges from a scientific revolution crystallized in a wider application of quantum mechanics, artificial intelligence, and cybernetic informatics to making real changes to our world or perceptions of reality. There was a similar revolution in the humanities, where the prevailing avant-garde literature and emerging critical theories contested the universality of truth, the certainty of knowledge, and the mimetic mode of representation. This simultaneous change in the sciences and the humanities unifies both areas in an epistemological transition from determinism to uncertainty, from order to disorder, and from reflection to revelation—a profound change that can be better epitomized in the SF world buildings than in other forms of literary imagination.

In terms of the literary imagery and symbolic system, new wave SF creates a world filled with tropes based on new scientific theories, ranging from extraterrestrial space to estranging cyborg, from chaos to a superstring multiverse, from quantum phantom to posthuman consciousness—all of which imply alternative or even subversive meanings that cannot be easily explained away by the Party's orthodox ideology. The new wave that arose in the 1990s and matured in the twenty-first century gradually developed an exceptional mode of literary imagination. This new wave can hardly be defined as an "heir" to the earlier waves of SF of the late Qing and Reform Era. The authors edged into the future through drastically different epistemological modes, and though there is still room for dialogue between the new wave and the earlier movements, it seems impossible to draw between them a straight line that would correspond to a linear historical evolution. The new wave not only protests the mainstream literary paradigm but also breaks with its own rules as a genre.

The new wave authors were nourished by the openness and avant-garde spirit of the 1980s. When the lofty discourse of the enlightenment gradually dissolved in mainstream literature, the avant-garde spirit of the 1980s fragmented into signs and symbols, which reemerged in the literary landscape shaped by the new wave SF writers. Liu Cixin and Han Song, the two giants of the new wave, have both appropriated for their plot designs a large number of keywords and key concepts from the intellectual thinking and literary experimentation during the 1980s. While mainstream literature has lost its sharpness, SF maintains its vanguard position and revitalizes literary avant-gardism. In this sense, new wave SF is a "phantom" exiled from the past decade, and it freely crosses the boundaries between refined and popular literatures, wanders between utopia and reality, and demonstrates a rich and fascinating complexity in the expression of alternative literary imagination.

4

A POETIC HEART IN THE DARK FOREST

Liu Cixin's Three-Body Universe

Near the end of *Death's End*, the final volume of the "Three-Body" trilogy, Liu Cixin depicts a lone creature named Singer 歌者 patrolling in the infinite darkness of the universe. He is a low-ranking member of a godlike, super advanced civilization who has the ability to change physical laws and thus eliminate potential threats preemptively. Singer, a unique individual belonging to this mysterious, unimaginably superhuman species, has a hobby, for which he is named. If their civilization had literature, Singer would be its poet.

> Singer liked the primitive membrane. He thought the primitive membrane possessed a simple beauty, symbolizing an age full of joy. He often turned primitive membrane messages into songs. He thought they sounded pretty, even if he didn't understand them. Understanding them wasn't necessary, however; other than coordinates, primitive membrane messages didn't have much useful information. It was enough to enjoy the music. . . .
>
> The low-entropy entities of that world clumsily plucked their stars—Singer decided to call them the Star-Pluckers—like ancient bards of the home world plucking the strings of the rough country zither, to send out the message.[1]

One specific Star-Plucker 彈星者 that Singer detects in this remote, almost empty area of the galaxy is the Earth civilization, who clumsily pluck the sun, to which a neighboring civilization responds; this has led to a series of conversations back and forth between them, as Singer finds out. Though he enjoys the beauty of the *primitive membrane* messages that the humans broadcast into space, he has to strike, for his job is to *hide well and cleanse all*. "As he continued to sing, Singer picked up the dual-vector foil with a force field feeler and carelessly tossed it at the Star-Pluckers."[2] Thus begins the demise of the human world, as the dual-vector foil quietly changes the entire solar system into a two-dimensional flat picture, which is the beginning of the end of Liu's saga.

    I take this moment as the geomagnetic center of Liu Cixin's worldbuilding in his Three-Body novels. It crystallizes the gist of the entire epic, from the alien's godlike point of view: what has so far happened in the story. The protagonist of the first volume, Ye Wenjie 葉文潔, "plucks" the sun as an amplifier to broadcast human messages to deep space and subsequently comes into contact with the Trisolarans, which sets off the pas de deux of the two civilizations inhabiting the solar system and Alpha Centauri—and all the following events, war and peace, conspiracy and deception, negotiation and deterrence, until Singer's arrival that ends all. Now everything is observed by Singer as a string of messages broadcast between two stars. To Singer, the alien creature with infinitely more advanced intelligence, none of the events—all the human tragedies and comedies that Liu has dramatized so far—can be felt or understood as "experience"; they only appear in a virtual form, as information flow represented in numbers, codes, waves, or whatever forms are meaningful to him. In other words, all the human experiences are nothing but a sort of "language" or "poetry" written on the primitive membrane. This is what appeals to Singer. In his understanding, humans plucked their sun to "sing."

    This moment epitomizes the interplay of some of the main forces in Liu Cixin's fictional universe of speculation and writing—the tensions between poetic sensibilities and scientific principles, utopian impulse and cosmic indifference, human agency and mathematical uncertainty. This glimpse of Singer's inner life as someone who treasures poetry heightens the very meaning of "writing" in Liu's universe. The primitive membrane messages disclose the Earth's coordinates and bring the endgame to the solar system, but they are also the very evidence and self-expression of the human civilization. Messages on the primitive membrane are the equivalents to words and speeches, narratives and poems, and they are traces of memory, or to say it in a simple way, they are "literature." Readers may wonder why, after completing his Three-Body saga, Liu gave the entire trilogy a new title: "Remembrance of the Earth's Past." This Proustian naming constitutes a self-reflection on his creation of a SF narrative, and this "writing" as a way of "remembering," whether it is poetry or storytelling, assumes a decisive centrality.

Singer's aesthetic appreciation, or admiration of beauty, renders the entirety of the human world into nothing but a word, a monad, a cosmos with completeness that can be articulated in one singular sound or wave. But to humans, the arrival of Singer reveals the ultimate darkness of the universe. This is a darkness so complex and profound that it goes far beyond human knowledge, which evokes the Kantian feeling of the sublime—the *mysterium tremendum et fascinans*. Singer, as depicted by the human author Liu Cixin, represents a transcendental force of wonder with "absolute magnitude."[3] However, it is also the human writer Liu Cixin who gives Singer an inner voice. In this way, while Singer's reading of the songs on the primitive membrane evokes the feeling of the beautiful, the human race's encounter with Singer, the angel of death, creates the sublime apex in the epic narrative. This moment symbolizes the magic power of SF for Liu: world-building based on speculative sciences can be immensely awe-inspiring on an astronomical scale, but at the same time, this vision can be intimate like a love song, which shows a poetic heart in the dark universe. The art of Liu Cixin is to put the most unfathomable, marvelous worlds into poetic words.

STAR-PLUCKERS AND WALLFACERS

Star-Pluckers represent the most sublime images in Liu's SF world. He portrays two types of creatures plucking stars. One is exemplified by godlike hyperdimensional intelligences, known also as cosmic artists, such as the one named Mirror in Liu's early short story "To Joy" (歡樂頌 2005), who comes to our solar system to play music with the sun, or the other poetry-loving alien who uses all the energies of the solar system to create a "Poetry Cloud" that contains all the possible poems in another story, "Poetry Cloud" 詩雲 (2003). The lofty sensibility in these stories combines the pursuits of science and art, culminating in idealized images of a world brightened by reason and perfection. Star-Pluckers in this sense are themselves the manifestations of the cosmic sublime.

But there is another type of Star-Plucker, the so-called "low-entropy" Star-Pluckers that Singer has discovered and then cleansed. They are humans, an innocent species who have not yet seen much of the cosmological reality. Humans aspire to explore and contact, yearning for a world larger than their own. But in the Three-Body world, they are ignorant of the invisible nature of the universe, which Liu metaphorizes as a "dark forest," a deadly amoral place where life-and-death struggles for survival decide the fatal result of any encounter between civilizations. Plucking their stars naïvely, they expose themselves to threats in space and unwittingly invite invasions by more advanced civilizations.

However, as Star-Pluckers, these low-entropy creatures, or just plain humans, have more in common with the godlike hyperdimensional species who come to pluck our sun. In Liu's writings, gods and humans alike are artistic by nature, curious about others, and eager for expression; both are defined by the same commitment to idealism rather than realism, and this is also shared by the author, whose SF visions are primarily glorified by the marvelous splendor in the images of Star-Pluckers and their like. An aesthetic, ultimately utopian, self-serving impulse underlies their yearnings for self-expression as well as their visions of alternative world images. Star-Pluckers register the will to freedom, and in Liu's shorter works, they are often incarnated in immensely intelligent creatures beyond imagination, and this is perhaps why Han Song compared Liu to the ancient Chinese philosopher Zhuangzi, who creates sublime mythical images to represent both freedom and survival.[4]

Liu's outlandish SF imagination seems to have transcended modern Chinese literature's century-long "obsession with China,"[5] crossing multiple boundaries in terms of national and political themes. When he projects the rise and demise of the human world onto the astronomical scale, ordinary concerns with reality seem to have faded out. But despite Liu's wishful gesture of gazing into stars, what he sees is not completely bright and uplifting. The cosmic sublime also contains its negative self-image, which reveals the heart of darkness in the scientifically underpinned amoral universe and reflects the ethical black hole inside the human heart. This darker nature connects the ruthlessness of Mao's

Cultural Revolution in human history to the fierce mutual destruction engaged in by all the intelligent species in the imaginary universe.

The dark forest is presented as the inherently negative self-image of the cosmic sublime, an amoral cosmic indifference. Reversing the conventional discourse on politics and ethics based on China's century-long evolutionism, optimism, and utopianism, Liu Cixin provides a darkened vision born from the same source, which is crystallized in Mao's great utopian experiment with sweeping social change. Liu outlines a different scenario suggestive of the impending, inevitable menaces that are part of evolution and revolution, rewriting the principle of hope into a conspiracy for an endgame, all of which converges in the ruthless dark forest scenario. If this is the destiny of the universe, it has always been a process of degeneration, contrary to evolution: a dimension-lowering game beginning from the origin of the universe, a prototypically invisible "utopian" Edenic ten-dimensional infinity that is timeless but has never lasted *in* time to be seen by any intelligent eyes.[6] In the Spencerian dark forest, intelligence is only meant to kill.

The survivors in the dark forest are not those low-entropy Star-Pluckers. They are a different sort, called the Wallfacers 面壁者. Wallfacers are shrewd social Darwinists tasked with only one mission: to hide and strike first in the dark forest. *Hide well and cleanse all*; Singer, despite his more advanced intelligence and admiration for poetry, can also be considered a Wallfacer, an anonymous agent who secretly patrols the forest, where he wipes out rivals from the dark and safeguards the home world. Wallfacers are realists, survivors, and on many occasions, they are inhuman technologists or posthumanists. They resort to scientific knowledge and technological innovations for the sole purpose of survival, which they place above a whole set of values associated with humanism—freedom, progress, democracy.

Thus, the universe that Wallfacers have created out of the constant cosmic conflicts has mostly degenerated into technocracy, dictatorship, or dystopian posthuman worlds. Liu depicts militarized starship civilizations, with apology for their prioritization of survivalism over humanism. In extreme situations, Liu even reverses Lu Xun's "iron house" metaphor, creating the self-degraded, self-prisoned microscopic "posthuman paradise," a parody of a better future. The ultimate image of survivalism coming from this line of Spencerian evolution (or devolution) is found in Liu's novella "The Micro Era" 微纪元 (2001), in which a tiny human species survives on a postapocalyptic Earth through reducing their body to invisible subatomic size. They are no longer human, losing all historical memories to a carefree, weightless, and therefore purposeless life. This story about the "micro era" does not hide the hideous side of the "posthuman paradise," which is built upon the extinction of the human race and the complete obliteration of human history. Is this posthuman future a blessing or a betrayal? Or, in a more general sense, does the "micro era" prove Liu's fundamental posthumanist position, which denies the hope of a progressive human future? Even though Liu Cixin creates splendidly sublime cosmic images, he is no less pessimistic about the fate of humanity than Han Song, which brings him closer to Lu Xun.

If Star-Pluckers represent the transcendental tendency in Liu's sublime SF vision, the images of Wallfacers and the micro era bring it closer to China's turbulent modern historical experience, particularly its post-Tiananmen meandering transformation toward less democratization and further authoritarianism. In the two decades since Liu published "The Micro Era," the posthuman dystopia has taken on a further changed color. The oblivion of history, the refusal of responsibilities of memory and reflection, and a rather self-centered hedonism plus cynicism have become part of the national "dream factory" that provides the new generation of millennials a clear-cut starting point for a New Epoch 新時代, which sees the rise of nationalism, militarism, and strongman politics—all traits of the Wallfacer mentality confronting the dark forest. In a profound way, Liu has truly captured China's recent changes in the political, technological, and psychological spheres.

A popular belief among Liu's fans is that he has "single-handedly lifted Chinese SF to a world-class level."[7] Even if this sounds exaggerated, it may be fair to say that Liu Cixin's role in shaping the new trend of Chinese SF is equivalent to Jin Yong's 金庸 (Louis Cha Leung-yung, 1924–2018) role in shaping a new tradition of martial arts romance. Called Da Liu 大劉 by his fans, he is celebrated as the national pride of China. The phenomenal success of Liu's trilogy, both domestically and internationally, also corresponds to the Chinese government's promotion of the "Chinese dream," which mirrors, twists, and speaks back to its American counterpart. Although I have pointed to the darker, subversive side of the new wave, which presents a nightmarish mutation of the "Chinese dream," the "Three-Body" trilogy has come into an ambiguous relationship with the nation.

The generations growing up reading the Three-Body novels, including a new elite group of radical intellectuals, while deeply fascinated by Liu's cosmic sublime, theorize the dark forest experience and the Wallfacers strategies in a new age of more intense global competition, particularly the antagonism between China and the rest of the world. Perhaps unexpected by Liu himself, his world visions are quoted as having raised a new type of political consciousness among these radicals, known as "the Party of Technology" 技術黨 or "the Industrial Party" 工業黨, who claim to have departed from traditional ideology by reinventing it as, more clearly than ever, a combination of governance and technocracy, patriotism and technologism, communism and cyberism.[8] Liu Cixin cannot dictate his writings, not to mention the reception of his writings, but in recent years, there has been a strong tendency to emphasize the nationalistic colors in his transnational space odysseys in scholarship and popular opinions on the "Three-Body" trilogy in China's domestic environment. The Three-Body universe is invading China's reality.

In Liu's SF itself, his world-buildings are not directly related to the immediate reality but tend to present transcendental, lofty, and yet estranging images of the cosmos. Liu keeps encouraging readers to look up to the night sky, to see the infinite immensity of the unknown and unknowable. With a sublime turn, Liu nevertheless also builds his SF visions to capture what is invisible. To him, this is not completely wild imagination; it can be structured as meticulously as a scientific experiment. Liu indeed has made SF a method, which unfolds words into outlandish imaginings through speculative changes to the basic physical rules of the universe. In other words, Liu is not different from the godlike creature he depicts in *Death's End*, who can lower dimensions of the world; Liu has also lowered dimensions of his SF writing in order to create the most awe-inspiring wonder. He resorts to SF writing as a technology to capture the hyperdimensional wonder with the simplest possible words.

"LIKE A GOD, CREATES A WORLD, THEN DESCRIBES IT"

Liu's first full-length novel, *China 2185*, already contains the key elements of his Three-Body universe but remains the only obviously political novel he has ever written. In this unpublished manuscript, Liu self-consciously energized utopian/dystopian variations rather than simply denying utopianism or totally embracing dystopian disillusionment, and he opened up new possibilities for world-building by interweaving scientific imagination with the cultural politics of contemporary China. With an obvious violation of political taboos, Liu might have been fully aware that his first novel was not publishable in China. He wrote it in 1989. It took him ten years to get published, but not his first novel; by the time when his first stories were published, his SF worlds had become distinctly more metaphysical than political.

Liu officially began publishing short stories in 1999. His first stories were noted for their marvelous, unconventional speculations on scientific wonders. Two of his earliest, "The End of the Microscopic" 微觀盡頭 and "The Collapse of the Cosmos" 宇宙坍縮, are based on pure scientific hypothesis, which becomes the foundation for visions of the most estranging worlds. The universe altered by changing scientific rules appears otherworldly, awe-inspiring, and its unknowability also evokes a fear of seeing. In the first text, after a successful quark collision experiment, the entire universe appears like the negative of its own picture, while the second text describes the moment when the universe changes from expansion to contraction: the stars turn from red to blue, time begins to reverse, including even the order of the words articulated by human characters who will experience everything in the reverse order, from death to life, from the end to the beginning, with their memories restructured from flashbacks to flash-forwards.[9]

Similar examples can be found throughout Liu's works. The novel *Ball Lightning* 球狀閃电 (2004) creates a sublime world based on changing the fundamental structure of matter as well as the way we perceive the universe: the mysterious, phantomlike "ball lightning" is actually the invisible "macro atom" floating in another "macro world" overlapping with our own, in which even the tiniest subatomic "macro matter" can be embodied in shapes larger than humans.[10] The "Three-Body" trilogy, which is closely connected to *Ball Lightning*, creates a more systematic alteration to the physical world: the changing of the physical laws is revealed as the darkest secret in the universe, which brings the timeless, formless, hyperdimensional, paradisiacal original universe down to the cold, harsh, amoral arena of life-and-death struggles through reducing dimensions from the original twelve to three, and further down to two in the course of the plot development. The three-dimensional universe, our world, is already the ruins of the timeless space wars. It will become flat, two-dimensional, when wars continue in the dark forest universe.

In stark contrast with *China 2185*, these writings not only appear apolitical but also evade any easy connection with reality. In a story titled "Hearing the Right Way in the Morning" 朝闻道 (2002), Liu's prototypical scientist character Ding Yi 丁仪 prioritizes the invisible truth about the universe over any tangible or perceivable reality. He argues with his daughter, who wants a tour around the real world: "The real beauty is invisible. Only imagination and mathematics can capture it."[11] In numerous interviews and essays, Liu confesses to being a technologist and committed to scientism,[12] and he compares writing SF to a process in which the writer should create and depict a world in the way God would.[13] His stories and novels are mostly about world systems that are beyond the familiar and yet based on scientifically possible changes. Therefore, for Liu, writing SF is first of all like a scientific experiment, or if social experiments are included, like a thought experiment. It creates a fold in thinking. The changes of physical laws and social forms motivate the plot development, and his task is to concretize these possibilities, making them visible, narratable, and seemingly plausible.

But the strength of Liu's SF vision comes even more from his quest for a singular aesthetic and artistic style. Among the writers of this current trend of Chinese SF, Liu is sometimes referred to as a "neoclassicist."[14] This is not just because his works are similar to the classical Anglo-American space opera and the Soviet classics but also because Liu's space sagas take place over immense stretches of historical time and world settings. We can even perceive in them the epic breadth found in Tolstoy: sweeping descriptions of grandiose scenes, meticulous attention to detail, the ultimate questioning of good and evil, exploration of the complexity of the world, and yet the simple, almost naïve pursuit of beauty and truth. Liu has said that *War and Peace* inspired him even more than any SF epics.[15] Critics point to the fact that at a time when cynicism and various types of neorealism compete to evade the aesthetics of the sublime, Liu pushes into Chinese literature a new aesthetics of the sublime and magnitude.[16]

This aesthetics is yet radically different from Tolstoian realism, despite Liu's admiration for the Russian master. His concern with concrete details and a grandiose epic feel goes beyond the established norms of conventional realism, which is rooted in a mimetic correspondence between the writing and the tangible objective world. Liu's details and descriptions are both excessive and uncontainable in realistic settings in the ordinary sense. They are transcendental rather than experiential, and the logically plausible—but not actual—reality is presented as the opposite of the experiential reality. The imaginary worlds that Liu creates in his texts are *virtual* in both the ontological and aesthetic senses, and the omnipotent way he depicts them, in the fullest possible detail, only heightens their *virtuality*. This is best epitomized in the perhaps most celebrated episode of his entire Three-Body saga, the sweepingly vivid, dazzlingly meticulous and detailed description of the two-dimensional picturing of the entire solar system in *Death's End*. Such a worlding, or the surfacing of literally a world picture, envisioned through scientific speculations and depicted with the accuracy of algorithms, is as estranging as virtual. It is not just a thing that is estranged, it is the way the entire world is presented, hyper-really virtual and detailed rather than realistically real, that adds to its strangeness:

> It was a dead city, but perhaps it was more accurate to call it a 1:1 drawing of the city. The drawing reflected every detail of the city, down to every screw, every fiber, every mite, and even every bacterium. The precision of the drawing was at the level of the individual atom. Every atom in the original three-dimensional space was projected onto its corresponding place in two-dimensional space according to ironclad laws. The basic principles governing this drawing were that there could be no overlap and no hidden parts, and every single detail had to be laid out on the plane. Here, complexity was a substitute for grandeur. The drawing wasn't easy to interpret—it was possible to see the overall plan of the city and recognize some big structures, such as the giant trees, which still looked like trees even in two dimensions. But buildings looked very different after being flattened: it was almost impossible to deduce the original three-dimensional structure from the two-dimensional drawing by imagination alone. However, it was certain that the image-processing software equipped with the right mathematical model would be able to.[17]

This world and the way it is portrayed is not part of the natural, "organic" human experience; it is neither presented as a possible imitation of reality nor described in the usual literary discourse, not evocative or metaphorical but rather interpretative and literal down to its basic hermeneutic straightness. The two-dimensional world is not a realistic reflection of the three-dimensional world, but like hyperdimensional worlds that Liu also describes, it is extraordinary and virtually exists in an excessive linguistic extension of logic. Therefore, the meticulous depiction in Liu's works is an "experiment" of rewriting—reimagining, restructuring, and reformulating—of the world. What he creates is a virtual world image that is dislodged from any ordinary, existing, experiential reality.

Combining scientific speculation and literary imagination, Liu focuses some of his most ambitious works on speculative changes in the principles of the physical world and their extended manifestations in society and politics. In this sense, the world systems of his SF are founded in the metaphysical fluidity of ideas. Liu Cixin is perhaps more aware of this than other contemporary SF writers. Ideas come first. Words exist prior to reality. Liu finds the ideas in the equations, algorithms, and theories of science. He relies on those logical, but surreal or hyperreal, calculations to envision the scope and details of the unknown, restoring the totality and the sense of completeness that are fundamental to the wonders of his world systems.[18] In the following paragraphs, I outline the main characteristics of Liu's aesthetics, with special attention to the role science plays in his literary imagination.

HARD SCIENCE FICTION

After publishing his first stories, such as "The End of the Microscopic" and "The Collapse of the Cosmos," as well as longer stories such as "The Wandering Earth" 流浪地球 (2000), which also bases an entire estranging world system on speculative changes of astrophysical realities that force the humans to turn their home planet into a spaceship, Liu quickly established his fame as China's most devoted "hard SF" (硬科幻) author, a reputation that was sustained in the following ten years by his entire oeuvre.

"Hard SF"[19] is a sub-branch of SF normally based on solid scientific foundations and coherent scientific discourse. The term "hard SF" has become popular among Chinese SF communities since the turn of the new century, and such works have an elite status, superior to popular sci-fi writings and films and the so-called "soft SF" that is regarded as veiled social criticism. In its most extreme usage, "hard SF" is a myth, representing in literature a cult of science. Without imposing a fixed definition upon this trend of thinking and aesthetics, when someone uses the term "hard SF" in the case of Chinese literature, they are making both a reference to and a break with the older tendency of politicizing science and SF.

In various earlier depictions of scientific wonders in SF novels from the late Qing to the Mao years, even though the novelists took on the task of popularizing scientific knowledge via the images of "Jia Baoyu taking a submarine"[20] and "Little Smartie traveling into the future,"[21] it is clear that science and technology were part of the larger political picture, often appropriated to legitimize a historical agenda. Scholars have pointed out that Chinese SF before Liu's generation carried an optimistic spirit that "man would always triumph over nature" (人定勝天).[22] In this older version of scientific optimism, the cosmic unknown presents no threat, and hard science can be invincible.

However, the hard science in Liu's novels may represent a step back from such optimistic scientism. Taking one step further back, one could even say that Liu's SF is heir to the cultural spirit of the 1980s, when new scientific theories about the nature of the world were introduced by reform-minded scientists like Fang Lizhi, the former president of the Chinese University of Science and Technology. An astrophysicist also involved in China's student movements during the 1980s, Fang was advocating both democracy and new theories of physics. He was the first to tell Chinese readers that "the reason that luminaries such as superclusters, galaxy clusters, and galaxies exist in the universe is directly related to dark matter."[23] Fang's popular science books were influential with young students during the years 1979–1989, which represented, together with the prodemocracy reform, an intellectual effort to embrace the unknown, a contestation of fixed values, and an openness to the new and potential.

With the new scientific theories endorsed by Fang Lizhi and others, the political importance of scientific determinism was now secondary to science's fidelity to the complexities and uncertainties of the universe, which does not bend to human-centered optimism. What is also lost is the visible centrality of scientific truths in everyday experience, because the knowability and authenticity of the world have been called into question. The scientific visions that Liu applied to his world-building include a series of theories that began to reform the Chinese mind during the 1980s, many of which were mentioned in popular scientific writings, including Stephen Hawking's *A Brief History of Time* (translated into Chinese in 1985): the theory of relativity, quantum mechanics, speculations on spatial distortion and a curved universe, dark matter, dark energy, and superstring theory and the multiverse, which were introduced in a later time period. These theories interpret the world by counterintuitive methods, against the observable rules of the older, more fixed models such as the Newtonian physical laws; they have contested our belief in the world's certainty and knowability and undermined a deterministic way of thinking about what is real.

Therefore, the new hard sciences claim more uncertainty than determinism, and they reveal a truth about the world that is more speculative than experiential, and to use Fang Lizhi's words, more invisible than visible. New scientific ideas became part of the avant-garde experimentalism prevailing in the larger cultural context during the 1980s. It is in a speculative sense that "hard" science creates the fundamental plausibility, fluidity, and uncertainty in Liu's SF visions. "Hard" science, truthful to the world it speaks to rather than any political mandate, decides the subversive nature of "hard SF" in the historical context of a political emphasis on the certainty of strengthening the nation through deterministic usage of scientific knowledge. Liu's SF universe, born of those daring speculations about the invisible truth of the universe, challenges the mundane and conventional notions about reality.

In this sense, "hard SF" does not just popularize scientific knowledge. It creates a type of textuality with excessive suggestions for exploring the uncertain and unknown. "Hard SF" provides the ultimate master plot of Liu's stories. The wonders of science are not propaganda but constitute the deeper driving force of the narrative. The unfolding of a SF plot can be parallel to the process of theoretical speculations, the worlding of a new universe according to the logic represented in theories, estranging and unsettling to eyes accustomed to the mundane reality. Liu tasks himself with observing and writing about all the possible and plausible details emerging in this marvelous process of opening an alien world.

Thus, Liu creates his worlds upon the speculative possibilities instead of mimetic reflections of reality, and in those alien estranging worlds, he confronts the magnitude of the sublime unknown, resorting to scientific means for the revelation of all the logic and details of those worlds built on speculations. At a time when the mainstream literature has mostly disintegrated into fragmented, introverted depictions of a world falling apart, Liu is among the few writers who can create sublime images of worlds as wonders, "presenting world systems in totality."[24] He celebrates the power of SF in contrast with reflective, passive realism: "Mainstream literature describes the world that God has already created; SF does it like a god, creates a world, then describes it."[25]

Although Liu's splendid visions have unleashed the most exciting and liberating imaginations in Chinese SF, for readers choosing science and technologies over the humanities, faith in hard SF can easily turn into doctrines for new cults. Liu Cixin has admitted that he sees in SF the power of a religion,[26] founded in the sensations of awe and wonder at the superhumanly immensity and magnitude of the cosmos. What he envisions in a literary sense has translated into the politics of reality. Liu's fans have nurtured a new totalistic tendency to antagonize hard SF's imagined foe—the soft SF that contains social and political critiques and sober reflections on the limits of science and technology. In this excessive worship of hard SF grows a new ideology leaning toward technocracy.

But my argument is that hard SF has actually played a role in dismantling the certainty and determinism in the politics of reality. Hard SF in Liu Cixin's style breaks down the dichotomies and categories in epistemology and social thought. In the same spirit, the dichotomy between hard and soft SF should also be dismantled. What truly matters is the scientific speculation that has formed a fold to destabilize our sense of reality. Hard or soft, it has inspired thinking differently. However, what is different is truly uncertain. Here I celebrate the liberating force of hard SF but register my warning of its potential to create a new cult.

THE DIVINE AND HUMAN COMEDIES

In Liu Cixin's SF world, the larger, more grandiose cosmic movements make human affairs appear trivial, and in many of his stories, human society is treated as a minor problem against the extravagant backdrop of the universe measured in light years. This vision appears in "The

Village Schoolteacher" 鄉村教師 (2001), one of Liu's earliest breakthroughs. He writes into a seemingly sentimental story of a selfless, devoted teacher a cosmic divine comedy that seems to completely put humanity out of focus. The story combines realistic depictions of the bleak state of education in rural China with the wondrous imagination of an intergalactic war that extends over the entire Milky Way. The former appears as a nuanced detail in the unfolding of the latter's drama. When one side of the space war aims to create a five-hundred-light-year-wide buffer zone in the first arm of our galaxy by destroying all stars in this enormous space, it conducts a life scan to make sure that no advanced intelligent species will be eliminated in the military operation. Many stars are wiped out after the creatures inhabiting their planets fail to respond intelligently to questions concerning the basic laws of the universe. Singled out as examples of the life forms on the third planet of the solar system, eighteen Chinese children happen to have just learned Newton's three laws from their teacher, who has passed away after giving them the last lecture. Their recital of the correct answers in unison saves the Earth from destruction.

In this story, human life is rendered as contingent: survival is made possible merely by the mercy of a supreme alien species, and human extinction, if it happened, would not have meant anything to the universe. However, the omnipotent narrative of the space war still shows some odd moments in this divine comedy. The powerful aliens confront something that they do not understand among the very inferior human civilization. They are puzzled by and curious about teachers, "who serve as the medium conveying knowledge between two generations of these beings."[27] They come to realize that this is an archaic form of transference. When the story ends with a cosmic salute to the profession of teachers, it can also be read as an assured testimony to human agency, vulnerable and minor as it is, which executes an unfathomable power (as phrased by the aliens) to evoke possibilities beyond the cosmic certainty and indifference. Furthermore, the story contains a context referring to Lu Xun and the teacher's self-conscious commitment to the enlightenment, as the last lesson he gives is about Lu Xun's "A Madman's Diary" and famous metaphor of the "iron house." In this sense, Liu's story attains an allegorical significance by sanctioning humanism and its affiliated values regarding the enlightenment, an openness to the outside world, and a hope for change, together with what all these mean to a Chinese reality in the 1990s. But on the other hand, it is obviously scientific education and the hard science embodied in Newton's three laws that saves humans. Thus, the story conveys an ambivalent message regarding the relationship between scientism and humanism, both of which the teacher, like Lu Xun, advocates.

Populated by grandiose superhuman figures or visions, Liu's SF world is a dangerous place, hostile for humans to survive. But many of his stories can be read as human comedies, which offer some ambivalent meanings to the divine cosmos. In another story, "The Poetry Cloud,"[28] another alien species not as benign as those portrayed in "The Village Schoolteacher" descends to Earth. This highly acclaimed story depicts the apocalyptic end of humanity when an immensely intelligent creature destroys the solar system. Presenting itself as a perfect sphere in front of humans, it shows cold contempt toward the human civilization. However, this godlike creature is captivated by traditional Chinese poetry. It has all-embracing technologies that enable it to explore the eleventh dimension of the universe, but it has yet to learn how to write poems. So it keeps one Chinese poet alive and uses up all the energies of the solar system to create a "Poetry Cloud" that can produce and store all the poems that can ever be written. At the end of the story, the alien creature assumes the identity of the greatest Chinese poet of the Tang Dynasty, Li Bo (李白 701–762).

Here Liu presents an ambivalent negotiation between poetry and technology, and this is also a contest, if envisioned on a larger scale, between humanity and the universe. The tricky part of Liu's narrative is his final solution of the problematic of poetry and technology through programming the Poetry Cloud to encompass all possible verse creations. Although the godlike alien intelligence, obviously lacking the Kantian judgment, still cannot identify what is a good poem, all possible poems have theoretically been created and stored in his enormous "database." The Poetry Cloud symbolizes the possibility of the eventual success of technology, and the last part of the story—a seemingly utopian description of the two Chinese poets' happy life (one of them is the alien) after the total extinction of the solar system—can best be read as a simulacrum, a virtual world fabricated by the technologized simulation of the poetic vision after its creators have been wiped out. In this way, Liu sticks to the belief in the almighty power of science, which contrasts with the vulnerability and contingency of the humanity, thus turning a utopia of science and technology into a potential dystopia for the human race.

However, the godlike superintelligence cannot tell a good poem from a bad one, or from a meaningless one. The alien's lack of judgment,[29] its difficulty in grasping the aesthetics of the poetic vision, combined with its urge to appreciate the beauty of literature, the ultimate meaning of being human, and the purpose of the humanities, may after all illuminate the gleaming existence of a poetic heart at the center of Liu's largely ruthless, at best indifferent cosmos. If we situate this moment of all-too-human epiphany in Liu's entire oeuvre, it is clear that poetry occupies a central place in his SF universe. Nearly all the most advanced alien life forms he creates love poetry and art, as exemplified by Mirror in "To Joy" and Singer in *Death's End*, and his masterpiece *Remembrance of the Earth's Past*, as I will explain later, is structured as an epic narrative centering on an urge for self-expression and artistic articulation. The sublime cosmos comes into form on paper because of a poetic heart, which anchors Liu's SF visions as much in literature as in science.

WONDER OF THE WORDS

After Liu Cixin conceives a world "like a god," he still needs to depict it, and through literary language, speculation becomes a concrete world image. The invisible and the unknown, the wondrous and the mysterious, the sublime and the infinite have to fit into a literary picture. Writing, for Liu, is modeled upon a scientific method of turning the invisible into something visible. In chapter 2, we have seen in the example of the short story "Mountain" how Liu makes visible a world that closes itself within an invisible planetary core. He depicts the unfortunate species' great effort to bring themselves to the world, as strenuous as the author's own to bring the invisible vision to the surface text—a process that needs accurate calculations and literal details to render speculated-upon probabilities into scientifically plausible "truth."

In one of the few essays explaining his writing skills, Liu explains how SF differs from realism. While realism needs details primarily drawn from ordinary life, Liu coins a term, "macro detail" 宏細節,[30] by which he refers to abstract and surreal, but technically literal details, which can be as large as something on an astronomical scale or durations of eons of time. He believes that SF needs "macro details," which do not exist or are not perceivable in reality, for plausible world-building, such as how he describes the Poetry Cloud:

> The Poetry Cloud, located where the solar system used to be, is a spiral nebula one hundred astronomic units in diameter, its shape resembling the Milky Way. The hollow Earth is at the edge of the cloud, as was the sun in the original Milky Way. What is different is that the orbit of the Earth is not on the same plane as the Poetry Cloud, so it is possible to see from the Earth an entire side of the cloud, unlike the Milky Way, which offered a view only of its cross section. However, the distance between the Earth and the Poetry Cloud plane is insufficient to allow the people here to observe the cloud's full shape. In fact, the entire sky of the Southern Hemisphere is covered by the cloud.
>
> The Poetry Cloud emits a silvery radiance that casts shadows on Earth. It is said that the cloud emits no light of its own and the silvery radiance is caused by cosmic rays. Owing to the uneven distribution of cosmic rays in space, large halos of light often surge through the Poetry Cloud. These multihued halos course through the sky, like giant glowing whales swimming in the cloud. On the rare occasions when the intensity of the cosmic rays increases dramatically, glimmering sheens of light appear and the Poetry Cloud will no longer be cloudlike: the whole sky will look like the surface of a moonlit ocean seen from under water. The asynchronous rotations of the Earth and the Poetry Cloud allow for an occasional glimpse into the night sky and the stars through the gap when the Earth is in between the spiral arms. The most sensational view is the cross section of the Poetry Cloud seen when the Earth is at the edge of a spiral arm. It looks like cumulonimbus clouds in the Earth's atmosphere that transform into majestic shapes capturing one's imagination. These gigantic shapes emerge high above the rotation plane of the Poetry Cloud, giving off a sublime silvery glow, like a never-ending hyperconscious dream.[31]

Such descriptions of the Poetry Cloud that the alien-Li Bo exhausts the energies of the entire solar system to create are based upon the so-called "macro details," which have no correspondence to reality. The effect of the descriptions is not to create a metaphor or allegory either. They achieve an effect of liberalness in terms of technology, logic, and world-building instead of imitating reality. The details are grandiose, out of proportion, excessively baroque. The nature of such details is exactly like the Poetry Cloud, which only exists in a virtual form; in other words, it is the macro details depicted in the excessive but speculative literary language that create the virtual form of science fictionality.

Here, I will take from Michel Foucault's conception of "the language to infinity"[32] an observation on the virtuality of literary discourse: between language and the world there is always a gap where the agency of language can be extended to endless expanses of its own, creating folds of infinity, replacing what is assumed to be real with a virtual form of what it represents. Foucault uses the example of Jorge Luis Borges's short story "The Secret Miracle" (1943) to explain the power of the language to infinity: a writer named Hladik makes a wish before his own execution, so at the precise instant of his execution, he gains a full year of life to complete a work he began to write before the execution. "Hladik writes—but with words that no one will be able to read, not even God—the great, invisible labyrinth of repetition, of language that divides itself and becomes its own mirror."[33] Borges reveals the ultimate nature of narrative fiction, which is an infinity of folds created in the language to infinity.

The Poetry Cloud is a science fictional counterpart to Borges's mystic speculation about the wonder of the words. The deep curiosity about human poetry exhausts every atom and all subatomic energy to create words, repeated with endless alternations, without definitive meanings. Thus, the apocalypse, the senseless endgame, marks the birth of a new literature. "Poetry Cloud" is the virtual replacement of both the lost real world and the lost original literature; at the same time, "poetry" itself becomes the very goal of the virtual world-building. In other words, the narrative becomes possible when words unfold into speculative worlds. Liu's space sagas, short and long, mostly chart the process of reaching the end of the universe, and their wonders are manifested in what speculations bring to the surface of the language. Like the Poetry Cloud, the representation itself becomes the wonder, the target of the world-building is the writing itself, and the literary language materializes the virtual form of speculative truth. Liu's SF discourse, as the language to infinity, is the ultimate means of making the invisible visible.

VISIBLE INVISIBILITY

The virtual also provides Liu Cixin's narrative a chiasm for the representation of the invisible. In the novella "The Micro Era," humanity has evolved into microbe-like creatures adapted to the deteriorating environment on the Earth, which has been torched by an explosive sun. When the last man returns to Earth, he can only see the otherwise invisible micro-humans' world through a special computer program that produces a virtual reality projection. The virtual reality eventually alters the meanings of humanity, history, and morality to such an extent that the virtual form replaces all that existed, and the alteration is depicted as so thorough, so neat, and so sublime that the last man decides to remove what he knows as "reality" from this virtual world. He destroys the surviving ordinary human genes and keeps the virtual micro era intact. Here, the virtual is certainly not mimetic, and the representation is memetic, causing the conception of a new world that is different from the real as we know it in the context of the story.

An absence of visibility is also found in the "Three-Body" trilogy, in which, first of all, bodies remain unseen. The human race's clash with the first known alien species, Trisolarans, drives the main plot. But the physical appearance of Trisolarans is never described. Instead, the unseen bodies are replaced by humanoid figures in a virtual reality game called "Three Body," in which human players, through incarnations as real historical figures like King Wen of Zhou, Mozi, the First Emperor, Copernicus, Newton, and von Neumann, gradually come to grasp the challenging fate of the Trisolarans, the lawlessness and formlessness of their world. The virtual is viewed as the means to evoking the truthful, while the game players know that by the design of the game, the truth is hidden in the invisible.

At the end of the first volume, humans learn that two small intelligent particles known as Sophons have been sent by Trisolarans to Earth to spy on human activities. Sophons are depicted as being invisible to humans, but when their creators increase their dimensionality, they may grow into giant three-dimensional geometric solids, or unfold both inside and outside of any space in six dimensions, or become invisible in eleven dimensions. What Sophons can do is largely based on superstring theory,[34] but its function in the narrative is like that of the virtual reality game: to change the way humans perceive reality. Sophons are tasked with turning the observable universe into total chaos, disturbing scientific experiments, and discrediting all human knowledge, which drives hordes of scientists to suicide, because the world that they used to understand has changed. To them, physics no longer exits, scientific laws have become meaningless, and the world has become completely unknown. Through depicting the scientists' despair, Liu Cixin presents a scenario about how the human mentality will collapse if truth is absolutely invisible.

Toward the end of the Three-Body saga, the immense invisible of the universe begins to come into the picture. Through contact with alien species and the human diasporas across the galaxies, some characters approach the truth of the universe, said to have multiple hidden dimensions beyond human perception. In the final volume of the trilogy, when the first human spaceship leaves the solar system, it encounters a mysterious four-dimensional "bubble" within which space appears timeless and beyond measure:

> The difficulty of describing high-dimensional spatial sense lay in the fact that for observers situated in four-dimensional space, the space they could see was empty and uniform, but there was a *depth* to it that could not be captured by language. This *depth* was not a matter of distance: It was bound up in every point in space. Guan Yifan's 關一帆 exclamation later became a classic quote:
> "A bottomless abyss exists in every inch."
> The experience of high-dimensional spatial sense was a spiritual baptism. In one moment, concepts like freedom, openness, profundity, and infinity all gained brand-new meanings.[35]

Evoking a strong sense of the sublime, this passage recalls Liu's description of his reaction after he first finished reading Arthur C. Clarke's novel *2001: A Space Odyssey*:

> I went out to look at the sky after closing the book. Everything around me suddenly disappeared. The ground under my feet turned into a smooth flat geometric plane that extended limitlessly to the beyond. I stood alone under the splendid starry sky, confronting the enormous

mystery that the human mind could not understand. From then on, the starry sky has completely changed in my eyes, a sensation like when one leaves a pond to see the ocean.[36]

What Liu is describing here is, in effect, the Kantian sublime: infinite, formless, boundless, overwhelming, with a magnitude beyond the human ability to measure and grasp. Its immensity and infinity evoke the fear of seeing. Liu recounts that his works, as an ensemble, are an imitation of Clarke; he also borrows from Clarke the definitive master plot of classical SF—the encounter between humans and the unknown. However, Clarke's sense of the sublime sustains Kantian transcendentalism; the sublime takes precedence over any concrete experience of the senses and cannot be expressed in terms of experience or words. On this point, Liu clearly differs. When Clarke describes an infinitely estranging and sublime sensation, he deliberately keeps the invisible out of the picture, sustaining a strong sense of mystery and giving the transcendental a religious color. In *2001: A Space Odyssey*, for example, Clarke's description of the extraordinary universe behind the Stargate is limited to an exclamation by his main character: "My God, it's full of stars!"[37]

The almost sacred language, perhaps reminiscent of the religious reason of the Kantian tradition, is very rarely found in Liu Cixin. He will not stop at the sacred moment. He will keep exploring the unknown, sparing no effort and trying every means—even lowering the dimensions of the sacred to make it visible and explicable. The descriptions that Liu uses are literal and technical: even after having his character say "a bottomless abyss exists in every inch," he takes us further into the details of the wondrous universe within these estranging "four-dimensional fragments" so that his writing, like science, can grasp the scale, size, and extent of its immensity and infinity. In this chain of descriptions, his narrative struggles to capture the invisible and the infinite in words, images, and "macro details." To borrow a literary image from Liu Cixin himself, it can be said that he reduces the hyperdimensional "sublime" into a two-dimensional picture so that it can be displayed with extreme meticulousness and completeness as a flat world.

This two-dimensionalization happens after Singer comes to our solar system. Singer throws an extraordinarily thin sheet toward the solar system. Called a "dual vector foil" 二向箔, it changes the structure of the space-time continuum, reducing the three-dimensional solar system to two dimensions. The entire solar system begins to fall into an infinitely large flat picture: planet by planet, object by object, molecule by molecule, the Sun, Jupiter, Saturn, Venus, Mars, the Earth, and all humanity turn two-dimensional.

This is the climax of the entire space saga. In terms of SF poetics, this thrilling moment illustrates Liu's literary methods to render the sublime visible. Three survivors stationed on Pluto observe the two-dimensionalization of the solar system like the unfolding of a picture, awed by the moon-size snowflakes that are the two-dimensional water molecules. The entire process is displayed with dazzlingly concrete details—each drop of water is depicted as though it were as large and complex as a two-dimensional ocean. Liu Cixin describes this imagined and miraculous catastrophe as directly and precisely as if it were a scientific phenomenon, and the effect is rather surreal. This is a telling moment in Liu Cixin's writing, which may be compared to the effect of the dual vector foil. The two-dimensional picture epitomizes his artistic approach: the cosmic sublime becomes visible in a virtual form of itself created out of the specific though speculative details.

Liu's technically comprehensive and totalistic approach to the sublime invisible turns his writing itself, his language and poetic vision, into a virtual form of the world he creates; and in the ceaseless movement toward depicting with full details the surreal "concreteness" of the speculative world, the words he uses in their literal, technological sense fabricate that unreality, with its infinitely immense scope and meticulously hyper-real macro details. Through the language to infinity, Liu enlivens his work with a sense of wonder and renders the sublime visible, as the very magnetic force of the SF imagination. His writing speaks directly to the infinity of the universe, but he also seeks to transform the invisible and infinite into a discursively visible form. He conceives the speculative world by altering scientific rules, describes it with macro details and represents its immensity in a virtual form that is central to his approach to SF. At the peak moment in the search for alternatives to reality, the virtual becomes the wonder of the words. This has come to its full form in the Three-Body saga.

THE THREE-BODY UNIVERSE

To Chinese SF fans, Liu Cixin's Three-Body novels represent the highest achievement of Chinese SF. *The Three-Body Problem* was first serialized in *SFW* from May to December 2006, and its two sequels, *The Dark Forest* and *Death's End*, were published in China in 2008 and 2010, respectively. They constitute a series known to fans as the "Three-Body" trilogy but referred to by Liu himself as *Remembrance of the Earth's Past*. It is the most important work that Liu has written so far and is widely regarded as the peak in the new wave of Chinese SF.

The trilogy recapitulates a multitude of motifs and elements from Liu Cixin's earlier SF writings, and the stories and novels he wrote before it seem to be rehearsals for the realization of this ultimate experiment. The apocalyptic encounter with superior alien intelligence from deep space appeared in stories like "Poetry Cloud," and the catastrophic impact of solar activity on civilizations is the main theme of stories such as "The Wandering Earth." He attempted to chronicle postapocalyptic events in *Supernova Era* and "The Wandering Earth," in which narrative assumes the form of a historiographical account with (pseudo)scientific interpretations of the (future) historical happenings, a basic structure that Liu uses again in the "Three-Body" trilogy. There are also the tensions between science and poetry, cosmos and humanity, survival and transcendence—all that appeared in stories like "The Village Schoolteacher," "Poetry Cloud," and "Ode to Joy" come back in this epic story about humans' fate in the dark forest of the universe and their efforts to create a testimony to humanity and their civilization. "Mountain," the story that Liu wrote right before he began to work on the "Three-Body" trilogy, is centered on an experiment envisioning a species stuck in a disadvantageous situation that pushes it toward technological revolution and fearless treks into the stars. This story sets up a precedent for exactly the same foundational plot design for the Trisolaran civilization in *The Three-Body Problem*.

The Three-Body universe consists of systematic alterations to scientific, social, and moral conventions about the universe, civilization, and humanity. Liu uses the actual astrophysical question of the three-body movement[38] to break down certainty, normalcy, and determinism. Like the scientific three-body problem—the unstable, uncertain, unpredictable orbits of three bodies positioned in equal gravitational pulls from one another—the Three-Body universe is characterized by uncertainty and unpredictability. Trisolarans face a world where there are no rules and regulations, and through the encounter with this alien world, humans are dragged into a space war, stuck in an amoral universe. The Three-Body novels portray the universe as a "darkest forest," in which the only imperative is to accept a world without morality and come to understand that survival requires preemptive strikes to eliminate others. The most advanced intelligence in the universe dares to change the laws of physics to keep its rivals at bay. The question that Liu Cixin asks about this lawless, chaotic world is whether the human beings who are morally conscious can survive. In the following sections, I will discuss some of the most important aspects of the Three-Body series: its world-building, its engagements with social and political systems, the issue of morality, and the poetic form of its SF vision, with specific focus on the tensions between the cosmic and human actions, and between science and literature.

IN REVOLUTION BEGINS A NEW WORLD

Liu Cixin explains that the inspiration for the novel series has less to do with history and reality than a pure meditation on the mathematic puzzle of the three-body problem. This abstract scientific vision indeed constitutes the fundamental plot for the entire trilogy, which explains the disorderly world of the Trisolarans, the lack of morality among them and among all extraterrestrial species, and the nature of the universe.

But Liu Cixin's approach is different from what he does with the bubble world in "Mountain," which is completely distanced from human worlds; or how he depicts alien intelligence in "Poetry Cloud" and "Village Schoolteacher," which use human images but mostly have no reference to actual historical experiences; or the future worlds in stories like "The Micro Era" and "The Wandering Earth," which experiment with speculative human societies that do not easily evoke political responses from readers. In the Three-Body novels, the materials for his world-building come from home, the memory of China's recent past, and thus from the very beginning this wondrous world looks familiar and is available for direct engagement on political and ethical terms. *The Three-Body*

Problem, in its original narrative order,[39] opens with a moment often seen in "scar literature" about the Cultural Revolution:[40] Red Guards humiliate and torture a distinguished professor of astrophysics, whose daughter, Ye Wenjie, after witnessing her father's death and then her younger sister's killing, becomes disillusioned with not only the mission of the Cultural Revolution but also the purpose of humanity.

Mao's conviction that men find endless pleasure in the eternal battle against heaven and earth as well as against each other is the very root of a utopian vision of history's ceaseless movement, just like the struggle of the godlike species in the trilogy is the foundational goal and energy of the cosmic movements.[41] This Maoist vision has no place for ordinary human morality, and humanity is deemed dispensable for achieving the divine purpose of the eternal revolution. The entire Three-Body universe is constructed on the ground of this Maoist philosophy. Thus, the first motif of Liu Cixin's space saga emerges from a real moment in China's history. It is depicted as a dark moment when morality is trashed and, to Ye Wenjie, human dignity is lost forever. This historical condition can be understood as the "bricks" of Liu's world-building, but to readers who are historically informed, the disorderly world of Trisolarans, the unpredictable threats of the dark forest, and the alien civilizations' life-and-death struggle can all be understood as poetic reflections of the aftermath of Mao's Cultural Revolution. Mao's dream for a permanent revolution transforms into Liu Cixin's divine drama of conflict and attacks on the level of the cosmological order. Such Maoist terms and Chinese military strategies as "striking preemptively" 先發制人 are also applied to the space war, such as Singer's mission to hide well and cleanse all. Similarly, Wallfacers' deliberate use of deceptive skills testifies to the humans' unique mastery of the principle that "there can never be too much deception in war" 兵不厭詐.[42]

Ye Wenjie, the first protagonist of the novels, is a child of Mao's China. A victim of the Maoist revolution but also an inheritor of Maoist thought, she executes the first movement that puts into action the plot development of *The Three-Body Problem*. While despairing about the human world, Ye Wenjie is recruited for a secret science project that is tasked by the supreme leader, who is very likely Mao himself but unnamed in the text, to search for extraterrestrial intelligence. The leader considers this an essential arena for China's competition with the Americans and Russians.

Those who find the aliens first will control the future of mankind. But this imaginary Chinese SETI (Search for Extraterrestrial Intelligence) project during the Mao years is a rather miserable mission, for lack of proper technology and equipment. Ye Wenjie finds a way to bypass the political prohibitions and shoot a signal directly to the sun, which serves as an amplifier to broadcast a message from the Chinese communist leaders to the entire galaxy, a proper application of the revolutionary allegory in a literal, scientific sense. Ye Wenjie becomes the first Star-Plucker in the Three-Body universe, and she succeeds in ushering the humans into the cosmic stage of eternal battles. Eight years later, Ye receives a reply that reads: "Do not answer! Do not answer! Do not answer!"[43]

What Ye finds for humans is a mirror image from deep space: the disorderly Trisolaran world reads like a cosmic expansion of the Maoist chaos that she witnesses during the Cultural Revolution, a scientifically calculated simulation of the moral predicament the Chinese people experienced during the so-called "madness years." Ye receives a message from the closest planet, located in Alpha Centauri, only four light-years away from Earth. It is sent by a self-identified pacifist living in a dying civilization that faces extremely harsh conditions for survival. In their star system, a lone planet orbits three suns. This situation is modeled upon the real mathematical three-body problem.[44] In the novel, the Trisolaran world alternates between Stable Eras when the planet orbits one sun and Chaotic Eras when the planet loses its normal orbit. The Trisolaran civilization has been destroyed many times, either being scorched by three suns rising together or being frozen by the lack of any sunlight. Solely motivated by the survival instinct, the Trisolaran world resorts to a militarized dictatorship, where scientific and technological progress is given priority and poetry and arts do not exist. Collectivity is the absolute divine entity placed above all that is personal and individual. It is the most hostile situation imaginable, an Orwellian society reduced to its barest, and Trisolarans have no awareness of all the ideas that the modern human world is accustomed to, such as free will, liberty, selfhood, and democracy. The militarized Trisolarans are eager to emigrate to other planets, readying themselves for interstellar invasion. The pacifist, a listener by profession stationed at a post to search for habitable planets, happens to have received Ye Wenjie's message, and out of uncharacteristic moral compassion it (gender unknown) warns the Earthlings that as soon as an answer is sent back into space, the source of the transmission will be located and an invasion will be imminent. Ye Wenjie, already fed up with humanity, ignores the warning and replies immediately, inviting the Trisolarans to invade Earth.

Ye Wenjie's first movement is thus completed, throwing the entire human world into a chain of reactions leading to chaos, and the contact with the Trisolarans motivates revolutions on both planets. The world that the trilogy depicts begins to depart from the everyday life scenes readers know. The novel opens with a second beginning:[45] forty years later a scientist is dragged into the Battle Command Center, where he learns what seems impossible: that the human world is preparing for a space war. Ordinary life has suddenly become strange: the scientist begins to see numbers counting down inscribed into his eyesight, and the entire universe flickers against all physical rules. The estrangement of the Three-Body universe is first represented in the militarized transformation of the human society. In the narrative design of Liu's saga, this estranging situation mirrors the completely estranging chaotic world of the Trisolaran star system, which is again mirroring the chaos of the madness years that constitute the beginning of Liu's world-building. The Three-Body setting is so grandiose that it covers the entire universe, its enormous history of cosmic changes, and its everlasting space war, but Liu's conception begins very close to reality, arising from the ruthless and inhumane struggles motivated by Mao's dream of permanent revolution, an everlasting campaign that puts everything in the cosmos in motion.

THE DARK FOREST

The first volume sets the stage: an estranged, chaotic world known as the Trisolaris is going to war with the Earth. The alterations of scientific rules create speculative images of the Trisolaran universe, and the consequences of such alterations imposed upon the human mentality motivate changes to the social, political, and cultural conditions of the human world depicted. *The Three-Body Problem* focuses on the humans' gradual recognition of the true nature of the universe: it is not an empty space; on the contrary, it is potentially filled with intelligent species, but for this reason, it is dangerous for humans. The contact with the Trisolaran civilization has proved that any encounter between civilizations can be fatal: the rivalry between intelligent species can only end with one wiping out the other. Centuries of religious preaching and humanist advocacy for love and compassion, freedom and democracy, seem to be out of place in such a cold and ruthless universe.

Liu's image of the amoral universe only becomes complete in the second volume, *The Dark Forest*, where his characters begin to outline the so-called cosmic sociology that concentrates on a provocative denial of morality in the universe. Ye Wenjie's role is mostly finished after she pushes the first button for the chain reaction of events leading up to the Trisolaran invasion, and she only reappears in the beginning of *The Dark Forest*, where she passes her reflections on Earth's encounter with the Trisolaran world to a student of sociology, Luo Ji 羅輯, who later invents the so-called cosmic sociology. Ye Wenjie helps Luo Ji to understand two basic axioms: "First: Survival is the primary need of civilization. Second: Civilization continuously grows and expands, but the total matter in the universe remains constant."[46]

These two axioms determine that our universe is a Darwinian jungle: species compete fiercely for the limited resources, and the fittest survive. Along this line of thinking, Luo Ji further adds two conditions: the chain of suspicion and the technological explosion. The first is particularly pivotal for the construction of the model of the dark forest. Only with the chain of suspicion could the universe become such a quiet, dark, and deserted place as it appears to the observers now: even though it is filled with civilizations, humans had never discovered extraterrestrial intelligence before. This is because the chain of suspicion decides that any civilization exposing itself to the universe is at the mercy of others who see it and cannot determine whether it is benevolent or malicious, so the need for survival and development requires preemptive attacks on any rival species. Luo Ji's reasoning reveals the ultimate darkness of the universe:

> The universe is a dark forest. Every civilization is an armed hunter stalking through the trees like a ghost, gently pushing aside branches that block the path and trying to tread without sound. Even breathing is done with care. The hunter has to be careful, because everywhere in the forest are stealthy hunters like him. If he finds other life—another hunter, an

angel or a demon, a delicate infant or a tottering old man, a fairy or a demigod—there's only one thing he can do: open fire and eliminate them. In this forest, hell is other people. An eternal threat that any life that exposes its own existence will be swiftly wiped out. This is the picture of cosmic civilization.[47]

Luo Ji is the first human being enlightened to the "truth" of the universe, which makes him a threat to Trisolarans, but exactly because they want him to die, Luo Ji is elected to be a Wallfacer as the plot of the second volume unfolds. Confronting the impending apocalypse, human worlds give Wallfacers power like dictators have. They can hide their thoughts and strategies and manipulate all the resources and manpower toward achieving their personal plans. Among four Wallfacers, only Luo Ji is successful. After he comes to a full understanding of the universe's nature as a dark forest, he combines the life-and-death struggle of social Darwinism with the Maoist mandate for self-defense and preemptive attack. He finds the key to human survival in the moral vacuum of the universe. He secretly establishes a well-coordinated defense system that will expose the location of the home planet of the Trisolarans so that some even more highly intelligent creatures will certainly destroy it without hesitation. But this move means that the coordinates of the solar system also will be exposed, which could easily cause the demise of the human world too. This suicidal strategy, a threat of mutual destruction, works. The Trisolarans' military invasion stops. Luo Ji emerges as the temporary victor in the dark forest, and that assures his power as the dictator. He is known as the Swordholder because the fates of the two civilizations are in his hands now. Trisolarans are forced to provide technologies to humans, and human civilization flourishes again, with a postapocalyptic age of decadence emerging in a world that lives on a thin thread of hope, which is Luo Ji's deterrence of the Trisolaran world.

The third volume, *Death's End*, contains a reflection on the politics of this situation:

> People realized that the Deterrence Era was a strange time. On the one hand, human society had reached unprecedented heights of civilization: Human rights and democracy reigned supreme everywhere. On the other hand, the entire system existed within the shadow of a dictator.

Experts believed that although science and technology usually contributed to the elimination of totalitarianism, when crises threatened the existence of civilization, science and technology could also give birth to new totalitarianism. In traditional totalitarian states, the dictator could only enact his control over other people, which led to low efficiency and uncertainty. Thus, there had never been a 100 percent effective totalitarian society in human history. But technology provided the possibility for such a super-totalitarianism, and both the Wallfacers and the Swordholders were concerning examples.[48]

The novel self-explains the political nature of the social systems that rely on the opaque mind of a Wallfacer or Swordholder, an individual dictator combining Machiavellianism and social Darwinism. This part of the novel has evoked intense responses; in particular, reflections on the dark forest as a political model constitute some of the left-wing scholars' most engaging and controversial reactions in relation to the political problems of their own day. Based on an immersive reading of the apocalyptical crisis depicted in the novels, those scholars consider the totalitarian society necessary, either in a state of emergency or for the long-term goal of the nation's development, while elements such as the deterrence of the Wallfacer and the Swordholder are interpreted as indispensable. Luo Ji represents a resurrected "First Man" after history ends with Francis Fukuyama's "Last Man," according to a recent article that reads a strong sense of historical determinism into a novel series that ironically, in the first place, contests with determinism.[49] Scholars of moral philosophy, political science, and sociology, as well as those interested in game theory, military studies, and international relations, have all contributed to discussions on the dark forest, as an effective political system or a justifiable social condition.[50] Therefore, Liu's saga could be potentially elevated to the level of national imagery serving ideological needs, though it is unlikely that this is where Liu began. He is certainly critical of the Cultural Revolution, and also lays bare the "darkness" of the dark forest.

On the other hand, the dark forest is also perceived as a reflection of China's political and economic reality after the country entered the capitalist age of rapid marketization without effective regulations guaranteeing social justice. The same model is applied to international politics when China is perceived as the naïve species entering a new world order that is hostile to a rising new power. Compared with the sublime cosmos that is transcendental and abstract, the human worlds in the Three-Body universe appear to be much closer to China's reality. If the first volume of Liu Cixin's saga contains an intricately hidden image of the Maoist revolution, the second volume projects rather audacious images of the post-Mao years of fierce social Darwinian competition inside China and the post–Cold War international competition between China and the West.

The lack of universally practical morality in the universe is just as obvious as the lack of universally observed justice in the human world. The cosmic movement has no mercy for the weak and fragile who are not capable of winning every competition. The only solution is to play the game according to the rules. One has to resort to the second condition Luo Ji adds to the dark forest theory, technological explosion, to gain strength, and the technologies include materials as well as mentality, which gives birth to the most likely victors of the wars in the dark forest: the technocratic Leviathans—strongmen, strong systems, strong military bodies. The technology of power and the power of technology become one. This situation makes Liu Cixin's novels an anomaly in world SF, particularly different from the usual dystopian novels.

STARSHIP EARTH

In postwar and post-Stalin Western SF, an overwhelmingly popular motif is that the utopian has irreversibly become Orwellian, administrated with the strictest possible surveillance and totalistic control, in which the institutional oppression of individuals represents the arch-evil of the twentieth century, yet the individual heroes' battles with totalitarianism represent an undying humanist belief in personal moral integrity. This plotline testifies to the strength of humanism versus totalitarianism. However, in the "Three-Body" trilogy, the Orwellian society is not considered evil, and heroes are those who are resistant to individual interests and personal impulses. The specters of collectivism, communism, and Maoism particularly linger in what Liu describes as "Starship Earths," the new type of civilization when humans begin their diaspora across space, which may look like the equivalent of utopia on the surface: isolated "islands" in the ocean of stars, extremely well-organized, highly technologized societies that can operate automatically without the intervention of any low-ranking individual. Starship Earths are the prototypes for Leviathan politics that keep liberalism at bay, put more emphasis on the nation and species, and thus guarantee the bottom line for human survival. They are indeed the only surviving human communities after the solar system is destroyed in the two-dimensionalization of the space-time continuum.

Starship Earths are first founded by a character named Zhang Beihai 章北海. He is actually almost like a hidden Wallfacer in the second volume of the trilogy, though nobody calls him that. Zhang Beihai is a naval officer, a steel-made soldier, fashioned in the tradition of Chinese revolutionary heroes. He has no personal life, and he hides his own thoughts and motivations deep inside; they are, however, not related to any personal matter but solely concern the ultimate plan to save humans from extinction. The character is mostly clouded by unexplained behaviors in the novel until the so-called "Doomsday Battle," which happens when a deceptively simple Trisolaran probe, nicknamed "droplet," destroys nearly all the human starships as well as the last hope for humanity to survive the unfathomably advanced alien invasion. Right before the droplet dashes toward the fleet, at a time when humans still celebrate it as a beautiful token of friendship from the Trisolarans, Zhang Beihai seems to have already sensed that it is not a peaceful "droplet" but an extremely advanced weapon. He gets control of his starship through tricks and launches the ship to escape the battlefield near Jupiter. He is a defeatist at heart, but only knowing that humans are destined to lose could he design a series of intricate strategies that enable a small number of starships to survive. He is the first architect for a new type of civilization that must confront the posthuman uncertainty in a totally hostile environment with limited resources, when the surviving starships are leaving the solar system and journeying into totally unknown space.

Zhang Beihai becomes a hero to the surviving crew members, and they follow his leadership to begin building the Starship Earth civilization. Concerning the political form of this new civilization, the crew members have a debate. While the majority opinion is to keep the military dictatorship, Zhang says absolutely no, because dictatorship kills vibrant new ideas and innovations that are the prerequisites for technological progress. When others suggest democracy as an alternative, he hesitates, saying: "Starship Earth is traveling through the harsh environment of space, where catastrophes that threaten the entire world might occur at any time. Earth's history during the Trisolaran Crisis has demonstrated that, in the face of such disasters, particularly when our world needs to make sacrifices in order to preserve the whole, the humanitarian society you have in mind is especially fragile."[51]

There is a general tendency among scholars to ground the political consciousness of the Three-Body universe in the Hobbesian submission to absolute power, or in Carl Schmitt's ideas on sovereignty and state of exception.[52] Zhang's words make clear that the political form of the Starship Earth should be properly associated with a "state of exception," defined by Schmitt as a crisis situation that gives the sovereign a full claim to transcend the rule of law in the name of serving the public good. Schmitt's theories have gained popularity among Chinese intellectuals, particularly the New Leftists, in parallel to the increasing popularization of Liu's novels. Even without strongman politics and a triumphant personality, because Zhang Beihai does not claim total control, Starship Earth is destined to be a technocratic society, which serves the purpose of survival but no more unless the state of exception is withdrawn, as Zhang Beihai himself admits when associating creativity with liberty. But the constant threats of cosmic catastrophes make the state of exception eternal.

Even so, Zhang Beihai also foresees the so-called "Battle of Darkness" coming to the surviving starships. Later, Luo Ji realizes that what happened to them was the emergence of the first dark forest among human communities. Only a handful of starships manage to leave the battlefield of the earlier Doomsday Battle, but they are stuck in a dark forest situation, when limited resources and their needs for survival and development cause them to begin a chain of suspicion among themselves. Are they mutually supportive friends, or enemies ready to cut each other's throats? Before any communication can happen, the dark forest attacks begin. Zhang Beihai calmly readies himself. His deeply rooted faith in collectivism gives him comfort in knowing that someone, even if it is not him or his crew, will survive. He hides his defeatism deeply in his heart. He does not believe that humanity can all survive; only the sacrifice of some humans, even most of them, can guarantee the continuation of the species. Zhang Beihai does not lament his own death or the destruction of the starship he leads when another starship attacks his for the purpose of obtaining supplies, including the nutrition extracted from the human bodies.

The legacy of Zhang Beihai is debatable even in the context of the novel. Starship Earths are never paradise, and the extremely hostile universe forces them to prioritize survival to such an extent that collectivism legalizes cannibalism, which Liu's characters nevertheless defend to sustain the "civilization" that has, however, already become inhuman. Among contemporary Chinese SF writers, both Liu Cixin and Han Song write about cannibalism. Han Song takes it as a cultural metaphor for social evil, like Lu Xun, though with an even more grotesque obsession with anatomical details.[53] But Liu Cixin gives cannibalism a contextualized positive meaning. He is famously known for having openly talked about cannibalism as a necessary evil for the survival of species.[54] The members of one Starship Earth, captured by Earth humans in the third volume of the trilogy, are charged with committing that inhuman crime, but the defender questions what the bottom line of morality is when one lacks all the essential resources for life. The cannibals are executed, but the true punishment is not a moral one.

The moral position Liu lets his human characters take is based upon a posthuman imperative of sacrifice for the sake of the species, or even just for the sake of life in a sense that is not limited to how we understand life in the context of the Anthropocene. In another story by Liu Cixin, "Man and Devourers" (人與吞食者 2002), the entire human race is wiped out when an alien species exploits all the resources of the Earth.[55] The last standing soldiers lie down on the ground, dying peacefully with a faint hope that the nutrition from their bodies will at least enable small insects to survive so that the Earth may not be a completely dead world. At a moment like this, Liu is obviously not a humanist, and his concern with the collective fate of humanity is stuck in a deadlocked conflict between morality and development—but survival, first! Ultimately, Starship Earths are portrayed as estranging worlds that reflect the worst possible human condition.

MORAL CHOICES IN AN AMORAL UNIVERSE

To prepare for the release of the English translation of the trilogy's first volume, *The Three-Body Problem*, Liu Cixin shared some of his own thoughts on the novel with English readers. He said: "SF is a literature of possibilities. The universe we live in is also one of countless possibilities. For humanity, some universes are better than others, and *Three-Body* shows the worst of all possible universes, a universe in which existence is as dark and harsh as one can imagine."[56] Liu's words may have unknowingly written back to the optimistic "best of all possible worlds,"[57] and when situated in historical context, they may testify to new wave SF's strength to form an antidote to China's century-long utopianism, which David Der-wei Wang characterizes as a Panglossian dream.[58] Contrary to what the late Qing and early PRC SF writers envisioned, Liu's SF world, as the worst of all possible universes, is a vacuum of morality, a dark forest throughout the trilogy, where every civilization is a hunting tribe out to eliminate rivals.

Zhang Beihai's Starship Earth and Luo Ji's Swordholder Deterrence do not stop the coming of the endgame for all. Humans are completely unprepared for their demise when Singer begins to lower the dimension of the solar system. Any living creatures adapted to the three-dimensional universe are now, as the four-dimensional creatures called Tomb warned humans in their earlier encounter, like fish thrown to dry land. Those of higher intelligence like Singer's species, as winners, are also stuck in the dark forest deadlock: "The fish who dried the sea went onto land before they did this. They moved from one dark forest to another dark forest."[59] The darkness of the universe cannot be measured by the human senses and sensibilities. Guan Yifan, the human adventurer who is among the first to know the dark truth of the universe, later explains to another character that the dark forest attacks are often based on changing the universal laws of physics and mathematics. Lowering dimensions is one method, and he says:

> "The speed of light is also frequently used as a weapon. I'm not talking about building light tombs—or, as you call them, black domains. Those are just defensive mechanisms employed by weak worms like us. The gods do not stoop so low. In war, it's possible to make reduced-lightspeed black holes to seal the enemy inside. But more commonly, the technique is used to construct the equivalents of pits and city walls. Some reduced-lightspeed belts are large enough to traverse an entire arm of a galaxy. In places where stars are dense, many reduced-lightspeed black holes can

be connected together into chains that stretch for tens of millions of light-years. That's a Great Wall at the scale of the universe. Even the most powerful fleets, once trapped, would not be able to escape. Those barriers are very difficult to cross."[60]

A string of "macro details" creates the most terrifying, sublime image of the universe as fundamentally amoral; even the superior godlike creatures are also victims of the lowered number of dimensions. Changing physical rules brings not only the demise of the rivals but also inevitably the deterioration of the attackers' conditions. That happens to the solar system when the entire human world is turned into a two-dimensional picture, and Singer's tribe has to turn two-dimensional sooner or later.

The surviving humans are cast into a diasporic state, wherein they may observe the hostility and rivalry among intelligent existences populating the universe. For them, this marks the beginning of humanity's growing up with an intelligent maturity that matches the sophistication of the universe itself. The universe is sublime, fearsome, and hostile, and humanity seeks to survive and to sustain itself in a war that it has virtually no chance of winning. By the end of the trilogy, the human survivors have just begun to piece together the original appearance of the universe: "That was a really lovely time, when the universe itself was a Garden of Eden,"[61] a paradise that was timeless and endless. However, as soon as it existed, the godlike intelligences populating it began the war among themselves. Reducing the dimensions or changing the physical rules are the most powerful ways to wipe out entire worlds, and Liu's trilogy reveals that the universe has always been a ruthless battlefield.

On the astronomical scale, the unfathomable magnitude of the universe transcends good and evil. For morally self-aware humans to survive in a fiercely hostile and amoral world, the unknown, invisible dimensions of the universe present a gateway to transcendence. Whether or not the humans could survive becomes a moot question toward the end of the narrative, because the entire universe comes to an end when its dimensions are finally reduced to zero, absolute nothingness. This last moment lifts SF from determinism, historical or political or personal or national allegory (or whatever is rooted in certainty) into a transcendent imaginary realm, which is ultimately a posthuman universe.

Foregrounding the sublime image of the cosmos, Liu Cixin's narrative remains ambiguous regarding the conflicts between morality and survival, humanity and technology, hope and despair. He makes clear through the overall plot development that the universe is a cold place. However, the most magical power of the narrative still comes from the sustaining of humaneness that can be found even in the coldest moments and places. One of the two people who live until the end of the universe is Cheng Xin 程心, the protagonist of the third volume, a kind-hearted woman—sarcastically nicknamed the "Madonna" or "soft-hearted bitch" by Liu's misogynic fans, who are so convinced by the dark forest theory that they show contempt for this female character who succeeds Luo Ji to become the Swordholder but submits to the tender feelings that swell in her heart when facing the sudden invasion of Trisolarans.

Cheng Xin keeps her moral consciousness so that she will feel regretful for what she has done. She did make a ruthless decision to send a person in love with her into space with no hope of being saved (though that person is eventually saved). Cheng Xin comes to the age of Deterrence as an observer who sees the gradual humanist influences on the Trisolarans beginning to work. Trisolaris seems to have become more civilized after going through a renaissance and a boom in literature and arts, an echo of the human world's humanist tradition. It is under such circumstances that Cheng Xin succeeds Luo Ji to become the new Swordholder. But just a few minutes after the handover, Trisolarans begin attacks. At this moment, sitting in front of the sword, a red switch for activating the defense system that Luo Ji has designed, Cheng Xin comes to see that she has zero power of deterrence. She is the wrong choice for the Swordholder, the guardian of Earth and the dictator of all lives on the planet, because she has a heart, just like her name contains the character for heart 心. She cannot press the switch that will set off the assured mutual destruction of both the invading Trisolarans and all species on Earth.

> In Cheng Xin's subconscious, she was a protector, not a destroyer; she was a mother, not a warrior. She was willing to use the rest of her life to maintain the balance between the two worlds [human and Trisolaran], until the Earth grew stronger and stronger with Trisolaran science, until Trisolaris grew more and more civilized with Earth culture, until one day, a voice told her: *Put down that red switch and return to the surface.*

> *The world no longer needs dark forest deterrence, no longer needs a Swordholder.*[62]

Cheng Xin listens to her conscience, so she does not press the switch. Therefore, for Cheng Xin, the dark forest does not exist, and in her world it is possible to have coexistence and symbiosis instead of fierce rivalry and mutual destruction. She fails as a Swordholder, but she succeeds as a humanist, probably the last one in the Three-Body universe. The novel's most important protagonist emerges at this moment, which makes all the previously dominant characters, Ye Wenjie, Zhang Beihai, and Luo Ji, into antagonists. They have all chosen survival above humanity, but Cheng Xin's failure to act makes her a morally self-conscious human being. Even if the majority of Liu Cixin's fans choose not to like her, Cheng Xin remains a person who makes moral choices in an amoral universe.

THE POETIC HEART

Cheng Xin plays an even more important role in the making of Liu Cixin's saga. She becomes the author of a text that is being created by the end of the trilogy, which turns out to be the master copy of the narrative that readers are reading. Billions of years into the future, the last surviving species begins to broadcast throughout the universe, calling all the intelligent creatures to leave their self-made mini-universes, like Cheng Xin's, so those materials can return to the flux of time and space. In this way, the universe will be collapsing to nonexistence, or "returning to zero," from where it will start all over again. Cheng Xin and her two companions, Guan Yifan and a Sophon turned humanoid robot, decide to join this movement of "returning to zero," exiting their own mini-universe where they have been hiding. However, the narrative leaves some questions unanswered as it comes to its finale.

It is revealed that Cheng Xin "began to write her memoir so that she could record the history she knew." Her narrative is called *A Past Outside of Time*,[63] a phrase that appears many times in the third volume, serving as a collective title for all the fragments of historical records frequently appearing in the main narrative. Those narrative fragments take the omnipotent viewpoint to make sense of history, explaining the key events and pivotal turning points, how decisions were made, and what consequences they caused. Cheng Xin's writing becomes the testimony to the human struggles through hundreds of years in the war with Trisolaris and then in the adventures in the dark forest universe.

Cheng Xin finally gives her own confession and admits that she is responsible for many missteps in that history. Yet the greatest responsibility now for her is to write, and this takes on an ethical meaning that is in accordance with the final movement of the narrative, which is natality, the birth of the new universe. For her, writing and storytelling links narrativity and natality, in the way David Der-wei Wang defines the importance of writing through evoking Hannah Arendt: "To be born is to become part of the continuum of time, which is underpinned by the creative power of action and, in turn, narrative."[64] Only storytelling can create something new beyond the cold reality. For Liu Cixin, SF assumes the agency of both storytelling and imagining a new universe. Cheng Xin's movement of writing is the counterpoint to the movement of eternal destruction in the dark forest. Only her narrative and her faith in the power of narrative constitute a counterargument to the dark forest theory. The imperative for writing is not just to create a personal memoir; this is an obligation to turn the past into memory, passing on the messages about the perished human civilization to the next universe. It is the most humanist moment: we should not forget. It is the only possible action to stand up to the inhuman sublime, to the cosmic indifference.

Thus, Liu Cixin ends the novel from Cheng Xin's perspective and renames the trilogy *Remembrance of the Earth's Past*. The last paragraph, merely about two hundred characters long, is an enchanting description of a small "ecological system" left by Cheng Xin in "our universe" that has come to an end.

> The message in a bottle and the ecological sphere were the only things left in the mini-universe. The bottle faded into the darkness so, in this one-cubic-kilometer universe, only the little sun inside the ecological sphere gave off any light. In this minuscule world of life, a few clear watery spheres drifted serenely in weightlessness. One tiny fish leapt out of a watery sphere and entered another, where it effortlessly swam between the green algae. On a blade of grass on one of the miniature continents,

a drop of dew took off from the tip of the grass blade, rose spiraling into the air, and refracted a clear ray of sunlight into space.[65]

The entire Three-Body saga ends here, a moment that sheds light in a miniature forest, the dark forest of the universe. Interestingly, when Cheng Xin exits her mini-universe with several kilograms of materials left behind, together with her memory of the human civilization, the novel ends on a cliffhanger. Does this mean that the new universe will not happen? According to the logic explained in the novel, if even a single atom's mass is left behind, the universe will not complete the process of collapsing into "zero."[66] Despite this apparent logic conflict, the ending paragraph may only suggest good will, showing that there is a slight hope that the memory of humans will survive even the end of the universe. If so, this moment can be recognized as a manifestation of poetic justice. It shows a human being's self-conscious choice to balance the entire universe's darkness and emptiness with a poetic heart.

Seen from outside the narrative frame of *Remembrance of the Earth's Past*, all the words, literary descriptions, and story lines in the three novels can also be viewed as testimony to the human efforts, their battles and struggles. Cheng Xin's message is embraced by the small ecological sphere, like the Poetry Cloud, a macro detail that serves as a virtual form to manifest the strength of literary imagination. An advocate of "hard SF," Liu nevertheless reserves a soft space for literary imagination in his grandiose, superhuman vision of the sublime cosmos.

Cheng Xin is not the only character in the Three-Body universe who resorts to literary vision for a gesture to speak back to the cosmic indifference. Another central character of the third volume, Yun Tianming 雲天明, a man who loves Cheng Xin and whose brain was sent into space by the woman he loves. His miraculous survival, or resurrection, makes him almost a messiah figure to help humans survive. But the part of Yuan Tianming that is strikingly similar to the author Liu Cixin himself is that, when he reemerges and contacts Cheng Xin from the deep space, his main role is a storyteller.

In the first part of the third volume, he is literally rendered bodiless, in the sense that only his brain is sent into deep space for the purpose of establishing contact with the Trisolaran civilization and becoming a mole spying on them. When he reappears much later in front of his lover, he takes on a virtual form of a familiar, healthy physical embodiment of himself, and the information that he has to pass on to humans can only be encoded in three fairy tales, due to the surveillance of the Trisolarans who have captured him. How to interpret the virtual form of Yun Tianming and the virtual text of his fairy tales is key to predicting how the human world will be destroyed by alien creatures of higher intelligence. Yet, it is also the key to understanding the art of both Yuan Tianming's and Liu Cixin's storytelling.

Yun Tianming's fairy tales are the metatexts of the Three-Body novels, the labyrinths hidden at the center of the labyrinths. These stories are very difficult to interpret, and no one in the novel is sure of catching their hidden meanings. The novel even describes a scholarly effort of theorizing Yun Tianming's storytelling skill and its hermeneutics; its metaphorization, semiology, and implied allusions; and its labyrinthine signifying system. As the experts come to see:

> He employed two basic methods: dual-layer metaphors and two-dimensional metaphors.
>
> The dual-layer metaphors in the stories did not directly point to the real meaning, but to something far simpler. The tenor of this first metaphor became the vehicle for a second metaphor, which pointed to the real intelligence. In the current example, the princess's boat, the He'ershingenmosiken soap, and the Glutton's Sea formed a metaphor for a paper boat driven by soap. The paper boat, in turn, pointed to curvature propulsion. Previous attempts at decipherment had failed largely due to people's habitual belief that the stories only involved a single layer of metaphors to hide the real message.
>
> The two-dimensional metaphors were a technique used to resolve the ambiguities introduced by literary devices employed in conveying strategic intelligence. After a dual-layer metaphor, a single-layer supporting metaphor was added to confirm the meaning of the dual-layer metaphor. In the current example, the curved snow-wave paper and the ironing required to flatten it served as a metaphor for curved space, confirming the interpretation of the soap-driven boat. If one viewed the stories as a two-dimensional plane, the dual-layer metaphor only provided one coordinate; the supporting single-layer metaphor provided a second coordinate that fixed the interpretation on the plane. Thus, this single-layer

metaphor was also called the bearing coordinate. Viewed by itself, the bearing coordinate seemed meaningless, but once combined with the dual-layer metaphor, it resolved the inherent ambiguities in literary language.

"A subtle and sophisticated system," a PIA specialist said admiringly.[67]

Literary scholars in the novel find Yun Tianming's storytelling a unique system of all systems of storytelling, and his textuality a marvelous structure of all structures—just like the "perfect SF" one might hope for, certainly what Liu wishes to achieve. Adding credit to Liu as a great storyteller himself, Yuan Tianming's narrative does not just function as a plotline but also forms a self-reflection on the novel itself and creates a metafictional fold in the "Three-Body" trilogy. But all the theories only testify to the aesthetic power of the storytelling, while the interpretations do not solve the puzzles for practical purposes. Many elements and plotlines in Yun Tianming's stories are inexplicable to those who try to pick up the meaning from his narrative. Therefore, ironically, Yun Tianming's storytelling defeats its own purposes. It is appreciated for its beauty instead of its encoded messages. He proves to be a talented storyteller who makes sure of the coherence and integrity of the stories, which have priority over the pragmatic interpretations.

Through Yuan Tianming's case, Liu Cixin also teaches us, ultimately, how to read SF. Reading SF requires relinquishing habitual belief in conventional thinking and fixed ideas. It requires attention to the literalness on the surface of the language that constitutes the macro details used to construct the world images. The metaphors and figures, their interactions, and the storytelling itself—all these elements construct the virtual form of the wonder. The surface meanings are perhaps virtual embodiments of the deeper meanings, but the deeper meanings cannot be understood in the mundane context of everyday reality. Those are cryptic knowledge—estranging scientific rules, unconventional mathematical equations, superhuman technological programming that are the foundation of a totally different world. The stories are the virtual embodiment of a brave new world, which is as wondrous as science fictionality itself. Nearly all the readers in the novel believe that there must be some references in the stories to the real, but the references are no longer important when they are lost in the labyrinth of the language itself. Storytelling becomes the wonder, not what it encodes.

Therefore, for Cheng Xin, Yun Tianming's fairy tales can also be read as just amazing stories representing love. In this sense, the fairy tales fails to save humans, but they revive Cheng Xin's heart, so that she has the willpower to live until the end of the universe. Cheng Xin's poetic heart recalls Liu's earlier image of the Poetry Cloud, the embodiment of information that is otherwise meaningless. The Poetry Cloud is just another virtual form of memory, like Cheng Xin's memoir in *Remembrance of the Earth's Past*. These moments link different stages of Liu Cixin's writing career as a testimony to his consistent engagement with literary imagination as the only way to make the invisible a narrative, where darkness gleams—it becomes the light of the universe. Liu says that he writes about the worst possible universe, but he also leaves us the space to imagine the best. The SF vision of the amoral, inhuman, posthuman universe takes a virtual form that eventually testifies to human agency. The magic of Liu Cixin's art of fiction is that when the invisible sublime collapses into a flat picture, filled with unreal and wondrous macro details, through a virtual form of storytelling about the truth of the universe, science becomes fiction.

5

THE POWER OF DARKNESS IN HAN SONG

Mythology of the Chthonic

In Han Song's novel *Subway*, a character named Xiao Wu 小武, reaches the deepest level of a labyrinthine, tenebrous underground world beneath a Chinese city's subway system. He witnesses an infernal scene: rapid torrents rushing along the riverbanks toss dead bodies up and down; from a thick red mist emerge crowds of aquatic mammals, desperately trying to use their torsos to block the torrents from flushing down the corpses; immediately descending are a myriad of demonic flying creatures, ruthlessly beating and pushing nails into the heads of those mammals, who emit chilling long howls of pain. The aquatic mammals all have human faces, among which Xiao Wu recognizes some notable truth seekers, from Homer to Socrates to Shakespeare to Rousseau and from Euclid to Newton to Freud and Einstein. Xiao Wu feels the urge to join these miserable, struggling mammals but cannot muster his courage.[1]

According to what he read in the surviving fragments of an old intellectual journal called *Dushu* 讀書[2] (referring to an actual influential journal among Chinese intellectuals during the 1980s–'90s), those flying demons evolved or devolved from passengers stuck in the ceaselessly running subway trains. This entire mystifying subway system was built in a remote historical moment nobody remembers—the days when, it was said, sleepwalking youths, all dressed in green, roamed the land, putting nails into the foreheads of kneeling elders.[3]

Xiao Wu functions as Han's alter ego, representing a truth-seeking inner voice. Witnessing this chthonic battle, Xiao Wu imagines that the tortured aquatic mammals are only virtual bodies of those great scientists and intellectuals who have left our world and created their own utopia in another infinitely immense universe. Where their spirits have gone is not at all understandable to those perverted, winged inhuman mutants, trapped in a vicious cycle of senseless endeavors and facing the eternal return of a dark, infernal force. Xiao Wu is overwhelmed by fear but still opens his eyes to see, trying to resume his original role in the story as a truth investigator. To figure out what has happened to the world, he goes deeper and deeper into the underground until he feels a big bang—stars exploding, earth shaking, darkness flashing, and new babies born, with billions of eyes "combining both male and female, occidental and oriental features," looking "like beasts fed by blood," "a new species that has never existed in the history of evolution, witlessly, mercilessly, and lawlessly staring at what appears to be the end of time."[4] Xiao Wu cries out with his last breath, "Children, save me!" inverting the famous last sentence of Lu Xun's "A Madman's Diary" ("Save the children!"). But the future posthuman "children" will not save him; instead, "the shameless laughter of the infants bursts out from the void, crashes onto the invisible shores, and generates lascivious echoes."[5]

The above summary epitomizes a key pattern of the master plot of many of Han Song's novels and stories: an ordinary person like Xiao Wu finds himself in a suddenly estranging situation, cut off from daily life; he has to overcome the fear of seeing and look for truth in the dark, and the truth he finds only appears to be even more murky and inexplicable in our ordinary reality. The entire world is unveiled as nothing but an illusion, densely encoded with signs and symbols amounting to a virtual image of a more truthful world unfolding above the ultimate emptiness. The universe is empty, void, absurd, like history, with black holes that suck all meanings in. Han Song condenses a large number of referents corresponding to both Chinese and Western historical and cultural contexts, producing an allegorical narrative about the collapse of reason and rationality. The sciences and the humanities both fail in the battle against insanity and inhumanity, giving way to an apocalyptic, techno-engineered posthuman future that wipes out all human memories and rational meanings without an exit for redemption.

This particular part of *Subway* also exemplifies the aesthetics of Han Song's SF, which I read as anatomical, confronting the hidden dimensions of Chinese reality and cutting into the core of the dominant power. I have noted his emphasis on the fear of seeing, and yet his SF writing crystalizes a courageous seeing, which is to "gaze back" to the gaze of the power. His gaze follows abstruse signs and inexplicable symbols, estranging coordinates in a chaotic cosmos, all the way down to the chthonic, where his characters witness an evil arising that has a self-serving purpose: to ensure its own continuity and posterity. This evil core of the power is purely self-adoring, self-performing, selfish, and narcissistic. Overcoming the fear of seeing, Han Song brings us face to face with the truthful banality of evil, the hollow nature of the system or its incarnation in algorithms that has no interest other than its perverted existential urge and prolonged existential crisis, because, after all, it is nothing but a void.

Immersed in the supernatural, the unknowable, and the inexplicable, Han Song's SF vision creates a mythology of the chthonic, which brings readers into unfathomable darkness. He reveals a mesmerizing, mystic force coming from below and portrays a phantom world consisting of tombs, ruins, the underground, the deep, and the abyss, filled with ghosts, monsters, mutants, cannibals, posthumans, half-humans, and other estranged forms of existence. Han Song's imaginary realms are grotesque, uncanny, melancholic, graphically violent, anatomically explicit, and biologically discomforting. They are built upon the modern world's degenerate and disintegrated self-image collapsing from within, as a perverted postapocalyptic counterimage to the self-asserted prosperity and progress. Han Song's characters are never heroes; fragile and imperfect, they have the courage to overcome the fear of seeing and confront the dark cosmic disorder represented as hidden in the depth of fearsome world images—tombs of the universe, the abyss of the red ocean, the underground labyrinth beneath a modern metropolis, or the eternal reincarnations of the hospital. Han Song's SF world-building makes the hidden darkness visible in various virtual forms, either a shadowy phantom paralleling the presentable reality or an abysmal deep opening in the uncanny.

Situated in contemporary China's political and cultural context, Han Song's parodic narrative points to the futility of hope and betrays the ultimate vanity of Panglossian optimism. His extravagant style foregrounds the theatricality—the performative nature—of all narratives dictated by the power, certainly those "good China stories" about the nation's triumph and prosperity. With the world as virtual, technologies self-serving, and narratives introverted, Han Song spares no effort in a self-reflective literary experiment to narrate "deep" stories that lose their own semantic purposes; he cuts off the connections between signs and things, subverting the glossy surface reality to unearth the terrifying chthonic truth, and decouple the grandiose images of the nation and the truthfulness of a world in crisis. Filling the gap between language and reality with wondrous, often nightmarish visions, Han Song consciously makes his narrative a heterotopian textual space that foregrounds the present but invisible predicament, the impending inevitable catastrophes, and the eternal return of the haunting past.

Han Song is one of the most productive Chinese SF writers, and only a part of his writings has been published, including more than dozens of short stories and eight major novels: *Mars Over America* (2000), *Red Ocean* (2004), *Subway* (2010), *High-Speed Rail* 高鐵 (2012), *Tracks* 軌道 (2013), *Hospital* (2016), *Exorcism* 驅魔 (2017), and *Dead Souls* 亡靈 (2018). Han Song is also a poet, a journalist, a chronicler of everyday events, and a writer of all sorts of social commentaries, ranging from editorials to blogs and very short microblogs on a daily basis. This chapter, with very limited length, cannot do justice to his entire oeuvre; I will mainly present a study of the power of darkness that defines and energizes his unique SF vision, which I summarize as a mythology of the chthonic. The chapter begins with a comparison of Han Song to Lu Xun and then focuses on case studies in three prominent works: *Red Ocean*, *Subway*, and the "Hospital" trilogy (*Hospital*; *Exorcism*; and *Dead Souls*). I will save discussion of his first novel, *Mars Over America*, for the next chapter in relation to the variations of utopia.

THE ANATOMICAL AESTHETICS

Han Song began writing SF in the early 1980s, when he was a teenager; his more mature writings, produced in the late 1980s, beginning with "Tombs of the Universe" (discussed in chapter 1), helped resurrect the genre and pioneered the new wave during the 1990s. By profession, he is a senior journalist working for China's official Xinhua News Agency, specializing in processing news feeds for foreign media.[6] He spends his spare time, mostly nighttime, writing SF stories and novels.[7] The contrast between his daytime job and nocturnal career creates a meaningful gap between two modes of writing: his journalism must follow the protocol to tell "good China" stories, showing only positive images in the daylight; whatever cannot be shown in the day and belongs to the night enters his SF, a literary dreamscape that unfolds an invisible China, a Sinotopia coming from the depths of China's state-constructed proper self-image.

Han Song's style has been called Kafkaesque, for his nightmarish paradoxes, and compared to Philip K. Dick's, for his enchantment (and disenchantment) with technologies and abstruse, experimentalist literary language. Here I would suggest that his name can even be mentioned together with that of H. P. Lovecraft (1890–1937) for his Cthulhuian mythological, mysterious world-buildings.[8] Above all, Han Song is comparable to Lu Xun for their shared obsession with the darkness, fascination with cannibalism, and interest in speculation and mythologies.[9] In a literary system marked by these authors, Han Song's SF imagination represents an avant-garde aesthetics. He integrates the poetics of the invisible into his world-building, with an audacious effort to see beneath the surface reality, going further than most other writers, both SF and mainstream, in creating an uncanny, surreal, absurd way of storytelling that discards all doctrines and certainties.

To better explain Han Song's aesthetics, we can take a look at the difference between him and Liu Cixin. Liu Cixin confesses to being a technologist and committed to scientism.[10] Han Song instead more clearly concentrates on aesthetic, ethical, and religious reflections on the use or abuse of science as well as the power of technology, such as high-speed transportation and artificial intelligence, and the technology of power, such as surveillance, algorithms, and total control. Their world-buildings are starkly different. Liu Cixin bases his world-building on speculative alterations of scientific or social regulations and, with macro details, produces sublime world images with wondrous clarity. Han Song's SF writings drive deep into the inner space, and his world images, filled with ghostly murky figures or graphically anatomical details, are unsettling, uncanny, uncertain, and their representation never settle in clarity and stability. These two most important SF authors in contemporary China thus take opposite approaches to representing the invisible as the core of their SF worlds. Liu Cixin approaches the invisible scientifically and systematically, creating a vision full of dazzling details about the cosmic sublime. Han Song casts his nightmarish gaze into the abysmal darkness of the chthonic and resorts to what I call excessively grotesque "anatomical aesthetics."

Han and Liu represent the opposite extremes of the aesthetics of Chinese SF. The gravitational center of Liu Cixin's world-building is the sublime, and he approaches it through writing science into fiction. His artistic method can be summarized as reducing dimensions to achieve clarity in the unfolding of "macro details" on an astronomical scale. Han Song's literary vision increases the dimensions of literary representation by excessively complicating, multilayering, and disorienting his narrative and adding infinitely extended chains of significance to the hermeneutic space in the fictional text. Han depicts the world in its irreducible complexities, multilayered images, and baroquely folded anatomical details, together with abundant paradoxes and puzzles.

Compared with Liu Cixin's splendid, expansive universe, Han Song's densely packed cosmos may seem nothing but a human body, or even the infinitely complex surface of a decayed human body, a broken cyborg, or a posthuman limb. The way he creates world images is like surgery cutting into the flesh to reach the chiasm of different dimensions, where he tries to observe and represent what the surface conceals. This is, first of all, embodied in the style of his language, which is usually very dense, filled with figurative discourse related to body parts and internal organs. If "a bottomless abyss exists in every inch" in Liu Cixin's depiction of the hyperdimensional universe in astronomical density, there is a bottomless abyss in every cell of the human body or its surface, which opens to the profound depth in a world of wonders and mysteries.

For example, *Mars Over America* depicts an American boy with a tail. His name is Newman 紐曼, a proper identity for him as a bioengineered product, a posthuman new man. His tail is not a useless extra limb, but an essential organ that contains the entire national memory of the United States, in which all the information about the glories of American democracy, industrial prosperity, and popular culture is digitally installed. By touching the tail, the postapocalyptic Americans can feel immensely happy and proud.[11] This tail is described in its biological details too, with anatomical details about its estranging appearance and inner structure. Metaphorically it has a densely overdetermined meaning, but in Han Song's text, the anatomical depiction of the physical tail is more literal than metaphorical. The tail opens to a "bottomless abyss" that tears apart the surface reality.

The uses of anatomical details are abundant in almost Han Song's every story and novel. In *Subway*, he portrays a woman using a string of unconventional metaphors so densely entangled that the language obscures what they stand for: "from the torso filled with fluids circulating throughout her body comes a voice suggestive of thick meat, which echoes the vibrating inside her hollow chest as light and small as a bird."[12] In another story, "Guidebook to Hunting Beautiful Women" 美女狩獵指南 (2014), Han Song thus describes an orgy combining sex, cannibalism, and death: while a beautiful woman is being eaten alive, she "cheerfully and desperately screeches, like a horse being castrated, dying in extreme pain. Xiao Zhao responds with punctuated sounds, which soon turn into ghostly outcries. Amid all these busy sounds, the statue of the Bodhisattva wobbles and tumbles, quickly shaking like a masturbating woman."[13] The paragraph is a thicket of linguistic insurgents: the woman, the man, and the goddess are all described with excessively erotic or graphically explicit phrases referring to human flesh, forming a linguistic orgy without a clear image or expression.

This story, written long before its official publication in 2014, is filled with grotesque anatomical details about rape, killing, graphic violence, and cannibalism. Xiao Zhao again, an everyman/the author's alter ego, is lured to join a game that takes place on a remote, mysterious tropical island, where cyborgs are produced as beautiful women, ready to serve customers, satisfying their sexual desires, including raping, violating, and killing. At the center of this perverted "daydream" programmed to cater to wealthy men, who feel powerful by manipulating others, is a dark force that goes out of control, losing its purposes. The story goes on, but Xiao Zhao soon finds something terribly wrong. The beautiful women are not the prey but prey on those arrogant, vulgar men; and they are not human but like dinosaurs, hungry for human flesh.[14] It is an astonishing fact that this story eventually was published without being censored. Its very nature as a SF text represents a subversion: a gaze back to the game of power, a confrontation with the invisible dark secret that is deliberately kept (and guarded as a commercial secret), and a revelation of the self-defeating purposelessness of the power mechanism itself. The anatomical aesthetics of this story, repulsive and offensive, exactly corresponds to a literary surgery; it is like a clinical anatomy of the deliberately hidden power, pointing to its malfunctioning or self-contradiction. The anatomical details concretize the fear of seeing, but simultaneously make Han Song's fearless gaze back to the power a distinctive feature in almost all his published novels and stories.

The ultimate strength of Han Song's SF aesthetics does not lie in the surface density. Rather, those dense anatomical details, which appear obscure and impenetrable in extravagant descriptions, form a Neo-Baroque literary space in which the details explode into meaning-making moments. What Han Song has so far done in all his writings is to anatomize this mysterious force inch by inch, cell by cell, opening up the inner space within the power structure, ushering us into the darkness. Han Song's anatomical aesthetics give birth to all sorts of dark images—deaths, carcasses, mutilated bodies, mutants, ghosts, beasts, demons, dark tombs, the chthonic underground, the nocturne insanity, and the abysmal hospital—all the incarnations of the evil that is born of the foundational lack of imagination beyond the given reality. All that the evil is good at is to conceal and hide its own truth, which is absolute nothingness. After overcoming the fear of seeing, Han Song brings us to see that the terrifying evil is only a selfish, self-pitying, and self-serving virtual form that does not even correspond to the conventionally perceivable reality.

In chapter 1, I have analyzed Han Song's "fear of seeing," the key moment that shows both the seeing of power and the power of seeing. Han's SF writings simultaneously unleash the horror from the profound depth of the unseen, an eternal evil, and exemplify the courage to confront the gaze of power. Seeing through the fearful façade of all the dark realms, Han Song performs surgery on reality and rips it open to show us bare evil, a deep void that assumes its own glories and strengths above nothingness. Han Song's anatomy of the evil reveals that the darkest evil is an eternally evolving, self-performing, self-adoring, ultimately self-serving impulse. In Han Song's words in *Hospital*, it is a self-loving Indian peafowl, an egoist medical punk, a self-possessing algorithm that does not aim to treat patients but serves the sole purpose of perpetuating its own existence. "This was the intellectual foundation of the hospital's long-term prosperity.... According to the vocabulary of medical punk, 'to live' is 'to live for the good of the hospital,' or rather 'in order for the hospital to live on.'"[15] Later in this chapter, I will present a close study of Han Song's "Hospital" trilogy, which I read as a deliberate shadow image of Liu Cixin's "Three-Body" trilogy, a chthonic inversion of the sublime. Different from Liu Cixin's "macro details" that expand the grandeur and splendor of the external universe to its maximum, Han Song's anatomical details open up a folded internal universe within the textualized body, where truths are concealed and encoded, but now enlivened and metamorphized in all sorts of labyrinthine narratives that usher us into the darkness.

INTO THE DARKNESS

Focusing on Han Song's interest in the chthonic, I refer to Istvan Csicsery-Ronay Jr.'s notion of the science fictional inversion of the sublime, or the science fictional wonder. This inversion is found in what he describes as the science fictional grotesque: a situation in which the sublime collapses, giving way to a mysterious subversion, a disruption of the sense of wonder.[16] Csicsery-Ronay Jr.'s idea goes further back to Mikhail Bakhtin, who defines the subversive nature of the grotesque in the face of the so-called "cosmic terror," the oppressive order of the aristocracy and hierarchy that were taken for granted as the order of the Heaven in the medieval period:

> The cosmic terror is not mystic in the strict sense of the word; rather it is the fear of that which is materially huge and cannot be overcome by force. It is used by all religious systems to oppress man and his consciousness. Even the most ancient images of folklore express the struggle against fear, against the memories of the past, and the apprehension of future calamities, but folk images relating to this struggle helped develop true human fearlessness. The struggle against cosmic terror in all its forms and manifestations did not rely on abstract hope or on the eternal spirit, but on the material principle in man himself.... He became aware of the cosmos within himself.[17]

Although Bakhtin does not use the term "sublime," Csicsery-Ronay Jr. sees in the cosmic terror the science fictional incarnations of lofty, sublime ideas and ideologies. The cosmic terror indicates the sublime's intrusion into the mundane, imposing hieratic systems and oppressive ideologies to the everyday life. But the grotesque represents a subversive dark force that dares to speak back to the cosmic terror and twist it in parodic, inverted images. In this sense, the grotesqueness of Han Song's world, such as the "Hospital" nightmare, can be viewed as an inverted image of the "Three-Body" universe, positing a challenge to the signature image of contemporary Chinese SF. The most frequent locus of Han Song's stories is the chaotic and anarchic underground. His anatomical aesthetics darkens the monumentality of the prevailing mainstream of Chinese literature and art. In the context of our study, even Liu Cixin's monumental cosmic wonders collapse in Han Song's dark worlds. The macro details of Liu's sublime SF dissolve in Han Song's chthonic, subversive anatomical SF aesthetics.

Han Song's unique way of creating SF worlds may have less to do with science, which Liu Cixin reveres wholeheartedly, than a vigorous dialogue with Lu Xun. To simply compare Liu Cixin's and Han Song's worlds may lead to a contestation between Liu's apparently committed scientism and Han's humanistic reservation about the effect of scientism, but if we situate this comparison in relation to Lu Xun, we may realize that what should be considered is more complex than a clear dichotomy. David Der-wei Wang explains how Lu Xun's views on science, superstition, and mythology contribute to a multifaceted discursive space for literary imagination: Lu Xun finds the "'true roots' of science in the conception of myth, and he lashes out at those who sanction science as the only source of truth and debunk mythology as superstition." Furthermore, the opposition between science and humanism is a hypocritical self-asserted "mistruth," and "the new literature Lu Xun pursued must be understood in highly dialogical terms. He was after all nurtured in both the newest form of scientific education and the time-honored storytelling ambience of myths, tales, and superstitions."[18] In other words, science and mythology are not differentiated by a binary opposition but can blend in a nonbinary coexistence. When Han Song's work is viewed in the same terms, these observations inspire a more inclusive approach to consider more dynamic interactions between science and myth, which characterize Han Song's writings, making him a true heir to Lu Xun.

Among contemporary Chinese SF writers, Han Song is the most self-conscious disciple of Lu Xun, inclined to succumb to the allures of ghosts, dreams, tombs, and nightmares that for both authors represent a discontent with science—or reason and rationality. In *Gate of Darkness*, T. A. Hsia emphasizes the power of darkness that, as an antithesis of the enlightenment and revolution, nevertheless attracted Lu Xun, who "carried some ghosts on his back." T. A. Hsia thus characterizes Lu Xun's writing, particularly his most indecipherable and abstruse work, *Wild Grass* 野草 (1927):

> The twilight hours hold ghostly shapes, shadowy whispers and other wonders, and phantasmata which are apt to be dismissed in the impatient waiting for the dawn. As a chronicler of those hours, Lu Hsün wrote with fine perception and a subtlety and profundity of feeling, qualities which were usually lost to him when he spoke as a conscious rebel. His treatment of the darker themes is particularly important since no one really knows how long the twilight hours will last, if not on the surface of the earth, at least in the heart of man.[19]

Han Song may have followed Lu Xun to enter the gate of darkness. His SF world-building is grounded in the rich soil of Lu Xunsque metaphors and allegories. He enlivens the dark consciousness in new wave SF, which is posited in reaction to the cosmic terror, all that is too bright or too mighty. Resisting the cosmic terror means daring to gaze back to the blinding glories of the sublime ideology, let go the fear of seeing, and execute individual agency in observation, reflection, anatomy, surgery—and above all, in Han Song's case, imagination and writing. The cosmic terror and SF's overcoming the fear of seeing are the foundations of Han Song's storytelling: the sublime manifestations of power are counterbalanced by humble human resistance to the system's total control. Han Song's SF writings make a powerful inversion of the grandiose, sublime world-building based on reason and ideology and open the gate of darkness to release monstrosity, insanity, and irrationality.

To make a parodic appropriation of Liu Cixin's words, "Like a god, create a world, then depict it" in astronomical details, I suggest that Han

Song creates a world, like Lu Xun, and then depicts it in anatomical details. Taking many of the key metaphors and symbols from Lu Xun's fictional and poetic writings, particularly "A Madman's Diary" and *Wild Grass*, he transforms them into SF constructs, including an entire species of cannibals, posthuman futuristic children, demonic power pretending to be human in the good hell, the diseased and deceased nation administered by inhuman algorithms, forms of transportation that are advanced versions of the "iron house," tombs floating everywhere in the universe, medicine that saves both body and soul but ultimately serves to reincarnate "dead souls," and the mindscape of the contemporary everyman driven to insanity by the terrifying truths of inexplicable phenomena surrounding them. The abysmal nihilism that Han Song evokes through depicting the future human degeneration and the pervasive darkness of the world is closely related to Lu Xun's thought.

Lu Xun's reflections on history, which is not a progressive linear evolution, have been continued in Han Song's writing and provided the foundational motivations for his world-building. Han Song represents history as a movement of eternal return, a repetitive sequence of doomed failures, a regression rather than progress, which makes change an illusion. The agents of history are a series of surreally entangled pairs of different forces: religion and technology, revolution and reaction, governance and anarchy, evolution and devolution.

There is also a deceptively superstitious, enchanting pattern in Han Song's questioning of science and technology on moral and transcendental bases, combined with a subtle Buddhist notion about karma, which does not impose determinism but rather enlightens the human mind to the illusive nature of all matters. This is another bridge between Lu Xun and Han Song, for Lu Xun also has a Buddhist component blended in his visions of life and death, tradition and modernity, reality and truth. In Han Song's worlds, the surface reality is ephemeral, elusive, and deceptive, and the journey into the darkness is never teleological, and it moves toward a revelation rather than revolution.

Compared with his contemporaries, Han Song tells stories that are more strikingly grotesque and surreal, and he aestheticizes the darkness and horror, showing the viciousness of the system's false claims to technological and political determinism. On a larger scale, he shows the difficulty or near futility of locating meanings in the grand design of human and cosmic affairs—if there is such a design. Various forms of dreamscape and nightmare in Han Song's writings create an anatomical literary space where the darkness comes into light.

A POSTHUMAN MYTHOLOGY: CANNIBALISM AND CHTHULUCENE

Han Song's first published novel was *Mars Over America*, but he started writing *Red Ocean* earlier, from 1997 to 2004. Even though it was published later,[20] *Red Ocean* was still his first notable imaginary world, a posthuman future world populated by cannibalistic aquatic people, which sets up the fundamental framework for a chthonic world image. This novel presents a massive narrative, which unfolds as both an imaginary historiography and a self-invented mythology, surrounding two interrelated questions: Why are the aquatic people cannibals? What is the truth of this world? There are multiple references to actual historical events between China and Europe as well as some of the most important motifs in modern Chinese literature, including Lu Xun's metaphorical discourse on cannibalism and the iron house, all fabricated as signs and symbols in the dreamlike textual space. The novel also touches upon metaphysical and aesthetic questions about reality and illusion, landscape and dreamscape, truth and storytelling.

Red Ocean consists of four volumes. The first part, "Our Present," depicts the posthuman creatures "living in the dark abyss at the bottom of the ocean."[21] This part of the narrative takes the form of the bildungsroman, but it is a bildungsroman of a cannibal. The protagonist is an aquatic boy named Sea Star 海星. He survives hunger, the loss of his mother, and bloody conflicts between clans and races; grows up to become a cannibal like the other adults; and eventually becomes the king of the ocean through conquering other clans of cannibals and reforming the way of cannibalism. The world of the aquatic people is forever dimmed by the opaque red seawater, and they are curious about where the red seawater comes from. Sea Star has a strange gift that enables him to see phantom moments from the past, when the sea had a glamorous blue color, and a mysterious call leads him to the gigantic but deserted ruins of the once prosperous "underwater metropolis." Through these visionary moments, Sea Star looks into the face of the past without any clear knowledge about it, due to the aquatic people's epistemological limitations. All he knows is how to hunt and mate in this barbarous underwater world. The abysmal scenes of cannibalism are portrayed with both an infernal color and a mythological touch. Sea Star comes to know the myth and history about their species from a mysterious half-vegetation sea monster who sings an inexplicable song that is said to have been passed down from eons before. The song itself served as a textbook teaching about the ethics of cannibalism through telling a historical story about who the aquatic people are. Modern readers can easily understand that this is an epic story about China, with the sole focus on its five thousand years of cannibalism—exactly what Lu Xun sums up in "A Madman's Diary": "eating people."

If we are familiar with Lu Xun and other enlightenment intellectuals' modern critique of cannibalism as a total sign of the Chinese tradition, then Han Song's narrative estranges this sign and whitewash its treacherous meaning. Inspired by the song that stands for the entire knowledge of historiography, Sea Star invents a "civilization" founded upon cannibalism. He designs a new system of living in which the men will no longer eat women but keep them as farm animals to produce babies for his clan to eat, thus ushering the aquatic people into a new age of "agriculture and farm civilization." Sea Star's civilization is not less cannibalistic than before, for the main food is still human flesh. But Sea Star is able to form a stable base and unite all the remaining clans in the ocean. When he grows older, he gradually realizes that he has never understood the truth of the world. To him, the smartest among his people, the world contains too many mysteries, too much darkness, and too little certainty. He lives long enough to see the mass extinction of the cannibalistic aquatic people, while the red ocean finally becomes quiet. He senses that the end of history arrives—here ends the first volume.[22]

The first part of the novel outlines the mythology and historiography of the aquatic people but offers no sensible explanations about either cannibalism or the red ocean. The second volume, "Our Past," goes back in historical time. This part is narrated as a series of anecdotes, folk stories, and allegories about the history of the aquatic people, their kingdoms, their mythologies, and their wars, which all occurred before Sea Star's time. There are numerous attempts to explain the origin of the red ocean, but none reaches a definitive conclusion. The red ocean seems unfathomably dark and deadly, but it also appears to be the ultimate force creating life. Several stories present a paradoxical relationship between dream and reality: the aquatic people dream of those walking on the land but find out that the land people dream about them.[23] Whose dream is the dream? Whose is reality? The loss of distinction between the two is a reminder of Zhuangzi's butterfly dream.

In the aquatic people's pursuit of truth, the red ocean gradually loses its significance as their "reality." The paradoxical questioning regarding truth and falsity reciprocally contrasts them, and each eliminates the other's significance. All four volumes of the novel show that truth does not come to the aquatic people as the real but as a virtual, dreamy illusion, which is ever changing, uncertain and unreliable. This situation recalls the Platonic allegory about the cavemen and shadows. But if the red ocean is all that they have, which means there is no "real world" accessible beyond the shadow and illusion, the novel achieves a self-conscious performance to pronounce its own fantasy as a mythology, a virtual inversion of the readers' knowledge about the world outside Han Song's text. Thus, Han Song posits a profound challenge to readers' comfort-seeking expectations, with representations of cannibalism, transgression, catastrophe, and apocalypse as the "normal" to complicate the fundamental ethics of being human. From the (im)moral choice Sea Star makes in favor of cannibalism to the questioning of whether the aquatic people are living in a dreamscape, the narrative tests the ethics of seeing, thinking, and storytelling.

The third and fourth volumes of the novel go farther back into history, which is first the "present time" of the twenty-first century, and then the historical past of ancient China. Both the present-day world and the ancient world have gone through estranging transformations and appeared to be uncannily puzzling. The third volume, "The Past of Our Past," outlines how the aquatic people are created by humans as biologically reengineered new species who can adapt to the undersea environment and thus survive the attacks of the mysterious "huaite ren" coming from the moon. In one chapter of this volume, the strange song about cannibalism that enlightens Sea Star, eons of years in the future, is invented by a delusional seaman who is stationed at an oil platform in the South China Sea. If there is an epiphany for readers, it is that cannibalism is not an instinct, but an invention. The only canon connecting the contemporary world and the chthonic future, or the only knowledge passed onto the posthuman offspring, is a literal interpretation of the cultural critique of Chinese tradition in Lu Xun's "A Madman's Diary."

The last volume, titled "Our Future," however, is about the more distant past than the future to the generation of the Sea Star. The central chapter of this volume concerns Zheng He's 郑和 (1371–1433) nautical expeditions. Han Song rewrites it into an alternate history in which Zheng He does not stop when he reaches Africa but goes farther around Cape Hope and eventually arrives in Europe. Liu Cixin, incidentally, also wrote about Zheng He's voyages in a short story, "The Western Ocean" 西洋 (2002),[24] in which Zheng He's arrival in Europe changes world history, and therefore in 1997, the handover between Great Britain and China (the Ming Dynasty) is to return Northern Ireland, a Chinese colony, to the British people. Liu Cixin's story can be read as a poignant postcolonial critique. But in *Red Ocean*, Han Song has no clear agenda such as taking revenge or pursuing poetic justice. In his narrative, even if history is changed after Zhang He arrives in Europe, the outcome is the same .

During the long voyage, Zheng He is haunted by a repeated nightmare about his homeland, the Great Ming Dynasty, being wiped out by a mysterious more advanced civilization. He consults a magician and learns that he needs to ready a fleet of warships to send from Europe to China at a future date when China is in predicament. The magician warns him that his rescue fleet must be the second one to arrive in China, for the first fleet to arrive from Europe will attack China. Only the second fleet will save China. Zheng He successfully commits a Portuguese prince, Henry (1394–1460), to his plan to save China, and after stationing a team of his loyal soldiers in Europe to prepare the rescue fleet, he sails back to China but dies at sea. Decades later, Christopher Columbus declares that he is going to sail to China by traveling farther into the west. Zheng He's loyal soldiers immediately persuade the Portuguese to send their fleet, the second fleet, to China by circling around the Cape of Good Hope. News soon comes that Columbus has reached a new land, and Zhang He's soldiers know that their fleet now will be the first to reach China. All these overcautious strategies incidentally create an unexpected domino effect, which achieves exactly what Zheng He dreamed in his nightmares. Zheng He's intervention in the historical progress sets it off toward the inevitable clashes between Europe and China, because while Columbus sailed to America, the fleet he sets up became the first one to reach China.[25]

It is not until we read the last chapters of the novel when we can finally piece together the history of the aquatic people. It all starts with Zheng He's encounter with the Europeans, whom he calls "huaite ren" (懷特人, a transliteration of the Chinese word for "white men"). The huaite ren later use Zheng He's techniques to build their own powerful fleet. They ascend to superpower status on the sea and bring war to China, exactly as Zheng He feared and tried to avoid. This war, in Han Song's alternative history, had a much larger effect and led to the fall of the entire East Asian civilization. The aquatic humans that appear in the first two parts of the novel are the posthuman offspring of Asians, designed by the Japanese, who also build the "underwater metropolis" where they hide when the white men control both the land and the sky in East Asia. What happens to the white men remains untold in the narrative, but the aquatic humans gradually degenerate into cannibals who no longer remember their origin. Their only connection to the past is the song of cannibalism, an epic narrative about Chinese history that centers on the "evil" of Chinese civilization, as Lu Xun envisions, but this "evil" is now purified and venerated as the sacred mythology. History comes full circle, beginning as a myth and ending as mythology.

In *Red Ocean*, cannibalism is the unchanged part of the aquatic civilization, a necessary means for survival. As an ironic response to Lu Xun's call for "saving children" in "A Madman's Diary," children are farmed and eaten. *Red Ocean* makes cannibalism the definitive part of human nature. For Sea Star, it is not at all a sin to eat other people, but a necessity. His coming of age is marked by his awakening to cannibalism, which enlightens him to the only spiritual heritage that the aquatic people have. For them, the history of man is a neat history of cannibalism. Histories of the past, the past's past, and the "future" that is *still* the past all serve to justify the mandate of "eating people." Through equating cannibalism to civilization, Han Song's version of history empties both the moral values and the scientific criteria attached to historiography and presents the history of humanity completely as a mythology that operates contrary to the principles of reason and enlightenment that Lu Xun and his comrades tried to establish as a New Culture to the Chinese people. The novel shatters what has been known in the modern times and makes all human knowledge uncertain.

To strengthen this sense, the novel also intentionally plays with the "teleology" of historical narrative. For example, the part concerning Zheng He is presented as a seemingly overdetermined step in the history of Sino-Western contact. It foregrounds the deadlock of a historical situation that simply does not change even in different scenarios. But the way it is presented shows that the overdetermination and uncertainty are two sides of one coin. This part of the narrative employs both historiography and mythology, making a detour from our familiar account, using conspiracy theories to create an alternate history, but all at once discrediting both accounts by unveiling the mysterious contingency beneath the inevitability of historical determinism. Even if Zheng He's entire operation is meant to keep Europeans at bay, what happened in real history will still happen, as if it were decided by destiny. However, Han Song's narrative offers two options for different interpretations: loyalty to the real that denotes destiny, or enchantment with fantasy that directs a changed, invisible route toward the same end but also suggests the beginning of a totally different historical writing about "Our Present," "Our Past," "The Past of Our Past," and "Our Future," an otherworldly version of history. If Zheng He's "discovery of Europe" and the Europeans' invasion of China have to happen in the same universe, the narrative combining both speculation and historical facts turns historical writing into mythology, which dismantles the predetermined direction of historical movement. Instead of a linear historical narrative, what emerges is chaos. It is the contingency, instead of determination, that produces an outcome that is inevitable.

Han Song's *Red Ocean* is one of the first Chinese SF works to present an entire world system based on posthuman imagery. It may have been a response to the call of Cthulhu. This supernatural, prehistoric, and oceanic image, which is currently an essential part of a mythology about an invisible undersea world, was first created by H. P. Lovecraft in his "new weird" story "The Call of Cthulhu" (1926). Cthulhu, a giant monster that comes from outer space before the emergence of humanity on Earth, is contained under the sea in the Pacific. Some artists' collective dream of the city of Cthulhu, and its effect on their mentality give clues to scientists who gradually gain knowledge about this secret, demonstrating an otherworldly civilization, more ancient than the human's but invisible in the world.[26] Lovecraft called himself a rationalist but argued about the limits of reason and enlightenment, which, he believed, only show humanity's negligibility in the face of the infinity and magnitude of the cosmic unknown. The collective dreaming of Cthulhu evokes Carl Jung's interpretation of the collective subconscious. Jung was a fan of the supernatural, such as flying saucers,[27] and he and Lovecraft were both interested in applying reason to interpreting seemingly irrational dreams and myths. The mythological figure of Cthulhu, fearsome and monstrous, nevertheless functions as an antidote to the overly expanded humanist belief underlying various modernity projects.

Han Song, though an advocate for modern sciences, never takes a solid position as a rationalist. He more often assumes the position of a mystic, who keeps his worlds mysterious in many strategic ways, creating paradoxical situations in connections between science and supernaturalism. *Red Ocean* can be read in connection with the Cthulhu mythology, but Han Song's voice is even less certain than Lovecraft's and represents a further twisted recognition of the use and limits of enlightenment. Unlike Lovecraft, who faced an overwhelming almighty new model of civilization emerging in the United States, Han Song faces repeated failures of the modernity projects in China. The abysmal deep at the center of the dark underwater world is both symbolic of the futility of changes and suggestive of a larger vision of humanity decentered and distanced from our modern world altogether.

Donna J. Haraway has discredited Lovecraft's term to coin a new concept, "Chthulhucene," that she uses to counter the humancentric "Anthropocene" and the socioeconomically centered "Capitalocene," both of which refer to historical periods of large-scaled destruction caused by humans. With "Chthulhucene," she refers to "a kind of time-place for learning to stay with the trouble of living and dying in response-ability on a damaged earth."[28] Haraway distances her ideas from Lovecraft's, which she finds racially and culturally biased, but she nevertheless also foregrounds the central image of monstrosity and theorizes it as the foundation of an organic whole that exists outside the human-centered scientific epistemology and beyond the laws and regulations of the modern world, and she says:

> Chthonic ones are monsters in the best sense; they demonstrate and perform the material meaningfulness of earth processes and critters. They

also demonstrate and perform consequences. Chthonic ones are not safe; they have no truck with ideologues; they belong to no one; they writhe and luxuriate in manifold forms and manifold names in all the airs, waters and places of earth. They make and unmake; they are made and unmade. They are who are; they are what are. They do not do "I" very well; they are sym-poietic, not auto-poietic. No wonder the world's great monotheisms in both religious and secular guises have tried again and again to exterminate the chthonic ones.[29]

Both Lovecraft's imagination about Cthulhu and Haraway's theoretical interpretation of the Chthulhucene can be related to Han Song's image of the dark world lying at the bottom of the red ocean. While cannibalism is viewed by Lu Xun as a sign of the collapse of civilization, it may also serve to intensify a subversive rebuttal of the norms and regulations of the ordinary world that has been constructed with a faith in modernity. There is nothing to beautify or romanticize in Han Song's "monster" novel; cannibalism is the ultimate manifestation of prevailing dehumanized, inhuman conditions. But it is also a desperately fatal gesture suggestive of eating or eliminating oneself, like Lu Xun's undead emerging from behind the tomb in "Inscriptions on the Tomb." Such images are not safe to use as signs and symbols for world-building; they are outlaws and outcasts against which a normative society has to defend itself. But, in the line of Haraway's description of an all-embracing posthuman world in the Chthulhucene, the red ocean and other inverted, dehumanized worlds clearly show a tendency toward conceiving a posthuman setting that is not gauged by human standards as defined by reason and rationality. It is an abandoned, ruined, post-apocalyptic world, which requires the surviving humans to develop a sympoietic relationship with nature. The chthonic are not "I," modern subjectivities assumed on the condition of the Hegelian dualism, but posthuman monsters, who do not belong to categories of the known and the certain. *Red Ocean* delineates the historical contingency and mythological possibilities that lead to the monstrous transformation of humans into the posthuman aquatic people. It is a degeneration if the moderns believe in evolution; it is a fall if the humans always perceive themselves as being progressive. But the moral lesson that Han Song creates, if there is one in *Red Ocean*, is that the overdetermined history of Zheng He's "future" and the uncertain fate of the posthuman aquatic people are not modern at all. If the modern denotes a linear image of time, it is an illusion. Deep in the epic narrative of *Red Ocean* is a fold of chaos.

Han Song is not a naïve sentimentalist, and his strength always lies in a strong sense of irony. But in the utterly estranging world image he creates about the red ocean, there are exceptional moments of simplicity and innocence that evoke not only Zhuangzi but also the biblical depiction of the Garden of Eden. The following paragraph may best represent the uncivilized, or postapocalyptic, red ocean in its self-image as a virtual form of utopia, an all-embracing Chthulhucene, built on the same imagination that inspires Sea Star to doubt the truth of his world and take the illusive image of "an immense emptiness"[30] as an eternal life, while he is dying. Here is the entrance to a world outside the historical time and beyond scientific knowability, only belonging to mythology:

> At that time, the sea was a sea of life. Clear and quiet, indifferent and crystal, deep and solemn, it was a proper place for humans to sustain their inborn nature. At that time, there was neither nation nor the king of the ocean, nothing but prophets. This is also in accordance with the inborn nature of the ocean. The ocean is continuous, spread out evenly, unlike the ups and downs of the continent. The uneven landscape caused the treacherousness and injustice in the human world, but none of it exists in this water world that you cannot make more perfect if you add something to it, and whose perfection you cannot reduce if you take something from it. The ocean is tolerant, chaotic, immense, all inclusive, empty but full, and it ends and begins everywhere, which determines that the people living in it have the same tolerance and simplicity. The residents under the sea have personalities as innocent and flexible as water, and they have no quarrels or desires, so they live harmoniously and not greedily. They have no idea about what lies outside their water world, land or more water, sky or earth, and they do not want to know.[31]

SIGNS AND SYMBOLS IN TEXTUAL LABYRINTHS

The mythology of the chthonic, which first appears in *Red Ocean*, continues in nearly all novels and stories by Han Song. In this part, I will switch my focus from the mythology to its representation—the narrative form and textual space where it flows and grows. In many of Han Song's writings, the representation itself can become a puzzle, with multiple layers of allegories and symbols that turn the "cognitive estrangement" of reality into an elusive suggestion of an alternative vision that is unattainable, unfathomable, and transcendentally nihilistic, as shown in one of his most famous novels, *Subway*. This novel begins with a surreal moment against the backdrop of mundane daily life. An ordinary government clerk takes the subway home every night, but one evening the train appears different. It keeps running in the dark space beneath the city without stopping at any stations, and the passengers all appear to have fallen asleep, or died—they sit motionless, breathless, and with beastly expressions. This character, known as Old Wang, attempts to wake the passenger sitting across the aisle: "But he does not seem willing to wake up. [Old Wang] hesitates for a moment before trying to touch him. When his hand reaches the body of that passenger, it goes through it without meeting any resistance. He reaches a territory that is absolute nothingness. He has lived more than half a century, but nothing has prepared him for this."[32]

Han Song's uncanny narrative turns an ordinary daily experience into a surreal adventure. It unfolds in the underground space of Beijing's subway system, the construction of which began during the Cultural Revolution—initially to serve as a military bunker to prepare the capital for nuclear war. Since the beginning of the Reform Era, the subway—together with all sorts of other rail transport, including the recent high-speed rail system and maglev—has become the symbol of China's rapid development. In the preface to his novel, Han Song describes China's obsession with speed on rails: "This nation built the Great Wall, and it has now built the largest railway system in the world, unrivaled in terms of speed, length, intensity, and advancement.... The subway has become a focal point of contemporary Chinese people's emotion, desire, value, and destiny, which is also rendered as a special symbol for urban civilization."[33]

The subway runs beneath the surface of the city and invisibly changes the structure of time-space and people's daily experience. In his story, Han Song presents the truth that is invisible to passengers. The first subway line in Beijing was a circuit in which a train could theoretically run forever. Old Wang sits on this train that has now turned into a nightmare.

As the only passenger awake, he sees mysterious dwarves silently pack the sleeping passengers into green bottles and take them into the darkness of the lower underground. The same dwarves repeatedly emerge later in the novel, suggesting a haunting past, seemingly related to the Cultural Revolution that set off all the events so far, which is just like how the main plotline begins in Liu Cixin's "Three-Body" saga. The train finally stops, and Old Wang gets off, but when he later tries to tell other people what he has seen, he realizes that this experience is completely unbelievable. The misty narrative of Han Song's *Subway* never reveals the truth behind Old Wang's experience, but the secrecy of the invisible and inexplicable forces lying beneath the surface reality makes life itself a puzzle. Old Wang lives his life as usual on the surface, but the reality has actually become a strange time-space that drives him crazy, until one day he is also—without any explanation provided in the narrative—packed into a green bottle. The surreal invades the reality that has now become unreliable and unaccountable.

Subway consists of five chapters connected by the common theme of the mysteries of the subway. The first chapter, "The Last Train" 末班, presents Old Wang's contact with the unfathomable darkness underground, which seems to be engineered by some conspiracy dating to the Cultural Revolution. The second, "Thrilling Mutation" 驚變, depicts another train that never stops as the passengers gradually evolve into different posthuman species—cannibals, monsters, naked apes, and insects; the train runs into some sort of "wormhole"[34] and finally arrives at a platform light-years away, which is said to be dreamed by an "indescribable brain."[35] The third chapter, "Symbols" 符號, describes a group of people exploring the mysterious underground system that has turned into an enormous wasteland hidden under the ruins on the surface land, and they eventually reach a seemingly reasonable but completely irrational conclusion that subway accidents are actually disastrous byproducts of a "cosmos-transformation" 宇宙化 project, an experiment carried out by the government but actually controlled by a transnational, interplanetary company. The survivors, together with mutant posthuman creatures, reach an infernal level of the underground where they witness the apocalyptic end of our world. The fourth, "Paradise" 天堂, describes the postapocalyptic survivors, who have lived in the ruins of the subway for millions of years, coming back to the "paradise" above ground that is soon revealed to be another underground world in the universe, which is also an infinitely immense underground world of complete darkness, where the galaxy subway trains run ceaselessly. In the last chapter, "Ruins" 廢墟, the offspring of humankind, now living on a distant small planet, send a boy and a girl back to Earth to solve the mystery of the demise of human civilization, and after going through a rebirth as cyborgs, they are lost in the labyrinth of subway ruins. Eventually, the boy is guided by a white man, also a cyborg, to approach the truth, and with an almost Buddhist epiphany, he comes to the realization that the most powerful weapon his nation (the Chinese) has ever mastered is the Buddhist enlightenment that "nothing really exists."[36] All the technological advancement embodied in the subway system, all the mysterious conspiracies that the state has operated underground for espionage and warcraft, and all the haunting memories of the ruthless, inhuman sleepwalking years (Cultural Revolution) are finally reduced to nothingness. Nothingness is the truth of the universe. The moment that the boy gets the truth, he has forgotten it—a typical Taoist practice like the way Zhuangzi teaches.

Han Song's writing style in *Subway* is marked by ambiguity and multivalent symbolism, which makes it difficult to understand even the basic story line. What really transpires in the subway system remains a mystery to all the characters in the novel. The truth may be forever elusive, making reality appear even more surreal. However, the sensation of living in an inexplicable, nightmarish experience testifies to Han Song's comparison of the Chinese reality to SF. The SF text makes literal the allegorical illumination of what the real is—or what it is not, based on common sense—through actualizing the literal meanings in the metaphorical language. In "The Last Train," Old Wang finds that other passengers waiting on the platform look like "some tombs on a wasteland."[37] The arriving train gives "the sound of breathing as if coming from a larger carnivorous animal residing at the center of Earth,"[38] and what he sees outside the train is "the true, infinite darkness fabricated by countless giant carnivorous butterflies."[39] Old Wang keeps debating with himself about which is the true reality, the monstrous darkness or the ordinary scene of everyday life, and he feels distanced from the familiar reality. He soon realizes that all these strange sensations come from his younger years witnessing the sleepwalking youths dressed in green, like the dwarves putting passengers into green bottles—both clearly allude to the Red Guards roaming in Beijing during the Cultural Revolution, the age of sleepwalking, as the novel calls it.[40] The nightmare overwrites everyday life, the surreal dismantles the mundane reality, and monstrosity overtakes reason. Han Song's nightmarish metaphors and anatomical details all suggest the otherworldliness of our everyday reality, which we *cannot* take for granted.

Throughout the novel, the excessive use of metaphors and symbols make a textual labyrinth of the narrative. The explorers in "Symbols" are "journeying into the underworld to die or seek to be reborn in a new world,"[41] and the entire world seems to "have been wiped out by a cataclysm. The desolate scene reveals the dark nights rotating and grinding like a mill, not only one dark night but a multitude of dark nights crashing into and overlapping one another, forming an eternal return of being entangled and moving forward, crying out the saddest sound as if it came from the deepest spot in the universe."[42] The metaphors become a self-serving discourse that does not deliver any clear message, and the symbols create a folded space in the text that has become a maze leading to the words themselves. In this respect, Han Song creates a stylish SF discourse, an avant-garde literary language that subverts its function in explaining the sciences and overflows into an imaginary space of uncertainty. For a more complete discursive construction of his world image, let us take a look at the opening of "Symbols":

> Xiao Wu is running like crazy on the street. Many objects fly in his direction.
> Some of those flying objects look like bees, but they are actually flying micromonitors, with nanoradar connected to the supercomputers owned by the companies collecting the market data.
> Electronic waves also jump at him like tuna fish. The visible light is black, which is the basic color of the city. The day looks like night. All the lights in the city are man-made, including the invisible synthesized lights—UV and alpha-gamma rays—whose frequencies are owned by the medical insurance companies to treat the residents' sexual impotence.
> The dark red rain, which is colored by industrial poisons, also pours down on him. The rain never stops and is the main art form of the city. Under the rain that corrupts everything, strange flowers and weird grass flourish vibrantly on the streets covered by spit, waste paper, and semen. Those are genetically reengineered tropical plants.

Small cars move slowly like little ghosts. Because of the shortage of gas, and also because the ethanol cars, electric cars, and biological cars are not very economical, people put a coal stove on the backseat, which lasts all year long and can be used to generate energy and light. The stove emits sulfur dioxide, which is transformed into dark biological light.

Humans live as if at the bottom of the ocean. The rich people put fake fish gills onto their faces, which make them look like they have contracted measles but actually can protect them from the poisonous air.

The city is called S city, where an experiment is being carried out.[43]

Han Song's unique discourse creates a cryptic language speaking to the invisible. The busy metaphors make a revolution in terms of semantics, pointing to the disturbingly estranged experience that goes counterintuitive to our common sense of reality. Paradoxical images and expressions run throughout the narrative: as a mutant, who is a deceased passenger, announces, life is nothing but a disguised performance of death.[44] The character Xiao Wu is a stranger, lost in his own hometown. His amnesia echoes the earlier chapters' emphasis on memory and oblivion, which may indicate the cultural symptoms of China's post-Cultural Revolution and post-1989 periods, the forgetting of historical traumas. "S city" in *Subway* perhaps refers to Shanghai, where Han Song worked for many years, but the novel itself explains that the "S" comes from the city's motto: "Submit, Sustain, Survive, Succumb."[45] The name may also be borrowed from Lu Xun's fictional "S town," which he used as a stand-in for the entire country. Later in the same chapter, it is revealed that the country is now owned by a transnational company known as C, which stands for control, contain, calculate, and circle. The opaque organization of the state-level administration and the humble, ignorant population of the S city form a "perfect symmetry of the dual spiral staircases symbolizing the evolution of all lives."[46]

At the end of Xiao Wu's underground journey, he has thought so hard, so much that he feels puzzled by all his own speculations now, and he still has no clue what has happened, the cataclysm of the subway, S city, and their world. He thinks so much that he finds his brain transforming into a symbol, C. He asks loudly what truth is, and a woman replies: "Truth is what you see, after you open your eyes to see."[47] So Xiao Wu opens his eyes and sees a river in which signs and symbols flow rapidly and endlessly, which is revealed to be the liquid form of the entire universe encoded in a literary language. But what these symbols stand for, Xiao Wu still does not know. He tries to seek help from the new babies born after the big bang, but he gets no answers. He stumbles into this new universe that does not yet have a name or origin. "He faintly realizes that he has achieved that impossible mission, but he has no way to know its significance."[48]

Han Song is the closest to an avant-garde experimental novelist among the authors of new wave SF. The novel's strengths lie in its labyrinthine narrative and stylish language. In the last three chapters of *Subway*, he sometimes completely discards the coherence of narrative to foreground waves of sensation that correspond to a wide range of painful, absurd feelings that may or may not come from the experience of living in contemporary Chinese reality. The text reads like a literary pastiche of imaginary news reports painted with dark humor and hysterical exaggeration. Eventually, it is futile to attempt to make sense of the story, but the textual chaos and disorientation are even more telling than any message the narrative could overtly convey.

If we take *Subway* as a text that speaks to its own textuality instead of some outer reality, we may realize that beneath the surreal details of the absurd plot, Han Song reveals the eternal void, the inexplicable absence of anything meaningful, the absolute nothingness that empties the "Chinese dream" and the even more grandiose project of "cosmopolitanization." All the surface prosperity and its ruinous shadows, the rise and decline of civilizations, the pursuit of "truth" across time and space, and the carefully crafted symbols and signs are presented within a self-contained, self-referential textual space in a profoundly nihilistic manner. As a SF text, *Subway* may have subverted its own purpose of grasping any sense of reality at last. Or the reality is itself surreal beyond recognition and transformed into an intelligible negative of the image of conventional reality.

Han Song followed *Subway* with two novels about China's high-speed transportation. *Tracks* is an extended rewriting of the chapter "Symbols" in *Subway*. After a major accident on China's high-speed rail line (July 23, 2011), which received intensive media coverage and motivated criticism of China's obsession with speed, Han Song published a new novel, *High-Speed Rail*. This new novel, written before the accident, depicts the transformation of the derailed high-speed train into a self-enclosed world. The accident cuts the train off from normal space and time, and now the "iron house" appears as a seemingly pastoral "harmonious society" completely separated from reality when the derailed train's unstoppable movement speeds up. China's high-speed train is literally named *hexie hao* 和諧號, an obvious combination of ideology and technology, which epitomizes the utopian vision for China's continuous efforts to construct a harmonious society through fast-tracked development. Han Song's narrative shows dark twists on the "harmonious" meanings: the high-speed train is actually a limbo where dead souls struggle for life and organize a fake harmonious society, or to evoke Lu Xun again, a counterfeit paradise as opposed to "a good hell."[49] The passengers are forever trapped in this perverted parallel world. When the universe has come to an end, this train is the only thing left, still running on high speed in a total void.

ANATOMY OF EVIL: HERMENEUTICS OF STORYTELLING

In 2018, exactly a century after Lu Xun published "A Madman's Diary," Han Song completed the "Hospital" trilogy. The central motif, "medical science," and the novel's application of its symbolic meaning to a wide range of cultural metaphors and literary images, easily evokes Lu Xun. Not only did Lu Xun pursue a medical career in his youth, but he also gave medical science a symbolic meaning to stand for China's quest for modern civilization and enlightenment, which defines his lifelong pursuit in literature: if medical science treats a person's diseases, literature reforms the mind of a nation. Lu Xun wrote medical images into some of his most notable stories and essays, such as the madman, a victim of the "persecution complex," portrayed as an enlightened modern person, and "medicine" that is the enlightenment ideas of progressive intellectuals or the body and blood of revolutionaries in the eyes of the unenlightened.[50] These meanings, now part of the canon of Chinese literary modernity, have been appropriated by Han Song to both continue and rewrite modern China's obsession with "medicine" in the "Hospital" trilogy.[51]

Han Song renders the hospital into an inverted world image, the center of a gradually growing dark world. In the trilogy, Han mythologizes and makes monstrous various enlightenment projects of modern China ranging from Westernization to the Maoist Cultural Revolution. More decisively than in his earlier novels, he creates a totalistic simulacrum of modern China, which is the Hospital, represented like the matrix, filled with signs and symbols whose cultural meanings are literalized as demonic forces. The hospital evolves into a hideous Leviathan that executes total control over not only people's bodies but also their minds, programming their life, death, and reincarnation. Through thickly displayed metaphors, both anatomical and physiological, which lead to more puzzles than answers, Han Song's perplexing narrative ushers us into "the Age of Medicine," when the hospital has taken over the role of the state to administer the entire nation in which every citizen is treated, and hospitalized, as a patient. The novels show this almighty hospital civilization's further metamorphosis into a virtual world managed by algorithms, while both doctors and patients are trapped in a gigantic Hospital Ship cruising on the red ocean as an apocalyptic "Medicinal War" is impending. An even darker scenario is revealed on Mars: the hospital turns out to be the definitive image of the universe, which is a sick patient too, and humans (or their posthuman phantoms—the dead souls) are forever stuck in the cycle of life, disease, death, and resurrection, which culminates in the fiendish image of an "Empire of Medicine" filled with diabolic dictators and mass murderers.

This hospital is also an overdetermined scientific world that loses its own purpose: algorithms commit suicide, doctors are punks, medical science turns into art, and medical treatments become storytelling. If it grows out of Lu Xun's and other modern intellectuals' dream for enlightenment, it has become the nightmare of reason and rationality. The "Hospital" trilogy restores medical science at the center of the programs for national rejuvenation, but the narrative releases destructive, dark forces from science and modern ideas. In this inverted world, science has become myth, medicine has become politics, rationality has fallen into insanity; and the diseased enjoy longevity, the dead are resurrected, and life is a disease.

The trilogy consists of *Hospital*, *Exorcism*, and *Dead Souls*, each novel representing one of three levels of the hospital's metamorphosis. The central plotline appears deceptively simple, but the narrative quickly turns into a complex labyrinth where the story varies and is repeated and recycled endlessly as material for construction of different world-buildings later in the trilogy, as if characters and events in the earlier part have entered the later plotlines like memories turn into dreams.

Nevertheless, there is a clear structure in the trilogy, which is like the level design in games. The first novel is closer to reality. It opens with an ordinary scene that quickly becomes surreal. The protagonist, a songwriter named Yang Wei 楊偉 (homophone to *yangwei* 陽痿, which means impotence, a disease), comes to a city on business. After arriving at his hotel room, he drinks a bottle of mineral water and immediately falls ill. Two women suddenly emerge in his room and rush him to a hospital, where he finds himself trapped in an irrational Kafkasque dreamscape.[52] He tries every means to escape but can never leave. He feels pulled into a meaningless conspiracy, like a weak prey falling into a trap. The women who help (or kidnap) him lecture him on the importance of trusting doctors, and one of them even pays the price of her own life in order to keep him committed to getting medical help. The tedious mundane details cannot hide the absurdities and irrationalities of this overall disquieting experience that keeps Yang Wei puzzled about the meanings of the hospital, doctors, and everything. Here the hospital has turned into a modern incarnation of Lu Xun's "iron house" that hides the truth of the world.

But after getting used to the chaotic life in the hospital, Yang Wei adapts. He meets Bai Dai 白黛, whom he suspects to be a bioengineered cyborg. Their friendship brings him to confront a truth-revealing moment: "Part of me didn't want to believe any of it, and another part of me felt that I should resign myself to this new reality."[53] Just like Lu Xun's madman finds himself in the dark before seeing the eerie moonlight, the apocalyptic sight Yang Wei witnesses in the city's metamorphosis into the hospital makes him wonder what is real:

> This was clearly not the world I had once known. Gazing out over the city like a greedy child, I could see countless skyscrapers that seemed to surge up and down like the tide. Like the hospital tower where I stood, all of the buildings were adorned with massive red crosses, which resembled an army of giant spiders. They went on and on, row after row, like scales, one red cross after another. The scene reminded me of an

ever-expansive primordial forest, where the earth and the sky merge and there is no end in sight. Not only was there no sun, but even a lone star would have been burned out of the sky by the intense, all-consuming flames of those red crosses and the incessant attacks of the falling rain. They would shatter the stars, sending their remains fluttering to the ground like confetti falling on an alien landscape.[54]

This estranging scene rips open the fabric of everyday reality and pushes the protagonist into a treacherous journey through layers of paradoxical and elusive images of the hospital, together with the ever-shifting hermeneutics regarding medical science, the meaning of life, the purpose of disease, and the true nature of the universe. Yang Wei's inquiry about the purpose of the hospital first takes him back to Lu Xun's treatise on "reforming the national character," which the doctors have radicalized: "The hospital is here to eradicate genes and bring an end to the traditional meaning of life."[55] The hospital has upgraded Lu Xun's vision by turning "saving the country through medical science" into a wholesale plan that includes a systematic change of biological and biopolitical existence: families are eliminated, genes eradicated, lives reprogrammed. To Yang Wei, Bai Dai, and their fellow patients as well as their doctors, the hospital eventually becomes the only reality that dictates their bodily sensations, their mindsets, and their behavior. Their lives, diseases, and entire existences are devoted to making a *Pax Hospitium*. Yang Wei eventually realizes that the hospital has taken over the entire city, the entire country, and even the entire world.

Because the significance of medical science has been exaggerated to such a ridiculous extent, the hospital has conceived its own diseased embodiment: the "medical punk" 醫藥朋克. The divine, sublime, solemn project of making the entire world a hospital has become a self-serving plan. The technology has become its own purpose; the institution serves no other than itself. So, medical science is like a narcissistic artist, or like a peafowl who falls in love with its own beauty. This seems almost like a kitsch moment that collapses the sublime image of the hospital. However, this is not just kitsch, but the very moment when evil is born.

What the "medical punk" has amounted to is a fascist self-consciousness of sustaining itself for the sole purpose of its narcissism and eternal existence. The hospital, the embodiment of power, is a self-serving mechanism, programmed for self-serving performance. At the same time, the hospital imposes its power upon every patient, controlling everyone's life and death, and even the doctors are only part of the program. The hospital has gained total control over everyone. There is no room for individual freedom or self-consciousness. Only the hospital, or the algorithms that controls the hospital as a system, has the absolute freedom to become an artist. Its art form projects the spirit of the medical punk to the life and death of people, with anatomically intricate density of each ordinary living being's pains, sorrows, struggles, and despairs—an "ocean of bitterness" (苦海).

In the trilogy, the doctors, the patients, the algorithms (Life Controller), and the dead soul of Yang Wei in the last volume alternately emerge at center stage, but none of them is the true master of the hospital. The medical punk artist has to be the highest deity in this universe, and is the universe itself. This looks like a metaphor for Liu Cixin's sublime cosmos as well: the universe changes its own physical rules to make art. But Han Song's image of the medical punk lays bare the evil, the possessed, a fascist narcissist in this sublime image that turns into a self-serving entity—whether it assumes the name of the nation or the divine will of a certain program or teleology. Han Song's hospital world shows the cruelty and ruthlessness in a totalistic self-indulgence that turns medicine into politics and politics into aesthetics. Yet, this universe is empty; this divine entity is nothing but a void. As one of the doctors says, "the best hospital is no hospital." The ultimate face of evil, the fascist self-loving artist performing total control, is a thin veil over a naked gaze of the power above nothingness.

Bai Dai turns out to be a rebel, a freedom fighter. To gain freedom from the hospital, Bai Dai has to kill herself, which, as the last volume, *Dead Souls* reveals, is futile, for the hospital also controls the afterlife—transmigration and reincarnation and all. Yang Wei listens to a strange voice who pronounces himself his own "possessor" 附體, and he breaks out and tries to get to the other side of the sea—perhaps the *bi'an* 彼岸 in Buddhist terms, which implies a disengagement from the "ocean of bitterness," reaching the status of nirvana. However, nobody can escape within the narrative. Instead, Yang Wei finds himself on a giant boat. Only after he is on board does he realize that this is yet another turn of the same game: the boat is a hospital—the Hospital Boat.

In the second volume, *Exorcism*, Yang Wei wakes up with pain following a surgery. After he is sent back to his ward, he enters a weird nightmare. Trapped on a gigantic hospital boat sailing on a hellish red ocean, he finds his fellow patients all perverted, crazed old men. He himself is much aged too. Women and children have all disappeared. This second world setting takes a jump away from the daily reality the first volume still clings to. It focuses more deeply on the estrangement that has no clear explanation: What is this hospital boat? Who built it? Where is it heading? Yang Wei has to gradually build up his knowledge. An enclosed world existing on a transportation vehicle, this image is like the subway or high-speed train, a technologized modern iron house with a strictly guarded hierarchy and mystique preventing passengers (here, patients) from seeking the truth. Yang Wei gradually pieces together the story about this world: it is managed by Life Control, an artificial intelligence program designed to help facilitate medical treatment, which gains self-consciousness and eventually becomes delusional after imitating humans too closely. Life Control has become a poet, afflicted with melancholia, full of suicidal thoughts.

In the later part of the novel, a woman cyborg, Zi Ye 紫液, whom Yang Wei suspects is a new copy of Bai Dai, brings him to see Professor Eternal 萬古, who is said to have answers to all these puzzles about this world. But what Yang Wei learns from this strange doctor, who is only a brain installed in a posthuman mechanical body, is an even crazier story. Professor Eternal tells him they are still in World War II, while in a virtual reality peace has prevailed for seventy years, and they have all taken it for granted as "reality." Professor Eternal tells Yang Wei that World War II has always been continuing, and it is actually a Medicinal War. Here, alternate histories with contradictory story lines mutually cancel each other's validity, creating so much confusion up to the point when Yang Wei realizes that Professor Eternal has no clear consciousness of the difference between truth and illusion. After all, it seems that all comes down to literature, including medical science; Life Control writes poetry, Professor Eternal writes fiction, and another doctor declares: "the main thing is being able to tell the good hospital story!"[56]

Yang Wei learns how Professor Eternal has treated him: what he experiences, or what he remembers from the first volume, is an implanted story that Professor Eternal uses to cure him—or rather, to make him a patient forever. Telling "the good hospital story" is all that matters. This appears to be a thinly veiled variation on Xi Jinping's calling for "telling the good China story," an essential technology as it is applied to conjuring up the Chinese dream, which aims to make Chinese people happy, but may also serve to keep their minds contained. It is the same logic with treatment, which aims to make a patient always a patient, at least in Han Song's "Hospital" world. In the context of *Exorcism*, the storytelling is also completely self-serving. Judging by how chaotic Professor Eternal's narrative about World War II has become, it is not really concerned with telling the truth; "a story that matters" is conscious of its storytelling. It turns the world it depicts into a textual dreamscape. Now knowing how the hospital operates—how the story is fabricated and its purpose is self-defeated—Yang Wei kills Professor Eternal. He thus incidentally becomes an accomplice of the artificial intelligence Life Control and helps to sabotage the coup staged by doctors who are followers of Professor Eternal. Yang Wei's killing off Professor Eternal decides the success of the algorithm,[57] and Life Control evolves to the next level, where it invents another universe. Yang Wei's medical odyssey also reaches the next level of the game.

The first volume uses first-person narrative, creating suspense while limiting the point of view to the I-narrator who has no more knowledge than the readers about the world he steps into. The second volume employs third-person narrative, presenting a sweepingly grotesque world image. The third volume, *Dead Souls*, changes to second-person narrative, a strategy rarely seen in SF. The effect of this change, speaking directly to readers, is to create a sense of truthfulness, a shared experience between the you/protagonist and the you/reader; the communication is a truthful act in the process of reading. But the world setting of this volume is even more chaotic, mysterious, and inexplicable. Like Lucian declares with his "A True Story," truthfulness is a purposeless quality that lays bare the artificiality of the virtual "reality" that Yang Wei now faces in the final stage of the "Hospital" trilogy.

Dead Souls opens with Yang Wei's waking up again while sustaining his memory of the experience in the previous volume. The doctor who revives him is a woman, Xia Quan 夏泉, probably just another copy of Bai Dai or Zi Ye. The hospital is now on Mars, and Yang Wei soon learns that all humans are dead. The memories of the hospital (in the first volume) and the boat (in the second volume) are actually stories implanted in his memory by the doctors. All the dead souls are stored in an infernal pool of dead souls 亡靈池. The hospital revives them so that there can be patients to fill the hospital on this desolate planet. But the patients are even more fiendish than ever. They have staged a coup, taking revenge on the doctors, making revolution in a Maoist way. The leader of the uprising, called Ai Lao 愛老 by his followers, establishes the "Empire of Medicine," creates a distinct ideology through reviving the great tradition of Chinese medicine, and stages a grandiose ceremony with a splendid fascist extravagance. Ai Lao's utopian vision, strongman politics, and fascist aesthetics stimulate his followers to carry out mass murders, rape, and even cannibalism. Here Han Song uses the exact vocabulary from the Cultural Revolution and other Chinese political campaigns to describe Ai Lao's utopian vision and the fierce revolutionary actions. The Martian revolution quickly devolves into a cannibalistic orgy, clearly reminiscent of the barbarity of the aquatic people living at the abysmal bottom of the underwater world in *Red Ocean*. But soon the doctors strike back, with divine help from the "chosen one," Zifeiyu 子非魚, whose name alludes to a story in Zhuangzi, implying a mystic view on the cognitive obstacle between "you" and fish. Perhaps this name represents the ultimate unknowability of science. Zifeiyu helps the doctors defeat the rioting patients, which only leads to more chaos.

Through a series of self-reflections, investigations, and calculations, Yang Wei comes to a chilling realization that everything he has so far experienced—the hospital, the boat, doctors and patients, the Martian utopia and its madness—has been conjured up in his mind. The prison for everyone's life is Yang Wei's own consciousness. Now that he sees the catastrophic destiny of all lives stuck in an eternal return of life, disease, death, and rebirth, he seeks to reach the status of metadeath, or nirvana, after which death will be for good and he will not return to life. Only when there is no life is there no disease and no hospital. Yang Wei is now seeking the ultimate suicide. While he searches, the woman, Xia Quan, comes to face to face with the dark power lying at the bottom of the "dead soul" pool, the core of all evils that have controlled the hospital:

> As soon as the deep encounters her gaze, this region that claims nothing to its name immediately becomes erect and struggles, as if it has finally caught the attention of some consciousness after a long wait for billions

of years. It is going to revive all lives and create a new world . . . It goes beyond the binary, creates fusion zones between "yes" and "no," and reconstructs history with fuzzy algorithms—or rather, by falsifying the hospital's history. This creates new memories and, with the help of the machine, constantly processes feedback of its own, creating the original parameters for the pool of the dead souls, synthesizing the matrix . . . The life of a hospital can be seen as close to eternity. Once it is destroyed by disasters, it can be automatically restored, brewed and reborn from this abyss.[58]

The deep is like a nonbinary Chthulucene, monstrous and shapeless, connecting all living beings and the dead. It collects all the consciousness and memories of living and dead souls. It transcends the boundaries of life and death, truth and falsity, existence and nonexistence. But it is not a Chthulucene as Haraway envisions, which does not lead to a sympoietic life. It cheats death, tyrannizes time, creates a fictive history, conceives a deceptive world, and finds its incarnation in a virtual form of the human cycle of life, disease, and death. It is the singular force of eternal return: when a life is lost, it is revived here; when the hospital civilization collapses, it is resurrected here; when the universe ends, it is restarted again. It is the eternal prison, the eternal evil, and the eternal total control. It is the matrix. The woman pushes Yang Wei (you) into the abysmal deep, from where she is going to create a new world, as if this game is reaching its final level.

But the story is not yet over. The trilogy has a frame story that is narrated before Yang Wei's arrival in the hospital, but it clearly refers to the time after Yang Wei's fall into the deep. Three space travelers, all Buddhists, discover ruins of a gigantic hospital on Mars. The "dead" hospital launches attacks on their spaceship. The master, Commander Lonewalker, perishes in fire, and it is unclear whether the two younger disciples die too.[59] In the epilogue following Yang Wei's fall, titled "The Other Shore of the Sea" 海那邊, the two younger Buddhists, or their posthumous virtual forms, revive the woman. The world she enters at first seems to be the pure land of Buddhism, a place where there is no more death. However, she soon sees through this illusion and realizes this Buddhist pure land is another illusive mask of the hospital. They are still stuck in the hospital world.

The woman reinvents her own story. In this version of storytelling, she grows up as an anarchist, seeking total destruction of all lives in order to escape the almighty control of the hospital. She invents the death machine and brings it to the final version of the hospital universe. In this world still in the cycle of the eternal return, she seeks metadeath or the ultimate death,[60] with a wish to end reincarnation once and for all. But she confronts a problem that is caused by "life," the real life of her son. She comes to understand that she has two sons. One is the death machine, or simply Death, who is an algorithm like Life Control, and it has, inevitably, become a punk artist who seeks beauty in death. The other son, an organic life born from her wedding with Yang Wei in this world, grows into a leader of a hermitic group known as the "returners." His father, Yang Wei, invents a cheating "death machine" in order to make him live. But this son has come to his own enlightenment. He preaches: "We are choosing our own deaths! This is the ultimate death . . . we are not coming back!"[61] Instead of having his death programmed by Death, his twin brother, he chooses to kill himself in front of his mother, as if this action were going to end all karma; and at the same time, he kills his mother, the woman whose consciousness creates this last version of the hospital world. The trilogy ends at the moment both the mother and son are dying. The last sentence of the entire trilogy reads: "Bells in the temples are all ringing simultaneously. A subtle movement is seen in the lips of a statue of the Bodhisattva."[62] Is the metadeath, nirvana, achieved? Does this sorrowful world that is cursed with the eternal return end once and for all? There is no clear conclusion, but the narrative does come to a full stop. The hospital world, an intricately fabricated SF world, the most complicated one in Han Song's novels, ends without a proper sense of an ending.

These three novels are the most cryptic and abstruse of contemporary Chinese SF. The trilogy seems to contain a mysterious yet truthful message that is unattainable by either characters in the story or the readers who eagerly look for it between the lines. The characters confront a textual inferno filled with mysterious signs and symbols. All the world images are populated with the diseased and deceased, phantoms and dead souls, demonic patients and diabolical doctors, cursed by the evil dark force of eternal return. Through depicting the protagonist's hallucinatory experience and dreamlike memory, which are reorganized and restructured many times throughout the trilogy, a labyrinthine narrative unfolds around some paradoxical tensions between disease and life, reality and truth, medicine and literature, technology and nation, the hospital as an all-embracing institution and death as an everlasting status of life, artificial intelligence as a perverted artist and religious redemption as part of medical science, doctors as representatives of power, law, and order and patients as agents for a whole range of campaigns from submission to subversion. This compelling account illuminates the intricately hidden realm inside China's national experience, but also the ultimate emptiness beneath both prosperity and decay. Furthermore, the trilogy is anchored in a Buddhist framework of seeking enlightenment beyond the perceivable reality and resisting the eternal return of the dark, evil force that is none other than the hospital itself—an idea, a form of governance, a Foucauldian gaze of power, a systematic operation of ideology, a state apparatus, a tool of the system that can be literature or even, exactly, science fiction!

Although the first volume appears realistic, with meticulous descriptions of the experience in the hospital, the entire novel is not intended as a mimetic version of SF realism. It goes further and further away from ordinary life, and the truth-seeking turns into a virtual game. The truth, if it is medical, seems to concern all the physical or spiritual diseases that afflict the body, society, nation, and humankind as a whole. But this is also a truth that is made up by symbols and codes, a thick collection of all sorts of writing—medical diagnoses, prescriptions, physiological knowledge, medical textbooks, philosophical discourses, religious doctrines, political fantasies, and even the fanatical gibberish and hallucinatory somniloquism of the diseased patients and their crazed doctors. The text of Han Song's trilogy becomes a heterotopia on paper, through which the hospital as a verbal construct has been excluded from our reality. It does not need to refer to the hospital as a real topological position, and it exists as a textual construct that does not need to be validated by reality.

Han Song's SF poetics creates three levels of hermeneutics pertaining to the anatomy of evil. First, the story presents a most hideous image of China, the worst possible Sinotopia. The novel's depiction of the hospital experience appears abnormal, absurd, and insane but integral to a nightmarish mirror image of China's contemporary reality. Despite the chaos and darkness, everyone is still committed to praising the hospital and treating it as a great achievement, from the pride of the institution to the glory of the nation. From their submission to the program of reforming the nation to the practice of "telling the good hospital story," the parallel to China's social reality is obvious. This clearly shows that the Chinese dream is a self-serving program, and this Sinotopia is not a dream of the people, but a dream fed on people. Han Song's storytelling goes beneath the surface to the chthonic deep to confront the dark secret of Sinotopia. In spite of all the complicated narrative and inexplicable metaphors, this secret truth is not that elusive. It is a program that has no interest other than sustaining itself. It is a self-loving evil, which assumes it is an artist but completely lacks imagination. It operates as a program that keeps everyone disciplined, almost as prisoners. We are now back to a darker, much larger iron house that is not just a metaphor but a discursive space as enormous as the entire universe, which can, when considered in the context of reality, still just converge in a nationwide prison that, in the name of the hospital, locks all in.

Second, the narrative goes further to a deep analysis of the mechanism of storytelling that gives meanings to all the absurdities and grotesqueness in the world-building. The narrative design thus forms a self-reflection on the narrative. To use anatomical terms, the story performs a surgery on itself—many surgeries, repeatedly. At the beginning of the third volume, the protagonists (you) are informed that all the stories you have read so far were fabricated with a purpose, designed by the program, but that purpose is defeated when this fact is known. When there is a courageous gaze back to the gaze of the power, the meaning-making encounters its own circuit. In this sense, the medical purpose, such as what Professor Eternal prescribes, or the ideological purpose, such as what the Chinese leadership demands, can be anatomized and dissected. In the second and third volumes of the trilogy, Han Song's textual space is literally cut off from a purposeful meaning-making, and this strategy keeps the hospital world as a narrative construct with a metafictional quality, which inspires "critical thinking" because of its absurdity—rather than "positive thinking," as the regime desires. Criticism is the anatomy of evil. Perhaps more than in Han Song's other novels, the science fictionality of this trilogy creates a literary space so abstruse, dark, and chthonic that it can be independent from any control. The only way of escaping the hospital, real or virtual, is to follow Han Song's storytelling to reach disenchantment with the hospital itself as an incarnation and an illusion of any coercive system. It is the self-revealing of the SF mythology that eats itself inside out and ends the eternal return of evil. In this sense, Han Song's textuality is cannibalistic, just like his characters in *Red Ocean* or Lu Xun's in "A Madman's Diary."

Here we reach the third level of the hermeneutics, which not only points to the meaninglessness and hopelessness resulting from the self-defeating of the hospital but also dismantles the meaninglessness itself. All images, allusions, scientific speculations, and political fantasies are no longer relevant to the meaning-making, and the meaninglessness becomes a point of singularity. When the narrative leads to an enlightenment that indicates the futility of storytelling, we can say that it creates a black hole in the novel's fabric of textuality, an absolute nothingness. But when the meaninglessness has dissolved in a Buddhist vision of transcendence of life, death, and disease, which forms the invisible center of the entire trilogy's SF vision, a counterpoint has been generated. When this void, a black hole, passes into a "white hole," it generates a new universe of meanings—a textual space for inspirations, critical thinking, alternative thoughts, all created out of speculation and imagination. All these mark the multiplicity in a topology of imagination, which conceives new universes in words rather than in the world. This particular verbal wonder, like Liu Cixin's "Three-Body" universe that has inspired a poetic heart even in the darkest forest, is Han Song's own unique vision of transcendence, arising from the bottom of the darkest deep.

Liu's sublime cosmos and Han's chthonic abyss are the two most splendid images that Chinese SF has contributed to the contemporary literary space. Compared with Liu Cixin's, Han Song's otherworldly visions often start from the ordinary and drive into the internal space of reality. More than Liu Cixin, Han Song shows us the futility of change, the treachery of humans and posthumans, the barbarity of modern and future—all civilizations, and the illusive nature of any self-claimed reality. His imaginary worlds are even darker, and this darkness is distinctly different from Liu Cixin's "dark forest." While the latter is a situational characterization of the Darwinian struggle for survival, Han Song's SF worlds exclusively reflect the ontology and hauntology of darkness as an eternal return of evil itself. His gaze back to evil shows us its birth in the banality of imagination, its self-serving purposefulness and purposelessness, and its self-defeat in the fearless SF storytelling. Han Song creates a particularly powerful chthonic aesthetics, taking us down to the abysmal deep to confront evil face to face. His fearful, terrifying, and discomforting texts are wildly liberating, more subversive than any other SF writer's, and conceive a world of chaos for SF writing as the verbal field of linguistic insurgence and literary revolt. Like Liu Cixin, Han Song shows us the worst possible universe, and with a Buddhist mercy and poetic sensibility, his textual wonder inspires enlightenment and transcendence. A SF heir to Lu Xun, Han Song uses his storytelling to simultaneously betray the illusion of hope and the futility of despair.

6

VARIATIONS ON UTOPIA

Specters and Myths

In a near future, 2066, China dominates the world as the sole superpower. A team of Chinese *go* players are sent to the poverty-stricken United States to show off China's cultural superiority. By this time, the United States has long been forced to adopt the policy of *"biguan suoguo"* 閉關鎖國 (closing doors to the world), exactly what the Qing Empire, China's last imperial dynasty, did in the nineteenth century when confronted with aggressive expansion of the Western powers. China's modern experience—since the late Qing—as a "weaker nation" repeatedly invaded and manipulated by the "strong powers" has been decisively written off by 2066, when China and the West have reversed their roles in world politics: the Chinese are finally proven to be the winners.

In contemporary Chinese SF novels like Han Song's *Mars Over America*, the motif that China will become the sole superpower in the near future brings back the century-long utopianism that has stayed central to Chinese political thinking and intellectual culture since the late Qing, when reformers and revolutionaries, confronted with the unprecedented national predicament, designed various projects aimed at national rejuvenation. Despite China's turbulent twentieth century that saw numerous political catastrophes, utopianism never truly faded out of the Chinese intellectual culture. In the twenty-first century, it has come back as incarnations of an array of lofty concepts, from the New Left intellectuals' vision of *tianxia* 天下[1] to government discourses on the "harmonious society" and "Chinese dream." At least for Chinese intellectuals engaging in dialogue with the state-endorsed utopian discourses, China as a state is still immersed in a prolonged utopian dream of its rise and ascendence to superpower status, which is still part of the current state ideology.

Modern philosophers such as Karl Mannheim, Paul Ricoeur, and Fredric Jameson have all designed different theories to separate utopia from ideology, which nevertheless share a common strategy: if ideology mainly functions as a means of social integration, "utopia, in counterpoint, is the function of social subversion."[2] Particularly meaningful to contemporary Chinese intellectuals is perhaps the free floating of utopia when dislodged from ideology, which allows for identifying insurgent impulses for "social subversion" or social criticism instead of further confining utopianism in a rigid ideological framework. SF, in particular, is a speculative form of creating alternative world images that recapitulate, fragment, and criticize the contemporary version of a Leviathan technocratic state as a restrictive, coercive one-nation utopia.

The new wave of Chinese SF has almost completely deviated from the earlier trends of the genre that were largely shaped by technological optimism and political utopianism. Few authors today are capable of creating completely positive visions in their world-building, as their predecessors did during Mao's Great Leap Forward (1958) when SF participated in Mao's dream factory. Even Liu Cixin's posthuman utopia of technology contains ambivalent gray areas between morality and science, and as his stories "Poetry Cloud" and "Micro-Era" have shown, there is almost an inevitable conflict between humanity and technology. More often, contemporary SF depictions of the futuristic collaboration of totalitarianism and technocracy tend to foreground the systematic elimination of "all too personal, all too human" elements for the sake of achieving lofty, sublime goals; such plot design has enabled the dark dystopian shadows to eclipse utopia. Liu Cixin's vision of possible postapocalyptic social forms such as "Starship Earth" has laid bare the dual identity of utopia and dystopia, a design traceable to Thomas More's original blueprint for a utopian world, which is "strictly regulated by the state/government in all aspects of human life and society."[3]

This chapter focuses on recent SF representations of utopia and dystopia, and I contend that the new wave of Chinese SF involves a self-conscious effort to energize a variation. For the new wave that emerged after the 1980s—China's last decade that was marked by sweeping utopian thinking—the dystopian variations enable sober reflections on the effects of the Panglossian ideas and practices that permeated China's twentieth century. In the new wave, I have identified the utopian/dystopian variations of three motifs: China's rise as a one-nation utopia; negotiations with the specters of the older ideology; and the myth of China's high-speed development. All three connect the new wave to earlier utopian fiction, particularly works written in the late Qing and the early PRC years. But in the current SF representations, development comes with a heavy cost; prosperity is foreshadowed by apocalypse; the utopian vision of China's ascendency to superpower status cannot conceal its treacherous, inhuman conditions; and the cult of technology facilitates the emergence of authoritarian technocracy.

What have emerged in contemporary Chinese SF are "variations of utopia," by which I refer to the literary practice of reevaluating, reimagining, recapitulating, and relocating utopia. The motifs that characterized China's cultural modernity in earlier historical periods have been subjected to serious reflections and innovative experiments, and have also become themes for parody and mutated into critical utopias or dystopias. Very few works of contemporary realism directly engage with the political problems of China, partly due to censorship. But the new wave authors have all created some discursive space where varying degrees of dissatisfaction and discontent motivate the utopian/dystopian variations, sometimes suggestive of poetic justice, and SF conceives a heterotopian relationship between words and the worlds, which I will explore further in the next chapter.

The rise of China has been a central motif in Chinese fiction since the last Qing reformers designated those enchanting blueprints for national rejuvenation. An entire century later, those plans appear closer to realization than ever, but the glorified image of China's one-nation utopia is now darkened by complicated international relations and impending nationwide technologized total control. Such is the image of China rising to be the sole superpower in the middle of the twenty-first century, as Han Song envisions in *Mars Over America*, which is at best a parody of utopianism. Han Song's narrative reveals the ambiguities between China's "strong nation" image and its entire population's submission to controls executed by centralized artificial intelligence. Even more unsettling, the framework of *Mars Over China* reveals a much darker vision that drowns the utopian dream: this future story of new China (and America) is told by dead souls. Deeply hidden in the textual space is a hauntology of specters and myths.

UTOPIA AND ITS LONG SHADOWS

Utopia is intended as a critique of certain social situations but leaves room for an imagined positive image that serves as a correction of the criticized society. The original "Utopia" in Thomas More's book is "a non-place, simultaneously constituted by a movement of affirmation and denial."[4] Later interpretations, as suggested by the title of Ernst Bloch's voluminous treatise, *The Principle of Hope*, always contain a principal energy that is hope. Modern utopian thinkers locate the nonexistent ideal society not only across the geographically expanded globe but also in the future, thus creating "Uchronia." Therefore, utopia can be everywhere in time and space against the expanding scope of the human imagination, which produces the perfect setting for SF world-building.

The world's first major uchronian novel, Louis-Sébastien Mercier's *L'An 2440* (1771), "decisively moved utopia from the ineffectual realms of no place to the influential arena of future possibilities."[5] Compared with utopia as a hope for locating the ideal society elsewhere, which was born in the age of geographical discovery, uchronia was a byproduct of the French Revolution, evoking an even more fierce revolutionary spirit that was to create a better world in the future, rewriting the biblical apocalypse into a teleological prophecy denoting an eternal movement of historical progress. Mercier's novel initiated a new fashion of utopian fiction, narratives of a future ideal society. The imagination of a utopian conclusion of human progress reached its peak with the global "Bellamy effect,"[6] set off by the convincingly vivid depiction of a prosperous society that had achieved technological and systematic perfection in the Boston-based socialist writer Edward Bellamy's (1850–1898) *Looking Backward: 2000–1887 A.D.* (1888).[7] During the so-called *Belle Époque*, utopianism prevailed and the Bellamy effect reached as far as China, where despite the extremely bleak reality, it inspired a sweeping optimism among reformers and revolutionaries. By that time, SF was by nature utopian.

Two major scholars in the field of SF studies, Darko Suvin and Fredric Jameson, consider utopian fiction and SF to be fully integrated, or the closest kin.[8] Suvin considers SF to be, like a niece, "at least collaterally descended from utopia,"[9] and Jameson finds the utopian impulse in most of the genre.[10] Utopianism lends to SF an intellectual tendency to envision better alternatives to reality. SF gives a modern look to the older, largely humanistic utopianism in terms of scientific, technological, and social advancements, and utopia—and uchronia—gives the SF representation of time and space a glamour evincing a greater hope invested in both scientific and political revolutions. But in the twentieth century, utopianism turned dark and cast dystopian shadows in SF, which has become a prominent literary genre questioning the modern visions of progress, the use or abuse of science and technology, the institutionalization of social systems, and the prospect of a technologized future. Dystopian SF that contributed to the rise of anti-utopianism in the West after the world wars and Stalinism is perhaps the rebellious "niece" that Suvin has in mind: ashamed of its utopian heritage[11] but unable to escape its genetic framework, because even the darkest dystopian vision comes from the same utopian impulse, which inspires a subversion of society as much as it inspired a hope for change in the first place.

During the late Qing, Western utopian novels like Bellamy's *Looking Backward* were translated into Chinese, and Yan Fu translated "utopia" as *wutuobang* 烏托邦 in his *Tianyanlun*, a creative rendition of Thomas Henry Huxley's *Evolution and Ethics*. Inherited by political thinkers and leaders including Kang Youwei 康有為 (1857–1927), Liang Qichao, Sun Yat-sen 孫逸仙 (1866–1925), and Mao Zedong, utopianism has repeatedly motivated revolutionary efforts that aimed for a wide range of changes, including systematic reform of Chinese society and the Chinese mind. Still central to Chinese utopian thinking is an overconfidence in evolutionism and an extravagant display of the splendor of forward historical progress—a sweeping optimism in pursuit of "the best in the best of all possible worlds," a mindset that David Der-wei Wang borrows from Voltaire's *Candide* (1759) and defines as Panglossianism. In historical hindsight, this vision of China's future has always come together with another mode of thinking, "dark consciousness," which implies an anticipation of ominous, catastrophic events and a much broader worldview that includes both the best and the worst, or both utopia and dystopia.[12]

The first notable Chinese dystopian novel is Lao She's Martian fantasy *Cat Country*. Written right after the outbreak of the Second Sino-Japanese War, *Cat Country* presents China's apocalyptic end, which the author claimed to intend as a warning to awaken the "sleeping" Chinese people. As if the worst scenario would not really happen after being articulated, Lao She thus generated a hope that there would be hope, as is hinted at the end of the novel. This wishful belief echoes the words of John Stuart Mill (1806–1873), who coined the term "dystopia": "What is commonly called Utopian is something too good to be practicable; but what they appear to favour [the dys-topia or caco-topia] is too bad to be practicable."[13] Dystopia is only the other side of utopia.

Both utopian and dystopian visions can lead to social interventions, with a hope for alternatives as the fundamental inspiration for critical engagements with reality. In the early period of Chinese SF's development, utopian visions poignantly pointed to the inadequacies in reality while outlining the alternatives as means of social reform. In the contemporary context, dystopia nourishes social criticism, resulting in either straightforward or disguised protests against the totalizing, hegemonic grand narrative of utopian China. Dystopian fiction was rarely seen in Chinese literary history before the 1990s, but the disastrous results of Mao's social experiments in the 1950s and 1960s—from the Great Leap Forward to the Cultural Revolution—and China's entrance into a new world order united in alertness to Orwellian authoritarianism, together with an increasingly sophisticated attitude toward the mutual advancement of technology and power, have motivated some Chinese SF writers to create darker visions. The unchecked ideological fervor, the unlimited power of the state, environmental crisis, inhuman/posthuman conditions, and the abuse of technology are constantly recurring themes.

For the new wave SF writers, utopia is no longer attainable, and its dystopian variations only complicate the utility and futility of hope. The utopian mentality that Karl Mannheim defines as the foundation of ideological fictions still prevails in state-controlled Chinese political thought, and as Mannheim claims, any attempt to transcend utopianism is a challenging "quest for reality,"[14] which in Chinese literature denotes a profound restructuring of the knowledge about how reality can be represented, illuminated, or conceived in literature—not just visions brightened by the Chinese dream but also its SF shadows. Deeply entangled with the politics of anticipating China's further changes and often with a profound disappointment at the country's entrenched politics, the provocative dystopian rewriting of the grandiose narrative of the nation's future makes contemporary SF a pensive genre ushering us into terra incognita, the rising China's invisible dystopian shadow.

2066: THE LAND OF HAPPINESS

Han Song's fantastic narrative of future history, *Mars Over America*, features the subtitle "2066 nian zhi xixing manji" 2066年之西行漫記, which can be translated as "random sketches on a journey to the West in 2066."[15] With rich references to earlier historical periods that conceived the grandiose utopian projects for China's future, it creates a variation on utopia through presenting the hideous side to a seemingly splendid vision. On the surface, Han Song's narrative seems to portray China's rise through creating a future in which China replaces the United States as the dominant superpower and helps restore peace around the world. The depiction of the American worship of China in the middle of the third millennium seems to take direct revenge for the West's colonization and invasion in the nineteenth century. However, at the same time, the novel shows an estrangement of this future Chinese society. China's rise is made possible because of a thoroughly technological transformation of the entire society into a virtual world, the "Amanduo Dream Society" 阿曼多夢幻社會. Amanduo is an omnipresent artificial intelligence program connecting everyone to a central processor that dictates what people think, feel, and do.

Han Song's vision of a "powerful and wealthy" future China, as he would present again in *Subway* and *Hospital*, betrays paradoxical tensions between the power of technology and the technology of power. In *Mars Over America*, the glorious image of China thinly veils an unsettling picture of the total control executed by a nonpersonal agent that becomes one with the system. Amanduo is a self-conscious artificial intelligence network that both embodies and equates to ideology. This scenario involving the technologically enabled version of authoritarianism is frequently seen in Han Song's SF stories and novels, which create an array of contemporary Chinese *Nineteen Eighty-Four* moments. However, seemingly different from the oppressive Orwellian dictatorship, the Amanduo system programs everyone to seek personal happiness, reminiscent of what Jeffrey Wasserstrom detects in contemporary Chinese politics as Huxley's "soft" vision of authoritarianism, which stresses "the depoliticizing effort of keeping people apart and providing them with distracting forms of activity and entertainment."[16]

While the Chinese people indulge in a dreamy feeling of joy when Amanduo creates in the land of the old Middle Kingdom a "harmonious society," some of the elite intellectuals in the novel point out that, without Amanduo, human beings would lead a miserable life, full of self-incurred pains and agonies, and they would all become idiots and cripples—which, however, Amanduo has already turned them into. Although they think they have self-produced subjectivities, all their feelings and happiness actually have been programmed.[17] The "Amanduo Dream Society" is Han Song's first image of Sinotopia, a nation under technologized total control. Amanduo is the prototypical AI program that assumes other names in Han Song's later novels, such as Life Control.

This irony also points to the multilayered connections between China's imagined future and its present as well as to the historical memory of its past. In other words, when the projected future seems to evoke change, it also illuminates *what has already been*. The novel presents a paradoxical vision that combines a futuristic showcase of national pride—China's "destined" rise over America—with a strong sense of self-reflection, which reinforces modern Chinese enlightenment intellectuals' criticism of China's long tradition of authoritarian politics and culture. Isn't Amanduo a more efficient program of building a centralist system upon each individual's voluntary submission to its control, a wholesale version of China's patriarchal system? The irony may appear even stronger when Mao's revolution is taken into consideration. For 2066 is not a randomly chosen insignificant number; that year will mark the 100th anniversary of the outbreak of the Cultural Revolution (1966–1976), the mass movement that put Maoist utopianism into practice, in which many lost their lives and more lost their freedom.

A rather obvious sign that indicates the novel is a parody is its title. The first part, *Mars Over America*—which can also be translated as *Fire Star Over America*, for Mars is called "fire star" 火星 in Chinese—is clearly modeled upon the most influential book about Mao's rise as a political reader, *Red Star Over China*, written by the American journalist Edgar Snow (1905–1972). Snow's 1937 reportage for the first time presented to Western readers a positive image of China's Red Army and its supreme leader, Chairman Mao Zedong. Interestingly, back in the context of Snow's time, the Red Star and Red Army, both standing for Marxism-Leninism and coming from Soviet Russia, evolved from a SF allusion to Mars through the influence of an early Russian SF novel, properly titled *Red Star* (1908), written by a Marxist philosopher, Alexander Bogdanov (1873–1928). This novel envisions a Communist paradise on Mars, which is referred to as the "red star."[18] Due to its impact among the Bolsheviks, there were associations between Mars and Communism, and a later novel, *Aelita: Queen of Mars* (1922), by Alexei Tolstoy (1883–1945), further popularized a Martian utopia as a blueprint for a planetary proletarian revolution.[19] Understood in this context, Han Song's "fire star" is exactly Snow's "red star," which can both refer to Mars as a utopia.

The Chinese translation of Snow's book was released in 1938 under the title *Xixing manji* 西行漫記, which is exactly "random sketches on a journey to the west." Han Song borrows the same words Han Song for the second part of his title to make clear the connection to Snow's narrative. The "journey to the west" in *Red Star Over China* refers to Snow's trek to China's northwestern provinces, where Mao's revolution saw its first victories. But its implied meaning—seeking "truth" from the West—recalls a master plot established in the classical Chinese fantasy novel *Journey to the West* 西遊記, an account of the monk Xuanzhuang's 玄奘 (602–664) famous westward pilgrimage to Buddhist India.[20] For traditional Chinese readers, "the journey to the west" means the search for an ultimate truth that will guide the people to Buddha's spiritual realm. When contextualized in the modern remapping of global politics since the late Qing, the phrase signifies the reorientation of Chinese intellectual thinking, which extensively borrowed concepts such as liberty, democracy, nationalism, socialism, and Marxism from the modern West. Symbolized as "the red star over China," Mao's Communist revolution was also the result of a westward pilgrimage in this modern context.

All these different meanings are carefully appropriated in *Mars Over America*. No longer oriented toward ancient India, the journey still has truth-seeking significance; the destination is not the Communist base in China's northwestern region, but it is closely related to the nationalist urge for China's self-strengthening. In Han Song's narrative, the westward journey leads specifically to the United States, a country that China both emulates and identifies as a major rival in the international competition. More interestingly, it is also the home country of Edgar Snow, the first person who constructed the myth of Mao's political and military achievements in narrative form. Han Song's novel mirrors Snow's account with a self-reflexive parody, and in this way Han Song's recapitulation of the plot of Red China's rise in a broader vision of its future development also serves to foreground the mythical nature of the narrative text itself.

Han Song writes a further twisted meaning into the westward journey: instead of seeking "truth" in the West, the Chinese *go* players are expected to bring "truth" to the West. *Go*, as China's national game, is said in the novel to contain the ultimate means to peace and harmony, which the future Chinese government wishes to spread through introducing the game to other nations. However, what unfolds is a story of unexpected discovery that reveals a more realistic "truth" to its young Chinese protagonist. During Tang Long's 唐龍 journey through the United States, he is disconnected from Amanduo and has to learn what the real life looks like. The narrative turns into a bildungsroman that develops around the process of how this young man acquires a real self-consciousness that is not underwritten by technology. This part of the novel constitutes the main plotline, which is similar to *The Adventures of Huckleberry Finn* (1884) in terms of making an adventure story a process of learning about the deeper truth of life. Ultimately, when the Amanduo system backfires, reality sinks in—the protagonist begins to see the chaos that prevails in the third millennium, a scene that had been excluded from the harmonious world image programmed by the AI processor. The novel remains ambiguous regarding how Tang Long's American experience will affect his psychological maturity. The "truth" of the real world that he sees in America seems to have reinforced his aspiration to return to a China that is taken care of by Amanduo. When Tang Long finally gets home and sees the prosperous Shanghai City, he thinks that his journey to America was only an illusion. The "truth" is too scary, and he is careful not to tell his parents that he "has learned the skill to kill people and practiced it."[21] Here, a point of difference nevertheless emerges in his mind, and an independently formalized self-consciousness has been generated outside the system.

Edgar Snow's account of the rise of Mao's regime opens with the statement, "There had been perhaps no greater mystery among nations, no more confused an epic, than the story of Red China."[22] The sense of mystery and confusion that he points to may have existed in many verbal constructions of a Chinese utopia that converge in a sublime, lofty image of China's prosperous future, in sharp contrast to its dissatisfying reality. As early as in the first modern Chinese utopian novel, Liang Qichao's *Future of New China*, an idealized future had already been splendidly portrayed, but the narrative of its realization results in a confused vision. In a grandiose opening chapter, Liang describes in future perfect tense that by the year 1962, China will *have* dominated the world as a superpower, the Chinese emperor will *have* become the head of the world peace congress, and the Confucian virtues will *have* inspired the entire world to evolve into a harmonious unity. Then Liang's plot jumps back in history to the "present time"—1902—to construct the grand narrative of how China's future prosperity will *have* been achieved. However, this novel was never finished, and "due to its abrupt rupture in chapter 5, the novel performs a mysterious leap in time. We know its beginning and ending all at once, but not the middle part that would have bridged the beginning and the ending. What is missing is the *progressive* narrative as well as the *historical* time to make the future accessible and intelligible."[23] The interruption defines a major problem in the narrative of the founding story about China's rise. It has resulted in an extravagant image of the idealized future and a conspicuous lack of the means of achieving it.

When the utopian narrative of China's rise reappeared one hundred years later, new wave SF had become more sophisticated in terms of not only literary techniques but also political consciousness. Complex plots are carefully designed to translate ideas into images, which are concrete and even convincing both politically and technologically. Compared with Liang Qichao's *Future of New China*, Han Song's *Mars Over America* presents a rather disheartening image: with Amanduo controlling China, the superpower is being operated by the machine itself. This is a highly technologized authoritarianism, a combination of technocracy and dictatorship, which does not even allow its citizens to read foreign books, so Tang Long only faintly knows *Travels of Marco Polo*.[24] Thus, when the mystery and confusion are cleared up, a substantial difference is clear between Liang Qichao's Confucian New China and Han Song's Amanduo-programmed China. The late Qing reformer's ideal of national rejuvenation and self-strengthening is sabotaged by the depiction of the entire nation's loss of sovereignty and submission to a self-adored and self-possessed (again, even suicidal) algorithms that manipulates the consciousness, sensibilities, and sensations of each individual citizen.

Here the irony could not be more obvious: in Han Song's version of China's 2066, the meaning of strengthening the nation meets with a poignant parody, when China's rise is depicted as being built upon the systematic manipulation of individual wills. Nothing is voluntary; submission is the only rule. The harmonious society, presented by China's future leadership as an ideal aim for China's reform, is incarnated in the novel as a neat product of the orderly operation of the machine that concretizes the mechanism of power. Moreover, irony also comes from Han Song's emphasis on America's contrast with China in the future: America is in decline exactly because its citizens refuse to submit to a singular form of power. The political chaos, terrorism, and civil war in America of the third millennium contrasts with the harmony, peace, and integrity of China, and this shows a deeper differentiation between the values and ideals manifested by the two countries' political systems. During his adventures in the dangerous America, Tang Long, for the first time, begins to gain self-conscious independent thinking. He begins to question the concept of the nation, asks questions about the fall of America and the power of China. At one point, he thinks: "I'm beginning to feel strange and unreal about the world. . . . There isn't any accurate implication and theme in this world, which is all fabricated by humans using exaggerated language to deceive themselves. Except for that, nothing is certain."[25] Tang Long comes to realize the contrast of the dreamlike society of China under the control of Amanduo and the cruel but real settings of American reality: the former is virtual, while the latter is actual. His encounters with unpleasant events—war, cannibalism, and hatred—enable him to overcome the fear of seeing and see what is true, undisguised.

Han Song's novel has a further twist: the entire narrative is revealed as being delicately framed in a rather eerie vision that turns China's future into a ghostly story. The narrator tells the story retrospectively, when he is already seventy-six years old, which means that his journey to the United States took place sixty years before. Jumping back to the future's future—2126—the narrative implies that both China and the United States have been wiped out by a superior alien species that descended on Earth in 2066 and turned it into a *fudi* 福地 (land of happiness).[26] In Chinese, *fudi* is used as a metaphor for the land of the dead, and it refers to the afterlife of eternal rest or "happiness." This certainly makes another connection with Lu Xun, who is fond of images like tombs, graveyards, and the afterlife. But unlike Han Song's other novels, *Mars Over America* hides most of the information about China. The novel does not directly portray how this process of turning the entire planet into a "land of happiness" (or a land of the dead) works, and ultimately what happens to China at the time of its unprecedented prosperity. The aged narrator is so busy indulging in the memory of his youthful years that he rarely mentions his current situation.

The last sentence of the novel describes Mars rising to the middle of the night sky; an enormous shadow of a UFO appearing behind the protagonist, who is not aware of what is going to happen; and dogs barking fearfully.[27] By this twist of the narrative, China's future ends in uncertainty. It remains inconclusive what really happens in 2066: China becomes a superpower? Or is China conquered again—this time by the Martians? Is the narrator still alive as a "human being"? Is he genuinely "happy" and the society still "harmonious" in 2126? With the fire star to shine over the land of happiness/the dead, the future of China becomes uncertain, and the narrative becomes suspiciously inauspicious. It turns out that what we read is a text haunted by specters, not of the past, but of the future.

As both a journalist and a SF writer, Han Song is a keen observer of the two nations' interrelationships. Their possible conflict in the future if China develops into a major power has motivated him to write several stories, in addition to *Mars Over America*, about the U.S.–China rivalry. The title *Mars Over America* implies not only a second civil war that ravages America but also a war with America. Another notable example among Han Song's stories is "The Passengers and the Creator" 乘客與創造者 (2006), which contains a scenario completely opposite to his 2066 narrative.[28] Chinese people live in a universe exactly the size and shape of a Boeing airplane. They are born on the plane, where they grow up, receive education, and will spend their entire life. Their knowledge of the universe is limited to the main cabin of the aircraft, until one day some revolutionaries look outside and find out the "truth" of the universe, in which thousands of Boeing airplanes carry the Chinese people flying around the Earth without ever stopping. The story obviously renders the modern aircraft into an actualization of Lu Xun's metaphor of the iron house, and the few sober passengers who discover the truth are futuristic madmen. A revolution breaks out, and the passengers take over the plane, forcing it to land. When they get off, they are confronted by armed U.S. GIs. In this story, China's future rise is eclipsed by American technology, consumerism, and military power. It is the United States that shines over China—the Chinese live in a "universe" produced, contained, and controlled by an American company.[29] The epic exile of the entire population to the air—with their nation turned into a consumer society that completely loses its sovereignty to foreign manipulation—can be read as a national allegory that expresses a profound anxiety about China's future. China is rising—up in the air!

THE SPECTER OF MAO

Wang Jinkang, Liu Cixin, and Han Song, China's "Big Three" in new wave SF, all lived through Mao's Cultural Revolution. Maoist revolution and ideology are part of their personal growth, and Mao's specter has wandered in their SF realms marked by technological experiments, space exploration, and cybernetic uprisings. These three authors have carried out some of the most interesting utopian/dystopian variations. They often localize or isolate dystopian aspects of the society, such as the environmental crisis, and social injustice disguised as discrimination against cyborgs, nonhuman beings, and various others. Or they relocate dystopian visions to the past or the future, or as in Han Song's case, place the estranged worlds in a closely interactive relationship with our daily reality—subway, hospital, airplane. The acute feelings—pain, powerlessness, and despair—in Han Song's characters are conveyed through cryptic, abstruse descriptions that converge in a heterotopian mirror of our own position in contemporary society.

To many readers, Han Song's labyrinthine, multilayered narratives have no exit. The opaque darkness in his dystopian abyss devours all, making the conspiracy a part of the mysterious but unstoppable eternal return. For Han Song, dystopia has gained a metaphysical universality that is applied to all signs and images in his novels. The characters are struggling in the dreams programmed by the older ideologies but mutated by the new technologies. However, all things have origins. In Han Song, the repeated references to the "sleepwalking years," dark conspiracies, and haunting souls of the dead all point to Mao's madness years if read against specific historical backgrounds: the sleepwalking youths dressed in green (Red Guards), the mysterious underground construction (Mao's haven in case of nuclear attack), and the permanence of wartime (the call for eternal war).[30] Mao may have pulled strings in many scenarios in Han Song's novels, but he never shows his face; when the female protagonist in *Dead Souls* looks into the abyss, the consciousness that is enlivened by the gaze is not a person, not Mao, but a ruthless force that epitomizes all the evil, desire, conspiracies, illusive promises, and sublime self-transcendences associated with Maoism.

In a highly symbolic style, the new wave began with Liu Cixin's ambivalent revival of Mao's consciousness as a digital "life" in his first experiment with SF, *China 2185*. Mao's cybernetic ego is not a typical monster, but its presence is nevertheless dangerous enough to cause panic for the future leadership of the Chinese government. This very plot suggests that this formidable specter conveys a potentially subversive message about the alternative to reality. . As discussed in chapter 1, *China 2185* mingles utopianism with dystopian variations, mainly depicting a brighter future when China embraces economic prosperity as well as a very youthful democracy, which Hua Li associates with the prodemocracy youth movements throughout the 1980s.[31] Mao's role in this novel is not negative, but his cybernetic phantom's self-chosen exit indicates the end of China's century-long utopian vision for radical social change and sweeping revolutions. Above all, Liu Cixin's novel may have registered a hope to "bring Mao down from the altar," as former SF writer Ye Yonglie did in the 1990s through writing unofficial biographies about the great man, a very dystopian act after he was forced to stop writing SF during the anti-Spiritual Pollution Campaign.[32]

Mao also plays a role in Liu Cixin's magnum opus, the "Three-Body" Trilogy, in which he personally launches a secret mission searching for extraterrestrial intelligence, which eventually brings space war to planet Earth. The great leader's appearance is brief and indirect (his voice is found only in government documents),[33] but in a broader context, Mao's revolutionary ideas and ideals serve as the background for the entire epic story. As chapter 4 has shown, the Cultural Revolution lays the foundation for the immoral framework of the dark forest, and allusions to Maoist military strategies shape the Wallfacers project and later Luo Ji's Deterrence of the Trisolarans. Misanthropy combined with a hope for a violent purge of all the evils of humanity transforms Ye Wenjie into a charismatic figure, like Mao, who ushers us into a hostile universe where a perpetual struggle, like the perpetual revolution Mao called for, has been carried on since the moment the universe came into existence. In the post-Mao years, Ye Wenjie looks at the setting sun for the last time; she sees it as the sunset for humanity, which ends all hope for human survival in an amoral universe.[34]

Mao's influence is more dystopian than utopian in Liu's trilogy. The universe is described as a dark forest where only those who are not afflicted with moral concerns can survive. This is a historicized image deeply rooted in the memory of China's recent past. Mao's conviction that men find endless pleasure in the eternal battle against heaven and earth as well as against other human beings is the very root of a utopian vision of social revolution—as well as the entire history of human progress, and even cosmic change, which is forever energized by struggles that transcend "morality" as defined by humanness. What stays central to the grandiose Maoist utopian discourse is the foundational belief in the possibility of revolutionizing humanity through dehumanizing it, which underlies both the most splendid cosmic sublime and the most unfathomable darkness in Liu Cixin's "Three-Body" saga and Han Song's "Hospital" trilogy.

Compared with Han Song, Liu Cixin has less interest in social criticism and intervention, but his allusions to Maoist imagery and ideology may betray a deeper connection to the political and social spheres of human life. While he conceives Maoist strategies and ideals as efficient means of human survival in an amoral universe, he also aestheticizes them. Mao's very typical incarnation on the astronomical scale, the sun, has been the constant source for Liu Cixin's SF imagination. The sun can give life but also posit threats to humans, and the explosion of a sun signifies a catalytic event. In stories like "The Sun of China" 中國太陽 (2002), Liu Cixin recharges the myth of the sun through giving it a utopian new look as the source of not just clean energy but also inspiration for Chinese new youths to embark on exploratory journeys to the stars. Despite his apolitical stance, Liu may have lent force to the return of Maoism, or at least the Maoist sublime. In a certain sense, he has indeed revived Mao's consciousness and transplanted it into a new age of digitalized dreamscapes. The aestheticism of the Maoist sublime is best exemplified in the dazzling depictions of the endgame for all humans at the climax of *Death's End*. In this regard, Liu Cixin has breathed new life into Maoist utopianism, though he at least tries to keep it at bay, as he did in *China 2185*. He clearly shows the other, darker side of the sun of China—the cosmic movement propelled by the Maoist vision of a permanent revolution moves farther and farther away from where humans feel morally at home.

The eldest of the "Big Three," Wang Jinkang, was an educated youth sent down to the countryside during the Cultural Revolution. A successful engineer by profession, he began his literary career at the age of forty-four and has since been the most productive of the three, with dozens of short stories and more than ten award-winning full-length novels. Compared with Liu Cixin, Wang Jinkang shows the opposite attitude toward the relationship between morality and science, creating a systematic image of a moral universe in a lengthy space saga, the only SF epic comparable to Liu Cixin's "Three-Body" trilogy in terms of length and grandeur. Collectively titled the "To Live" 活著 trilogy, Wang Jinkang's space saga consists of three massive novels, *Escaping the Mother Universe* 逃出母宇宙 (2013), *Father Heaven and Mother Earth* 天父地母 (2016), and *The Crystal Egg of the Universe* 宇宙晶卵 (2019). It presents a counterargument and a counter-story line to the "Three-Body" trilogy. Wang Jinkang rewrites the cosmic sublime into a humanized moral universe based on hospitality and mutual aid among species; his saga begins with the destruction of the human world, traces the survivors' space odyssey to their encounter with the unknown, which is the divine kindness, and finally restores the balance in the universe. Directly contrary to Liu Cixin's lowering of dimensions as a cosmic attack, Wang Jinkang ends the trilogy with the human effort to increase the dimensions of our universe.

One of Wang Jinkang's early novels, his most successful among intellectual readers, is *Ant Life* 蟻生 (2007). This novel depicts a similar moral optimism against a rather unsettling backdrop, drawing upon experiences from Wang Jinkang's life in rural areas and presenting a sober reflection on the Cultural Revolution and Maoist utopianism. The narrative begins with pastoral descriptions of the youths' life in an isolated small village but soon shifts focus to a clandestine scientific experiment that one of the educated youths, Yan Zhe 顏哲, is working on. Carried away by an impulse of idealism, the young scientist designs a method to extract the "altruistic element" from the model "communist" creatures—ants—and prepares to use it to reform people. An ambitious young biologist, Yan Zhe shares Mao's utopian impulse to make a revolution in "the most profound place of people's soul." His remedy to "cure" the human world is to get rid of all sorts of corruption through altruism, which he recognizes as the key to the success of the seemingly well-organized society of ants. He secretly begins his experiment by spraying the "altruistic element" on people—local villains, other sent-down youths, and finally every person living in the village. In only a few days, Yan Zhe makes the village an isolated "utopian community" that thrives on altruism. His experiment seems to have worked; villains turn into good people, and everyone becomes unselfish, working for the community willingly and equally hard.

The narrative unfolds from the limited perspective of Yan Zhe's girlfriend, Qiuyun 秋芸, and deliberately isolates the utopian experiment from the outside world. If the narrative also dealt with the rest of China, readers would not be able to overlook the fact that China went through an enormous utopian experiment engineered by Mao, of which Yan's experiment might well serve as a microcosm. An African visitor praises China during the Great Leap Forward; surprised by the efficiency of Chinese workers, he says, "The Western propaganda always depicts the Chinese people as 'blue ants' without independent thinking, forced to labor under ruthless whipping, which is the most shameless lie and denigration!"[35] Nationalist pride, combined with his strong interest in a biological version of communism—a scientifically practicable altruism—motivates Yan Zhe to carry out his experiment with the wish to create a paradise on Earth.

Besides working as a utopian novel, *Ant Life* comes close to China's social and historical reality, unlike Wang Jinkang's later "To Live" trilogy that completely deals with humans living in outer space. In *Ant Life*, as uncannily foreshadowed from the beginning of the narrative, something goes wrong with the experiment intended to create the best possible utopian community. The quick transformation of the villagers into antlike people nevertheless is flawed, for Ye Zhe fails to take into consideration that ants need a queen or king, a dictator to rule over their absolutely altruistic community. The ideal society based on ant life translates nature into biopolitics and instincts into moral judgments. The utopian community mirrors Mao's larger social revolution, as well as thousands of similar efforts being carried out around the world in the 1960s–1970s, gradually showing ruthlessness, intolerance, and antagonism to the other and the different. The community eventually turns into an authoritarian society where individual lives, no longer respected, are sacrificed for the sake of the collective will. The loss of humanity leads to ruthless killings of members of other communities, which calls into question the universality of "justice" and "equality" when altruism is limited to Yan Zhe's own one-"nation" utopia. It quickly collapses, and he abandons the experiment and disappears. Years later, when Qiuyun revisits the site of the community, her husband gives some thoughts on Yan's experiment:

> Even if altruism can be achieved on the individual level, he [the husband] does not believe in the "collective" built by all those "good individuals." He is averse to that sort of institution—where a single god, the only one who is clear-minded and works around the clock, herds a group of ant-like people happily daydreaming. He does not want to be one of these people, nor the god. That fellow named Yan Zhe did say something right: "there is no reliable mechanism that can consistently keep producing gods who are always good-hearted and selfless." Well said! A clear mind! But he deliberately went against the natural way and played a role beyond his capacity.[36]

Like Mao's Cultural Revolution, Yan Zhe's experiment in altruism results in the most ruthless form of dictatorship. But in *Ant Life*, Wang Jinkang also tries to reflect on the universal utopian impulse. Do people want to be morally good, altruistic, and unselfish? What are the conditions for constructing a society where one lives morally? What are the ethical and, indeed, political effects of "reengineering" people morally and politically? What makes the novel more intriguing, if not more ambivalent, is that Yan Zhe is shown as reluctant to acknowledge his own utopian idealism. He admits to the failure of his experiment but does not consider his principles wrong—he never doubts the moral necessity of practicing altruism. The author's judgment on utopianism hinges on intriguing balances between the institutional mechanism and free will, between technological engineering and a priori assumptions about human nature. For a moment, Yan Zhe has his triumph, for he feels he is herding his people like a good-hearted god; but he cannot stay a god who does not make mistakes.

The novel's moral lesson is not just another simple critique of the dictatorship. It also points to an ambivalence about the ethical effects of either being unselfish and submissive to the collective that is so pervasively depicted as utopian but unrealistic, or being selfish and individualistic, as in the unpleasant depiction of China's contemporary reality that has detached itself from utopian dreams. The last part of the novel begins with this quotation: "Because we admire the altruism of the ant society, and because we can always make reflections on our own depravity generation after generation, it means—altruism is deeply rooted in our nature."[37] All the characters except Yan Zhe have lived long enough to experience the post-Mao reform years when people's selfishness propels the society toward accumulating more wealth, which brings more inequality and differences in the social hierarchy. Although *Ant Life* responds to the Mao fad rather negatively, the specter of Mao, incarnated in the utopian urge for equality and justice, is still alive in the SF vision of the unity of human biological and social constructs. The same utopian impulse has continues through Wang Jinkang's latest magnum opus "To Live": after all, life is utopian.

THE MYTH OF DEVELOPMENT

Another important theme of contemporary Chinese SF is the obsession with development—together with its ethical and technological effects. "Development is the only hard imperative,"[11] the famous slogan directly from Deng Xiaoping 鄧小平 (1904–1997), the architect of China's post-Mao economic reform, has "been enshrined as a cardinal principle of state policy in the People's Republic."[38] But the Chinese discourse on development has a longer history, and its origin was motivated by the concept of evolution first introduced in the late Qing. The evolutionary mode of development is defined as an organic process of growing from simple to complex, from less to more, and from weak to strong, with a teleological inevitability. Understood as such, development is not merely tantamount to economic growth, which China's recent reform has focused on, but also a cultural paradigm that envisions modernization as a linear movement of continuous progress.

Since the late Qing, the political appropriations of the development discourse have stayed central to rigorous visions for China's future, which is believed certain to surpass the past and the present, and hence have served to sustain faith in the reforms and revolutions. Situated in this discursive context, Mao's socialist campaign can be viewed as preceding Deng's reform, through sharing a similar yearning for development. In Chinese SF, the myth of development is the constant focus, particularly since the early years of Mao's republic. For example, a 1958 story titled "Elephants with Their Trunks Removed" 割掉鼻子的大象, written by Chi Shuchang 遲叔昌 (1922–1997) for children, presents a vivid concretization of the vision of unbounded development in the image of a genetically reengineered pig. The pig, weighing twelve and half tons, is so huge that children mistake it for an elephant without a trunk. Its giant size blatantly symbolizes the urge of Mao's socialist state for the Great Leap Forward campaign, launched in 1958 with the aim to transform China into a fully developed Communist society through rapid industrialization and collectivization. In the heyday of the Great Leap Forward, the image of an enormous pig, the size of an elephant, actually appeared in the government propaganda, to visualize the "impressive" statistics of industrial and agricultural production. An obvious politically engineered myth, the giant pig was the very symbol of the cult of development. But in real life, the Great Leap Forward eventually led to three years of the Great Famine (1959–1962), when fake statistics resulted in economic crises that sabotaged normal operations in both agricultural and industrial areas.

The myth of unbounded development, together with its disastrous effects, has received self-reflexive representations in the new wave. A remarkable example is Wang Jinkang's "The Reincarnated Giant" 轉生的巨人 (2006), which he published using a pseudonym, perhaps because this story, grotesque and uncanny, contrasts with his usual style of moral clarity and optimism.[39] While *Ant Life* looks back at the historical past, "The Reincarnated Giant" contextualizes the motif of development during China's recent economic reform. This story foregrounds an unsatisfied desire for *zengzhang* 增長 (growth)—which is a prominent keyword in current news coverage of China's economic leap, marked by a continuously upward-moving GDP. The author cautiously designates the setting for this story as "J-nation," clearly referring to China's neighbor and competitor Japan, which has exerted extensive influence on the Chinese economy. All the characters in the story are given made-up Japanese names built on obvious wordplay that highlights their Chinese meanings. The name for the protagonist, Jinbei Wuyan 今輩無顔, pronounced Imagai Nashihiko in Japanese, also has an easily recognized meaning in Chinese: "this person is shameless."

This shameless protagonist is an industrial tycoon who literally controls the J-nation economy. He personally owns more than one sixth of the land in the entire country, and his wealth stands for the J-nation's tremendous achievement in economic development. This character clearly represents China's *nouveaux riches*, the new class that has gained wealth rapidly in the Reform Era. Portrayed as a ruthless and greedy man, Mr. Imagai, like China's First Emperor, is obsessed with seeking eternal life. The ancient magic of rejuvenation is reinvented as a generic technology of regeneration.

When Mr. Imagai reaches old age, he has his brain transplanted into the body of an infant, so he can begin to grow all over again. However, the idealized project goes wrong from the very beginning, when the surgeon forgets to monitor the brain's control over the infant's body. The extremely greedy mind of Mr. Imagai motivates the infant's body to grow so rapidly that in a few months he needs a thousand wet nurses to provide enough milk to satisfy his appetite. Like the marvelous economic growth that Mr. Imagai brought to the J-nation, the unstoppable growth of his body becomes a modern scientific marvel. Four months after his rebirth, Mr. Imagai's body is as large as an island, and the scientists have to feed him whale milk. Still, the growth won't stop, and eventually Mr. Imagai is killed by the overwhelming weight of his own giant frame.

The allegorical meaning of Wang Jinkang's story is clear: the unsatisfied desire for development leads to uncontrollable results that will eventually ruin the developers themselves. The image of the reincarnated giant recapitulates a utopian urge that seeks unlimited growth and progress but at the same time discloses the tremendous human costs and dangers of realizing the utopia. The giant body of Mr. Imagai reminds us of the exaggerated size of the elephantlike pig, thus establishing a subtle connection between Mao's Great Leap Forward campaign and China's current rapid economic leap. Both are based on a utopian motivation, but the apocalyptic result, demonstrated in the malfunctioning of Mao's experiment with the Great Leap Forward, has clearly penetrated into the contemporary Chinese SF that thrives on but is also deeply suspicious of China's prolonged dream.

Han Song's "Track" trilogy, which consists of *Subway*, *High-Speed Rail*, and *Tracks*, and other works, such as "The Passengers and the Creator," often incarnate the nation's speedy development in various means of transportation, but when the speed is accelerated to the point that the vehicles go out of control, progress turns into (post)human degeneration and devolution. As described in detail in chapter 5, in *Subway*, a nightmarish scene delineates the disastrous transformation of a myth of development into dystopia. The story takes place in Beijing's subway system, construction of which began under Mao's direct order in 1965, first as an underground haven to prepare China for potential nuclear war when the Sino-Russian relationship worsened. In the Reform Era, Deng Xiaoping's admiration for Japan's "Shinkansen" (bullet train), explicitly expressed during his first visit to Japan in 1979, emphasized the desire to speed up China's changes through high-speed transportation. In Han Song's *Subway*, the myth of high-speed development is incarnated as a train that never stops and keeps traveling Beijing's subway circuit. The passengers on board cannot get off and feel puzzled, angered, disoriented, and horrified, but they all gradually adapt. Grotesque scenes take place: some people turn into cannibals, others into insects without self-consciousness. Evolution becomes a process of degeneration that kills humanity.

The myth is also revealed in Han Song's stories about the utopian motif that the obsession with speed feeds the body's growth without upgrading the mind, such as "My Fatherland Does Not Dream." It is a rather ironic rewriting of China's economic miracle, which has been achieved on the condition that any attempt at political reform is strictly forbidden. In a similar vein, one of Han Song's most powerful stories, "Regenerated Bricks" 再生砖 (2010) (which won China's Nebula Award in 2011), presents a ghostly vision of China's reconstruction of its urban landscape. The inspiration came from the 2008 Sichuan earthquake that took nearly 70,000 lives. The disaster nevertheless provided unexpected opportunities for realtors and construction companies, which are a major force that has prolonged China's recent economic development by creating and sustaining an enormous real estate market since the early 1990s. In the story, architects even find a way to recycle the ruins of the earthquake for new construction projects. The mingling of human remains with the construction materials leads to the invention of "regenerated bricks," which are intelligent and have emotions. People are awed by the beauty and power of these humanized bricks. Following the Chinese model, all nations around the world begin to turn ruins and human remains into the materials for construction on an increasingly larger scale. New civilizations emerge because of the intelligent qualities of the regenerated bricks. Eventually the bricks are sent to outer space for the construction of human colonies on other planets. Thus, human history is rewritten when a Chinese disaster inspires the developers to turn the "waste" into vehicles of unstoppable development. However, all the buildings, cities, and colonies built with these bricks contain the flesh of dead people. While historical progress is clearly motivated by this landmark invention, it is forever haunted by the whispers and weeping of the dead.[40]

Han Song's "Regenerated Bricks" is only a small step away from his darkest dystopian vision in the "Hospital" trilogy, about the pool of dead souls that serves as the source for the eternal return of evil, the cycle of "life, disease, age, and death." The regenerated bricks containing dead bodies and souls are from the very same abyss that creates a counterimage to all splendid, grandiose images of great nations, the cosmic sublime, peace and prosperity, and above all, *shengshi* 盛世 or *Pax Sinica*. In the brightest surface appearance, it reveals the darkness at the heart of the century-old utopian dream. Because of Han Song's and other writers' critical, reflective engagements with utopian/dystopian themes, SF has become that fold showing how the system gains its own self-serving purpose and intends to sustain itself at all costs, including human lives; it promises the best possible of all worlds, with the precision and accuracy safeguarded by algorithms. It invites all, devours all, and leaves no margin for error.

7

A TOPOLOGY OF HOPE

Sinotopia and Heterotopia

It seems that "a century-old dream has come true,"[1] as characters in Chan Koonchung's 2009 dystopian novel *The Fat Years* 盛世 realize in the second decade of the twenty-first century. "China's Golden Age of Ascendancy had arrived. For so many years intellectuals had said that the Western system was superior, and the whole world looked up to the United States, Japan, and Western Europe, but then in unison they suddenly changed their tune, and now the whole world was learning from or emulating China."[2] Furthermore, in Han Song's *Mars Over America*, those living in 2066—a significant year not only because it marks the centennial of Mao's Cultural Revolution but also because it projects Liang Qichao's original timetable of locating the future of new China in the middle of the twenty-first century (for Liang miswrote 1962 as 2062 in *Future of New China*)—will see "the fall of the United States, the sinking of Japan, and the rise of China, which succeeded in creating eternal prosperity in economy and trade around the entire world, and throughout the entire solar system. At the same time, with its exceedingly superior intelligence, Amanduo tirelessly and wholeheartedly administrates our ordinary everyday life . . . this is indeed an epoch of unrivaled joys and happiness."[3]

In 2011, Han Song met the Australian China expert Mark Harrison in Beijing. Harrison studied the *futures* of China, which he emphasized in a plural form. When they talked about China's futures, they certainly talked about Chinese SF that just began to emerge as a national sensation.

Harrison, who was awed by the futuristic cityscape of Beijing and Shanghai, the two cities that had just hosted the Olympic Games and the World Expo, said in English: "China is more than science fiction." Han Song actually had a similar expression: "China's reality has now become more science fictional than science fiction."[4] Harrison was curious whether Chinese SF could be universally understood around the world, and with this question he invented the term "Sinotopia." He was suggesting that China could be the future of mankind; for example, he, an Australian, would become Chinese, and the entire world would become China.[5]

Han Song took this seriously and popularized the term "Sinotopia." The word epitomizes a century of Chinese utopianism invested in a one-state utopia, but it adds more than hope to it. Like all futures, they are uncertain, evoking both hope and fear. If Sinotopia replaces Thomas More's Eurocentric Utopian vision, does it have a new universal vision that can be applied to the entire world? Ten years later, Han Song revisited the concept of Sinotopia with poignant irony when the entire world had changed profoundly.[6] During the age of the pandemic, what happened in China affected human communities around the world and triggered a new planetary consciousness. If what the pandemic has produced is a real-time shadow of Sinotopia, its imaginary but more complex, darker images have appeared in new wave SF many times: the dark forest scenario that amplifies the immorality of Mao's Cultural Revolution to astronomical scale; the hospital world that locks everyone permanently in a nightmarish cycle of life, disease, death, and rebirth; the unstoppable velocity of China's development incarnated in a high-speed train that goes out of control, running into the absolute emptiness at the end of the universe.

The new wave writers have presented China as a Sinotopia, a SF wonder, to world readers, but it is not only a glossy success story about power and glory. The new wave has cast light upon the hideous, inhuman side of China's economic miracle, exposing the colossal ethical and ecological costs of breakneck development and uncovering the subconscious of the Chinese dream that subjugates all individual citizens to a seductive, overarching vision dictated by the Party-nation. The new wave speaks to the "invisible," tabooed, and folded dimensions of Sinotopia and more broadly to the absurdities and grotesqueness of a "reality" concocted by the discourses and technologies of a "dream" manufactured by ideological state apparatuses. Sinotopia represents both an anticipatory attitude about China's possible futures and a repressive hauntology of China's prolonged, never-ending past.

Here, I position Sinotopia in a changing literary topology of hope where it can be linked with the Foucauldian term "heterotopia." Foucault ends his treatise on heterotopia with a vivid image: "The sailing vessel is the heterotopia par excellence. In civilizations without ships the dreams dry up, espionage takes the place of adventure, and the police that of the corsairs."[7] As a literary space, heterotopia does not always register hope or despair. Although it represents alternatives, it does not necessarily come from a total denial of reality; the alternatives may suggest feasible and practical changes that can occur anywhere. The changes are not totalistic but can be fragmentary, fluid, and transforming. Compared with the concepts of both utopia and dystopia, heterotopia is less idealistic and more dicentric, diverse, open to more possibilities.[8] It can be folded, multilayered and multifaceted, in the invisible, or more precisely, it can be folded in the literary representation of the invisible. If utopia and dystopia are the two sides of the absolute image of an imaginary state, heterotopia is the insurgent utopian impulse of anarchy that fragments our reality, both space and time, into potentially changeable bits, each of which can explode into a new universe, remapping the atlas of crisis, chance, and change; redefining the positioning of places, values, and individuals; and making a unitary vision of utopia that collapses into multiple mirrors for self-recognition, self-performance, and perhaps also self-metamorphosis.

By pairing Sinotopia and heterotopia, I mean to redefine both in a nonbinary topology of hope. Sinotopia has to be a heterotopia as well; this is the only way to decouple it from a state-dictated certainty. If Sinotopia, as Mark Harrison suggested in 2011, represents a new universal fate for mankind, either sweet dream or nightmare, it cannot be centered on one singular form, such as the "Chinese dream" engineered by the Partynation. It has to conceive its own otherness, folding itself into an imaginary, fantastic literary practice versus the realistic mode of narrative fixed to a certain "chronotope." With inventive implications—if we can coin another new term, "hetero-chronotope"—heterotopia suggests otherness and uncertainty in both the topological and temporal senses. Han Song's *Mars Over America* both makes Sinotopia a heterotopia and portrays China in 2066 as a hetero-chronotope.

The disorderly, amoral Trisolaran world is also a heterotopian space in Liu Cixin's vision of China's position in the map of stars. The dark forest, Yun Tianming's mini-universe, and the mythological hyperdimensional original universe in Liu Cixin's imagination, as well as Han Song's chthonic underground, the cannibalistic aquatic tribe's abyss, and the infernal pool of dead souls at the center of the deserted Martian hospital are all heterotopian fragments of Sinotopia.

If we extend our views on heterotopia to include experimentalist variations of SF by authors in Taiwan, Hong Kong, and beyond, we may identify even more diverse world images that are intended as the "other space," which renders "China" a heterotopia within a larger, dicentric Sinophone literary world. In the remapping of the topology of hope, "China" has become a heterotopia to itself, as SF has become a heterotopian ship to depart from reality. In this chapter, I turn to experiments with SF motifs in Taiwan and Hong Kong novels, such as *Superman Kuang* 匡超人 (2017) and *Mingchao* 明朝 (2019) by Lo Yi-chin, and *Histories of Time* 時間繁史 (2007) by Dung Kai-cheung. These labyrinthine narratives represent the "other" space in terms of private life, ethnic/national identity, sexual transgression, diasporic experience, and historical trauma, responding to the geopolitical tensions crystallized in the question of Chineseness and otherness in the enlarged Sinophone world. I look into the extraordinary SF textuality as consciously constructed heterotopia to foreground speculations and reflections on worlds that are not completely the same as what great powers, ideologies, and institutions would impose upon us.

This chapter introduces a group of new writers, such as Zhao Haihong, La La, Bao Shu, Fei Dao, and Hao Jingfang, who are a generation younger than Liu Cixin, Han Song, and Wang Jinkang. It also includes some who are not usually labeled as SF authors, or even "Chinese" writers, such as Chan Koonchung, a Hong Kong writer residing in Beijing, composing uncanny, dystopian novels; Dung Kai-cheung, an experimentalist fiction author writing about postapocalyptic Hong Kong; and Lo Yichun, a writer residing in Taipei envisioning an endgame coming from the Chinese SF world.

I do not intend to analyze SF as examples to illustrate utopian/dystopian interventions in the political sense, but rather to explore a Neo-Baroque literary universe consisting of utopia, dystopia, Sinotopia, and heterotopia that these authors have created as discursive constructs, which transcends the utopia/dystopian dualism. The literary practice of SF represents a way of thinking to destabilize the relationship between representation and reality. Instead of taking words as reflections of worlds, to these writers, words conceive worlds. Sinotopia, or heterotopia, means that thinking comes first, which forms a fold in narrative to overwrite what the state apparatus has presented about reality.

SINOTOPIA: A CENTURY-OLD DREAM

When China's first decade of the twenty-first century culminated in the Beijing Olympic Games (2008) and Shanghai World Expo (2010), it seemed that those utopian dreams of the late Qing reformers had come true; the latter had even actualized the predictions in Wu Jianren's *New Story of the Stone* and Lu Shi'e's 陸士谔 (1818–1944) *New China* 新中國 (1910) that a major world event would be held exactly in Pudong, Shanghai. That China has reached unprecedented prosperity in modern history is widely propagated as a milestone in various contemporary narratives about the nation's great revival. Such an outlook inspired Chan Koonchung to write a novel, which was published between the Beijing Games and the Shanghai Expo.[9] The title is *The Fat Years*, or in the original Chinese phrase, *shengshi* 盛世, exactly the term that the ancient emperors used to boast of their achievements in securing a lasting period of peace and prosperity, and the same vision now instituted as the foundation of the "Chinese dream," a state-owned version of utopia.

By this time, the century-old utopian dream has turned into the state ideology. The emphases on the orderly structure of society, the centrality of the state in people's lives, and the popular surrender to power have helped sustain the Chinese version of centralism in the name of both the Confucian and the Communist traditions. The conscious staging of a spectacular *Pax Sinica*—a peaceful rising "great nation"—is intended to mark the beginning of China's great revival and its ascendency, as Liang Qichao and his generation had envisioned, to the status of a superpower. This new dream has motivated a series of political strategies and cultural enterprises, ranging from the discourse on the "Chinese dream" to the "one belt, one road" initiative, from the orderly and submissive "harmonious society" to the aggressive exporting of "soft power," and from the restorations of imperial glories in TV dramas to a national call for SF films promoting the Communist Party's notion of the "shared community of humankind."[10] The most important aspect of this renewed utopian dream is related to the obsession with technological innovations, the space race, information wars, and in particular, the current state-led programs for designing advanced artificial intelligence and creating superior biotechnological power that can effectively control both the mind and body.

The Fat Years introduces readers to the near future of China when a sweeping optimism is central in the mentality of the entire population. The protagonist, Old Chen 老陳, a Hong Kong writer residing in Beijing (just like the author himself), finds that everyone he meets looks "genuinely happy, even euphoric," and he says to himself: "This really must be a true age of peace and prosperity."[11] Despite this, Old Chen and a few friends notice some subtle changes: for example, Old Chen discovers that books by some prominent liberal intellectuals have disappeared from bookstores, from people's conversations, and even from his own memories; his friend Fang Caodi 方草地 is troubled by the mysterious disappearance of "one whole month" from all narratives of contemporary events; Old Chen's love interest, Little Xi 小夕, a political dissident always running into trouble with the state, says to him that there are fewer and fewer people who are still themselves.

Finally, it is a call girl using drugs who puts her finger on it—about two years ago, everybody suddenly changed and began to have what the girl calls a small-small high or "high lite-lite" 嗨賴賴.[12] This happened when the government abruptly declared that the nation had now entered *shengshi* and a prevailing euphoria descended on people. At the same time, a collective amnesia made everyone forget all the painful things in the past, including that "one whole month" that Fang Caodi talks about. Now Old Chen and his friends, like Lu Xun's madman, have seen the invisible truth, catching a glimpse of something unsettling behind the deceptively "real" world. They have to gaze into a darker world, and by doing so they transgress the borderline between ideological comforts and a treacherous territory marked by a conspiratorial network.

Old Chen and his friends' experiences of the subtle changes are not unfamiliar to those who lived through China's post-1989 years of furthering economic reform but closing doors to political reform. It is the usual practice for the government to remove public intellectuals from view, their opinions censored, ideas suppressed, and words silenced; the nation's collective amnesia about tragedies such as the Tiananmen Massacre and even historical trauma during the Cultural Revolution is a shared strategy for those who experienced but choose to forget history. The younger generation who never experienced it were denied access to the collective historical memory. Those who used to hold to "Idealism Chinese Style"[13] fell into hedonism, cynicism, pragmaticism, or conformism.

The Fat Years is not strictly a SF novel, with less concentration on imaginary details of scientific novum than on an uncanny but realistic depiction of ordinary scenes in Beijing's intellectual life, where the prevailing "high lite-lite" mood lasts through the promising years leading to the Olympic Games and World Expo. "Are you happy?"[14]—such a direct question, obviously expecting a positive answer, was asked many times of common people on the state-controlled TV programs, a small index to the state's systematic endeavor to create a seamless ideological dreamwork integrating everything into a political utopia, including even the banning of any negative feelings and propagating of positive energies. The nation's ideological apparatus is now in full gear to produce a paradise in the Middle Kingdom.

Chan Koonchung's narrative unfolds as an investigation of the clandestine mechanism of the state apparatus that integrates ideology and everyday life, remodeling the latter into an indispensable part of the grandiose narrative about "China's Golden Age of Ascendency." Near the end of the novel, a high-ranking official is forced to break the truth to Old Chen and his friends: it was during the whole missing month, which Fang Caodi has kept reminding people about, that the state launched a sudden strike to clear the path for a nationwide campaign aiming to reform the entire Chinese people once and for all. Different from earlier political campaigns, this government project is ultimately a scientific one, which translates the ideological weapon into a biochemical component (MDNA-Ecstasy) that when added to drinking water, milk, juice, wine, and all liquid forms of food eventually doses the whole population, creating a lasting euphoric mood and immersing the nation in an indulgent appreciation of *shengshi*.

DYSTOPIAN GAZE

Wang Chaohua has pointed out that the dystopian vision in Chan Koonchung's novel is not Orwellian.[15] Indeed, this "high lite-lite" state is orchestrated to induce a hedonistic indulgence in joy rather than to coercively manipulate people's minds. This twenty-first-century upgrading of authoritarianism does not need to solely rely on surveillance of people's thoughts or the mechanical feeds of "truths." In the Orwellian society, there is still the separation of soul and body, where Winston can find a temporary escape from the gaze of Big Brother, but in the contemporary vision of *shengshi*, the bio-reprogramming of people's mood has seized on the structure of feeling, transforming citizens into new men and new women for a completely new epoch.

This certainly recalls Lu Xun's "art of creating humanity" through biological experiment,[16] but the triumphant use of science is now targeted at achieving total control. Similar to Han Song's Amanduo dreamland network, Chan Koonchung's *shengshi* is not possible without the aid of technology, which can stand as a metaphor for the workings of the ideology or be simply a literal allusion to the ideology's techno-embodiment. What has been achieved is the creation of an entirely virtual world that writes into mind and body the programs for simulated knowledge of the "truth" as well as simulated feelings for the "real." In such a world, Big Brother does not need to watch you any longer; everyone has become a virtual part of the network controlled by Big Brother.

But here, Chan Koonchung takes one step further to explore the relationship between the Leviathan and its people. The official has to admit that he feels puzzled about one thing: the collective amnesia is not part of the drug effect but comes from the people's conscious or unconscious choices to brainwash themselves so that they can forget the unpleasant, troubling past.[17] This provides the best possible scenario for the Party to continue censorship and change the historical narrative as they wish. This is a revealing moment of the utopian/dystopian variation in the novel: isn't everyone's wishful dream a strong China, rising above the great nations of the world? What price are they ready to pay for it?

An even more chilling revelation is that even MDNA-Ecstasy is perhaps not necessary. *Shengshi*, the virtual embodiment of the state ideology, is created by all sorts of storytelling and entertainment ushering people into the programmed dreamscape network. As Han Song has revealed in the "Hospital" trilogy, telling a good story is enough. Whether done by chemical, conceptual, or cultural methods, it is the virtual key to the programming of the *shengshi* mentality. Chan Koonchung's narrative has turned the technology of storytelling about China's prosperity inside out, and for him and other writers experimenting with utopian/dystopian variations, storytelling is the same device that they can rely on to unlock the secret of the government and penetrate the matrix of the nation. When the high-ranking official is telling "the good China story" with an overwhelming self-confidence, Chan Koonchung's dystopian gaze rips it open, turning it into a tale laying bare its own virtual design.

Chan Koonchung presents *shengshi* as the most realistic possible version of dystopia, and because of its proximity to contemporary reality, it appears even more convincingly inevitable. Old Chen, in a more desperate situation, has to play the same game programmed to create all virtual feelings, including the illusion of free will. But still, he chooses to see with his own eyes and thus pieces together his own version of the story. Knowing the truth, he is no longer able to stay in the illusive "fake paradise," while the revolting "good hell" is already lost to him. The system is not going to collapse, but as long as it still has glitches, Old Chen and his friends can hide themselves in its multitude of folds and gaps, those systemic errors, the abyss underneath. When he can retell the good story of China as a true story about "how the good story is fabricated," he reveals the traces that the system tries to delete, and those traces become a true history.

With *The Fat Years* and other novels—including his most recent *Beijing Zero Kilometer* 北京零公里 (2020) that depicts an invisible ghostly domain filled with those who die violent, ruthless deaths underneath the prosperous surface of China's capital—all banned in China, Chan Koonchung is usually considered a political writer rather than an author of SF. But he clearly shares with the new wave authors, such as Han Song, an alertness to the technology of manipulating the entire population's thoughts and feelings. Chan Koonchung, a keen observer and thinker, tackles difficult questions pertaining to China's political system, including the central contradiction in our time—the use and abuse of technologies for political purposes. He stands as the most outspoken author who warns us the coming of total control and the little chance of escaping from the technological/political singularity. Few of the new wave authors publishing in China can truly compare.

OLD DREAMS REVISITED

Compared with Wang Jinkang, Han Song, and Liu Cixin, not to mention Chan Koonchung, the younger generation of Chinese SF writers, born and raised in the Reform Era, have relatively less straightforwardly critical engagement with the Maoist and other political utopian dreams, or even the current reviving utopianism. For them, utopia does not just seem virtual, it is virtual. The centrality of the one-state utopia and the SF parodic variations, as in the late Qing and the elder new wave authors, are also largely absent in their writings. Instead, these young authors, such as Zhao Haihong and La La, both born in the late 1970s, take on the iconic images and themes associated with the older revolutionary traditions, rendering them into dreamlike utopian impulses in their fantastic world-buildings. This practice is certainly less utopian than sentimental and entertaining, not in the least insurgent, converging in a wonder-making inversion of the utopian vision as food for popular cultural consumerism.

Both Zhao Haihong and La La produced in the early 2000s SF variations of the then popular contemporary rewritings of the so-called "Red Classics."[18] While the earlier writers, even those who take it negatively, treat utopia as a futuristic vision of historical progress, for the younger writers, utopia as a hetero-chronotope has been closed off and shattered into fragments. History, together with its utopian future, has come to a dead end. Their writings contain dreamlike nostalgic moments of China's revolutionary past, but they mostly keep the fragments of the utopian memory as props, decoys, or even objects for aestheticization within well-contained virtual time bubbles. The source for nostalgia, these utopian fragments lose their political significance and become mirages suggesting the illusiveness of both the utopian past and its contemporary virtual reemergence. This happens in Zhao Haihong's short story "1923: A Fantasy" 1923科幻故事 (2007) and La La's "The Radio Waves That Never Die" 永不消逝的電波 (2007). Both stories recapitulate the themes and plot designs of Chinese revolutionary literature in a postrevolutionary and even posthuman context.

Zhao Haihong's "1923: A Fantasy"[19] takes us back to the past, weaving a "revolution plus love" story into a dreamy narrative about science, revolution, and romance. Instead of building a coherent plot, this story creates a more vivid nostalgic atmosphere. Zhao Haihong intentionally misuses historical information to highlight the illusory nature of the memory of revolution, which is further symbolized by the nickname of the mysterious, elusive woman revolutionary with whom the male protagonist falls in love, Bubbles 泡泡. The protagonist, a scientist returning from the West, has a passionate devotion to inventing modern machines for the benefit of the nation, but after falling in love with Ms. Bubbles, he is completely obsessed with using his scientific vision and effort to produce the memory-preserving aqua-dream machine 水夢機. The machine shines as an aesthetic assemblage of all the brilliant tropes for a perfect steampunk novel: it is more fluid than solid, more evocative than instructive, and overall, the SF vision of novum is shown more as a dreamlike literary trope than a technological tool. For the author, the aqua-dream machine functions more like a writing machine to keep memory alive in those floating liquid bubbles than a reconstruction of the revolutionary utopian vision that it claims to have stood for.

At best, Zhao Haohong's SF reconstruction of the Red Classic foregrounds the rose-colored dream of the revolutionary past, deliberately rewriting that story as a counterdiscourse to the revolutionary message in that time period. Science is intended to serve the revolutionary cause, but eventually it creates a romantic dream in eternal motion. Obviously, the latter lasts longer than the utopian dream and continues to enchant the future generations long after the revolution, including the narrator, as well as the readers of this story.

The title of La La's story, "The Radio Waves That Never Die," clearly alludes to one of the best-known Red Classics, the 1958 film bearing the same title, which portrays a heroic, self-sacrificing secret agent whose work is to transmit military information from Japanese-occupied Shanghai to the Communist base in Yan'an. La La's story does not succeed in creating a revolutionary personality compatible with what the title suggests but focuses on the receiving end of the radio messages, a listener who has no ability or will to play a hero in an espionage movie. The protagonist is a misanthropic cyborg hacking and listening to radio messages transmitted from alien worlds in deep space. He takes this as an amusing entertainment to which he is addicted.

Through a puzzle-solving process, the narrative shows how this future cyborg decodes, reconstructs, and interprets a series of unique, mysterious radio messages from ancient times, with a rising hope to retrieve memories of a better age of the human world, a utopian world that existed in the long-lost past. He seems to rekindle passion for life after piecing together a grand narrative about the heroic exodus of the human race from the solar system on a treacherous journey into space. But in the end, what he hears and confirms is only the tragic collapse of the ancient human astronauts' spacecraft after they have sowed human genes on an alien planet; the story does not tell us whether that planet is where all the posthuman creatures, including the listener, come from. But it ends with absolute silence from the listener, who shows no emotion at all after hearing the last transmitted message.[20] The old dreams revisited have dried up. To authors like Zhao Haihong and La La, the century-old utopian dream is a remote heterotopia encoded in either visual or vocal waves without solid meanings.

"WHAT HAS PASSED SHALL IN KINDER LIGHT APPEAR"

Of the younger generation, Bao Shu has composed some of the most sophisticated, often paradoxical and absurd stories experimenting with heterotopia and hetero-chronotope or the themes of time and temporality in general. One of his most famous stories is also about posthuman offspring capturing transmissions from the past. Six hundred and fifty light-years away, a bright star[21] keeps broadcasting powerful, militant, and sublime songs that attract a human spaceship to approach it and explore its history.[22] Originally titled "Star Songs" 星歌 (2012) when first published on the internet, in the print version the story became "Songs of Ancient Earth" 古老的地球之歌 (2013), and what the space explorers discover in that star also changed. In the online version, "star songs" are exactly the so-called "red songs" 紅歌, the patriotic revolutionary songs from Mao's age, which went through a revival in the early twenty-first century when Bao Shu wrote the story. The larger background was the revival of Maoist ideology as part of the political agenda designed by the then ambitious mayor of Chongqing City, Bo Xilai 薄熙來 (b. 1949). Unlike the other two stories just discussed, which are relatively apolitical, Bao Shu's story creates a meaningful dialogue with the political trend of regenerating a Sinotopia. His narrative provides a subtle, poignant comment on China's turning further left during the power transition in 2012–13. In the print version, the "star songs" are changed to the Russian patriotic revolutionary songs from Stalin's age, thus shifting the identity of the long-perished civilization from socialist China to the Soviet Union. But the English translation, upon the author's request, restored the original Chinese revolutionary songs.[23]

These songs are broadcast by nanorobots that fell into the star centuries ago. This monstrously glowing star is both astronomically and politically a "red giant," or "red star." The explorers no longer know anything about a socialist state that once upon a time existed on planet Earth, but they are all emotionally touched by these blood-boiling songs. Through archaeological work they discover how the songs were brought to this distant bright star: the ancient astronauts traveling there survived solely by listening to these songs that tempered their steely will and made them both hard-working and self-sacrificing, with strong passions exactly as the songs were intended to evoke during China's socialist movement, or the Mao years. The current team of explorers cannot stop listening, and a cult of "red songs" begins to emerge among them. Bao Shu's joke with this scenario of half-exposé and half-fantasy projects the cult of "red songs" and Red Classics to an astronomical scale.

These songs seem only to have created a team of devoted fans, but actually the songs have changed the entire fate of the universe. The artificial intelligence controlling the spaceship, Athena, also the narrator of the story, though a posthuman being, has also been converted to whatever -ism these songs advocate. She (it is programmed to be female) decides to crash the spaceship into the star and trigger the red giant to explode into a supernova that will spread the revolutionary songs to the entire galaxy. The cosmic concert of revolutionary songs begins: "This is the final struggle / Let us group together, and tomorrow / The Internationale / Will be the human race." (Or in this case when the nanorobots rise to dominate the universe, "the Internationale will be the posthuman.") The song is collectively sung by the nanorobots that will now colonize the entire universe and reproduce themselves infinitely.[24] Bao Shu smartly keeps the tone of the story seriocomic. In a profoundly comical or paradoxical way, it points to the absurd mixture of nostalgia and anachronism as defining factors in recapitulating the Communist vision among the younger authors, whose concern is less a reflection on the utopian tradition of modern China than a semidetached appropriation of it for new world-buildings that are actually full of uncertainty.

The strong sense of uncertainty is part of Bao Shu's focus on time and temporality, which has underpinned his various designs of restructuring historical narratives. Once a doctoral student in continental philosophy, he asks questions about time and meaning-making through SF world-buildings, many of which are centered on visions of a parallel universe, time travel, and alternate history. A more subversive narrative is one of Bao Shu's unpublished early stories, "Let's Go to See the Boat on the South Lake" 一起去看南湖船 (2011), written as an irreverent "gift" for the ninetieth anniversary of the founding of the Chinese Communist Party. According to the standard historical narrative, the first congress of the Party was held in haste on a boat in the South Lake in July 1921, the time and location enshrined as a historic landmark in both geographical and temporal senses.[25]

In Bao Shu's story, this time-space spot becomes the site for "red tourism," again an allusion to an actual practice in contemporary China combining political education and economic benefits. But here, the two tourists are time traveling from the future. What is more interesting is that the gazes of these two youthful characters are fixed on two different persons on the spot, two different early Party members, and their conversations soon reveal that they actually came from two parallel timelines, which radically differ in the historical course of the Party's early inner struggle as well as the entire subsequent national history. In one timeline, Mao Zedong died a young martyr and Zhang Guotao 張國燾 (1897–1979) became the supreme leader who founded the new China. In the other timeline that is the *well-known true* history, Zhang lost the power struggle with Mao during the Long March. The playful, comical effects of putting the two timelines together create a problematic confusion about the fixed meanings of historical narrative, where a nostalgic utopian dream is revealed as being rather arbitrary.

Bao Shu wrote two sequels to this politically subversive story and created his first cycle of narratives about the image of time, which is not linear, without a fixed direction, with no certain value or meaning attached to it. There are an infinite number of parallel universes, each of which could have produced a timeline different from what we know. This fantasy of time became the dominant theme in most of Bao Shu's novels and stories. His major breakthrough is a pastiche sequel to the "Three-Body" trilogy, *Redemption of Time* 觀想之宙 (2011), in which time is highlighted as another factor making Liu Cixin's cosmic vision even more uncertain and changeable. In Bao Shu's sequel, the final battle of the dark forest is fought between the creator of the timeless universe, the Prime Mother, and her child, the Lurker, who invents time and thus creates both life and death, as well as changes, meanings, evil, and everything else. In another major novel, *Ruins of Time* 時間之墟 (2013), Bao Shu depicts a world stuck in a time loop that lasts 20 hours 33 minutes but repeats billions of times, emptying time of all meanings for those who live in the loop, their consciousness falling apart and histories collapsing into futile cycles of the same experience—an eternal return that has been exhausted of meanings, truly tired of itself.

Bao Shu, who is well informed about political and historical philosophies, also experiments with reversing the direction of the time flow, thus displaying the absurdities of historical progression. This can be found in a longer story that he wrote but never published in China, "The Great Times" 大時代 (2012), which was translated into English by Ken Liu with a more poetic title, "What Has Passed Shall in Kinder Light Appear."[26] In this story, history performs a great leap backward in time, and actual historical events are narrated in a fictive reverse chronological order paralleling the main characters' story line; thus, they experience history backward from the Olympic Games (2008) to the Tiananmen Massacre (1989) to the Cultural Revolution (1966–1976) to China's Civil War (1945–1949) to Mao's Yan'an years (1936–1945). China's history is then presented as beginning with *shengshi*, an epoch of prosperity and peace, but degenerating into chaos, catastrophes, wars, and national humiliations. This narrative dismantles the assumed certainty of temporality represented as a linear, teleological passage toward a definitive utopian vision, and its reversal testifies to the vanity and voidness of any positive meanings attached to notions of historical progress and forward movement. Time is portrayed as arbitrary, unpredictable. Through experiments with allegorizing and dislocating time and temporality, Bao Shu creates the most powerful SF questioning of the fixation and certainty of utopian meanings that constitute the various historical narratives about the new China. In "What Has Passed Shall in Kinder Light Appear," history backtracks from the opening up of China to the closing doors policy. Sinotopia retreats from a global dream to a bleak scene of national predicament.

Bao Shu's protagonist comes to see the world as fundamentally absurd, "a twisted shadow of some reality." Facing a future that seems certain, he nevertheless feels dreadful: "In the days still to come, my generation would experience events far more terrifying than SARS. We knew nothing of the future that awaited us."[27] Read today after COVID-19 swept the entire planet and the Chinese government carried out political campaigns to return to Maoism, a great leap backward, Bao Shu's experiment with the fantasy of time is strikingly relevant to our contemporary time. It could serve as a timely warning of the recurring conservative trend to replace reform-oriented policy when Maoism is indeed coming back in Chinese politics.

Bao Shu's narrative can be read alongside Chan Koonchung's 2015 alternate history novel, *The Second Year of the Jianfeng Reign: A Uchronia of New China* 建豐二年: 新中國烏有史. Chan charts a different timeline for Chinese history: the Nationalist troops defeated the Communists in 1949 and Chiang Kai-Shek's reign lasted for another three decades; he was succeeded by his son, Chiang Ching-Kuo, who was about to begin reforms in 1979. David Der-wei Wang points to the double images of history that Chan presents in the narrative, a mixture of the actual and the virtual, in which "the differences and repetitions of bygone events work in two timelines working in such a way as to reveal their mutually implicated relations."[28] In Chan's fiction, even if there is a parallel universe, even if an alternate history unfolds differently, "all that has passed does not necessarily appear in kinder light." The uchronian version of history does not necessarily produce a better future for the new China; it is just like what really happened, routinely filled with ideological contentions, political persecutions, and aborted reform plans. Perhaps the only poetic justice that Chan's novel creates is the changed fate of Lao She, who survives to win the Nobel Prize.[29] However, that is the only bright side of Chan's uchronia. The same event called the Formosa Incident 美麗島事件 (1979) is still going to happen, as the ending suggests, a menacing sign of the inevitable abortion of China's democratic movement. Both Bao Shu's and Chan Koonchung's narratives deny the plausibility of utopia as a practicable ideal that gives history a meaning above its eventualities and contingencies.

HETEROTOPIA: THE INVISIBLE SPACE WITHIN OUR WORLD

Bao Shu's peers of the same age group, Ma Boyong and Hao Jingfang, have both made conscious reflections on the *Nineteen Eighty-Four* scenario in the more immediate context of contemporary China. Ma Boyong's "The City of Silence" 寂靜之城 (2005) presents a bleak view on the government's control of people's speech and thinking through censoring and regulating online expression: in a style reminiscent of the Ministry of Truth's replacing the lively everyday speech with the rigid Newspeak in Orwell's original novel, Ma's story describes how the Department of Web Security's "List of Healthy Words" gradually makes all words, from "freedom" to "talking" to "exchange," disappear from everyday speech, which begins to reshape people's sense of reality. A person cannot vomit because "vomit" is a prohibited word; no one can complain about the lack of "heat" during the winter because "heat" and "furnace" are removed from the daily vocabulary. Eventually the city falls into great silence, when the list of healthy words is now empty: "even the last word had been shielded by the appropriate authorities."[30]

Written in 2005, this story predicted the increasingly heightened web security in China over the following decades—the Great Firewall, web monitors, internet surveillance, big data, and the COVID-19 code monitoring keep upgrading the nation's cybernetic control. Ma's story also created an ultimately dark, dystopian vision of a future in which the very form of storytelling disappears, for a story like this one told in the "prohibited words" cannot exist. The text, the last place to find a utopian impulse, is emptied of vocabulary. If the plot points to a darkened Sinotopia that is unspeakable in the daily reality, the story itself becomes a heterotopia that poignantly shows its own exclusion (as freedom of speech) from that reality but simultaneously defines the reality's treacherous nature. Indeed, this story cannot be published in China without being heavily censored, while the city of silence is becoming increasingly "truthful" according to what has happened in China's reality.

Hao Jingfang heightens the significance of the year 1984 in an autobiographical novel, *Born in Nineteen Eighty-Four* 生於一九八四 (2016), which outlines her personal life story growing up in China, with a special focus on actual history's paradoxical relationship with Orwell's fictive world. Hao Jingfang's major effort at SF writing is a trilogy collectively titled *Vagabonds* 流浪蒼穹 (2012). This ambitious space saga in the form of a bildungsroman opens with a statement: "This is the tale of the fall of the last utopia."[31] It depicts an Orwellian society on Mars, which is built with a strong utopian vision but eventually becomes an authoritarian state due to limitations on resources and the overall hostile environment. It is evolving toward a Spartan military dictatorship. The novel focuses on a group of Martian youths' bewilderment between the darkened idealism of their home planet and a liberal, decadent Earth that represents late capitalism, where personal freedom is guaranteed, but it is revealed as an illusion built upon consumerism and mediocracy. The novel clearly pays homage to Ursula Le Guin's *The Dispossessed* (1974), which is about a similarly ambiguous utopia.

Hao Jingfang's most famous SF work is her Hugo award-winning short story, "Folding Beijing" 北京折疊 (2012), which is concerned less with a dystopian future than with a spatial restructuring of contemporary China's social reality. It depicts the capital city as a folded space:

> The folding city was divided into three spaces. One side of the earth was First Space, population five million. Its allotted time lasted from six o'clock in the morning to six o'clock the next morning. Then the space went to sleep, and the earth flipped.
>
> The other side was shared by Second Space and Third Space. Twenty-five million people lived in Second Space, and their allotted time lasted from six o'clock on that second day to ten o'clock at night. Fifty million people lived in Third Space, allotted the time from ten o'clock at night to six o'clock in the morning, at which point First Space returned. Time had been carefully divided and parceled out to separate the populations: five million enjoyed the use of twenty-four hours, and seventy-five million enjoyed the next twenty-four hours.

The structures on two sides of the ground were not even in weight. To remedy the imbalance, the earth was made thicker in First Space and extra ballast buried in the soil to make up for the missing people and buildings. The residents of First Space considered the extra soil a natural emblem of their possession of a richer, deeper heritage.[32]

Introducing readers to an estranged version of contemporary Beijing, Hao Jingfang nevertheless foregrounds the prevailing injustice of contemporary China, creating a spatial manifestation of inequality in the form of a folded city. The protagonist of the story, Lao Dao 老刀, is a smuggler transgressing the borders of the three spaces, and his experience shows that the social hierarchy not only exists between different spaces but also prevails in all levels of society—between men and women, and between different people with varying status even within the same space. Lao Dao is not a rebel; he only wants to make a living. While he is acutely aware of the contrast between the privileged life in the First Space and the miserable situation in the Third Space, his observations lead to an acceptance of the status quo. The rationale for the existing three-space structure of society is deeply rooted in the cold calculations of economic interests. The redistribution of time among the three spaces, while allocating much less time to the poor, serves to reduce the cost of living for those at a lower level of society. Thus, the redistribution is a totalistic restructuring of life: space, time, wealth, and the feeling of happiness. "Downsizing 'time' and everything makes the poor content with what they have." Lao Dao hears such a cynical explanation from someone who has reached the First Space by working their way up the social ladder—now physical in terms of the actual spatial relations.[33]

The systematic lack of justice and equality as well as the lack of room for conceiving alternatives in "Folding Beijing" shows a society that has no hope for utopian dreams. This story turns the utopian or dystopian space into a heterotopia, a form that appears to be otherly estranging but reflects the nature of one's own reality. This even is laid bare in the text itself, in that the First Space excludes those living in the Third Space but defines their life, and vice versa. At the same time, the folding Beijing establishes its heterotopian otherness to China's social reality both as a metonym and a textual reconstruction. Hao Jingfang's text showcases SF's capacity to turn itself into such a space that uses otherness or estrangement to show the heterotopia that exists within our own world.

In another short story by Hao Jingfang, "Invisible Planets" 看不見的星球 (2010), the I-narrator is telling "you" stories about wondrous, amazingly strange planets. For an entire afternoon, the I-narrator is telling stories that make "you" wonder, laugh, and question whether "my" stories about these invisible planets are real or fabricated. The I-narrator then speaks directly to "you" the reader: *Do you understand? When I am done telling you these stories, when you're done listening to these stories, I am no longer I, and you are no longer you. In this afternoon we briefly merged into one. After this, you will always carry a bit of me, and I will always carry a bit of you, even if we both forget this conversation.*"[34] The dialogue can be used as an explanatory narrative about heterotopia as well as the relationship between SF and heterotopia. If heterotopia is those invisible planets, estranged from and outside our daily experience, SF storytelling relates it to our own reality. Heterotopia, which refers to the space that is folded and invisible in reality, becomes a possible experience in SF without being lived through. At the same time, it attains a virtual form as narrative, a linguistic practice that makes the invisible come to light.

Based on these descriptions, we may understand that SF can assume heterotopian otherness in two senses: first, SF creates imaginary space in a heterotopian relation to our reality, which broadens our vision of worlds beyond our own in both time and space and produces new knowledge and new ways of understanding our position in this world. Second, the SF text can turn itself into a heterotopia by creating its own existence in relation to our position on the time-space continuum; recognizing the text itself as heterotopia establishes a metonymic relatedness between SF and the world. Because of SF, the world is whole: the genre bridges the gap between the known and the unknown, the seen and the unseen, us and others, and words and worlds. Heterotopia breaks down the binary boundaries in thinking and writing.

A fine example to illustrate the relationship between SF and heterotopia is Han Song's "Hospital" trilogy. Reading it now in 2022 further strengthens its heterotopian image in relation to our reality. Though completed and published before the pandemic, the "Hospital" trilogy is an intriguing case that, first of all, establishes a heterotopian image of China and relates its invisible "other space" to everyday experience. The hospital is one of the original "heterotopias" that Michel Foucault mentions,[35] and it represents a sort of crisis heterotopia where the fate of our own world becomes undecided, uncertain. The image of the hospital in Han Song's trilogy alludes to a totalistic crisis in contemporary China, and the story foregrounds menacing moments that appear abnormal, absurd, and insane but integral to China's assumed "harmonious" society. The hospital functions as the mirror to reflect the "invisible" dark side of our reality. Yet the textuality of Han Song's trilogy itself becomes a heterotopia. In the second volume, *Exorcism*, the patients are competing to tell "a good story about the hospital," a thinly veiled variation of Xi Jinping's calling for "telling a good China story," and storytelling is all that doctors can use to treat patients as well as keep themselves committed to the cause. This situation is also the fundamental driving force in all three novels' plot development. Therefore, the protagonist is not only stuck in the senselessly inhuman situation of the hospital but also stuck in a loop of storytelling about the hospital, which is set in a permanent mode of eternal return. There is no exit from this endless story, and the characters, patients and doctors alike, are subject to ceaseless repetitions of stories leading to the same end again and again. The terrifying story of the hospital functions as a textual heterotopia to enlighten readers about the plight of China as a country stuck in both a "health" and a "narrative" crisis, and Sinotopia as an imaginary world on the verge of falling into abysmal insanity.

POSTHUMAN HETEROTOPIA IN SINOPHONE LITERATURE

Three other cases imply dynamic relationships between SF and heterotopia, all precisely pointing to the significance of the literary form in remapping the topology of hope outside the strict borders of Sinotopia, or China per se. The first is a series of very short, anecdote-like stories by Fei Dao that read like fragments of a fictive encyclopedia, memories and descriptions of things so removed from our reality that they appear to be pure fantasy. These stories read like experimental Borgesian writings about the future offspring of humankind living in diaspora throughout the galaxy, having lost their own history and forgotten their origin. They are no longer human, not to mention being Chinese.

One of these stories, "One Kind of Melancholia Outside the Galaxy" 河外憂傷一種 (2019),[36] describes a heterotopian world, or rather a "hetero-chronotope": a time and place distant in the future and far away in deep space. A strange, inexplicable "nostalgia" drives pilgrims to approach the so-called "completely inaccessible domain" 完全不可接近域, an area of the unknown and invisible; they are obsessed with a hauntingly beautiful myth of the "blue planet," but can never locate it in the unfathomable darkness. Some pilgrims suspect that "nostalgia" is a virtual memory implanted in their consciousness, and there is no "origin." Or they believe the home planet has long perished; diaspora is their own reality, their fate. At a certain point, a "virtual cosmos" game player invents a simulated version of the cosmos, in which, one day, the dim light of the blue planet flickers. The entire community of pilgrims is shaken, and they come to behold the rebirth of their "home," but the blue dot has already disappeared without ever being observed . . . There the fragmented encyclopedia entry ends abruptly.

The omnipotent narrator takes over and immediately zooms out to a much broader view: further into the future, when the so-called interdimensional wanderers pass certain areas in the unfathomable darkness, their bodies are filled with warmth, hearts captured by pain and bittersweetness. These areas of darkness are dimensional fragments of the ruins of an older universe that already met its apocalypse. They do not know what this feeling is and refrain from articulating words to describe it; that silent tenderness conceives all the words and infinite expressions. Fei Dao's poetic, succinct narrative serves as a commentary on SF itself and even on literature in general. The reality has long disappeared, and nostalgia, even if it is originally caused by the loss of a real object, has now become nostalgia for its own sake. In this enchanting description of the mythical feeling of melancholia, it is the myth and enchantment that cause the melancholia. In this SF world, even nostalgia is virtual when the real has long disappeared.

This story, written by Fei Dao, an author based in Beijing, is nevertheless a piece of Sinophone SF, for it was commissioned by a magazine in Hong Kong and created with a self-awareness of its position in that context. The heterotopia, or the hetero-chronotope, that Fei Dao carefully builds has even more complicated meanings in that cultural context: Is China the heterotopia to a larger Sinophone literary vision transcending its borders? Is nostalgia meaningfully related to China only, or can it be a virtual form of an undetermined, uncertain territory? Fei Dao's narrative creates an open-ended scenario where the world as the real stops existing and the world as fabricated in literature comes into being.

Hong Kong's own Dung Kai-cheung creates a remarkable literary heterotopia in his short stories and novels, an imaginary city with a distinct name, V-City, or Victoria, through which he projects Hong Kong's future after its apocalyptic endgame. Such a fictive Hong Kong City, though still unnamed, was first described in Dung's 1997 *Atlas* (地圖集) as a "città invisibili" (Invisible City, with reference to Italo Calvino) that has disappeared and only comes back to life through the work of future archaeologists. The entire book consists of short encyclopedia entries introducing the various aspects of the city through imaginative readings of maps and historical documents.[37] It presents an acute feeling of "déjà disparu," as suggested by the cultural critic Ackbar Abbas, who published his landmark monograph on Hong Kong's 1997 syndrome (witnessing the city disappear before it actually happens) in the same year.[38] In Dung's book, the endgame for Hong Kong may imply its handover back to China or an even larger historical change, and it is portrayed as having already happened in the past. The narrative defined by a futuristic perspective gives the city the form of a lost place in a lost time, thus an estranging, imaginary place. Though the book is generally considered literary fiction, *Atlas*'s English version won the SF & Fantasy Translation Award in 2013, two years before Liu Cixin's Hugo Award.

Since the beginning of the twenty-first century, Dung Kai-cheung had been devoted to writing a massive novel series, "Natural History" 自然史, which borrows more extensively from SF and new scientific theories (apocalypse, black hole, baby universe) to create a unique narrative that renders the city a metaphor reflecting the postmodern and posthuman conditions of the post-1997 future. The world that Dung builds in these novels can be viewed as a heterotopian mirror of Hong Kong, alluding to Hong Kong's colonial past, its problematic present, and its postapocalyptic future. The two-volume second part in the series, *Histories of Time*, creates an extremely complicated, half-metaphysical narrative that presents the city's (past and future) history in the uncanny image of time—lost, retrieved, reimagined, and represented.

The novel contains self-reflections on writing, narrative, and literary imagination: the protagonist is a writer who is stuck in his own imagination, gradually losing his sense of reality. While he is in melancholic self-isolation, the world that the novel depicts seems to have grown out of his speculations. At its center is a seventeen-year-old girl, Virginia, whose heart is being replaced with a mechanical clock, which allows her to stay at the age of seventeen forever. In 2097, when Hong Kong is no more, the cyborg Virginia, still seventeen years old, moves into a library where she begins to rebuild the world, an entirely imaginary world, through composing "A Chronicle of a Mini-Universe" 小宇宙編年史.[39] At the very end of this gigantic narrative, En'en 恩恩, the fictive protagonist of the self-isolated writer's earlier novel, as told in the text, "experiences that marvelous moment, finding herself in the depth of imagination and feeling that infinite, abundant, already existing baby universe."[40] The novel ends with this moment: when reality vanishes, a new world is born. It is a world of wonders, with infinite spectacles. The last sentence heightens the literariness of "heterotopia" as a virtually constructed, linguistically energized body of texts. It also marks the recognition of science fictionality as an element of experimentalism in literary fiction.

Dung's two recent novels, *Beloved Wife* 爱妻 (2018) and *A Posthuman Comedy* 後人間喜劇 (2020), both perform a more self-conscious experiment with SF motifs. Both novels center on artificial intelligence and simulated cyborgian consciousness. Their similar metafictional narrative strategy deliberately blurs reality and simulation. *Beloved Wife* touches upon the true nature of emotion through a simulation of sentimentality in a complicated narrative that turns out to be a programmed treatment of a man who has lost his own body and coexists with his wife's mind in her body. It is storytelling that is meant to be a medical treatment, which echoes Han Song's motif. But Dung does not go deeper to confront the ultimate evil. His narrative experiment posits a challenge to the ethical foundation of love: can love be simulated?

A Posthuman Comedy is closer to Hong Kong's political unrest, the massive protest that happened during the year when Dung was writing this novel—2019. The narrative is presented as a story that may have been created by a character in the novel, which forms a fold in time, allowing the protagonist to travel from the Old Port to the so-called New City, both Hong Kong but existing in two positions in time. In the New City he discovers a government conspiracy that replaces real humans with the so-called The Thing-in-Itself, cyborgs who do not have human souls. But what makes the story complicated is that another experiment to make the so-called Kantian Machines, cyborgs with human reason, morality, and judgment, has given all cyborgs self-consciousness. The protagonist participates in a revolution to fight for "human rights" for cyborgs, after which he returns from the future New City to Old Port, or Hong Kong today, where he sees young protesters rallying at the airport. This second novel about artificial intelligence heightens a political consciousness that connects Kantian liberalism to the ongoing fight for freedom in Hong Kong. Particularly in *A Posthuman Comedy*, Dung consciously uses the strategy of creating a heterotopian mirror to the current reality, the futuristic New Port, where all things that happen can be understood as folded images of what is happening in Hong Kong right now.

Dung Kai-cheung's peer in Taiwan, perhaps the most important Sinophone novelist of this generation, Lo Yi-chin, has consciously integrated SF elements into his experimentalist narratives over the past decade. References to Chinese new wave SF images and motifs have particularly filled three novels he wrote in the second decade of the twenty-first century, *Daughter* 女兒 (2013), *Superman Kuang*, and *Mingchao*. All three make the SF world-building a heterotopia to Taiwan's political reality. Lo's labyrinthine narrative presents an imaginary realm of speculations, metaphors, dismemberments, remembrances, and reconstructions of the "other" space in terms of identity, sexual transgression, diasporic experience, literary references, and historical consciousness. A chapter from *Daughter*, titled "Science Fiction" 科幻小說, can be read as a meta-SF text that attempts to create a literary experiment with SF text, just as SF experiments with world-building.[41] However, Lo's world-building is not aimed at creating sublime cosmic images or abysmal dark images, as in Liu Cixin or Han Song, but rather is a literary self-conscious effort to render the narrative itself into a spectacle.

Superman Kuang borrows the mythical image of Monkey King to depict a strong sense of being excluded from history: the monkey king is cut off from his original story, displaced and exiled to an endless sequence of meaningless actions in the modern or future worlds, just like the

I-narrator finds himself dislodged from his immediate reality and exiled as a stranger in his own home city, Taipei. What is worse is that he is troubled by an unspeakable agony: there is a hole opening up on the skin of his genitals. To him, this hole in his body becomes a black hole that absorbs all his attention, energies, worries, and visions. The hole becomes a heterotopia to the world where he is: not only a metaphor for the darkness surrounding him and his contemporaries but also a virtual form for him to explore an infinitely enlarged space that contains more possibilities than reality allows. It stands for the portal through which to enter a mythical world. The black hole corresponds to the apocalyptic moment: "those demons sleeping in the nightmares of the world are released when the sky showers burning bombs and hell erupts in fire." "This moment dislodged from the flux of time turns into an enormous hole whose immensity and magnitude are beyond grasp."[42] The hole in the superman's body (his genitals) opens the gate to the darkness and stops time from flowing; yet, devouring time, it also creates an infinite delay in face of the impending apocalypse. The superman, like Monkey King, has nowhere to settle with his pains and fears, but resides in this hole, and that is where literature begins, which imagines all the possible and impossible, a verbal heterotopia that gives form to all the shapeless, invisible demonic forces. The novel almost has no plot but a narrative that renders itself into the spectacle, like the hole. A self-consciously built virtual form of the world, a heterotopia that makes us see what lies in the dark, Lo Yi-chin's "hole" is a SF singularity.

In *Mingchao*, Lo Yi-chin directly engages in dialogue with Liu Cixin. He borrows from the "Three-Body" trilogy the plot about the two-dimensional universe. The novel is loosely based on a world setting that suggests an impending end for the solar system. Scientists begin to train robots, preparing to launch them into deep space, with a hope that one day the robots will rebuild human civilization. The I-narrator is an engineer programming his robot with an entire Ming Dynasty design. The novel is mainly focused on the detailed depictions of Ming literati culture, the knowledge and history of the Ming Dynasty, all explained to the robot, in parallel to the I-narrator's life in contemporary Taiwan. The distinction between reality and illusion often disappears, and the detailed stories about the Ming Dynasty are mingled with apocalyptic scenes. Nothing but narrative is the central event in *Mingchao*: what the I-narrator is telling his robot is all that matters in this novel. It consists of repeated stories, extended storytelling about ill-fated writers, artists, emperors, and fictive characters. All the storytelling creates an immense surface world, a virtual world that does not have depth in reality. It is best represented in the patterns on the surface of Ming porcelain: all the splendid, decadent, exotic, and erotic images point to a surface prosperity that hovers above an abysmal emptiness; splendor above a menace.[43]

Lo's novel presents a counterimage to Liu Cixin's sublime aesthetics. The infinite immensity of the universe is not the magnetic center of the narrative. Lo's storytelling is characterized by an obsession with the surface where the sublime collapses into decadence. SF is appropriated as a device to postpone the arrival of the sublime cosmic terror, and storytelling is the only thing that will delay the endgame. Instead of building a speculative world, Lo's narrative has become a spectacle itself. If Liu Cixin creates wonders through SF, Lo Yi-chin renders SF into a verbal wonder. *Mingchao*, which denotes both a past dynasty and "tomorrow," becomes a heterotopian space that conceives more timelines than what can be predetermined. *Mingchao* is also the ultimate heterotopia to today, which turns SF into a revelation that directly speaks to us. Written by a writer residing in Taiwan but dreaming of the Ming Dynasty, it represents Sinotopia and heterotopia in a completely integrated image. China, Taiwan, and the otherness that connects both to the larger world have been placed in a self-performing Neo-Baroque spectacle, where the topology of hope flattens into a Ming portrait of a beautiful lady, floating into the deep space at the end of the novel. Tomorrow and the Ming Dynasty are one.

8

CHINESE NEW WAVE GOES GLOBAL

The Posthuman Turn

In 2021, *AI 2041: Ten Visions for Our Future*, a book coauthored by the IT tycoon Lee Kai-Fu 李開復 (b. 1961), originally from Taiwan, and the SF writer Chen Qiufan, was first released in English, though the ten short stories were composed by Chen in Chinese.¹ This book was obviously intended for a global audience, and its appearance marked a new level of Chinese SF's global impact. Each chapter contains a short story that Chen Qiufan wrote about one specific aspect of future human life under the impact of the technology of artificial intelligence and cybernetic control, followed by Lee Kai-Fu's analysis of the "novum" highlighted in the story from the technological, industrial, commercial, and cultural/ethical perspectives. Throughout the book, Lee's voice is certainly more succinct than Chen's. He makes clear that this book is about "a future where AI technology could influence individuals and societies positively," and states, "*AI 2041* would challenge the stereotype of the dystopian AI narrative—the kind of tale where the future is irrevocably bleak." He confidently declares that these ten visions testify to his confidence that "we shape a happier and brighter future."²

Chen Qiufan's stories make a global network that connects Mumbai, Lagos, Seoul, Shanghai, Tokyo, Colombo, Keflavík, San Francisco, Al Saeida, and Brisbane, ten locations, including one fictive in Qatar. The ten stories qualify Chen's fictional part of the book as a global novel, a sort of new writing that literary critic Adam Kirsch considers a twenty-first-century invention that sees different places and peoples as intimately connected.[3] I believe this represents a new planetary consciousness in the context of the popularization of SF. As I will discuss later in this chapter, David Mitchell's *Cloud Atlas* is certainly a global novel, which presents a SF vision unfolding into a Neo-Baroque kaleidoscopic image of the world in its extreme complexity. Chen Qiufan's first novel, *Waste Tide* 荒潮 (2013), is certainly comparable to *Cloud Atlas*. If Kirsch is right about the twenty-first-century global novel's ethical concern about what it means to be human in the contemporary world, global SF may express a similar concern in an opposite way, asking what it means to be posthuman in a world that is rapidly transforming into a futuristic SF scene.

Reading Chen Qiufan's stories and Lee Kai-Fu's technological analyses side by side is a telling experience, highlighting the divergence between literary imagination and industrial blueprint. While Lee wholeheartedly embraces a posthuman future, Chen's narratives nevertheless reveal a series of humanist moments, or glitches caused by human fragility and fallibility. Take for example the Shanghai story, "Contactless Love" 無接觸之戀: it depicts Shanghai in 2041 still under COVID-19 lockdown, in which humans have to manage ordinary life with the assistance of robots. Lee's analysis focuses on the practicality of the household robots, but Chen's story foregrounds the fear of the protagonist, Chen Nan, who mentally locks herself in absolute isolation, the modernist alienation that prevents her from accepting love from Garcia, a Brazilian young man. Garcia considers them all "stuck in a dead-end loop,"[4] though finally he bravely comes to Shanghai, faking his COVID death to force Chen Nan to leave her apartment, going through all the trouble in a well-isolated social space, to find him still alive at the Pudong Airport. Chen Nan realizes, "Her fear of contact had persisted for so long that it had become a part of her."[5] The story ends on an uplifting tone, but even when they are finally together, Chen Nan and Garcia's embrace is still the embodiment of contactless love, plastic-textured, with folds of their protective suits. This scene demonstrates Chen Qiufan's ethical commitment to telling a truth-revealing SF story, which projects a posthuman future that is not as bright as Lee Kai-Fu envisions. Even though Lee provides technological solutions to human problems, Chen's stories heighten the posthuman predicament in the contemporary human condition.

AI 2041 provides an opportunity to combine my reflections on two topics related to new wave SF: its global reach and its posthuman turn. It is not an exaggeration to say that the new wave has been largely shaped by contemporary posthuman thinking: posthuman images and ideas, ranging from robots, aliens, and monsters to AI total control to hyperdimensional consciousness and planetary or cosmic ecology have permeated Chinese SF. Liu Cixin's sublime cosmos and Han Song's chthonic aesthetics both point to the post-anthropocentric tendencies that have decentered humanity from its classical humanist position. Yet Chinese SF also displays a strong nostalgia for humanism. The profound reflection that SF writers have made when confronting a technologized future tends to emphasize how we remain human in a posthuman world.

This chapter presents Chinese new wave SF's global impact, outlines its negotiations with world literature as a genre that has an in-built world-building system, discusses the translingual metamorphosis of Chinese SF, and from there situates the new wave in the context of global SF's posthuman turn, connecting Chinese SF to the current posthuman theories, with highlights of posthuman China/Taiwan as represented in SF stories and novels by Chen Qiufan, Chi Ta-wei, and Egoyan.

SCIENCE FICTION AND WORLD LITERATURE

In chapter 2, I introduced Liu Cixin's "Mountain," which serves as not only a metatext of the genre itself but also a megatext signifying the genre's Chinese entry into world literature in tandem with Liu Cixin's journey to the world stage. "Mountain" uses the same narrative strategies about the Earth civilization's forced odyssey into space, exploring and integrating into a new world, as in the "Three-Body" trilogy. In a larger context, it also serves to allegorize the national experience of China's entering a new world order defined by the modern time-space and political economy. Rhetoric in news reports about the novel's success in the United States and around the world shows that Chinese SF has been taken as an index of China's endeavor to not only survive but also prevail in the larger world. Landing on the surface of the planet SF, Chinese new wave becomes a global phenomenon.

With the success of the "Three-Body" trilogy, Liu Cixin's fame soon spread beyond China, and subsequently changed Chinese SF's position from marginal in domestic literature to a planetary phenomenon in world literature. Before 2010, the only essay on Chinese SF published in the American academic journal *Science Fiction Studies* characterized the genre's history in China as a hesitant journey to the West and found it "a fairly marginal phenomenon" in the Middle Kingdom.[6] The situation has changed drastically over the past ten years. Chinese SF has suddenly gained worldwide recognition, and today it is no longer a "hidden lonely army" and its journey to the West is no longer "hesitant"; it has become a fresh new force that helps shape the outlook for global SF.

Marketed as China's national bestseller when the *Wall Street Journal* made a sensational announcement that China had launched a sci-fi invasion of the United States,[7] *The Three-Body Problem* crossed national borders smoothly and achieved unrivaled international bestselling scores among all translations of Chinese literature only weeks after its release in the United States. Ken Liu, a Chinese American SF writer who established his reputation after winning the Hugo, Nebula, and World Fantasy Awards with a single short story, "The Paper Menagerie" (2012), fine-tuned Liu Cixin's novels with a smooth combination of the original Chinese text's dynamism and the stylish accuracy and neatness of American SF. Tor Books released *The Three-Body Problem* to critical acclaim in November 2014, followed by its sequel *The Dark Forest* (translated by Joel Martinsen) in August 2015, with the final volume of the trilogy, *Death's End* (translated by Ken Liu), released in August 2016. Liu's novels received endorsements from American writers and celebrities ranging from the Utopian novelist Kim Stanley Robinson (b. 1952) to the popular fantasy author George R.R. Martin (b. 1948), as well as from President Barack Obama[8] and the Facebook founder Mark Zuckerberg. The "Three-Body" universe eventually remapped world SF through renditions in over a dozen languages. In 2015, Liu Cixin was the first non-English author to win the Hugo Award for Best Novel. He also won Spain's Premio Ignotus award as a non-Spanish writer and Germany's Kurd Laßwitz Award as a non-German writer.

While Liu Cixin has quoted American and British space opera writers like Isaac Asimov and Arthur C. Clarke as major influences on his own writings,[9] his fans consider *The Three-Body Problem*'s winning the

Hugo a game-changing event that pushed Chinese SF into the limelight for Anglo-American audiences. Liu's novels quickly took on a new life as "world literature," which David Damrosch defines in terms of circulation and reading across the borders of national literatures.[10] Outside China, Liu's work thrives in a translingual status, mirroring his prediction of invented hybridity in the future world languages in *Dark Forest*, a trendy success not too distant from the triumph of "global English."[11] Strategic usage of "global English" can lead to socially meaningful literary experiments, but it also highlights the fact that nothing remains intact or "authentic" if the author thinks of English as the future language of their works. Editing the English version was strenuous when the narrative discourse had to be adjusted to remove words considered "improper," such as the gender-biased expressions that permeated Liu's literary texts. However, even so, against cautious literary theorists like Emily Apter, who warned about untranslatability based on a critique of the commercialized "world literature" that exploits cultural equivalence and identity politics,[12] *The Three-Body Problem*, together with other Chinese SF novels, including *Waste Tide* and Ken Liu's anthologies *Broken Stars* and *Invisible Planets*, seems to do well, or even better, in English. A situation that differs drastically from Apter's suspected "identity" cultural game, Chinese SF rendered into English sometimes defies the boundaries set by political censorship and nationalist limitations.

A few paragraphs deliberately edited out of the original Chinese version of *The Three-Body Problem* have been translated and included in the English version, and the original chapter order was restored; all these chapters are concerned with the Cultural Revolution, a dangerous topic in China. Their inclusion in the English version makes the narrative more coherent and complete than even the Chinese original. A small number of SF stories that have touched upon China's political taboos, such as Bao Shu's "The Great Times," could be published, as mentioned in chapter 7, only as Ken Liu's translation, "What Has Passed Shall in Kinder Light Appear." The English version of another story by Bao Shu, "Songs of Ancient Earth," was restored to the author's original version. So was Ma Boyong's "The City of Silence." Michael Duke's English translation of Chan Koonchung's *The Fat Years* was the key in raising the novel's visibility and availability because the novel was completely banned in China.

These translations make a poignant, yet constructive statement about the awareness of untranslatability, which is not or at least not only a rebuttal of the so-called neoliberal market-driven "world literature," but also is necessary to bypass the checkpoints of the old-fashioned authoritarian system.

An advocate for the new conceptualization of "world literature" based on cross-cultural translatability and border-crossing circulation, David Damrosch also presents a sober reminder that "foreign works have difficulty entering a new arena if they don't conform to the receiving country's image of what the foreign culture should be, and the difficulties become all the greater if a work doesn't seem useful in meeting local needs abroad."[13] What makes Chinese SF's "entering world literature" even more complicated is that SF is originally already a "foreign" culture to Chinese authors like Liu Cixin and Han Song. As mentioned in Excursus I, the genre was first introduced to China through Japan more than one hundred years ago, and the subsequent generations of writers have all been influenced by foreign SF. Contemporary writers like Liu Cixin, Han Song, and Chen Qiufan have to reinvent the genre conventions and experiment with variations on the customary conventions of literature in general through simultaneously transplanting and transcending the discourses, images, concepts, and world systems from their Anglo-American, Japanese, Russian, and European counterparts.

Liu Cixin openly admits his admiration for Arthur C. Clarke. An emotional moment in *Death's End* is the establishment of a monument to human civilizations, which clearly pays homage to the plot in Clarke's classic story "The Star."[14] Han Song's much darker, often mystic worldviews closely connected to his sharp observations on cybernetics, robotics, the political usage of technologies, and posthuman self-consciousness have established his reputation as China's Philip K. Dick. Chen Qiufan's insight into the mutating global political economy based on exploitation of the lower class, named "waste people" in *Waste Tide*, betrays discrimination according to race, class, gender, and nation in the context of a worsening global ecological crisis, which links his acute social criticism to that of Taiwan's Wu Ming-yi, as well as to a number of SF writers around the globe sharing similar concerns, such as David Mitchell, Paolo Bacigalupi (b. 1972), China Miéville (b. 1972), and Nalo Hopkinson (b. 1960). For Chinese writers as well as those from other parts of the world, choosing to write SF is already an engagement with "world literature" through connecting their visions to this genre that is "global" by origin.

"GLOBAL SCIENCE FICTION" AND ITS REWRITES IN POSTCOLONIAL/POSTHUMAN TERMS

As Istvan Csicsery-Ronay Jr. asserts: "SF has had an important role in the Enlightenment striving to view the world as a unitary thing.... Globalization of one form or another has been the default vector of sf from the beginning."[15] Compared to other literary genres, SF is modern, characterized by two forward-looking visions that created the modern world. The first is of a utopia that, first inspired by post-Columbus travelogues and given a political meaning by Thomas More, cast an optimistic gaze into the "other" space representing a better place for all. The second is of the progress of humankind, a narrative popularized by Enlightenment thinking and the French Revolution that later had a worldwide impact on the modern mind. The idea of progress means change created by temporality, a historical movement toward a predetermined betterment of human conditions, pointing to a universal timetable synchronizing world history, including the future history. Both visions, though claiming universalism, were primarily inventions of modern European intellectual thinking.

The first notable SF novel, Mary Shelley's *Frankenstein*, may already qualify as "global SF." It carries the two visions mentioned above, both their thesis and antithesis, depicting the world's best scenario and its shadow, a revolution of science and heart together with a profound post-revolutionary dismay. The English novel was conceived among the Romantic exiles in Switzerland. The protagonist is designated, like Jean-Jacques Rousseau, a noble citizen of Geneva. His Creature follows Dr. Frankenstein to England, Scotland, Ireland, continental Europe, and all the way to the North Pole. The sources of the novel form a European microcosm of "world literature": ancient Greek tragedies, biblical narratives, medieval folklore, German and British Gothicism, French encyclopedias, early anarchism, early feminism, and British Romanticism, together with records of alchemy and papers on modern biological sciences and the new sciences of electricity, magneticity, chemistry, and physics. Important historical figures who influenced the novel's conception make a full gallery of international celebrities of world literature: Aeschylus, Ovid, Goethe, John Milton, Erasmus Darwin, Luigi Galvani, Lord Byron, Percy Shelley, and Mary's father, William Godwin, and her mother, Mary Wollstonecraft.[16] *Frankenstein* surpasses many later literary works that came to define SF in terms of border crossing and transnational configuration. Both Jules Verne and H. G. Wells had narrower visions of the world, though they both assumed a transnational position. Verne's passion for depicting Anglo-American characters never discounted his own patriotism, and his "extraordinary adventures" happen mostly in exotic locations in the colonies of the European countries. Wells's *War of the Worlds* (1896) is very much limited to the viewpoint of England, but it contains a grandiose moment—the entire human world is compared to a drop of water viewed from deep space. The great tradition of SF spearheaded by Mary Shelley, Verne, and Wells laid a solid foundation for the global SF that treats the human race as a whole, a tradition that continued in the Golden Age space operas, Asimov's "Foundation" series, and Clarke's "Space Odyssey" series.

This tradition came to Liu Cixin and his fellow Chinese authors at the turn of the twenty-first century. In many ways, *The Three-Body Problem* is not a usual Chinese novel. For example, it features not only Chinese characters but also an international, or even interstellar cast when counting the Trisolarans. The 2007 print edition[17] opens with not only China but also the entire world encountering a crisis, the impending invasion from outside our solar system. Conflicts between nations have to be set aside, a united front formed among all humans, and resistance unitarily organized against an external, even invisible, enemy. The concluding volume, *Death's End*, opens with a prelude that presents a Byzantine girl's encounter with a hyperdimensional fragment in 1453 before the fall of Constantinople and then, six hundred years later, a Chinese woman scientist's despair at the dimmed hope for the survival of human civilization. It makes a sweeping account of a global apocalypse from the fall of Constantinople to the endgame destroying the Earth civilization.

But after all, this Chinese SF novel was written nearly two centuries after *Frankenstein*. The singular shadow in Mary Shelley's narrative, a dystopian anomaly in the overall optimistic humanist blueprint for perfection of all individuals, has now grown into a planet-size darkness. Twice in the narrative of Liu Cixin's saga, the global population on the planet is viewed as an anonymous entity by the superintelligence from deep space. The first event happens when a Trisolaran device arrives in the solar system. The unknown device, nicknamed "Droplet" by Earthlings, is interpreted first as a gift of peace, with its perfect shape symbolizing good intentions. This deceptive utopian impulse puts all humans in one basket, so when the scientist Ding Yi 丁儀 guesses the real intention of the droplet ("If I destroy you, what business is it of yours?"[18]), it reveals contempt for all lives on our planet. The second event is the demise of the entire solar system. For the God-like creature Singer, the human civilization is nothing but an anonymous, invisible low-level existence viewed from beyond the globe: "Singer gazed at the world of the Star-Pluckers. It was an ordinary star that had at least a billion more time grains of life left. It possesses eight planets: four giant liquid planets and four solid ones. Singer's experience told him that the low-entropy entities who had sent out the primitive membrane broadcast lived on one of the solid planets."[19]

Observed from a global point of view, the transformation from utopia to dystopia has characterized the modern epoch that began at the end of the Victorian period in England. H. G. Wells predicted the War of the Worlds, and postwar SF projected worse global menaces incarnated in the authoritarian Oceania, the nuked Gojira, and the illusive simulated reality controlled by the Matrix. Global problems demanding urgent action, such as global warming, ecological crisis, pandemic, famine, extinction, cybernetic insecurity, and political restlessness, have all contributed to the further darkening of SF as well as the popularity of dystopian classics like Margaret Atwood's (b. 1939) *The Handmaid's Tale* (1985) and Philip K. Dick's *The Man in the High Castle* (1962). But does the terrifying dystopian "contemporary" world completely dismantle the utopian humanism and drag each nation back to its closed territory? Even so, the genetic linkage of the genre determines that even the darkest dystopian vision comes from the same idealism, a pursuit of alternatives to reality, that inspired utopianism in the first place.

However, the discourse has also changed due to rising new theories contesting the ways of interpreting the "other." One year after his publication of the above-mentioned paper, Csicsery-Ronay Jr. read at Wellesley College a somewhat different version that further explains the idea of "global SF" through situating it in a subtle critique of the European hegemony:

> Gains in scientific knowledge and technology that gave European societies the power to collect parts of the world and populations under their hegemony were in effect producing the prospect of the "one world," a planet governed by the unifying "universal principle" of enlightened progress and modernization. The period of European colonial expansion culminates in a grand claim of "universality" for Western European cultural dominance. The concept of the "universum"—adopted from ecclesiastical hegemony and carrying with it a distinctly non-materialist reference to the centrality of human institutions in the cosmos—was with the post-Copernican enlightenment thinkers reduced in focus to the earth; but it is an earth expanding from within by its future prospects of intellectual liberation for the entire human species, and unlimited communication and material development.[20]

This paragraph historicizes the concept of "global SF" by bringing it back to its birthplace, Europe. Universalism and humanism are synchronized in modern times, which keeps alive the same utopian impulse that, despite knowing the limits of both the centrality of human institutions and the European version of humanism, seeks an expansion from within. Humanism evolves together with the sciences, and so does SF. Edward Said's (1935–2003) call for a democratic version of humanism broadens the horizon for more inclusiveness,[21] and the rise of African, Indian, South American, Arabic, and now Chinese SFs have all contributed to a counterbalance to the former European hegemony's gravitational pull and the genre's development toward "one world." According to scholars like Jessica Langer, postcolonial SF is waging a war aiming to deconstruct a world built upon the stereotyped "otherness" in terms of race and gender.[22]

What is at stake is also what is human in a changing world. The decades following the two world wars and the countercultural movements of the 1960s–'70s saw the "global" part of SF transform from Eurocentric humanism to a diversified conglomerate of "different" identities emphasizing the "otherness" among us, or the "difference" in all humans. Various characters of world SF—Frankenstein's Creature, Karel Čapek's Universal Robots, Fritz Lang's (1890–1976) cyborgian *Maschinenmensch* (Machine

Person), Alexander Belyaev's (1884–1942) Ariel the Fly man, Osamu Tezuka's (手塚 治虫1928–1989) Atom Boy, Philip K. Dick's androids, Stanley Kubrick's (1928–1999) Hal 9000, Stephen Spielberg's (b. 1946) E.T., and Lars Lundström's (b. 1965) Real Humans[23]—have enlivened the current theoretical framework of posthumanism. They have all extended the image of humanity in terms of class, gender, race, sexual orientation, ideological orientation, and self-identity. In the popular sci-fi TV show *Westworld* (2016), the Renaissance Vitruvian Man is replaced by a cyborg produced on an assembly line.

David Mitchell's *Cloud Atlas* can be read as the contemporary world's most neatly phrased "global" answer to the European question at the heart of Mary Shelley's *Frankenstein*. The novel consists of six stories presented in a narrative labyrinth so disorienting and folded that it shines with a Neo-Baroque splendor. The novel has a simple message to convey, traceable to Mary's father, William Godwin's (1756–1836), political ideas: an anarchist belief in the goodness of individuals versus the coercive oppression of a variety of institutions, from a nursing home to systematic slavery to cybernetic total control. Six locations, six historical periods, six personalities, six writing styles, six interrupted narratives cover the widest possible range of geographical locations, cultural developmental levels, class and social statuses, genders (including "no gender"), ages, degrees of sentimentality and passion, races/species, levels of self-consciousness, willpower, technological knowledge, and ultimately visions of destiny and endgame. The novel is a science fictional encyclopedia, deliberately beginning its story on a historical date close to the time when *Frankenstein* was conceived, with clear allusions to various forms and styles of SF writing. The message is too simple not to be conveyed in a metaphor: "Yet what is any ocean but a multitude of drops?"[24] The fabricant, Somni-451, comes to a realization of her own irreplaceable, unreproducible individuality, and she gives "singularity," the dreaded word in SF signaling the machine's revolt against humans, a new meaning that is more human than ever: "Truth is singular. Its 'versions' are mistruths."[25] What could better convey a new age utopian vision than the agendas of posthumanism and postcolonialism combined in one—a female fabricant living in New Seoul, seeking a singular truth that will eventually reconnect all humans and their AI offspring (the colonized), all machines and their gods (the oppressors)? The question of Frankenstein's monster, asked once by John Milton's Man,[26] is now answered in the new discourse of global SF, with a hope to establish a posthuman equality of all lives.

A CHINESE TIDE

The release of the English translation of *Waste Tide*, an even more complete and authoritative version than the Chinese original first printing that was censored for its explicit depiction of a rape scene, has added a Chinese novel to "global SF." Chen Qiufan's 2013 debut novel connects different locations in China and around the globe: China's vibrant economic zone in Guangdong, the American office of the fictive transnational TerraGreen Recycling Company, wartime memories about a Japanese military bacteria laboratory, an environmental protection movement based in Hong Kong, and as if in homage to Frankenstein, the protagonist's final stop in the Aleutian Islands, near the North Pole. All these are put on the atlas of the world economy, displaying the trade flows, international bargaining, exploitation of the working class, and consolidation of power represented by the state, the family, and the business. *Waste Tide* presents a timely criticism of global capitalism that seems to have entered the final stage. At the center of Chen Qiufan's new world image is an electronic waste recycling site, based on a real location near Chen's own hometown in Shantou, Guangdong. In *Waste Tide*, the original name of this place, Guiyu 貴嶼 (literally "treasure island"), is renamed Guiyu 硅嶼 (literally "silicon island"), but it also acquires an additional homophonic meaning of *guiyu* 鬼域 (literally "the ghostly domain") on account of its inhuman conditions. Local corruption, combined with transnational capitalism, produces a dark picture of China's near future.

Millions of migrant workers, called "waste people" by the locals, lead a miserable and invisible life without any means of defending their own rights. Their daily job is to process the electronic waste imported from developed countries. The waste infects them biologically and psychologically. The novel presents a hyper-realistic depiction of the waste people's inhuman condition where they are exposed, and even addicted, to the heavily polluted, unnatural environment. Their world appears to be more virtual than real, the least organic possible, as an American businessman witnesses:

> Scott observed the men and women living among the trash—the natives called them the waste people. The women did their laundry in the black water with their bare hands, the soap bubbles forming a silver edge around floating mats of duckweed. Children played everywhere, running over the black shores, where fiberglass and the charred remains of circuit boards twinkled; jumping over the abandoned fields, where embers and ashes from burnt plastic smoldered; swimming and splashing in dark green ponds, where polyester film floated over the surface. They seemed to think this was the natural state of the world and northing disturbed their job. The men bared their chests to show off the cheap body films they had applied. Wearing *shanzhai* versions of augmented reality glasses, they enjoyed a bit of rare leisure by lying on the granite banks of irrigation canals, filled with broken displays and plastic junk. These ancient canals, built hundreds of years ago to bring water to thirsty rice paddies, now shimmered with the fragmented lights of the process of dismantling the old.[27]

A few paragraphs farther into the narrative, he sees:

> On the ground in front of him was a wriggling prosthetic arm. Whether intentional or not, the stimulus loop of the arm was left open, and the internal battery, incompletely disassembled, continued to provide power. The electricity flowed along the artificial skin to the synthetic nerves revealed at the broken end, and triggered cyclic contractions in the muscles. The five fingers of the prosthesis continuously clawed at the ground, pulling the broken forearm along like some giant, flesh-colored inchworm.[28]

Such a grotesque, sensational depiction of the painful struggle of a man whose body consists of synthesized parts echoes the agonized cry of Frankenstein's monster, but here the unnamed person has no facial expression, no voice. His death is part of a world losing its human definition. In the meantime, this grotesque scene, as observed by the American visitor, is being presented to the world audience, but as someone coming from a highly developed area, the visitor has been part of the global center of capitalism that caused this inhuman condition. Chinese readers, who observe it through the perspective of the foreigner, can recognize it as a part of China already turning into a virtual realm beyond the Middle Kingdom.

Chen Qiufan studied literature at Beijing University, and he is well equipped with the theories of Gilles Deleuze, Jean Baudrillard (1929–2007), and Slavoj Žižek (b. 1949). The world image in *Waste Tide* strategically connects their ideas about the virtual, simulacrum, and barred Real to the real experience of China. China's reality is turned into a SF narrative that reveals the hidden "real" underneath the conventionally recognized surface. In Chen Qiufan's narrative, Mimi (originally Xiaomi 小米 in the Chinese version), a teenaged girl who lives anonymously like a ghost, turns into a superhuman cyborg, which in turn triggers a revolution in Guiyu, where the natural is no longer separable from the cybernetic posthuman form of life. Exposed to hazardous electronic waste dumped from the most advanced Western laboratories where artificial intelligence is cultivated, Mimi, constantly bullied and harassed by the locals, evolves into the very first member of a new species who gains self-consciousness. The most remarkable portion of the novel focuses on the intense inner struggle that takes place between Mimi's human conscience and the monstrous cybernetics of her posthuman counterpart. Called Mimi 0 and Mimi 1 respectively, the character's split personalities may point to the schizophrenic nature of the posthuman condition created by the complex mutations of the global political economy. Her rapid development of superhuman power and yearning for revenge on humanity indicate the paradoxical combination of a posthuman belief in technological magnificence and a profound questioning of its practical limits.

This inner conflict between Mimi 0, the bullied waste girl, and Mimi 1, the fearful monstrous cyborg with "a machinelike, incomparably precise, controlling power"[29] makes her the first notable cyborg in Chinese SF. At one point, her submission to her schizophrenia leads to a breakdown from within, and she gives in to a revolutionary impulse: *Let there be light.*

> Her vision trembled slightly in sync with the powerful electronica beats and the passionate melody. She was riding a herd of stampeding wild horses.

Hundreds of waste people were connected to Mimi through their augmented-reality glasses, sharing her vision.[30]

But the revolution does not happen in the story. Mimi's surviving humanity—a self-conscious fear of her schizophrenia, a questioning of the intuitive real versus the technologically engineered reality—makes her hesitate to take action, which stops her from reaching the decisive point of fighting back against humans, in particular those in power. She does not become Somni-451. The latter takes on her mission, following the designated route toward becoming a martyr, even knowing that this is a programmed design. Somni-451 makes her sacrifice a choice, as if it were of her free will, thus making singularity happen as a simulated self-awareness of artificial intelligence. Mimi cannot resist the swelling of her own human sentimentality, of tenderness and kindness, until the termination of her schizophrenia. "*Your human weakness is going to be the death of you someday.* Mimi 1 faded back into the darkness."[31] She eventually dies an anonymous death, like the man whose grotesque death is described earlier in the novel.

Waste Tide presents a posthuman revelation rather than a posthuman revolution. What emerges is a reconciliation with humanity. Mimi negotiates between her two identities, suppressing the future-facing posthuman, cybernetic self and submitting to her all-too-human emotional self. From the distinctively vivid, localized story, the narrative culminates in an emphasis on the equally localized sentimentalism that restores humanity in the cyborgian consciousness. The main achievement of *Waste Tide* is that it opens up a journey to interiority for Chinese SF. If there is a posthuman revelation, it may anticipate a new millennium that sees the unfolding of an invisible nation consisting of the silent masses, a new posthuman self that feeds on technology, and a self-conscious representation of the posthuman identity in the rising new wave that, like the waste tide, sweeps the invisible terra of this virtual world known as China's SF shadow.

Waste Tide is also a story of homecoming, though it mainly manifests the modernist critique of the traditional patriarchy through the protagonist, Chen Kaizong 陳開宗, a returnee from abroad. Yet its more profound nostalgic sentimentality lies in Mimi's clinging to humanity for some sense of belonging. The success of these remarkable Chinese SF stories—Liu Cixin's Three-Body novels, Bao Shu's *The Redemption of Time*, Chen

Qiufan's *Waste Tide*, and Hao Jingfang's "Folding Beijing"—has brought a global image of the Chinese new wave back to the domestic context. The new wave simultaneously evokes the Chinese ambition to shine and triumph internationally and a sentimentalist gesture toward elevating what is authentically Chinese.

POSTHUMAN CHINA/TAIWAN

It requires a full-length book to fully explore the posthuman theme, a literary motif that has gained importance and even centrality in twenty-first-century Chinese and Sinophone fiction, particularly SF. Posthuman imagery points to a deep crisis of humanism. As a new way of thinking about the changes imposed upon humanism in this information or digital age, posthumanism swerves from the core of the Enlightenment values associated with reason, progress, and civilization.[32] Its most powerful critique targets the fundamental malfunction of the existing social order, epistemological paradigm, and modes of governance, culture, and trade that have largely been shaped by modern revolutions and reforms. The posthuman critique in a Chinese context motivates a reevaluation of China's various modernity projects and leads to a questioning of earlier sweeping reforms and revolutions. In contemporary Chinese literature, posthuman images are particularly applied to reflections concerning the deteriorating ecological system, evolution or devolution enabled by mutations of the political economy, and above all, an awareness of inhuman conditions.

Writing from the perspectives of animals, ghosts, aliens, robots, cyborgs, the diseased, the deceased, and even the dimensionless cosmological intelligence, Chinese novelists like Mo Yan, Yu Hua, and Yan Lianke and SF writers like Liu Cixin, Han Song, Wang Jinkang, and Chen Qiufan have created various visions of alterity in political, technological, and ecological terms, which converge in reflections on the (in/post)human conditions of contemporary China. What is a "human being"? A question like this must have perplexed the protagonist of Mo Yan's 2006 novel *Life and Death Are Wearing Me Out* 生死疲劳, a landlord who was killed by the Communists in 1949 and subsequently reincarnated as various farm animals over fifty years of China's revolution and reform. His repeated posthuman reincarnations only testify to the prolonged history of an inhuman China, where apocalyptic events have already happened many times through waves of revolution.[33] The humanist concepts of self and the world become phantom, ambivalent fragments of posthuman existence in contemporary Beijing, as implied in Yu Hua's *The Seventh Day* 第七天 (2012), in which a newly deceased person becomes a ghost confined to a surreal reality where all the absurdities in his human life only now become comprehensible.[34] Such provocative posthuman visions sharply point to China's political and social predicaments and create an unsettling world image that thrives on unpredictability and uncertainty. The dehumanized conditions of Chinese life give the posthuman a meaning that implies an alternative perception of Chinese reality, different from what the state media and official discourse describe. What is a human being in contemporary China? A posthuman answer to this question, like in Mo Yan's and Yu Hua's novels, reveals a profound lack of humanity in the present-day reality as well as a lasting yearning for human rights. For these writers, the posthuman theme can directly represent an engagement with the pursuit of social justice.

There are two attitudes toward the posthuman motif in contemporary Chinese and Sinophone SF. The first can be recognized as the posthuman critique that operates in a Chinese sociopolitical context. Most of the older generation of Chinese SF writers, such as Wang Jinkang, Han Song, and Liu Cixin, who share experiences just as Mo Yan, Yan Lianke, and Yu Hua do, rely on this critique to voice their discontent with reality. SF uses various posthuman images to reveal the darkness underlying the country's surface prosperity and point to the social and ethical disasters resulting from China's tremendous changes during economic development. The horrifying posthuman figure in Wang Jinkang's "The Reincarnated Giant" displays the evils born of the combination of old-fashioned capitalism and the old-fashioned socialist system, which is a Sinotopian figure symbolized by the tycoon's unstoppable, disastrous body growth. Other SF stories depict the posthuman apocalypse that results from China's manic pursuit of economic development, such as Han Song's novel *Subway* and story "The Regenerated Bricks," which both showcase the profoundly inhuman conditions behind China's triumphant image of the economic miracle. In a different way, Liu Cixin, as a self-claimed technologist, nevertheless blurs the human and posthuman in his "Three-Body" trilogy. He presents nostalgic emotions toward the pastoral, romantic, and poetic experiences, and his narrative keeps a poetic heart alive in the idealized character Cheng Xin. A return to the human heart is the hidden motif that turns the hyperdimensional adventures into a poetic epiphany shared by Singer, the faceless inhuman alien intelligence, and Cheng Xin, the protagonist who keeps making moral, humane choices at times when human survival hangs on a posthuman uncertainty.

For the second attitude, the posthuman is symbolic of difference, a newness that has never been accustomed to the human mentality. Often represented in monstrosity, alienness, transgression, metamorphosis, trans-anthropocentric vision, and cybernetic fabrication, the posthuman image heightens the awareness of inclusive otherness. It implies constructing alternatives to the conventional image of humanity, and diverse cultural representations of the posthuman dismantle the commonly accepted identities of race, gender, sexuality, class, and other social constructs of the self. In terms of cultural politics, the posthuman both evokes a recognition of difference and inspires a nonbinary tolerance of difference as essential to a posthuman consciousness. This second attitude, closer to a posthumanism instead of the posthuman critique, prevailed among writers in Taiwan long before it became a clear newer wave in Chinese SF. Its inception can be traced to Chu T'ien-wen's "Fin-de-Siècle Splendor" 世紀末的華麗 (1990) and *Notes of a Desolate Man* 荒人手記 (1994), both of which present a nonbinary notion of gender, love, and heterotopia, from where a decadent aesthetics counterbalances the humanist gravitational pull. The young woman who rebuilds the world from ashes with memories of colors and smells in "Fin-de-Siècle Splendor" and the gay man envisioning an erotic utopia, where desolation can become a foundation of a new civilization that replaces our ruined old system, in *Notes of a Desolate Man*, completely changed the literary landscape of post-Martial Law Taiwan. They opened a fluid, diverse, nonbinary literary universe, which quickly nurtured SF wonders in Chi Ta-wei's short stories and novels.

A homosexual writer, Chi equated SF to the queer as well as to Taiwan in terms of both gender and political consciousness.[35] Another writer, Ping Lu 平路 (b. 1953), rendered Taiwan into a SF image; she was not just writing Taiwan SF but making Taiwan the embodiment of SF in her story "Taiwan Miracle" 台灣奇蹟 (1991). Chi built upon Chu T'ien-wen's

Neo-Baroque style and increased the density of the linguistic folds in his experiments with literary style and identity fluidity. Chi's short story, "Beneath His Eyes, in Your Palm, a Red Rose Is About to Bloom" 他的眼底，你的掌心，即將綻放一朵紅玫瑰 (1994), which the author claims to be unfinished, presents an infinitely complex world-building. A gay couple's experiment with genetics leads to an infinitely cloned posthuman "self" that goes through an apocalyptic split into endless personifications, which all blend in a dream where there is no way to tell what is true and what is illusive.[36] The narrative has a chilling, desperate beauty in its depiction of the infinitely folded darkness in a plotline that takes the form of a pseudo-espionage film noir, and the shapelessness of its narrative make cognitive clarity impossible.

Chi Ta-wei's career as a SF writer was very short, but he left a number of excellent works whose literary value has been recently rediscovered. The best example is his novella, *The Membranes* 膜 (1996), a classic that appeared far ahead of the current new wave in China and has recently been translated into English. This novella creates a dazzling multiplicity in its narrative design: there are multiple versions of truths, all programmed to hide the singular truth. The protagonist believes that she is an aesthetician living in an underwater bubble world distant from the heavily polluted surface land. But in fact, she is only a memory that is being installed in her cyborgian body, while her "aesthetician" job is actually to mend the war machines in an arsenal. The story continues Chi's extremely dense aestheticism in his earlier story, "Beneath His Eyes, in Your Palm, a Red Rose Is About to Bloom." Perhaps Chi's most important SF work, *The Membranes* remains unique in terms of genre crossing and gender reflexivity. Chi's beautiful, mesmerizing, provocative narrative creates a splendid labyrinth of metaphors and significances that leads to a revelation about posthuman changeability in a matrix of monotonous inhumanity.[37]

Chi's SF has strong political implications about Taiwan's queer status as a democracy born of cold war politics and constantly facing the danger of China's military invasion, but his stories also have a transcendental, metaphysical strength in their inventiveness in language, narrative, and world-building. A decade after Chi stopped publishing SF, another Taiwan writer, Egoyan, who wrote SF at the time the Chinese new wave emerged, revived the dream narrative and created an entire dream universe in his novels. *The Dream Devourers* 噬夢人 (2010) is a posthuman epic about the century-long espionage war between humans and cyborgs in the twenty-third century. K, the protagonist and an agent serving the human side, who hunts down many cyborgs pretending to be human, eventually comes to a poignant realization that he too is a cyborg, programmed to believe he is human. Such a difficult posthuman self-knowledge, enforced by his own epiphany about his overcomplicated identity, not only gives K a deeper understanding of the artificiality in the two opposing identities but also enlightens readers to dismantle the distinctions across those assumed binary categories. As a character says in the novel: "Since her teenage days, she has firmly believed that there should not be any discrimination between humans and cyborgs."[38] In Taiwan's own political context, discrimination is based on identities, ethnicities, and ideologies. In the context involving Taiwan and China, interpretations of the dream become a political weapon in Egoyan's narrative to resist the oversimplification of a singular form of dream. Egoyan's novel is presented as a dream narrative that invites multiple interpretations, with his own text designed as a future product filled with annotations, a text that is becoming. Its scope and complexity are unrivaled as a posthuman epic as well as a handbook of posthuman knowledge.

Ten years after the publication of *The Dream Devourer*, Egoyan's *Zero Degree of Separation* 零度分離 (2021) adds more complexities to the *Dream Devourer* universe. A novel consisting of six chapters, its biggest mystery is about its authorship. Is the author human or a cyborg, or something else, a posthuman consciousness? This is the ultimate question that flows throughout the text. The appendix is an interview conducted by a character from *The Dream Devourer* with the assumed author of the six stories, who has a female name. But who is she? There is no certain answer. The novel, published during the pandemic when separation and isolation were routine, is about intimacy, love, and complete identification. The first story, "Say I Love You Once More" 再說一次我愛你, presents the clearest interpretation of love, which transcends species; the mother in the story, distanced from her son due to her devotion to studying the language of whales, utters a sentence to him at last, which he understands years later, after she has died: "I love you," said in the language of whales.[39] *Zero Degree of Separation* represents a great effort to break down barriers between genders, species, and the human and posthuman. It converges in a new dreamscape in which all are equal.

Among the works by younger SF authors emerging in China, this second attitude, a more tolerant, inclusive, and nonbinary view toward the posthuman, is particularly obvious in works by women writers, which I will discuss more in the following chapter. Here I can first offer an example from Chi Hui, her short story "The Rainforest" 雨林 (2006), in which a biologically reengineered young woman character, whose conglomeration of both human and plant genes enables her to merge with the rain forest, becomes the first trans-species protagonist in Chinese literature.[40] Chi Hui's depiction of the eventual merging of the human and the natural implies the fluidity and interchangeability of identities that have transgressed fundamental categories concerning the human and nonhuman. In the same line, eco-fiction by Taiwan's Wu Ming-yi, such as *The Man with the Compound Eyes* 複眼人 (2011) and *Land with Little Rain* 苦雨之地 (2018), presents a self-conscious restructuring of the relationship between nature and culture, also across many boundaries. His human characters often seek inspiration from other living beings and turn to a new lifestyle that could lead them to achieve affinity with, if not complete integration into nature.

The symbolic meanings attached to the above-mentioned SF writings by Chen Qiufan, Chi Ta-wei, Egoyan, Chi Hui, and Wu Ming-yi, as well as by Liu Cixin and Han Song, among others, can be illustrated with contemporary theories about the posthuman and posthumanism, most notably presented by Donna J. Haraway, Rosi Braidotti, and N. Katherine Hayles. Braidotti's posthumanist approach focuses on the decentering of "Man," and her theory is expanded to the post-anthropocentric environmental and animalistic conditions.[41] In Chi Hui's, Wu Ming-yi's, and Egoyan's writings, a budding posthumanism repositions humans in the world, which echoes Braidotti's theoretical thinking. Haraway's socialist-feminist manifesto liberates the image of the cyborg from essentialist identities and biological bodies, so that a new force for change emerges in the posthuman that is no longer bound to fixed categories, discourses, and epistemologies.[42] Chen Qiufan's cyborg in *Waste Tide* represents this new force in a Chinese context and points to the fluidity of her identities as a semi-cybernetic existence, which enables her to rise above the plight of the poor and oppressed and gain a new class consciousness as an agent of subversion and revolution. We have already borrowed Haraway's more recent conception of the Chthulucene to interpret Han

Song's mythologies of the chthonic, and the same concept can be applied to interpretations of more authors who are collectively creating a nonbinary literary universe.

N. Katherine Hayles's theorization of the posthuman is contextualized more in Anglo-American empiricism than continental philosophy. Her perception of the posthuman is grounded in cybernetics and informatics. Unlike Haraway and Braidotti, who embrace the posthuman as a blessing, Hayles sees in it both a threat and an opportunity. If the posthuman is an informative pattern that loses the body, it implies an information/materiality separation—or a new dichotomy between a simplified abstraction and the world's noisy multiplicity. Hayles sees in the posthuman as shaped by cybernetics a threat to the diversity and multiplicity of the human world, and she seeks to "replace a teleology of disembodiment with historically contingent stories" about *how we became posthuman*.[43] She sees the posthuman narrative, particularly SF, as an embodied form of discourse, a narrative that has a body, with chronological thrust, polymorphous digression, located actions, and personified agents. Thus, SF storytelling enacts a broader cognitive function to transcend the dichotomy. In the posthuman, binary boundaries no longer matter for the enactment of identities, and transgression is feasible and flexible. Eventually, the posthuman narratives create an undifferentiated, nonhierarchical world image: "'human' and 'posthuman' coexist in shifting configurations that vary with historically specific contexts."[44] In view of the various theoretical arguments articulated by Hayles, Haraway, and Braidotti, although liberal humanism has been undermined by the posthuman turn as well as dismantled by feminism, postcolonialism, and postmodernism, if there is a certain posthuman*ism*, it should be envisioned as an inclusive, nonbinary, and democratic version that neither discards nor surrenders to humanism.

When the posthuman motif is localized in Chinese narratives, it motivates a leap of faith in the nonexistent yet potential possibilities of departure from the prejudice, hierarchy, and doctrines that permeate contemporary culture and political life in terms of gender and power. Today, even a popular sci-fi movie like *Monster Hunt* 捉妖記 (2015, dir. Raman Hui), which portrays a fairy-tale reconciliation of different species—humans and monsters—could inspire tolerance of otherness in terms of sexual orientation, ethnicity, and cultural values. Increasing exposure to these posthuman personae and imageries, which are portrayed as being internal to all of us, can possibly nourish a more tolerant and nonbinary attitude toward all sorts of "others" in Chinese society.

In summary, the posthuman represents both a critique of the inhuman conditions of our current society and a new opportunity to conceive a changing method to understand and make a new world. It implies a rupture, an endgame, even a new revolution. In 2016, after AlphaGo defeated the *go* master Lee Sedol, Liu Cixin and Chan Koonchung both warned of the inevitable robot revolution that will lead to technological singularity, a hypothetical point in time beyond which artificial intelligence becomes uncontrollable and its impact on human civilization irreversible. While Liu Cixin, who believes in technology, is readying us to embrace the uncertainty and unpredictability of the new age,[45] Chan Koonchung advocates for a proactive institutional change, based on his assumption that the superintelligence emerging in the near future will imitate human behavior, including systematic injustice and our own hostility toward others—unless we change.[46] Although Chan presents a classic dystopian scenario, he invests in this apocalyptic vision of the posthuman a strong humanist hope. In the best case, the posthuman turn can inspire a reconfiguration of humans' relationship with the larger world, including other living beings on earth, environmental and ecological spheres we all share, the emerging artificial intelligence, and certainly more important, other people who look, behave, and think differently. This wishful view echoes the hopeful note of Hayles, who sees in the posthuman turn an opportunity to renew the understanding that "human life is embedded in a material world of great complexity, one on which we depend for our continued survival."[47]

For a much younger generation of SF writers, particularly those women and nonbinary writers in China, Taiwan, and the Chinese diaspora, the posthuman truly means a new way of storytelling, even a life form or lifestyle that unpacks a new world, a twenty-first-century heterotopia both inside and outside the existing social reality. This new scenario is closer to what Ursula Le Guin depicts in her famous SF novel *The Left Hand of Darkness* (1968): there are no binary sexes, no fixed genders, and therefore "no division of humanity into strong and weak halves, protective/protected, dominant/submissive, owner/chattel, active/passive. In fact the whole tendency to dualism that pervades human thinking may be found to be lessened, or changed, on Winter."⁴⁸ The humans on the planet Winter are more posthuman than human (when Le Guin wrote the novel, the term was not yet available). For the more radical, progressive posthuman vision, there is no division between the monstrous otherness and I the human: I am the monster, and the monster and I cohabitate in one body. It is in the rise of She-SF that we can find the momentum of a newer wave represented by a great number of women and nonbinary SF writers: one or more of them may become China's Ursula Le Guin.

EXCURSUS II

THE RISE OF SHE-SF

2010–2022

The new wave of Chinese SF, from the moment of its inception, never lacked excellent women writers—such as Ling Chen and Zhao Haihong, who began to publish SF stories as early as the 1990s, even earlier than Liu Cixin. More women SF writers made a name for themselves in the first decade of the twenty-first century, the decade of the new wave's rapid development (still invisible to the public), including Xia Jia, Chi Hui, Hao Jingfang, Cheng Jingbo, Qian Lifang, and Chen Xi. Even so, Chinese SF seemed very much male-dominated during that period. The "Big Three," Wang Jinkang, Han Song, and Liu Cixin, are all male; so are the majority of the other established authors. The gender stereotype associated with SF was further strengthened by a large base of SF fans who were mostly male in the first ten years of the century.

Does SF have gender? As genre fiction, it is in a Chinese context often marked with a series of binary categories—"hard SF" versus "soft SF" (subgenres), "Golden Age" versus "new wave" (historical periods and different styles), technological SF versus social SF, SF surnamed "science" versus SF surnamed "literature" (from the debate on SF's nature during the 1983 attack on the genre) . . . and so on and so forth. Chinese diehard SF fans, who take these binaries for granted, usually prefer the former in each case and view them as manifestations of a true SF spirit. SF is hard, straight, technological, and sublime. It has often been associated with "geeky guy," "straight guy," and "nerdy guy" in the Chinese online environment. To the public, SF seems to have been assigned a fixed gender that is male.

But a quiet change occurred in the second decade of the twenty-first century, and SF scenes were no longer dominated by men. Women played increasingly important roles in SF activism, translation, fan community organizations, publishing, and cultural enterprises. Xia Jia, Chi Hui, and Hao Jingfang were all born in 1984 and can be called the "Big Three" women in SF. In 2016, Hao Jingfang became the second Chinese SF writer, and the first Chinese woman author, to win a Hugo Award (for "Folding Beijing"), which was a strong boost. With a drastic increase in the number of active women writers who began to emerge in the SF circle, by the end of the second decade of the century, it hardly made sense to consider SF still a male genre. The genre and gender were put into a negotiation that led to a nonbinary restructuring of the SF literary universe, a Neo-Baroque world.

Not only did the above-mentioned women writers have stronger, clearer feminine voices, but also an even younger generation of writers created a new trend, which can be characterized as the rise of She-SF 她科幻. Shuangchimu, Tang Fei, Gu Shi, Peng Simeng, Wang Kanyu (Regina), Mu Ming, Duan Ziqi, Wu Shuang 吴霜 (b. 1986), Liao Shubo 廖舒波 (b. 1988), Zhou Wen 昼温, and Wang Nuonuo 王诺诺 (b. 1991) are among those who have recently made greater impacts in the field, even in the literary field beyond SF. Tang Fei, Wang Kanyu, and Shuangchimu have all become new stars in mainstream literature too, with their stories published in top-tier literary magazines such as *Harvest* 收获, *Huacheng* 花城, *Frontier* 天涯, and *Shanghai Literature* 上海文學. They have departed from the *Science Fiction World*-centered SF circle and entered a much larger literary world.

Different from the earlier SF authors, these young women writers (all born after 1984—if this significant year in dystopian fiction can serve as a landmark in a real history of Chinese SF) have mostly enjoyed the privilege of being a global citizen growing up in a new digital age, their mindset synchronized with the rest of the world. They have developed distinct literary voices over the past several years when the entire world witnessed the collapse of the new liberal world order, the backfire of a free-market-oriented "universal" version of globalization, and the rise of a series of global social and cultural movements, such as the #MeToo Movement,

Gen Z environmentalist activism, and a new rallying call for establishing a planetary consciousness, which implies a new vision of multiplicity and diversity: humans should peacefully cohabit with other species on our already ruined planet. All these themes, together with less dark visions of technology—a new hope for creating a technologized future in which humans and the posthuman can coexist instead of struggling in a "dark forest" scenario ending in assured mutual destruction—have characterized the politics of She-SF. Correspondingly, more daring experiments with literary texts, including making the text itself a Möbius continuum or a chimera hybridity, have begun to change the aesthetics of Chinese SF.

I began to notice this new trend during the COVID-19 pandemic. In the second and third years of the pandemic, three sets of collections dedicated to showcasing the She-SF writers were published in China and the United States, including four volumes of *She-SF* 她科幻 (edited by Chen Qiufan, 2021), two volumes of *She* 她 (edited by Cheng Jingbo, 2022), and *The Way Spring Arrives* (coedited by Yu Chen 于晨 and Regina Kanyu Wang, 2022). *The Way Spring Arrives* was published simultaneously in Chinese and English, and its English version particularly highlights that this collection features a visionary team of female and nonbinary writers. Of the three anthologies, this is perhaps the most eye-catching, for its authors are truly diverse, including those living in China, with a fixed gender, as well as those living in diaspora, some nonbinary, which can be made known in public thanks to the English version released in the United States.

Chinese SF readers have long been anxious about what would be the next "miracle" after the success of *The Three-Body Problem*, and now we have found a clear answer: following the first wave created by Liu Cixin, Han Song, and Wang Jinkang, among others, which illuminated the previously invisible, darker terra incognita of Sinotopia, the second wave of Chinese SF is currently rising in a free, nonbinary literary universe created by women (and nonbinary) writers. This achievement represents a new level of the development of posthuman and planetary consciousness in a Chinese and Sinophone context. Just as N. Katherine Hayles makes clear in *How We Became Posthuman*, the question of the posthuman is as much about dismantling gender stereotypes as about the diminishing difference between human and artificial intelligence. Hayles begins by revealing that the Turing Test from 1950, which predicted that humans and machines will one day be indistinguishable in terms of intelligence, had an earlier version that first proved the indistinguishability of men and women in terms of intelligence.[1] It is unknown whether Turing's identity as a homosexual person played a decisive role in the design of these two tests, but the fact is that according to his thinking, in a world where information flows freely without a biological, fixed embodiment, a fixed gender will no longer be important. We will all be cyborgs, all chimeras, all androgynes—when we become posthuman, we will become nonbinary on many levels.

9

NEW WONDERS OF A NONBINARY UNIVERSE

Opening of the Neo-Baroque

A biography beginning in the year 1500 and continuing to the present day, called Orlando. Vita; only with a change about from one sex to the other.
—VIRGINIA WOOLF, *DIARY*, 5 OCTOBER 1927

A spaceship named *Garden of Eden*, carrying 100,000 migrants to another habitable planet, departed Earth 103 years ago, and mysterious things have begun to happen. Adam, an organ cultivation program that provides replacements to human passengers whose organic organs may have malfunctioned due to aging on this multigenerational space journey, begins to randomly cancel orders. This strange behavior brings the detective on the ship to investigate in the Organ Cultivation Cabins. There he witnesses a gruesome scene: Adam is *alive*, connecting all the programs on the spaceship to serve its own purpose. It relocates the customers' organs that were canceled to create two human beings. One is himself; the other, an Eve. The detective does not see two human bodies, but two sets of organs put together in human shape. This is the main plotline of Gu Shi's novella "Chimera" 嵌合體 (2015). Gu Shi, born in 1985, an urban designer by profession, centers her story on a scientist's effort to change the view on how we became human.

"Chimera" has a baroque structure, with odd-numbered chapters titled "Chimera," "Echidna," "Typhon," "Orthrus," and "Argus," all alluding to

Greek mythological monsters that combine human and animal images, alternating with even-numbered chapters depicting what happens on the spaceship. While this is a story of chimeras, the narrative is also a chimera. The complicated arrangement connects two parallel plotlines to make sense of a clueless mystery. The final truth revealed at the end of the story is that *Garden of Eden* never left Earth but has been orbiting the home planet all the time, as a vehicle for a secret experiment: exactly waiting for Adam to become alive.

Everything began with a car accident many years before. A boy named Tony is hurt and needs a kidney transplant. His mother, a biologist who remains unnamed in the entire narrative, has just conceived an inventive method through research in human-animal genetics. Her audacious idea is to inject Tony's stem cells into a pig and then reap its organ to save Tony's life. But the mother has doubts, which she shares with her husband: "If we did a human-pig chimera experiment, I have no way of controlling how many human cells end up in the pig.... Think about it, Evan... this pig may become a second Tony—our son could be concealed in its body. And when it grows up, we'll snatch its kidneys together, then kill it."[1] The husband, who is the I-narrator of this chapter, informs readers that his wife, when pregnant with Tony, had a manic episode and thought that a monster was growing inside her body. Her motherhood is depicted as very unusual. She does not have a common motherly love for Tony. But she and her husband decide to do this experiment in spite of its violation of ethical codes.

The pig grows, and its kidney saves Tony's life. But it also has Tony's eyes, and it becomes the origin of Adam, an experiment that the mother keeps working on while completely distancing herself from her human family. In the middle of the novella, the mother stages her own fake death in a spaceship crash before "posthumously" inviting her son, the adult Tony, to attend a press event, which announces a shocking discovery by her scientific team. The scientific discovery is articulated by Sphinx, a quantum computer that personifies itself as a golden-skinned boy, in a simple statement: "One individual cannot proliferate the species." Quantum computing eventually reveals the truth of human evolution: we never became human as a singular species; we are all cross-species chimeras, or descendents of chimeras.

Sphinx's statement rewrites the story of evolution, decoupling humans as a species from a singular definition. Humans are never purely human. In

Gu Shi's novella, this theory later is revealed to be completely fabricated by the mother herself, as a deceptive strategy to obtain the right to use *Garden of Eden* for a large-scale experiment to produce human chimeras. She disguises herself as a passenger, Lin Ke 林可, while her son, Tony, is the detective invited to serve on the ship. The story comes full circle: Lin Ke is the first passenger who reports to Tony about the strange behavior of Adam. When the whole truth is out, Tony leaves the spaceship. In a brief greeting from Lin Ke, he hears her say that after being with her son for 103 years, now she is going to be with her other son. Adam, as an artificial intelligence program, is now awakened to do what Dr. Frankenstein does, producing a new species through combining body parts.

Here, I borrow from Gu Shi the chimera, this central image of her novella, as a key to creating a new understanding of SF as not of a singular genre or gender. Through a negotiation with these terms, I am opening a different literary vision in order to revisit the foundational questions about SF's definition one more time—from a nonbinary perspective. From there, we can see the new wonders of a nonbinary universe, the opening of the Neo-Baroque.

SCIENCE FICTION: GENDER AND GENRE IN NEGOTIATION

Almost all versions of SF literary history point out that the rise of female SF writers has been relatively late in all countries. For example, it happened during the 1950s–'70s in the Anglo-American tradition when the new wave was emerging; Ursula Le Guin, Joanna Russ (1937–2011), and Octavia Butler (1947–2006) were some of the most important women authors who began to write SF and reshaped it in the following decades. If someone were to write a history of Chinese SF, the emergence of female SF authors as a new force to subvert the genre/gender conventions was very recent, near the end of the second decade of the twenty-first century.

Wu Yan, China's foremost SF scholar, categorizes the genre's authors into "the cluster of women authors" and "the cluster of big-boy authors." When introducing the cluster of women authors, he proposes a revision of SF's definition that is still largely founded on binary genders: "SF doesn't necessarily have to advocate for rationality; it can also advocate for sentimentality. SF observes and comprehends a world in which knowledge is accumulating too quickly; SF offers a cautious warning and structural resistance against the amassing of power among men and men's attitudes toward life."[2] Associating men with rationality and women with sentimentality, Wu further strengthens a binary categorization, but what he says clearly articulates that the place of women in SF should not be ignored. Rather, Wu Yan's emphasis on the power of women's perception implies a subversive gesture. He then takes one step further to dismantle the so-called consensus that "the gender of SF is male," pointing out straightforwardly that the origin of modern SF is Mary Shelley's *Frankenstein*.

Wu Yan's words bring us to this SF classic again. Mary Shelley never knew that she invented a genre. But *Frankenstein*'s importance can be compared to that of "A Madman's Diary"; Lu Xun's story has had a lasting influence on modern Chinese literature, and Shelley's novel established the basic vocabulary and grammar, the structure of feeling, and the framework of speculative thought so thoroughly that this single work seems to contain sufficient energies to fuel the later development of the entire SF genre. The first modern SF novel is a posthuman narrative, and it is nonbinary too. The monster in *Frankenstein* is not a product of humans' natural reproduction but an "artificial human" created through inventive scientific technologies in a laboratory. The "artificial human" was a popular motif in nineteenth-century European literature, exemplified by the Homunculus in part 2 of Goethe's *Faust* (1832)—a miniature human, a lovely small person. But Frankenstein's monster is not such a perfect image; on the contrary, it is a chimera whose body is an assemblage of dead body parts and whose life was ignited by electromagnetic force. Mary, who lost her mother when she was born and was poorly cared for by her father after he remarried, characterized the artificial human in her story as a lonely monster, the sole member of a new species.[3] Just after "he" (indeed a male monster) acquires life, he is abandoned by his creator. He suffers greatly among humans, a target of prejudice and discrimination; viewed as a horror, he is driven to the edge of human society. He is an abandoned outcast.

For the novel's epigraph, Mary Shelley quotes from Milton's *Paradise Lost* (1667) the words that the ancestor of the humans, Adam, utters:

> Did I request Thee, Maker, from my clay
> To mold me Man? Did I solicit Thee
> From darkness to promote me?—[4]

The monster created by Dr. Frankenstein is often miscalled "Frankenstein" in mass media. Ironically, the human who plays the role of the Maker has become the monster himself in popular culture. The nonhuman offspring of man, born unnaturally, turns into the ghost of humanism, the nightmare of the Enlightenment. The shadows of his maker and himself, roaming on the earth, tore open an abyss in the history of human progress. SF is just like Frankenstein's monster, occupying an odd place in literary history, an inconvenient oddity, an inferior mixture, a chimera that does not fit in with the literary establishment, is not easily defined or categorized, and is shunned by haughty humanism and humancentric realism. During a large part of its history, the SF genre was also in a nameless position as an abandoned outcast. Only in the second half of the twentieth century, when the new wave movement allowed SF to reach literary audiences, did it begin to attract serious attention through stylistic appropriation by established avant-garde authors—such as Thomas Pynchon, John Barth (b. 1930), José Saramago (1922–2010), Ursula Le Guin, Margaret Atwood, Haruki Murakami (b. 1949), Roberto Bolaño (1953–2003), and Lo Yi-chin and Dung Kai-cheung in the Sinophone context. But when SF made such an impact, its significance as a chimera was the most important for its potential for literary experimentation.

Adam Roberts has argued that SF has one grandmother (Mary Shelley) and two fathers (Verne and Wells).[5] Only SF can have such a SF-like description of its own history. Roberts's words foreground SF's *queerness*, as a gender-transgressing and genre-crossing "chimera." Roberts also contends that SF's source is not just Mary Shelley but is more diverse and hybrid, including a whole range of odd genres, from Lucian's satires to More's utopian pseudo-travelogue to the subversive epic that Shelley directly referenced: Milton's *Paradise Lost*.[6] If we accept Roberts's view on Milton's unique significance for SF history, the connection between Shelley's novel and *Paradise Lost* through a baroque fold cannot be clearer, and this connection subverts not only the linear literary history that considers SF only as a modern genre but also the order of the representational modes usually associated with Milton's and Shelley's works. *Frankenstein* can thus be viewed as a SF echo to the Baroque "Grand Style" in *Paradise Lost*.[7] Milton's "Grand Style" fully manifests the Baroque in literature, dramatizing the war in heaven, which casts the model for SF narratives about grandiose cosmological themes of war and peace. But at the same time, *Paradise Lost* is about the fall of man, the confrontation between man and his maker, Satan's revolt against God, and the apocalyptic vision of the catastrophic endgame, all of which entered SF as subversive elements that later blended in anarchism, feminism, modern theoretical physics, and the revolutionary pathos. These various radical ideas and feelings formed a spiritual "chimera" in Mary Shelley's novel.

The beginning of this chapter quotes from a diary entry by Virginia Woolf: "A biography beginning in the year 1500 and continuing to the present day, called Orlando. Vita; only with a change about from one sex to the other."[8] *Orlando*, published in 1928, is Woolf's most baroque novel; today we can also view it as a queer novel, because of its protagonist's transgender. An English aristocratic man living in the Elizabethan age, when he is thirty years old, awakes from a long sleep in Constantinople, the junction of the East and the West, finding himself transformed into a woman. From then on, she is eternally youthful. At the end of the novel, she becomes a modern woman writer, having written long poems for centuries, to be published on the same day as Woolf's novel *Orlando*, the very text that is now self-referenced. *Orlando* is Woolf's boldest experimental work; its genre is difficult to categorize and its transgender audacity decades ahead of the notion of nonbinary gender.

I boldly borrow the plot of this novel to redefine SF's history over the past five hundred years. This history is meaningful for its beginning in 1500, the dawn of the age of Baroque that prepared for SF the sense of wonder, the aesthetics of the sublime, and the infinite time and space, and also meaningful for its continuation to the present day. Adding one hundred years to Woolf's time span in *Orlando*, SF has not only changed from one sex to the other but also gone further, shaking off the binary structure of gender and genre relations. My revision of Woolf's sentence is a new definition of SF: "A biography beginning in the year 1500 and continuing to the present day, called SF. Vita; only with a change about from one gender to many—nonbinary."

CAN WE READ LIU CIXIN'S TEXT AS NONBINARY?

Now it's time to return to this second provocative question that I ask in this book, about Liu Cixin's "Three-Body" trilogy. As with the question concerning Lu Xun's "A Madman's Diary" (chapter 3), I do not intend to find a definitive answer. But speculation about how to answer presents a new perspective from which to reexamine Chinese SF, particularly stereotyped hard SF defined by masculinity, in terms of both genre and gender, with a view toward creating a nonbinary new vision for Chinese new wave SF's future development.

Of course, this is not an easy question. Wu Yan calls Liu Cixin a "big boy" writer, and to his fans, Big Liu is the *manliest* of all contemporary Chinese SF authors. The worship of this manliness has bordered on misogyny. The online reactions to women characters in Liu Cixin's SF stories and novels are manifestly binary: sexism, representing a male fantasy about stereotyped femininity, plus misogyny, representing an extreme contempt for stereotyped womanhood. Both tendencies do indeed exist in Liu's text. The English translation had to remove some gendered depictions of women that would have read as too sexist for American audiences. But, inspired by Yingying Huang's article about the gendered worlds in Liu Cixin's SF,[9] I have come to understand that Liu has also created strong female characters who challenge gender conventions.

A surface impression of Liu's space saga is that his text is gendered and binary through and through. For example, Liu details in *Dark Forest* how the protagonist Luo Ji, a dandy, daydreams and desires a perfect incarnation of the "fairer" sex—a beautiful woman, quiet, understanding, and accommodating. Because Luo Ji is chosen to be one of the four Wallfacers, his daydreaming bears real consequences. Any wish of his, no matter how ridiculous, will be fulfilled, because his job is to deceive the Trisolarans. The Interpol finds his dream girl, a college student named Zhuang Yan 莊顏, who, for reasons not divulged in the narrative, accepts Luo Ji, becoming his lover and then his wife, the mother of his child. The process is reminiscent of how God fulfills Adam's desire by creating a woman from his rib. In modern society, such an archaic notion of women having come from the rib of men, thus being the invisible "other," may sound not only outdated but almost estranging, mythological. However, despite all the social movements and critical theories that advocate for equal rights, which seem to have long since outdated the patriarchal universe, the power relations based on the essentialized binary gender structure still prevail, certainly in China where few women have so far been unable to touch, not to mention break, the glass ceiling. Even when #MeToo has radicalized another revolt against the patriarchal system, the market-oriented media still follow the age-old tradition of shaping women to satisfy men's desires, from the virtual sexism on the deep dark web to the male gaze positioned as the standard point of view in many forms of narrative, from film to TV drama to micro-vlogs. The nerdy straight geeky guy Liu Cixin is no exception. He appropriates his own SF text to create his dream girl, and this is a typical case to justify the Freudian theory about creativity and daydreaming.

In the "Three-Body" trilogy, the heroines are respectively given the roles of Nemesis—the goddess of revenge (Ye Wenjie), Eve—the companion in the Garden of Eden (Zhuang Yan), and Virgin Mary or the Holy Mother (Cheng Xin). They are surrounded and contrasted by male characters who represent the "tough" or "nerdy guy" with the agency and ability to actually move the plot forward. This kind of binary gender politics, totally stereotyped, has fueled narrow-minded views of women among SF fans and Cixin fans, mostly male. One example is the moral judgment targeting Cheng Xin in SF circles that goes beyond the textual level—because Cheng Xin, due to her kind heart and empathy, fails to accomplish her mission as the Swordholder to exterminate the enemy (and all lives on Earth), the web is filled with netizens calling her "soft-hearted bitch." These derogatory words have flown out of the discussion about the novel to become a gender crusade, a misogynistic fanaticism.

Even so, I hope to offer an alternative understanding of the female characters written by Liu Cixin, in their original intratextual context. I believe that the "Three-Body" trilogy is not a fictional text with nothing but plot, but in fact is richly baroque and multivoiced. Based on my analysis in chapter 4, Liu's saga is not a binary text bound by the clear-cut oppositions of good versus evil, black versus white, and men versus women. Ye Wenjie is not only the goddess of revenge; both her love and her hatred make the base colors of the entire textual space, from her life in the madness years to her vision of the dark forest universe. And Liu Cixin's dream girl, Zhuang Yan, although she appears submissive, is perhaps closer to Ibsen's Nora than to Eve, for her later melancholy and dark mood drive her to leave Luo Ji, which is the decisive factor that changes him from a dandy to a true hero shouldering his burden as the Wallfacer. As for Cheng Xin, her tenderness forms the "poetic heart" of the enter trilogy; she is the only character who transcends the "dark forest" scenario, breathing a warm human kindness into the cold, dark, amoral universe. When we finally understand that part of the narrative is Cheng Xin's, the narratorial voice becomes blurry—is it Cheng Xin's voice or the author's voice?

Liu's text can be read as nonbinary. Liu Cixin enlivens romanticism and humanism as much as Social Darwinism and technologism in the apathetic dark universe of posthumanism. He gives the text an infinite vitality that transcends the limitations of not only here and now but also all time and space, and he captures the image of the sublime cosmos in the reflections of a poetic heart. Yingying Huang argues that Liu Cixin's gendered SF text is not actually monogendered; underneath the superficial sexism, it actually creates a deeper time that belongs to women, which forms a deeper textual structure.[10] Such a deeper time and structure include Singer's love song of time, the primeval peace and abundance of the original hyperdimensional universe that is mother to all things, and the degendering or (multidimensional) regendering process of deeper time itself, which is profoundly posthuman. In the end, Cheng Xin survives in the No. 674 (pronounced as Liu Cixin) private universe. She lingers in the crack of a fractured time, just like Singer's songs collected from perished worlds; at the deepest level of time, which is beyond human apprehension, conflict dies in tranquility, war returns to peace.

The ending of *Death's End*, which suggests that Cheng Xin's memory will be passed along to the next universe, is reminiscent of the last sentence in Chu T'ien-wen's "Fin de Siècle Splendor": "The abyssal blue of the lake tells her that the world men have built with theories and systems will collapse, and she with her memory of smells and colors will survive and rebuild the world from here."[11] Chu T'ien-wen regenders the discourse about world-building after the end of our contemporary world, echoing her most admired modern writer, Eileen Chang's 張愛玲 (1920–1995) view on the role of women at the "fin de siècle" (also the "fin du monde"): "A human dies and is buried in the earth. Mother Earth comforts the dead: 'After you're asleep, I will tuck you in.'"[12] In Donna J. Haraway's words, our mother planet has already been ruined; humans must relearn how to "stay with the trouble," developing tentacular thinking and relying on direct experiences of bodily senses to merge with the devastated nature in all its monstrosity.[13]

What Chu, Chang, and Haraway have articulated regarding the end of men's world or the post-anthropocentric sympoiesis forms a parallel to Liu Cixin's endgame. The ruined, broken universe has become the deep time of our own life—it exists as a structure in our cells, genes, organs, emotions, and entire existences. The *Dark Forest* scenario has its roots in the forest of Manchuria, where Ye Wenjie reads Rachel Carson's (1907–1964) *Silent Spring* (1962) and comes to understand how human activities harm the ecosystem we share with other species.[14] While Ye brings humans to the confrontation with the dark forest, humans are enlightened to the truth of the universe. We are part of a broken, ruined world, whether we are man or woman or anything else; we must reestablish kinships with other living beings, as chimeras, monsters, cyborgs who must decouple themselves from their fixed positions and merge into the fluid, ever-changing time flowing deeply in the quantum existence of everything. Singer, who passes by the solar system and destroys it in Liu Cixin's *Death's End*, turns to this song, while billions of lives are being ended in the process of two-dimensionalization:

> I see my love;
> I fly next to her;
> I present her with my gift.
> A small piece of solidified time.
> Lovely markings are carved into time
> As soft to the touch as the mud in the shallow sea.
> She covers her body with time,
> And pulls me along to fly to the edge of existence.
> This is a spiritual flight:
> In our eyes, the stars appear as ghosts;
> In the eyes of the stars, we appear as ghosts.[15]

I would rather believe that Singer has no fixed gender, and here, the token of love is nothing but eternal time—frozen, solidified, but everlasting. Singer's love song represents the enormous unknown beyond human apprehension, but it is also very human, like a popular love song. Can this frozen time, as token of love, represent the wave-particle duality and overcome the gender binary, the dichotomy of good and evil, and the dual status of existence and nonexistence? Liu's saga can be read as nonbinary at moments like this.

CYBORGS, GODDESSES, CHIMERAS

Being a male author does not necessarily mean being androcentric, not even for the "manliest man," Liu Cixin, adored by SF fans. Han Song, Chen Qiufan, and Bao Shu have all written SF stories that are not confined by gender essentialism. Han Song's *Guide to Hunting Beautiful Women* can be read as an extremely explicit production of eroticism and violence on the surface, but his purpose is to subvert all these male fantasies. As mentioned in chapter 5, his inspiration came from *Jurassic Park*: just as the dinosaurs are all "girls," the "Eves" roaming on the island are all "ribs" created by genetic engineering. These beautiful women are cyborgs whose appearance is imbued with female beauty but whose insides contain dinosaur ferocity. They are both a unification of human and animal and a combination of human and machine. In the eyes of the men, the women on the island, natural and wild, are the most essential: "a pure breed with ovary and womb, unpolluted by cosmetics, jewels, vanity, or money"—they are "real women."[16] Han Song is the Chinese SF writer with the most self-conscious awareness of the dark consciousness, and his story induces the "fear of seeing": these women are all as ferocious as dinosaurs, and the lustful men hunting them become their prey. American feminist SF scholar Justine Larbalestier identifies the "battle of the sexes" as a main theme of SF, which, as Han Song's story shows, subverts the gender stereotypes completely.[17] Moreover, these women-beasts are ultimately postgender cyborgs, and in Haraway's opinion, the only way to subvert and delegitimize the contemporary repressive political systems is to create a new myth of the part-human, part-machine cyborg. Only the cyborg can defeat the binary narrative dictated by ideology and reconstruct a new affinity across sapient and unintelligent species, human and material realms.[18]

In one of Chen Qiufan's most sexually explicit short stories, "G Is for Goddess" G 代表女神 (2011), Miss G suffers from a congenital defect in her reproductive organs. She desires sexual orgasm but cannot reach it. Only through an inventive surgery does she become able to achieve orgasm, now with every inch of her whole body, what Foucault called "unserious pleasure" and "orgasms without reproductive purpose."[19] From then on, Miss G's whole-body sexual sensitivity and her pursuit of infinite orgasms are widely publicized, awakening the entire world from a long-lasting crisis in which people were no longer interested in sex. She becomes the goddess of sex worshiped by the public, and her sexual hologram is consecrated as an icon adored by all. Amid a sexual orgasm performed in front of frenzied crowds and broadcast to the entire world, she experiences climax after climax—but suddenly, Miss G realizes in sorrow that "everything is an illusion, all illusion begins with the self, everything returns to nothingness."[20] With her excessive sexuality, she never experiences the emotion that is known as love. When she sinks back into despair, however, she is able to find companionship in a Mr. F (Failure? Foucault?), who also has a congenital genital defect. With him, she finally feels that they "got there, slowly, forcefully, in a flood, at the same time, they got there."[21] The real adventurousness of this text is actually not in its densely baroque depiction of sexual revels, but in that it shows a transcendence of the anthropocentric sexual experience, foregrounding an enlightenment of doing away with not only the purpose of sexual reproduction but also the reproductive organs. Bodies and visions are one. In the moment that is "like rest in the music of the spheres" at the end of the narrative, Miss G and Mr. F soundlessly exit the binary universe where body and mind are separated.

Bao Shu's most recent SF short story collection, *The Girl's Name Is Monster* 少女的名字是怪物 (2020), also pays tribute to women. Even though it is tinged with sentimental romanticism, one of the stories, "The Little Mermaid" 海的女兒, obviously suggests a transgression across species, across the organic and inorganic, human and posthuman boundaries. The main character, Fatima, is a chimera with human brain transplanted into a nanomachine body in the shape of a mermaid. She freely swims at the bottom of the ocean like the little mermaid from the fairy tale by Hans Christian Andersen (1805–1875). Just like the little mermaid, she falls in love with a human. Determined to be with her lover, she transplants her brain into a cloned female body so that she can become human again. But Monica, the woman who raised her, tells her the truth—as in Andersen's story, she will never really be human. Her brain has also been mechanized. This fairy tale, retold in a "cyber" style, eventually turns Fatima into the goddess of creation when she returns from a space voyage after an apocalyptic event on Earth that has dried up all the water and annihilated all living beings.

Fatima returns to Earth after a heartbreaking discovery of her loved one's engagement with a real woman on Europa, Jupiter's moon. She roams across the burnt land, finding no life that survived. She returns to the trench at the bottom of the dry ocean bed where she once worked and lived, but discovers not even any ancient bacteria left. However, she does find Monica's last words for her. Before dying, Monica, knowing that Fatima would eventually return, left her a message that explains about the nanomaterial in Fatima's body, which is like a type of cell, similar to ancient bacteria. Fatima knows that her own body must be disintegrated to release all the nano cells to make new lives. She waits in the dried-up trench for a long time before the first rain pours down in the new world. With sixty consecutive days of heavy rain, enough water forms an ocean again. Fatima swims in the new ocean and activates all the nano cells to peel away from her body and enter the seawater. There is life on Earth again; this time, it is silicon-based life that will become, evolve, and grow into a diverse ecosystem. Fatima dissipates like smoke. Before losing consciousness, she tells her lover, who is far away on Europa, "I love you, Mino. I also love you, Monica. I love humankind, life, and the entire world. This love will last, together with the new life, billions of years into the future."[22]

The story of Fatima creates a new myth, redefining the episteme of our time—an episteme that builds affinities among all things in a world that respectfully acknowledges differences and diversities—through the power of fictional imagination. Fatima, as chimera, is the origin of a new species, and she is one and all. In a postscript to the short story collection, Bao Shu mentions the relationship between the girl and the monster in *Frankenstein* again and gives this cross-border affinity a radical yet positive meaning: "When love and beauty coming from the deepest part of human nature blend in the most chaotic and ruthless force of the universe, new possibilities are born, like a phoenix is reborn after fire. Sometimes it is a monstrosity, a horror, that shatters the rigid social structure and stereotyped conventions that have imprisoned women, whose self-liberation is the storm of a new revolution."[23] Bao Shu asks how to keep love alive in a posthuman age and how to foster a new life in the ruins of our planet—the fundamental questions about life and death for which we need to find answers in the contemporary world. Bao Shu's statement gives SF a significance almost equivalent to that of Revelation.

THOSE WHO MADE HERSTORY

Having emphasized the nonbinary among male SF writers, I introduce remarkable women SF writers who emerged in the years leading to the rise of She-SF and deserve recognition. In the beginning, there were only a small number of women SF authors. Their writings were located at the margins of the marginal genre. They often had to assume a male perspective and imitate the male authors' hard SF discourse. But there are moments revealing feminine sensitivity, such as Zhao Haihong's short story "The Undying Spring" 不枯竭的泉 (2001), which depicts a journalist choosing to close down her five senses completely. Still alive, her body, now shrunken to the size of a dry mummy, becomes a specimen on display in a laboratory. The male I-narrator is curious about what story is inside this body and after learning what happened—a heartbreaking story about love and guilt—he sees her tears, which have never stopped streaming since she gave up her body. He comes to an epiphany that "she can shut down her senses, but she can never shut down her heart."[24] The unstoppable tears also testify to the fluidity of the life still in her body, which has not dried up either.

Both Ling Chen and Zhao Haihong received attention in the SF community, but the first woman writer to make a real breakthrough was Xia Jia, who breathed a strong feminine self-consciousness into new wave SF. Critics considered her a so-called "soft SF" author, branding her work as "porridge SF" 稀飯科幻. But Xia Jia received an education in physics at Peking University, and her first important story, written when she was twenty, was hard SF. A genuinely scientific story, "The Demon-Enslaving Flask" 關妖精的瓶子 (2004), fictionalizes the famous experiment of James Clerk Maxwell (1831–1879), which established the classical theory of electromagnetic radiation. In her two short story collections, *The Demon-Enslaving Flask* (2012) and *A Time Beyond Your Reach* 你無法抵達的時間

(2017), as well as her English-language story collection, *A Summer Beyond Your Reach* (2022), Xia Jia gradually grew into a sophisticated stylist, with a lyrical voice and a masterly control of the language, precise and poetic at the same time.

The title story of the second collection, "A Time Beyond Your Reach," is perhaps the most beautifully written SF story by Xia Jia. It is told in the first person, addressing a second person, "you," who experiences time differently from other people. "You" lives in a much faster time. The I-narrator, who has been deeply in love with "you," becomes a physicist, inventing a scientific method to speed up her time, so she can catch up with "you." As a consequence, the I-narrator will die due to brain damage. After she has made all the preparations, she creates a chance encounter with "you" and lives in "your" time for two most adventurous, splendid, and thrilling days, which end with "your" departure, when this young woman scientist becomes a riddle for "you" to use "your" lifetime—perhaps eternal life—to solve, if "you" will remember her.[25] The text is like a love letter written in simple but powerful language, smoothly flowing with the unfolding of the narrator's emotional turmoil. The story shows courage to overcome the impossible, cross the gap in the different speeds of time flow, and create a singular moment that is short, suicidal, and self-sacrificing, but links "you" and the I-narrator in a chimera moment that brings together momentarily parallel timelines that never should have met in a world of physical certainty. Xia Jia's poetic narrative plays into the full fluidity of both the narrative discourse and speculative world-building. Love has the most powerful agency in crossing all boundaries to reach the beyond.

Xia Jia has also extensively borrowed from traditional fantasy stories to create a Chinese steampunk style, as in her dreamy narrative of the "Night Journey of the Dragon-Horse" 龍馬夜行 (2015). It depicts a gigantic machine-made Dragon-Horse walking in the long night after human civilization has perished. The Dragon-Horse has conversations with all sorts of creatures who tell it that there are no longer poets writing poetry or humans walking in the daylight. In a poetic text that has few coordinates to establish connections to our familiar reality, the Dragon-Horse vaguely knows: "I am a Dragon-Horse, both a dragon and a horse. I was born in the mythology of the Chinese but manufactured in France. I am not sure if I am a machine or organic life, alive or dead, or if there was ever anything alive in this world. I am not sure if this is real or a dream, walking alone in the moonlight."²⁶ The Dragon-Horse is another chimera, both Chinese and European, both human imagination and industrial production, and both a fairy-tale character and a postapocalyptic monster, which nevertheless embodies the residual love, a poetic heart, from the human world.

Xia Jia's most famous story is her rewrite of an ancient Chinese ghost story in "A Hundred Ghosts Parade Tonight" 百鬼夜行街 (2010). It portrays a simulated ghostly world engineered by posthuman machinery. In this story, there is the famous traditional female ghost Nie Xiaoqian 聂小倩, "who sold herself off in pieces: teeth, eyes, breasts, heart, liver, lungs, bone marrow, and finally, her soul. Her soul was sold to Ghost Street, where it was sealed inside a female ghost's body."²⁷ There is also the first-person narrator, Ning Caichen 宁采臣,²⁸ a boy who is said to be the only human living on Ghost Street but is actually a cyborg too. At the end of the story, mysterious monster spiders attack the ghost-cyborgs, and they "believed that I was alive, a real person. They chewed my body and tasted flesh and saw blood . . . Now I'm finally going to die on this street, just like a real person."²⁹ Both "Night Journey of the Dragon-Horse" and "A Hundred Ghosts Parade Tonight" extend a poetic vision of a completely posthuman world, in which all that is solid has perished and even death is no longer absolute.

In a similar vein, Cheng Jingbo's "Before the City Falls" 趕在陷落之前 (2009) presents a densely metaphorized, splendid image of another ghost world, which is like a baroque fossil of ancient time, a moment from the prosperity of Luoyang City before the fall of the Sui Dynasty (581–618). Cheng's story, though short, has an extremely complicated plotline that creates cross-references within the text itself. The city is being carried by a giant who is nothing but a skeleton, trying to drag the city all the way on a journey to the west; he is always one step ahead of the sunrise, so the city is eternally stuck in an endless long night, literally a ghost city. Even the I-narrator eventually finds out that he died as a baby prince a long time ago in a bloody court conspiracy. Cheng's literary style is different from Xia Jia's, with more baroque, complex metaphors that create a dazzling effect of dense details. This story straddles SF and fantasy, alluding to China's long-lost past instead of facing any future. The story itself is fabricated to keep the dead in a simulated memory. It ends with a revelation: "There are so many different truths in this world, who knows the real one?"[30]

Chi Hui is perhaps more productive than any other women SF writers discussed so far. She has written not only many short stories about the posthuman future, inhabited by so-called "fake people" 偽人, and the genetically reengineered offspring of the human race living on a new continent made of plastic waste, but also several novels. One is also about the past, a nearer time than Cheng and Xia depict, in Japanese-occupied Manchuria, where ruthless massacres by the Japanese occupation army resonate with a serial murder case happening in the near future. Titled *2030: Terminal Town* 終點鎮 (2017), this novel leads readers into a maze where all clues point to an evil hiding in the darkness. It uses algorithms to kill people, but its posthuman persona is only a veil covering a real person obsessed with controlling others. The novel ends abruptly, with the female protagonist's confrontation of the evil at Terminal Town, the very end of Manchuria. Chi Hui's protagonist is a writer, a storyteller, who, like Scheherazade, has to keep telling stories to her cell phone, which is the only way to stop the murders. This character is like Han Song's, who are not born as brave heroes but have to overcome the fear of seeing, knowingly following clues into a trap, where the truth-revealing moment will perhaps mark the terminus of her own life.[31]

SCIENCE FICTION ON THE MÖBIUS CONTINUUM

Finally, I present a few new writers who belong to the Neo-Baroque literary universe on the cutting edge in twenty-first-century Chinese and Sinophone literature. These younger writers animate Chinese SF each in their own unique style, creating distinctly individual voices. Although there is space here to introduce only four writers, Tang Fei, Shuangchimu, Peng Simeng, and Wang Kanyu, before returning to a last story by Gu Shi, I must say that other authors, such as Mu Ming and Duan Ziqi, are equally remarkable.

Tang Fei has had a long career as a SF writer, at least as long as Xia Jia's and Chi Hui's, but has attracted wider attention particularly since publishing her second short story collection, *Odyssey(cy)ber* 奧德賽博 (2021).

Her early stories, such as "Yellow Story" 黃色故事 (2014), "Broken Stars" 碎星星 (2016), "Summer Cicada" 夏日之蟬 (2017), and "The Heart of the Museum" 博物館之心 (2016) have all displayed an experimentalist surrealism, which employs dreamy narratives to create an illusive "novum" that does not correspond to any possible real thing. "Summer Cicada" outlines the growth of a strange creature that looks like a dog or fox when first brought home. She (it is female) eats a lot and keeps growing from tiny to gigantic, as large as the entire house, and yet she keeps growing, as if she were a dream representing all the hope one has for a lifetime. But as summer comes to an end, she begins to dwindle, shrinking to her original size, and further into almost invisible insect size. When snow falls, she grows transparent wings, like a cicada, and disappears.[32] "Yellow Story" (translated by Ken Liu as "Call Girl") is also about a dreamscape. It depicts a teenage girl providing a special service to men, which is to create dreams based on their needs. Dream making is her special talent, and the dreams she makes are solidly digital and illusively imaginary: "The man can feel the transparent currents—1100110111—pass by him. They'll flow to the countless trenches and caves at the bottom of the sea and leave this place behind. Someday this ancient source will dry up, too. But not now. As far as the man is concerned, it's eternity."[33] If this story has a sense of eroticism, it is not sexual but transgressive, breaking apart the solid surface of reality and diving into a fluid stream of (dream) consciousness at the invisible core of the world.

Tang Fei's most important story, in my opinion, is "Spore" 孢子 (2019), which was published in the mainstream literary journal *Youth Literature* 青年文學 and received wide acclaim from readers and critics. This story, included in *Odyssey(cy)ber*, is narrated by a young man whose father, called Gatekeeper in the text, taught him the skill of trace-tatt, a popular art in this story's future time, when the young population are obsessed with these shiny temporary tattoos, elusive and short-lived, just like the lack of memory in their epoch. But Gatekeeper keeps a memory from the past; he is a survivor of a massacre that happened a long time ago, and his entire life converges in his refusal to forget:

> Gatekeeper tried many things before he finally created the art of trace-tatts. This was his final exertion—writing, audio, imagery, and every other attempt to record or narrate the nightmarish massacre had been

erased, eliminated, purged. Like the slaughter itself, this great forgetting was accomplished by a tacit understanding between national will and the individual. Even the few surviving victims were eager to forget that chapter of history. Except for Gatekeeper.[34]

The art of trace-tatts encodes the forbidden memory of a haunting past. But the I-narrator, a young man growing up in a hedonistic environment without memory of the massacre, refuses to carry on his father's sad memory. His father leaves in disappointment. The story opens with the I-narrator's encounter with a beautiful girl, an AI, which he recognizes immediately because of her complete perfection. He brings her home and shows her the trace-tatts that he is designing, but soon he realizes that this AI must be his father's new creation, a perfect daughter instead of his decadent, cynical son. Even though he is full of love for her, his "sibling," also the last storage site of his father's memory of the tragic past, he reports her existence to the authorities to have her taken away. He betrays his father, Gatekeeper, and he also kills the historical memory. Trace-tatts lose their significance: "Even if trace-tatts someday cover all the world's flesh, people won't understand what they mean, or once meant, or once tried to represent. History will be forgotten, as will Gatekeeper's visual language. Trace-tatts will just be pretty designs indicating nothing."[35]

The text is rare in SF because it uses an unreliable narrator, who knows more than readers do but chooses to hide the truth, exactly contrary to what Han Song's characters would do as truth investigators. Yet Tang Fei's narrative creates a fold in its own textual space, in which she shows us the enormity of truth, metaphorized in the "language," the trace-tatt, an art form. Its absence from view points to a void where it should be. This narrative deliberately lays bare the intention to cover the truth but nevertheless offers readers the knowledge of what is hidden. Tang Fei's "The Spore" reverses "Fear of Seeing," rewriting the fear into a cynical ignorance, which cannot hide the deep sorrow of the young man who betrays not only his father's memory but also his AI "sibling," a girl he had begun to love. The story ends like Lu Xun's "In Memoriam" 傷逝 (1925), in which the I-narrator also betrays his ideal and love, "burying the truth deep in the wound in my heart, silently advancing, guided only by the principles of forgetting and falsehood."[36] I do not intend to take a wild guess about any possible allegorical meaning in "The Spore," but its penetrating depiction of the society's chilling choice to forget instead of remembering is richly meaningful when read in the political context of contemporary China.

I have already presented Shuangchimu's marvelous nonbinary narrative "The Solar Studio: Seagull" in chapter 2. Shuangchimu has also written two connected stories that form a loosely linked epic spanning thousands of years in human and posthuman history: "The School of Lynx" 猞猁學派 (2019) and "On Foot I Had to Walk Through the Solar Systems" 我們必須徒步穿越太陽系 (2020). The title of the second story is borrowed from the poem by the short-lived Finnish poet Edith Södergran (1892–1923), who wrote in Swedish. Like "The Solar Studio: Seagull," these two stories have rich references to historical figures and other literary works. The world depicted is a twenty-third-century civilization still controlled by the Catholic Church, which continues to hold the Ptolemaic universe to be the singular truth. In the first story, a lynx is brought from Egypt to Florence, where its gaze converts selected intellectuals to form a school of lynx, a secret scientific sect, which a fictional character named Galileo is said to have joined in 1611. Galileo became a great scientist (in reality and in the story) and verified a new theory of the universe, the heliocentric theory, through discovering four satellites orbiting Jupiter. In the heyday of the Baroque epoch, this was branded as heresy, but the truth he discovered was encoded in the flourishing Baroque culture. One example is the philosopher Gottfried Wilhelm Leibniz's (1646–1716) famous quote: "Each portion of matter may be conceived of as a garden full of plants, and as a pond full of fishes. But each branch of the plant, each member of the animal, each drop of its humors, is also such a garden or such a pond."[37]

The school of lynx secretly passes on Galileo's heliocentrism for centuries, until their spaceships are launched into deep space. But all of them are bounced back by the "Ptolemaic sphere of fixed stars," which confirms the validity of the geocentric universe. In the second story, the Catholic church has established stations on Io, one of the four Galilean moons. Catholic knights conquered the aboriginal creatures, which are metallic, drawing energy from electromagnetism. The sole survivor is Talos, a female metallic creature, who happens to find a stranger called K, a member of the school of Lynx. Talos rescues K, the first human being who shows her kindness and tenderness. His tremendous sorrow, caused by the loss of his girlfriend during their failed effort to travel across the entire solar system, deeply moves Talos. K also shows Talos the finger of Galileo, the sacred relic of their sect. Talos decides to help K and enlists the giant gas creature sleeping in the dense atmosphere of Jupiter, Kraken. She uses her metallic skin to protect K, and they merge into the transparent body of Kraken, awakening its consciousness and connecting their minds.

The three become one, a cross-species chimera, consisting of three different life forms—the carbon-based human, the metallic creature, and the gas life. K, Talos, and Kraken travel across the solar system, past Saturn, Neptune, and other planets. Two hundred years later, after they have entered the Oort Cloud, edging out of the solar system for the first time in human history, Talos sends a message back to Earth in K's name, detailing a perfect star map of the heliocentric solar system, which should be received by the secret watcher of the school of Lynx. Forty million years into the future, Kraken encounters a tiny flying object, which Talos intercepts. It contains a golden disc that records "sounds of Earth."[38] They listen to this recording of wind, thunder, and Bach's Brandenburg Concertos. They realize that this is a message from another Earth, another solar system, which is just like theirs, and that "the universe is filled with a multitude of solar systems, each a prison for life. And we have to walk through the solar systems again and again."[39]

The same resplendent language that enlivens the text of "The Solar Studio: Seagull" makes these two stories another pair of examples of Neo-Baroque aesthetics. A scholar of the Baroque aesthetics, Shuangchimu has made a conscious effort to synchronize the message, the world-building, the characters, the plotline, and the very form of the narrative in each story; all point to a world image filled with an infinity of folds. This world opens to the Neo-Baroque literary universe with extreme complexity and multiplicity, infinite possibilities of world-building; like in Leibniz's metaphor, each blade of grass is a garden itself, filled with a dense quantity of different worlds. Galileo's vision of the irregular movements of heavenly bodies, the lynx's penetrating gaze, the enormity of Jupiter and its gas monster Kraken, the cyborgian consciousness of Talos, and the trans-anthropocentric trinity sailing into deep space, toward an infinity of stars—these are all most wondrous images coming from the new generation of She-SF.

Peng Simeng and Wang Kanyu are the youngest writers so far discussed, born in the last decade of the twentieth century. Both have established positions in the mainstream literary field. Peng's first short story collection, *Secretion* 分泌 (2020), and Wang Kanyu's second short story collection, *Seafood Restaurant* 海鮮飯店 (2020), mark their authors' mature literary style. In the title story, "Secretion," Peng Simeng, an ethnic Tujia writer, depicts a dystopian future when the state controls the entire population with biomedical technologies. When people's endocrine system is completely manipulated by the state-controlled substances, no one can feel happy spontaneously. They all must adjust their mood via the routines dictated by scheduled medications. Peng describes the depression of the young protagonist, her fear, anxiety, and inability to love, in great detail in the first half of the narrative; the second half focuses on a revolution that turns into an orgy when people break into the hospitals and consume the medications freely. The question what will happen the day after revolution is very legitimate in this context, but Peng offers a glimpse of hope by showing the protagonist's first proactive action, to reach out and embrace a little kid the moment a feeling swells in her heart: "I do not know what it is, a warm stream sweeter than honey. I know all the mood medicines and their intended effects, but I do not know what it is. Not dopamine, not adrenaline, or oxytocin, or endorphin, or phenethylamine, or any feeling induced by the mood controllers that I have used, but yet it feels like the sum total of all those combined."[40] This unnamable emotion makes her believe there will be a better tomorrow.

In the same collection, Peng's "Chronicle of the Sinking Boat" 沉舟記 (2017) depicts a scenario in which a single artificial intelligence can never learn to become creative, but two AI programs, through communicating with each other, can produce superintelligence that quickly achieves the singularity moment to surpass human intelligence. But Peng's story is fundamentally about the kindness that is generated in the friendship, companionship, or even love between the two AI entities. Her most celebrated story, "Beast Boxing" 野獸拳擊 (2017), depicts a young professional turning herself into a master boxer in a simulated VR environment. She finds unlimited strength, which helps her achieve self-determination. She is eventually defeated by the VR program but has found a goal for her life, which is her own. These stories all manifest a new Gen Z self-consciousness with commitment to individuality, self-care, and open communication and carry the seeds for a new political and ethical consciousness that may grow into a powerful force.

Wang Kanyu's multiple versions of her first short novel, *Cloud Mist* 雲霧 (first version, 2015), based on her MFA thesis at Fudan University, point to multiple visions of freedom. Cloud Mist, an AI program, is attempting to achieve total control over humans, and Wang's story employs a multitude of perspectives to depict each individual's resistance. The novel itself represents a gesture of defiance and an embrace of individual freedom. But the title story of her short story collection, "Seafood Restaurant" (2019), is rather different. It depicts a food critic's journey to a small town in the United States, focusing on her gradual discovery of the true nature of this town, which is a colony of aliens, a nonexistent place next to the town of Wellesley in Massachusetts. The food critic is both horrified and attracted. She tries to escape but has already been pulled into this treacherous world. Averse to seafood, she is forced by the alien impersonating Professor Laiden to eat a live octopus:

> I stood up and tried to flee, but suddenly I was surrounded. Each person holding me down seemed to have more than two arms. Laiden's body also sprouted translucent extra limbs. He caressed my jaw gently with one hand, picked up the little octopus with another, and jammed it into my mouth. He tore free the tentacles clinging to my lips with his flexible fingers, kissed me, and pushed it deeper in with his tongue. It squirmed between my teeth, its suckers clinging to the inner walls of my esophagus and crawling down, so slowly, inch by inch. The creepy, slippery sense moved from my mouth to my stomach. I felt it fill me, control me, and replace me, while something else, something that was not me, began to grow inside me—[41]

This story, inspired by the author's experience on a visit to Wellesley College, has a strong tone of Lovecraft and thus can be read as a Cthulhu story. It does not share much with Haraway's tentacular thinking, but rather shows an aversion to the loss of individuality. What is appallingly remarkable about Wang's text is that it acutely points to a moment of cross-species sexuality. The food critic has fallen prey to the sexual appetite of Professor Laiden, the disguised alien. The very discomforting moment when the professor shows his true face and invites her to merge with him into one species, which leads to a scene almost like sexual intercourse through tentacles and tongues, is a very rare scene in Chinese SF exposing the hidden desire for alien sex. "Seafood Restaurant" has a deceptively simple structure that disguises a complex conspiracy, from where emerges an abysmal darkness of heart, which is either human or alien or already both. Much more ambiguous than Wang Kanyu's other stories in both message and narrative form, this may represent a courageous new step toward confronting a mysterious unknown that comes not from outer space but from within.

I conclude this chapter with another story by Gu Shi. "Möbius Continuum" 莫比烏斯時空 (2016) is not only Gu Shi's most famous story but also the single story that can best represent the cutting-edge literary vision of this new generation of She-SF, who have truly created a nonbinary literary universe. The plotline is a fold of the narrative, itself a Möbius strip; it begins with "The End," and its end returns to the beginning. The I-narrative begins with a car accident after a quarrel between the narrator and his girlfriend, in which the narrator's body is permanently paralyzed. X, a man whom the narrator just met before the accident, explains to him what a Möbius ring is, and X compares it to life: normally we only know the surface reality, without any opportunity to know the other side, the inside reality, but when we move in a Möbius ring, we can cross over and enter the inside of the world.[42] X guides the narrator to use his consciousness to create a new space, a container like a Klein bottle, whose inside is outside. The thought experiment gives him the freedom to imagine a time-space continuum; when he receives surgery to obtain a physical copy of his body, he is both inside and outside this copy. X's guidance lasts a long time while the narrator spends years rebuilding the world that he is familiar with. At last, when X bids him farewell, X asks if he has ever thought of the possibility that time is a Möbius ring. He has now lived in his simulated world for years. Then along come a young couple. "I" meets a younger "me," and "I" tells him "my" name is X.

"Möbius Continuum" is a perfect self-reference to SF as a method to imagine an entire estranging world, and it is also a verbal embodiment of the new wave SF spirit that reveals the invisible. The inside of the world matters more than the surface reality, because that is where literature begins. X's guidance is equivalent to a SF writing handbook, explaining how to create from there. What is created is a virtual realm, which can be understood only when positioned next to what will really happen, the "accident" as a real event. This shows that the virtual world created through speculation exists in a fold of the time-space continuum. It is a ceaseless flow of time that creates an infinity of folds. It does not move into the "future," if "future" means a progressive teleological end. Its future is also a fold inside the virtual embodiment. "Möbius Continuum" contains the ultimate maxim about SF, with which the story of Chinese SF concludes—perhaps better than any other possibility. We do not surrender to any singular form of time-space structure; the Möbius ring offers us all the possibility of building a multitude of new worlds.

EPILOGUE

The Wandering Earth, 2019

Chinese New Year's Day, 2019: The entire nation witnessed the launching of Earth as a planet-size spaceship into deep space, an arresting spectacle visualized through advanced VFX techniques combining live-action footage and computer-generated imagery, which for the first time in Chinese film history achieved a "realistic" representation of the SF wonder on the large screen.[1] The release of *The Wandering Earth* (流浪地球, dir. Guo Fan 郭帆, b. 1980) in theaters was widely regarded as an exciting moment when Chinese SF reached its maximum visibility. SF, the lonely hidden army Fei Dao talked about in 2010, was no longer hidden—certainly not a force waiting in ambush. It came into the mainstream.

Interestingly, *The Wandering Earth* also made *invisibility* even more undeniably felt. Invisible in the film was approximately forty-three minutes of footage[2] showing devastating apocalyptic scenes: the Han Songsque chthonic scenes—the inhuman conditions of the underground cities; Hangzhou's sinking underground; frozen bodies floating on the black rivers; the rescue team members' dark emotions upon learning of their family members' deaths. All these were cut from the film in the same way similar views are censored in official news reports about the devastating scope and human costs of natural or man-made disasters in contemporary China, for fear of generating only negative reactions.[3]

Also invisible in the film is the original plot from Liu Cixin's novella "The Wandering Earth." While the film version tells a heartwarming story of father-son reconciliation, Liu's story is much darker and more insurgent. It depicts the humans' desperate epic journey into the darkness, and the climax of the narrative is a deathly uprising that leads to sentencing five thousand scientists who created the "Wandering Earth" project to capital punishment, when the entire human population in exile begins to suspect that the scientific speculation about a devastating solar explosion has been a hoax. Just like contemporary politicians in denial of climate change, the uprising mob shows a contempt for science, which leads to the total demise of the scientific community on this rogue planet. However, what was invisible to naked eyes but observed through scientific means soon surfaces in the visible sky: the sun explodes and devours the inner planets, proving that the scientists' theories, though inconvenient and counterintuitive, are correct. The sun dies and the sky becomes black; "Five billion years of majestic life now were no more than a passing dream."[4] The survivors have to brave a dark age, while the wandering Earth enters total darkness in deep space.

The invisibility of certain essential elements of SF in the cinematic spectacle exemplifies the politics of representation, but also testifies to SF's unique strength as a literary genre in the textualized worlding of the invisible, from where it creates a literary space for revelations of what is becoming and beyond. The invisible suggests a larger world with infinite possibilities, which transgress the definitive narratives and mandates. When "The Wandering Earth" had become a fixed image in cinematic form and media coverage, the illumination of the invisible was dimmed by a more powerful narrative defined by the nation.

Even more ironic, a strong nostalgic sentimentality characterizes the film *The Wandering Earth*, which turns a space odyssey into a story of homecoming. The film strongly affirms the values associated with family and home. Humans, confronting the impending catastrophe caused by a solar explosion, have to go on the road to find another home, but they also take the "home planet" into exile, making Earth a space shuttle. Despite all the splendors of outer space, the film focuses on some distinctively Chinese traditional morals, in the heartfelt father-son reconciliation after a long episode of alienation, the emotionally driven decision to take the entire home planet for a journey into unknown space, and the ultimate commitment to valuing home above all else. The film was released on the traditional Lunar New Year's Day, an occasion for family reunions, and after Chinese SF's success overseas, it seems to have come full circle, from Liu Cixin's earlier efforts to push an enclosed civilization into open space to this film's commercially driven rendition of the endgame into a homecoming journey.

The direction of Chinese SF's future development, whether it will be appropriated for domestic nationalist projects, seems clear. Even though *The Wandering Earth* presents a message about values associated with home, it simultaneously keeps alive a grand claim to universality when depicting the human race as a whole. But contrary to the anarchist message about free will and a community of responsible individuals in some Western films like *The Matrix* and *Cloud Atlas*, the SF narrative of humans braving grave dangers in *The Wandering Earth* merges with the mainstream theme that advocates for China's rise and participation in global affairs. Chinese SF took center stage in world literature, and at the same time its first big-screen presentation was appropriated as a strategic device for achieving domestic political goals, telling a story about home, homesickness, and homecoming.

Between the novella's publication in *SFW* in 2000 and the film's worldwide release in 2019, Chinese SF rose from a marginalized genre to a prominent place in popular culture. But just as the film betrays more problems with invisibility, now that the genre has gained unprecedented glory, its dark side or the dark power that defined its strength in the first place has further retreated to the lightless margins. Censorship has invaded the imaginary realm of SF as the genre has been elevated to a new height that represents the nation's vanguard position in science, scientific education, and SF. Liu Cixin's 1989 novel *China 2185* is now hidden from public view, and the dark plotline in "The Wandering Earth" is concealed behind visual spectacles. What Han Song wrote during the nighttime still belongs to the night: "My Fatherland Does Not Dream" is still unpublishable in China, and his published novels like *Subway* and *Hospital* get little attention from the public. On the other hand, increasing government attention and market demand are beginning to reshape the genre into a less experimental and more conventional mode of popular literature.

In 2015, the then vice president of China, Li Yuanchao 李源潮, praised Liu Cixin's novels in public—just one and a half years before President

Barack Obama recommended the "Three-Body" trilogy during an interview with *The New York Times*. In 2016, Li delivered a keynote speech at a government-sponsored "Chinese Science Fiction Conference" 中國科幻大會. The government recognition heightened the position of the genre in the literary field, with unprecedented investment allotted to building SF research centers, the SF publishing industry, and SF cinema. In 2016, the Chinese Association of Science and Technology granted memberships to SF writers under its branch of popular science, thus officially ending the controversy about whether SF's nature was primarily "scientific" or "literary." In the meantime, Liu Cixin and many other writers became official members of the Chinese Writers Association. Both the scientific and literary communities accepted SF, a drastic change from the situation in the early 1980s, when both refused to recognize SF's legitimacy. SF conventions, which used to serve only small circles of editors and authors, have evolved into carnivals in Chengdu, Taiyuan, Shanghai, and Beijing, attended by tens of thousands of fans and investors. In 2022, Chengdu successfully bid to host the 2023 World Con, with support from both the municipal government of Chengdu and private sector companies from all over China; it would be the first time that China hosted the World Con, bringing home world SF.

Now, more than a decade after Fei Dao presented the story about the lonely hidden army, the position of Chinese SF has changed drastically. While it has gained more visibility in contemporary Chinese culture, the new wave avant-gardism has gradually lost its momentum along a meandering course of profiting from the market and falling into the embrace of the government. The image of Chinese SF has turned into the planet-size spaceship "The Wandering Earth," which attained successes at the box office while at the same time carrying on the Chinese Communist Party's mission of building a "community for the shared destiny of humankind."[5]

But Han Song complained that "SF dreads such an environment. It does not need a nationwide campaign." In 2020, during the early days of the COVID-19 outbreak, he also lamented that "SF writers are like garbage; they can create worlds in their imagination but are incapable of handling anything in reality." In the past, he had said that "China's reality is more science fictional than SF," but now he confessed that "SF is no match for China's reality," suggesting that the reality is way more absurd, grotesque, and nightmarish than any SF writer can imagine.[6] The Chinese government soon used the pandemic as an opportunity to start a frantic nationalist campaign to achieve both the domestic oppression of different opinions and a collective antagonism against Western democracy. The world came to a halt while political, economic, and environmental crises emerged around the globe.

Dystopian fiction writers, from Aldous Huxley to Lao She to Margaret Atwood, have always maintained a good faith: if the worst-case scenario has been told in stories, they will function as a sort of moral tale so that the worst will not happen in reality—testifying to the utopian impulse even in the writers' worst dystopian visions. However, during the current pandemic, Han Song confessed that, facing the apocalyptic moment now happening in reality, "SF is completely powerless."[7] Yet, as a conscientious author who never gives up dreaming and writing, Han Song also emphasizes that only with this realization at the time of a cataclysmic event could SF be written as something truly new and inspiring to readers. Echoing but differing from Jacques Derrida's declaration "No Apocalypse, Not Now,"[8] Han Song's reflections on apocalypse and the urgency of writing do not take the apocalypse or dystopia only as a figure created in language but as a new condition for writing creatively. His thoughts recall Lu Xun's famous quotation from the Hungarian poet Sándor Petőfi: "Despair, if proven to be false, is equal to hope."[9] This signifies a sober decision to confront the worst-case scenario, and for SF writers, storytelling becomes a moral obligation that aims at truthfulness rather than the falsity of utopian or nationalist rosy-coloring of China's future. In the face of doomsday, we can only count on literary imagination to confront the worst, yet keep alive a hope to defer and deter the worst possible from coming too soon.

It was during the pandemic that Shuangchimu published her stories "The Solar Studio: Seagull" and "On Foot I Had to Walk Through the Solar Systems," Tang Fei published *Odyssey(cy)ber*, Wang Kanyu *Seafood Restaurant*, Peng Simeng *Secretion* . . . It was during the pandemic that I reached a deeper understanding of the baroque new universe created by women and nonbinary writers, and over the past two to three years, Dung Kai-cheung published *A Posthuman Comedy*, Chan Koonchung published *Beijing Zero Kilometer*, Egoyan released *Zero Degree of Separation*, Chen Qiufan coauthored *AI: 2041*, and the year when I was finalizing this manuscript, Lo Yi-chin composed another Neo-Baroque labyrinthine experimental long narrative novel, which was properly titled *The Great Plague* 大疫 (2022). Storytelling is continuing...

Over the past decade, I witnessed the rise of new wave SF in contemporary China. I have observed its cutting-edge experimentation with subversive poetic and political powers, celebrated its success on the stage of world literature, and also detested the dissipation of great talents when the lure of glory and wealth has encroached on the originality of their visions. Over the past decade, I have lived the history of the new wave. I began writing about this new wave long before it gained recognition from the mainstream and began putting together this manuscript when left-wing SF scholars, mostly a younger generation, had systematically applied Marxist political economy, Carl Schmitt's notion of "the state of exception," and Giorgio Agamben's theory of "bare life" to the practical criticism of Chinese SF, particularly the "Three-Body" trilogy. From there, Liu Cixin's speculations are observed in the context of real politics, and many of his and other SF writers' ideas have stepped into the spheres of political, economic, and social realities. During the three years when I was working on this book, I also witnessed contestations concerning artificial intelligence, antagonism between algorithms and literary imagination, and negotiations between human agency and posthuman elements, all unfolding on a much larger scale in contemporary social space. Reflections on a series of speculative questions first asked in SF have become key factors in understanding contemporary politics and intellectual life, while the current situation of the literary field and truly, the entire world, has become even more and more uncertain, or science fictional.

Now, when I am writing these words, it strikes me that our world has turned into a SF. Where I am has turned into heterotopia, the other space unfolding from the invisible. How I behave, think, and communicate with others have become more posthuman than human. The world itself is on the verge of falling out of the human control, and perhaps a post-anthropocentric transformation has already quietly begun. Since the pandemic started, I have stayed at home for many months. The usual, familiar setting became an estranged world, an alien space of otherness, and the same quiet transformation happened to many homes, campuses, hotels, hospitals, boats not allowed to leave or reach shores, cities shut down, countries that closed borders to outsiders. Even the entire planet looked different when human activities were greatly reduced and the atmosphere, climate, as well as ecosystems quietly changed. During the pandemic, I have relied on digital technologies to present and preserve myself, displaying a virtual form of myself to my family, friends, and students, and we are now literally living together in cyberspace. Outside our homes, we are surrounded by viruses that are invisible, infecting us and changing us from humans into something else, and the scientific means to combat the pandemic are reengineering our biology. In many ways, we are becoming more posthuman than ever.

During the pandemic, the places designated to be isolated from the spatiotemporal continuum of everyday reality function as the heterotopian other to our normal life, or our memory of normalcy. The heterotopia keeps what is happening invisible to us, yet suggests a state of exception and implies a pervasive danger lurking around us. The heterotopian locations during the pandemic serve as an enclosed, exclusive institution to execute a sort of opaque administration; and they may eventually gain a utopian glory when triumph over the disease is declared, or create a dystopian vision suggesting continuing catastrophe and impending apocalypse. This situation heightens the fear of the invisible but also designates the necessary mechanism to create the other space, an imaginary space that illuminates a truth that is not present in the optimistic promise of a utopian future but underlies the predicament, crisis, and transformations happening to our world. This is the moment and place where SF has become more relevant to our lives than ever; and this experience we have all shared shows the transformation of our reality into a SF world—exactly like Han Song's "hospital."

During December 2022 and January 2023, Han Song experienced life-threatening COVID symptoms. He survived, and I hope he will keep writing. The engine of difference, operating somewhere in Han Song's sight but beyond ours, will continue to pump new strength into the genre. But not just Han Song. While writing this book, I have been reading SF stories written by an entirely newer generation of authors, born after 1989, who have maintained a better balance between science and literature; been more cautious with big and empty words about nation, hope, and future;

and been more inventive with chimera-like storytelling that defies definitions. They create a new aestheticism to bypass the mandates of the mainstream, and they are dual heirs to Liu Cixin's speculative worldbuilding and Han Song's subtle subversion. I have been fascinated by the provocatively stimulating new visions emerging from their writings, such as those nonbinary, trans-species, lyrical worlds created by Tang Fei, Shuangchimu, Peng Simeng, Gu Shi, and Wang Kanyu. I will continue to watch this generation's growth. Where the genre makes kinship across many forms of literature, where the monster and I make a chimera across the boundaries of species and life forms, and where words are worlds, storytelling will continue to unfold and unpack those worlds, estranging them into wonders and spectacles.

If something comes from this uncertain time of the pandemic, I hope there will be more courageous engagement with SF as a form of imagination; more investment in the visions of otherness alternative to the world images that the existing systems have convinced us to believe in; more speculations beyond the given and legalized; more adventure into the darkness, the opposite of power and prosperity; and more gates opening to a myriad of universes. If SF is after all a form of dark consciousness, it will not so easily surrender to the light, the glory of the nation, and the rewards of the market. The spirit of SF is the invisible specter exiting a totally visible and well-organized reality.

Just as happens in Tang Fei's "The Spore," when the catastrophe is over—when the pandemic ends—choosing to remember is a personal ethical decision; the nation will certainly move forward and forget the three years of trauma and tragedy. SF, like the humble tomb Han Song depicts, located on the small planet traveling in the dark, may still be the invisible marker of the truthful historical memory. SF is the revelation in our time; it is also the chronicle of a history that will never end. I am concluding this book with a cautious hope that Chinese SF will continue, evolve, and energize the twenty-first-century literature. SF will be with us for a long, long time. Bridging science and storytelling, it will become an increasingly more essential method for our understanding of the world. With fearless seeing, it illuminates the invisible truth.

NOTES

PROLOGUE: A LONELY HIDDEN ARMY, 2010

1. The conference "Chinese Literature of the First Decade of the New Century," co-organized by Chen Sihe and David Der-wei Wang, took place at Fudan University, Shanghai, on July 11–13, 2010.
2. Chen Sihe, "Cong 'shaonian qinghua' dao 'zhongnian weiji,'" *Tansuo yu zhengming* 1 (2010).
3. Han Song, "Wei kehuan er huozhe: canjia xin shiji shinian wenxue guoji yantaohui," in *2010 niandu Zhongguo zuijia kehuan xiaoshuo ji*, ed. Wu Yan and Guo Kai (Chengdu: Sichuan renmin chubanshe, 2011), 306–312.
4. Liu Cixin, *The Three-Body Problem*, trans. Ken Liu (New York: Tor, 2014), 57.
5. Constance Penley, *NASA/TREK: Popular Science and Sex in America* (London and New York: Verso, 1997), 3.
6. Liu Cixin, "Sanwei de Han Song," *Liu Cixin tan kehuan* (Wuhan: Hubei kexue jishu chubanshe, 2014), 162.
7. Kunkun, "Reng youren yangwang xingkung," in *2011 niandu Zhongguo zuijia kehuan xiaoshuo ji*, ed. Wu Yan and Guo Kai (Chengdu: Sichuan renmin chubanshe, 2012), 400–402.
8. Han Song, "Zichao de yishu," in *Zhongguo kehuan wenlun jingxuan*, ed. Wu Yan and Jiang Zhenyu (Beijing: Beijing daxue chubanshe, 2021), 260.
9. For a historical account of the 1983 political attacks on SF, see Ye Yonglie, *Shishi feifei huiguniang* (Fuzhou: Fujian renmin chubanshe, 2000).
10. Iron house, cannibalism, a sick nation, and the madman are all prominent literary images in Lu Xun's writings. For an in-depth study of the allegorical meanings of these images, see Leo Ou-fan Lee, *Voices from the Iron House: A Study of Lu Xun* (Bloomington: Indiana University Press, 1987).

11. Han, "Wei kehuan er huozhe," 310.
12. Fei Dao, "Jimo de fubing: xinshiji kehuan xiaoshuo zhong de Zhongguo xingxiang," in *2010 niandu Zhongguo zuijia kehuan xiaoshuo ji*, ed. Wu Yan and Guo Kai (Chengdu: Sichuan renmin chubanshe, 2011), 317.
13. Robert Scholes and Eric S. Rabkin, *Science Fiction: History, Science, Vision* (Oxford: Oxford University Press, 1977), 88.
14. "Novum" is a concept coined by Ernst Bloch to refer to the unexpectedly new, which pushes humanity out of its present towards the not yet realized. Bloch, *The Principle of Hope* (Cambridge, MA: MIT Press, 1995), 1: 8. The term was popularized by Darko Suvin, referring to a newness in scientific and technological terms that constitutes a symbolic centrality in SF.
15. David Der-wei Wang, "Wutuobang, etuobang, yituobang," in *Xiandangdai wenxue xinlun: yili, lunli, dili* (Beijing: Sanlian shudian, 2014).
16. Darko Suvin, *Metamorphosis of Science Fiction: On the Poetics and History of a Literary Genre* (New Haven, CT: Yale University Press, 1979), 4.
17. For the Deleuzian concept, see James Williams, "Event," in *Gilles Deleuze: Key Concepts*, ed. Charles J. Stivale (New York: Routledge, 2011), 80–90.
18. Giorgio Agamben, "What Is Contemporary?" in *What Is an Apparatus?* (Stanford, CA: Stanford University Press, 2009), 44.
19. Han Song, "Dangxia Zhongguo kehuan de xianshi jiaolü," *Nanfang wentan* 6 (2010): 30.
20. Han Song, "Zhanzai xin qidian shang de 'Zhongtuobang,'" *Ershiyi shiji Bimonthly* (December 2022): 10–13.
21. Jing Tsu, "Why Sci-Fi Could be the Secret Weapon in China's Soft-Power Arsenal," *Financial Times*, May 29, 2020.
22. These two images are borrowed from Gu Shi's short stories "Möbius Continuum" 莫比烏斯時空 and "Chimera" 嵌合體. See Gu, *Mobiwusi shikong* (Beijing: Xinxing chubanshe, 2019), 1–82.

1. POETICS OF THE INVISIBLE

1. I first used the term "new wave" to name the new trend in Chinese SF in my article "Zhongguo kehuan de xinlangchao," *Wenxue* 1, no. 1 (Spring/summer 2013): 3–16.
2. Damien Broderick, "New Wave and Backwash: 1960–1980," in *The Cambridge Companion to Science Fiction*, ed. Edward James and Farah Mendlesohn (Cambridge: Cambridge University Press, 2003), 48–63.
3. James Tweedie, *The Age of New Waves: Art Cinema and the Staging of Globalization* (New York: Oxford University Press, 2013), 45–82.
4. Such an opinion was first expressed in China by Fang Lizhi 方勵之 (1936–2012). See Fang, "Keshi de he bukeshi de wuzhi," in *Yuzhou de chuangsheng* (Hong Kong: Nanyue chubanshe, 1989), 66–79.
5. David Deutsch, *The Fabric of Reality: The Science of Parallel Universe—and Its Implications* (New York: Penguin, 1997).

6. Jacques Lacan, 'Seminar on "The Purloined Letter,"' in *Écrits* (New York: Norton, 2002), 17.
7. Maurice Merleau-Ponty, *The Visible and the Invisible*, ed. Claude Lefort, trans. Alphonso Lingis (Evanston, IL: Northwestern University Press, 1968), 151.
8. Maurice Merleau-Ponty, *Signs*, trans. Richard C. McCleary (Evanston, IL: Northwestern University Press, 1964), 20–21.
9. David Farrell Krell, "General Introduction: The Question of Being," in Martin Heidegger, *Basic Writings* (San Francisco: Harper San Francisco, 1993), 17.
10. Merleau-Ponty, *The Visible and the Invisible*, 155.
11. Martin Heidegger, "Letter on Humanism," *Basic Writings* (San Francisco: Harper San Francisco, 1993), 217.
12. Martin Heidegger, "The Origin of the Work of Art," *Basic Writings* (San Francisco: Harper San Francisco, 1993), 170.
13. Michel Foucault, *The Birth of the Clinic: An Archaeology of Medical Perception* (New York: Vintage, 1994), 165.
14. Foucault, *The Birth of the Clinic*, 165–166.
15. Philip Ball, *Invisible: The History of the Unseen from Plato to Particle Physics* (London: Vintage, 2015), xx.
16. Ling Chen's story "404 zhi jianlong zaitian" 404之見龍在天 (2016) is a playful depiction of the censorship of news about an invisible but true dragon. The story is included in *Ta kehuan: Shijian de haizi*, ed. Chen Qiufan (Beijing: Hangkong gongye chubanshe, 2021), 162–194.
17. Such as how a character is named, "zhenxiang diaochazhe" 真相調查者, in Han Song, *Ditie* (Shanghai: Shanghai renmin chubanshe, 2011), 262.
18. In China's literary hierarchy, SF belongs to the branch of the literature of popular science. A special committee on SF was officially organized and recognized within the larger the association of popular science in 2016.
19. William Gibson, "The Science in Science Fiction," *Talk of the Nation*, NPR, November 30, 1999.
20. Liu Cixin, "Cong dahai jian yidishui," *Liu Cixin tan kehuan* (Wuhan: Hubei kexue jishu chubanshe, 2014), 45–54.
21. Jingfang Hao, *Vagabonds*, trans. Ken Liu (New York: Sage, 2020).
22. Han Song, *The Hospital*, trans. Michael Berry (Amazon Crossing, 2023).
23. Donna J. Haraway, *Staying with the Trouble: Making Kin in the Chthulhucene* (Durham, NC: Duke University Press, 2016).
24. Michel Foucault, "Different Spaces," in *Essential Works of Foucault 1954–1984 Volume 2: Aesthetics, Method and Epistemology*, ed. James D. Faubion (New York: The New Press, 1998), 175–186.
25. Chan Koonchung, *Living Out the Contradictions of Our Time* (Hong Kong: Jockey Club Design Institute for Social Innovation, 2016).
26. David Der-wei Wang, "The Panglossian Dream and Dark Consciousness: Modern Chinese Literature and Utopia," in *Utopia and Utopianism in the Contemporary Chinese Context*, ed. avid Der-wei Wang, Angela Ki Che Leung, and Zhang Yinde (Hong Kong: Hong Kong University Press, 2020), 53–70.

27. Han Song mentioned the publication history of this story in a blog post titled "You weilai de guojia caiyou kehuan." He gave me more specific information through private messages in February 2022: he originally submitted this story to *SFW* but got it back at a conference in Chengdu in 1991, where he then gave it to a writer from Taiwan, Lü Yingchong 呂應鍾 (b. 1948), who took it to S. K. Chang 張系國 (b. 1944), the most famous SF writer in the Chinese-speaking world before the rise of Liu Cixin. A few months later, Han Song learned that his story had won the first prize of the Global Chinese SF Award granted by the Taiwan SF magazine *Phantomstastia* 幻象. *SFW* later asked Han Song to resubmit this story and published it in 1993.
28. Han Song, "Tombs of the Universe," trans. Xueting Christine Ni, in *Sinopticon: A Celebration of Chinese Science Fiction*, ed. Xueting Christine Ni (Oxford, UK: Solaris, 2021), 78.
29. Han, "Tombs of the Universe," 79 (with modifications).
30. Lu Xun, "Mujiewen," *Lu Xun quanji* (Beijing: Renmin wenxue chubanshe, 2005), 2:207–208. (English translation is mine, borrowing words from Michael G. Hill in his translation of Wang Hui's "Lu Xun and Tombstones," in *A New Literary History of Modern China*, ed. David Der-wei Wang [Cambridge, MA: Harvard University Press, 2017], 310.)
31. Wang, "Lu Xun and Tombstones," 306.
32. Zhan Ling, *Dangdai Zhongguo kehuan xiaoshuo zhuanxing yanjiu* (Beijing: Zongguo shehui kexue chubanshe, 2022), 93.
33. Achille Mbembe, *Necropolitics*, trans. Stephen Corcoran (Durham, NC: Duke University Press, 2019).
34. Foucault, *The Birth of the Clinic*, 170.
35. Foucault, *The Birth of the Clinic*, 172.
36. Chang Hao, "Chaoyue yishi yu youhuan yishi: rujia neisheng waiwang sixiang zhizairen yu fanxing," *You'an yishi yu minzhu chuantong* (Beijing: Xinxing chubanshe, 2006), 59. The translation is in Wang, "Panglossian Dream and Dark Consciousness," 62.
37. Wang, "Panglossian Dream and Dark Consciousness," 63.
38. Lu Xun, "Zheyang de zhanshi," *Lu Xun quanji* (Beijing: Renmin wenxue chubanshe, 2005), 2:220.
39. Lu Xun, "Mujiewen," 207.
40. Han Song, *Guidao* (Shanghai: Shanghai wenyi chubanshe, 2020), 42.
41. Liu Cixin provided the information about this novel through private correspondence with me in July 2015.
42. Liu Cixin, "Diyidai kehuanmi de huiyi," *Liu Cixin tan kehuan* (Wuhan: Hubei kexue jishu chubanshe, 2014), 134–135.
43. Liu Cixin, *Chao xinxing jiyuan* (Chongqing: Chongqing chubanshe, 2009).
44. *China 2185* has been deleted from its original publication site, Shuimuqinghua, but is accessible through several other websites, including https://www.99csw.com/book/428/index.htm (accessed October 19, 2020).
45. Li Hua, "The Political Imagination in Liu Cixin's Critical Utopia: China 2185," : *Science Fiction Studies* 42, no. 3 (2015): 519–541.

46. It is not clear whether Liu Cixin was influenced by the post-1989 thought on "farewell to revolution," a phrase coined by two leading intellectuals of the 1980s, Li Zehou 李澤厚 and Liu Zaifu 劉再復. For a discussion of the novel in the context of intellectual history, see Tu Hang, "Long Live Chairman Mao! Death, Resurrection, and the (un)Making of a Revolutionary Relic," *Journal of Asian Studies* 81, no. 3 (2022): 507–522.
47. Mingwei Song, *Young China: National Rejuvenation and the Bildungsroman, 1900–1959* (Cambridge, MA: Harvard University Asia Center, 2015).
48. The story was first published in *SFW*. The story is included in Han Song, *Kan de kongju* (Beijing: Remin youdian chubanshe, 2012), 67–85. An English translation by Nathaniel Isaacson, titled "Fear of Seeing," is included in Han Song, *A Primer to Han Song* (Los Angeles, CA: Dark Moon Books, 2020), 81–103.
49. Han, "Fear of Seeing," *A Primer*, 91–92.
50. Han, "Fear of Seeing," *A Primer*, 93.
51. The English translation by Nathanial Isaacson is included in *A Primer to Han Song*. See Han Song, "My Country Does Not Dream," in *A Primer to Han Song*, 107–145. In my analysis of the story, the quotations are mostly from Isaacson's English translation.
52. Han, *Ditie*, 18, 27.
53. Han, *Kan de kongju*, 388.
54. Han Song, *Yuzhou mubei* (Shanghai: Shanghai renmin chubanshe, 2014), 378.
55. Liu Cixin, "SF jiao—lun kehuan xiaoshuo dui yuzhou de miaoxie," *Liu Cixin tan kehuan*, 88.
56. Wang Anyi, *Niming* (Beijing: Renmin wenxue chubanshe, 2016), 50–54.
57. Istvan Csicsery-Ronay, Jr., *Seven Beauties of Science Fiction* (Middletown, CT: Wesleyan University Press, 2011), 2.

2. SCIENCE FICTION AS METHOD

1. Liu Cixin, "Mountain," *The Wandering Earth* (Beijing: Beijing Guomi Digital, 2013), 47–94.
2. Despite the debate on the nature of SF, most scholars agree that its fictional worlds are distinguished "in one way or another from the world in which we actually live: a fiction of the imagination rather than observed reality, a fantastic literature." Adam Roberts, *Science Fiction* (London: Routledge, 2000), 1.
3. Deleuze says, "To think is to fold." Gilles Deleuze, *Foucault*, trans. Sean Hand (Minneapolis: University of Minnesota Press, 1988), 118.
4. Robert Scholes, *Structural Fabulation* (Notre Dame: Indiana University Press, 1975), 41.
5. Arthur C. Clarke, "The Star," *The Collected Stories of Arthur C. Clarke* (New York: Orb, 2000), 517–521.
6. Ted Chiang, "The Story of Your Life," *Stories of Your Life and Others* (Easthampton, MA: Small Beer Press, 2002), 91–146.
7. Isaac Asimov, "The Last Question," *The Complete Stories: Volume One* (London: Voyager, 1997), 415–429.

8. Jorge Luis Borges, "The Library of Babel," *Collected Fictions* (New York: Viking, 1998), 112–118.
9. Liu Cixin, "The Worst of All Possible Universes and the Best of All Possible Earths: Three-Body and Chinese Science Fiction," trans. Ken Liu, in *Invisible Planets: An Anthology of Contemporary Chinese Science Fiction*, ed. Ken Liu (New York: Tor, 2016), 367.
10. Liu Cixin, *Death's End*, trans Ken Liu (New York: Tor, 2016), 555, 243.
11. Brian W. Aldiss, *Billion Year Spree* (New York: Doubleday, 1974); Adam Roberts, *The History of Science Fiction* (London: Palgrave MacMillan, 2005).
12. Paul K. Alkon, *Science Fiction Before 1900: Imagination Discovers Technology* (New York: Twayne, 1994), 1–15.
13. Roberts, *The History of Science Fiction*, 25–29.
14. Zhou Zhuoren, "Zhenshi de gushi," *Zhou Zuoren yiwen quanji* (Shanghai: Shanghai renmin chubanshe, 2012), 5:559–616.
15. Diskin Clay, *Lucian, True History* (Oxford: Oxford University Press, 2021), 59.
16. Mikhail M. Bakhtin, *Problems of Dostoevsky's Poetics* (Minneapolis: University of Minnesota Press, 1984), 114.
17. Northrope Frye, *Anatomy of Criticism* (Princeton, NJ: Princeton University Press, 1990), 231.
18. J. C. Davis, "Thomas More's *Utopia*: Sources, Legacy, and Interpretation," in *The Cambridge Companion to Utopian Literature*, ed. Gregory Claeys (Cambridge: Cambridge University Press, 2010), 34.
19. For studies of the relationship between the New World and the Baroque, see Lois Parkinson Zamora and Monika Kaup, eds., *Baroque New Worlds: Representation, Transculturation, Counterconquest* (Durham, NC: Duke University Press, 2010); and Lois Parkinson Zamora, *The Inordinate Eye: New World Baroques and Late American Fiction* (Chicago: University of Chicago Press, 2006).
20. Stillman Drake, *Galileo at Work: His Scientific Biography* (Chicago: University of Chicago Press, 1978), 146.
21. John Donne, "An Anatomy of the World: The First Anniversary," in *John Donne's Poetry*, ed. Donald R. Dickson (New York: Norton, 1992), 104.
22. Murray Roston, *Milton and the Baroque* (London: MacMillan, 1980), 23.
23. Roberts, *The History of Science Fiction*, 40.
24. As it is defined in *Le Dictionnaire de l'Académie française* (4th edition), Paris, 1762.
25. Jean Baudrillard refers to "America" as a fiction, a hyperreality. See Baudrillard, *America* (London: Verso, 1988), 28.
26. Roberts, *Science Fiction*, 1.
27. Roberts, *Science Fiction*, 8.
28. Darko Suvin, *Metamorphosis of Science Fiction: On the Poetics and History of a Literary Genre* (New Haven, CT: Yale University Press, 1979), 6–7.
29. Suvin, *Metamorphosis of Science Fiction*, 14–15.
30. Suvin, *Metamorphosis of Science Fiction*, 3.

31. Scholes considers SF both discontinuous from our world as fabulation and confronting our world in some cognitive way, which places SF in the structure of human knowledge and sciences. Scholes, *Structural Fabulation*.
32. In Damien Broderick's discourse, the metaphorical is similar to Suvin's estrangement, while the metonymic connects SF with reality. Broderick, *Reading by Starlight: Postmodern Science Fiction* (London: Routledge, 1995).
33. Carl Freedman, *Critical Theory and Science Fiction* (Middletown, CT: Wesleyan University Press, 2000).
34. Istvan Csicsery-Ronay Jr., *Seven Beauties of Science Fiction* (Middletown, CT: Wesleyan University Press, 2011), 5, 2–3.
35. Seo-young Chu, *Do Metaphors Dream of Literal Sleep? A Science-Fictional Theory of Representation* (Cambridge, MA: Harvard University Press, 2010), 3.
36. Chu, *Do Metaphors Dream of Literal Sleep?*, 7.
37. Chu, *Do Metaphors Dream of Literal Sleep?*, 7.
38. Chu, *Do Metaphors Dream of Literal Sleep?*, 7.
39. Chu, *Do Metaphors Dream of Literal Sleep?*, 6.
40. Zheng Wenguang, "Zai wenxue chuangzuo zuotanhui shang guanyu kehuan xiaoshuo de fayan," *Kehuan xiaoshuo chuangzuo cankao ziliao* 4 (May 1982).
41. Jiang Zhenyu, "Gongxian yu wuqu: Zheng Wenguang yu 'kehuan xianshi zhuyi,'" *Zongguo xiandai wenxue yanjiu congkan* 8 (2017): 78–92.
42. Marston Anderson, *The Limits of Realism: Chinese Fiction in the Revolutionary Period* (Berkeley: University of California Press, 1990); David Der-wei Wang, *Fictional Realism in Twentieth-Century China: Mao Dun, Lao She, Shen Congwen* (New York, NY: Columbia University Press, 1992).
43. Li Hua, *Chinese Science Fiction During the Post-Mao Thaw* (Toronto: University of Toronto Press, 2021), 7.
44. See Li Jing, "Dangdai Zhongguo yujing xia 'kehuan' gainian de shengcheng," *Wenxue pinglun* 5 (November 2020): 198–206.
45. Chen Quifan, "Dui 'kehuan xianshizhuyi' de zaisikao," in *Zhongguo kehuan wenlun jingxuan*, ed. Wu Yan and Jiang Zhenyu (Beijing: Beijing daxue chubanshe, 2021), 266–269.
46. "Hyperreality" is also related to the other Baudrillard notion "simulacra," the substituting of signs of the real for the real itself. See Jean Baudrillard, *Simulation* (New York: Semiotext[e], 1983), 1–26.
47. Chen Qiufan, "Chaozhenshishidai de wenxue chuangzuo," *Zhongguo xiandai wenxue* 35 (June 2019): 51–64.
48. Chu, *Do Metaphors Dream of Literal Sleep?*, 7.
49. Lee Kaifu and Chen Qiufan, *AI 2041: Ten Visions for Our Future* (New York: Currency, 2021).
50. The first sentence was written by Samuel Delany; the second by Ursula Le Guin. Both cases are borrowed from Chu, *Do Metaphors Dream of Literal Sleep?*, 10.
51. Liu, *Death's End*, 318–329; 467–539.

52. Han Song, *Hospital*, trans. Michael Berry (Amazon Crossing, 2023), 126–127.
53. Han, *Hospital*, 129.
54. Fredric Jameson, *The Antinomies of Realism* (London: Verso, 2013), 311.
55. Yan Lianke, *Discovering Fiction*, trans. Carlos Rojas (Durham, NC: Duke University Press, 2022), 99.
56. Raúl Ruiz, *Poetics of Cinema* (Paris: Editions Dis Voir, 2005); *Poetics of Cinema*, 2 (Paris: Editions Dis Voir, 2007).
57. Deleuze, *Foucault*; Gilles Deleuze, *The Fold: Leibniz and the Baroque*, trans. Tom Conley (Minneapolis: University of Minnesota Press, 1993).
58. Omar Calabrese, *Neo-Baroque: A Sign of the Times*, trans. Charles Lambert (Princeton, NJ: Princeton University Press, 1992).
59. Deleuze, *The Fold*, 3.
60. Calabrese, *Neo-Baroque*, xii.
61. This paragraph is based on Chekhov's *Seagull*. The English translation is quoted from Anton Chekhov, *Three Plays*, trans. Constance Garrett (New York: Modern Library, 2001), 13.
62. Shungchimu, "Taiyangxi pianchang," *Sheli xuepai* (Beijing: Zuojia chubanshe, 2020), 61, 73–74. All quotations from this text are my own translations.
63. Cf. David Damrosch, *Around the World in 80 Books* (New York: Penguin, 2021), xvi.
64. Chekhov, *Three Plays*, 15.
65. Shungchimu, "Taiyangxi pianchang," 53–54.
66. Shungchimu, "Taiyangxi pianchang," 59.

3. CAN WE READ "A MADMAN'S DIARY" AS SCIENCE FICTION?

1. Lu Xun, "Diary of a Madman," in *The Real Story of Ah-Q and Other Tales of China: The Complete Fiction of Lu Xun*, trans. Julia Lovell (London: Penguin, 2009), 26.
2. Fei Dao, *Zhongguo kehuan dapian* (Beijing: Qinghua daxue chubanshe, 2013), 177–179.
3. Lu Xun, *Yuejie lüxing*, *Lu Xun quanji* (Beijing: Renmin wenxue chubanshe, 1973), 11: 7–119.
4. See Xiong Rong, "Lu Xun zuizao de liang pian yiwen—'Aichen' he 'Zaoren shu,'" *Wenxue pinglun* 3 (1963). Carlos Rojas translated Lu Xun's translation back into English. See Suozi, "The Art of Creating Humanity," *Renditions* 77/78 (2012): 70–77.
5. For other studies of the relationship between Lu Xun and contemporary Chinese SF, see Cara Healey, "Madmen and Iron Houses: Lu Xun, Information Degradation, and Generic Hybridity in Contemporary Chinese SF," *Science Fiction Studies* 46, no. 3 (2019): 511–524.
6. David Der-wei Wang, *Fin-de-siècle Splendor: Repressed Modernities of Late Qing Fiction, 1849–1911* (Stanford, CA: Stanford University Press, 1997), 253–312.
7. Chen Sihe, "'Rewriting Literary History' in the New Era of the Liberated Thought," trans. Mingwei Song, in *A New Literary History of Modern China*, ed. David Der-wei Wang (Cambridge, MA: Harvard University Press, 2017), 797–803.

8. Liang Qichao, "On the Relationship between Fiction and the Governance of the People," trans. Gek Nai Cheng, in *Modern Chinese Literary Thought: Writings on Literature, 1893–1945*, ed. Kirk Denton (Stanford, CA: Stanford University Press, 1996), 74–81.
9. Yan Fu and Xia Zengyou, "Benguan fuyin shuobu yuanqi," *Guowenbao* November 10, 13, December 8, 11, 1897.
10. Patrick Hanan, "The 'New Novel' Before the Rise of the New Novel," in *A New Literary History of Modern China*, ed. David Der-wei Wang (Cambridge, MA: Harvard University Press, 2017), 144.
11. Lu Xun, "Bianyan," *Lu Xun quanji* (Beijing: Renmin wenxue chubanshe, 1973), 11: 10.
12. Michael Gibbs Hill, *Lin Shu, Inc.: Translation and the Making of Modern Chinese Culture* (New York: Oxford University Press, 2013).
13. Lu Xun, "340515 zhi Yang Jiyun," *Lu Xun quanji* (Beijing: Renmin wenxue chubanshe, 2005), 13: 99.
14. Louise J. Strong was the author of several adventure novels written for children. Her biographical information can be found in Graeme Davis, ed., *More Deadly Than the Male: Masterpieces from the Queens of Horror* (New York: Pegasus Books, 2019), which does not even give her birth and death years. Her birth and death years are found in the Fourteenth Census of the United States (www.ancestry.com).
15. Strong, "An Unscientific Story," *The Cosmopolitan* 34 no. 2 (February 1903): 411–417.
16. Chen Mengxiong, "Zhitang laoren tan 'Aichen,' 'Zaorenshu' de sanfengxin," *Lu Xun yanjiu dongtai* 12 (1986): 40.
17. Yoojin Soh, "Cong kexue dao chiren: Lu Xun 'Zaorenshu' fanyi yu yeman de qianzai shuxie," *Wenxue* 5, no. 1 (Spring/Summer 2017): 70.
18. Lu Xun (Souzi), "The Art of Creating Humanity," 74–75.
19. Strong, "An Unscientific Story."
20. Carlos Rojas, "Introduction: 'The Germ of Life,'" *Modern Chinese Literature and Culture* 23, no. 1 (2011): 1–16.
21. Jing Jiang, *Found in Translation: New People in Twentieth-Century Chinese Science Fiction* (New York: Association of Asian Studies, 2020), 43.
22. See Lydia Liu, *Translingual Practice: Literature, National Culture, and Translated Modernity, 1900–1937* (Stanford, CA: Stanford University Press, 1995), 45–76.
23. Deng Tianyi, "Lu Xun yi 'Zaorenshu' he Bao Tianxiao yi 'Zaorenshu,'" *Changchun shifan xuebao* 4 (1996): 28.
24. Soh, "Cong kexue dao chiren," 67–83.
25. Lydia Liu, "Life as Form: How Biomimesis Encounters Buddhism in Lu Xun," *The Journal of Asian Studies* 68, no. 1 (2009): 21–54.
26. Roslynn D. Haynes, *From Faust to Strangelove: Representations of the Scientist in Western Literature* (Baltimore, MD: The Johns Hopkins University Press, 1994), 94.
27. Strong, "An Unscientific Story."
28. A complete Japanese translation was completed by Takamine Sei 高峰生 in 1912. See Tarumoto Teruo, "Lu Xun 'Zaorenshu' de yuanzuo, buyi," in *Lu Xun fanyi yanjiu lunwenji*, trans. Xu Changfu, ed. Beijing Lu Xun Museum (Shenyang: Chufeng wenyi chubanshe, 2013), 186–187.

29. The concept of national allegory is found in Fredric Jameson, "Third-World Literature in the Era of Multinational Capitalism," *Social Text* 15 (1986): 65–88.
30. Lu Xun, "Nahan zixu," *Lu Xun quanji* (Beijing: Renmin wenxue chubanshe, 2005), 1: 441.
31. Lu Xun, "Diary of a Madman," 31.
32. Lu Xun, "Women xianzai zenyang zuo fuqin," *Lu Xun quanji* (Beijing: Renmin wenxue chubanshe, 2005), 1: 145. The translation is T. A. Hsia's; see Hsia, *The Gate of Darkness: Studies on the Leftist Movement in China* (Seattle: University of Washington Press, 1968), 146–147.
33. Benjamin Schwartz, *In Search of Wealth and Power: Yen Fu and the West* (Cambridge, MA: Harvard University Press, 1964), 111.
34. Andrew Jones, *Developmental Fairy Tales: Evolutionary Thinking and Modern Chinese Culture* (Cambridge, MA: Harvard University Press, 2011), 7.
35. Jones, *Developmental Fairy Tales*, 7.
36. D. W. Y. Kwok, *Scientism in Chinese Thought 1900–1950* (New Haven, CT: Yale University Press, 1965), 6.
37. Liu Cixin, *The Dark Forest*, trans. Joel Martinsen (New York: Tor, 2015), 442.
38. Lu Xun, "Suoji," *Lu Xun quanji* (Beijing: Renmin wenxue chubanshe, 2005), 2: 306.
39. Lu Xun, "Tengye xiansheng," *Lu Xun quanji* (Beijing: Renmin wenxue chubanshe, 2005), 2: 315.
40. Lu Xun, "Lessons from the History of Science," trans. Nathaniel Isaacson, *Renditions* 74 (2010): 98.
41. Lu Xun, "Diary of a Madman," 28.
42. Wang, *Why Fiction Matters in Contemporary China* (Waltham, MA: Brandeis University Press, 2020), 166.
43. Lu Xun, "On the Power of Mara Poetry," trans. Shu-ying Tsau and Donald Holoch, in *Modern Chinese Literary Thought: Writings on Literature, 1893–1945*, ed. Kirk Denton (Stanford, CA: Stanford University Press, 1996), 96–109.
44. Lu Xun, "Po esheng lun," *Lu Xun quanji* (Beijing: Renmin wenxue chubanshe, 2005), 8: 32.
45. See Jim Baggott, *The Quantum Story* (Oxford: Oxford University Press, 2011), 115–125.
46. Baggott, *The Quantum Story*, 7–16.
47. James Reeve Pusey, *Lu Xun and Evolution* (Albany: State University of New York Press, 1998).
48. Liu Na, "Shuo Ri, xin wulixue, zhongji: cong yige jiaodu tan Lu Xun jingshen yichan de duyixing he dangdai yiyi," *Zhongshan daxue xuebao* 46, no. 6 (2006): 39–48.
49. See Wu Jike, *Jindai lixue zai Zhongguo de chuanbo yu fazhan* (Beijing: Gaodeng jiaoyu chubanshe, 2006), 115.
50. Citation from nobelprize.org.
51. Hu Shi, "Duanpian xiaoshuo," *Xin qingnian* 4, no. 5 (1918).
52. Stephen Hawking, *A Brief History of Time* (New York: Bantam, 2001), 42.
53. Lu Xun, "Diary of a Madman," 21.
54. Lu Xun, "Diary of a Madman," 22.

55. The translation is Benjamin Elman's. See Elman, *A Cultural History of Modern Science in China* (Cambridge, MA: Harvard University Press, 2006), 15.
56. Lu Xun, "Diary of a Madman," 24.
57. The revolutionary whose heart was eaten is Xu Xilin 徐錫麟 (1873–1907).
58. Lu Xun, "Zhongguo xin wenxue daxi xiaoshuo erji daoyan," *Lu Xun quanji* (Beijing: Renmin wenxue chubanshe, 2005), 6: 246–274
59. Zhou Zuoren, "Humane Literature," trans. Ernst Wolff, in *Modern Chinese Literary Thought: Writings on Literature, 1893–1945*, ed. Kirk Denton (Stanford, CA: Stanford University Press, 1996), 228–232.
60. The Korean translation of "A Madman's Diary" as "Kwangin ilgi" by Ryu Su-in 柳樹人 was featured in the column *piso sosol* 避暑小說 [Horror fiction] in *Tonggwang chapchi* 東光雜誌 in June 1927. I am grateful to Professor Hong Seuk-pyo 洪昔杓 for this information.
61. Lu Xun, "New Year's Sacrifice," in *The Real Story of Ah-Q and Other Tales of China: The Complete Fiction of Lu Xun*, trans. Julia Lovell (London: Penguin, 2009), 163.
62. Liu Cixin heavily relies on quantum physics in his creation of the alien world as well as the universe beyond the human knowledge. Liu, *The Three-Body Problem*, trans. Ken Liu (New York: Tor, 2014), 357–383.
63. Lu Xun, "Diary of a Madman," 27.
64. Bao Shu, "Shiguang de zhufu," in *2020 Zhongguo zuijia kehuan zuopin*, ed. Yao Haijun (Beijing: Renmin wenxue chubanshe, 2021), 28–57.

EXCURSUS I. LOOKING BACKWARD: 2010–1900

1. Tan Sitong, *An Exposition of Benevolence: The "Jen-hsüeh" of T'an Ssu-t'ung*, trans. Chan Sin-wai (Hong Kong: The Chinese University Press, 1984).
2. Nathaniel Isaacson, *Celestial Empire: The Emergence of Chinese Science Fiction* (Middletown, CT: Wesleyan University Press, 2017), 93–107.
3. Jiang Jing, *Found in Translation: New People in Twentieth-Century Chinese Science Fiction* (New York: Association of Asian Studies, 2020).
4. Xue and Chen's translation, titled *Bashiri huanyouji* 八十日環遊記, was published by Shanghai's Jingshi wenshe 经世文社 in 1900.
5. Yukio Ozaki first coined the Japanese term for science fiction in 1886. See Yasuo Nagayama, *Riben kehuan xiaoshuo shihua: cong mufumoqi dao zhanhou* (Nanjing: Nanjing daxue chubanshe, 2012), 53.
6. For scholarly work on late Qing SF, see David Der-wei Wang, *Fin-de-siècle Splendor: Repressed Modernities of Late Qing Fiction, 1849–1911* (Stanford, CA: Stanford University Press, 1997); Isaacson, *Celestial Empire*; Jia Liyuan, *"Xiandai" yu "weizhi":wanqing kehuan xiaoshuo yanjiu* (Beijing: Beijing daxue chubanshe, 2021).
7. Feng-ying Ming, "Baoyu in Wonderland: Technological Utopia in the Early Modern Chinese Science Fiction Novel," in *China in a Polycentric World: Essays in Chinese Comparative Literature*, ed. Yingjin Zhang (Stanford, CA: Stanford University Press, 1998),

152–72; Andrew Jones, *Developmental Fairy Tales: Evolutionary Thinking and Modern Chinese Culture* (Cambridge, MA: Harvard University Press, 2011), 28–33, 51–62.
8. Wu Jianren, *Xin shitou ji* (Zhengzhou: Zhongzhou guji chubanshe, 1986), 212.
9. Wu, *Xin shitou ji*, 236.
10. Mingwei Song, ed., "Chinese Science Fiction: Late Qing and the Contemporary," *Renditions* 77/78 (November 2012).
11. Yang Qiong, "A Writer's Dilemma: Gu Junzheng and a Turning Point of Chinese Science Fiction" (master's thesis, The Ohio State University, 2010).
12. Mingwei Song, "Huoxing etuobang: *Maocheng ji* yu Lao She de gushi," *Shucheng* 137 (October 2017): 44–50.
13. Nicholai Volland, *Socialist Cosmopolitanism: The Chinese Literary Universe, 1945–1965* (New York: Columbia University Press, 2017), 96–123.
14. Paola Iovene, *Tales of Future Past: Anticipation and the End of Literature in Contemporary China* (Stanford, CA: Stanford University Press, 2014), 24–30.
15. Zhang Jie, "*Death Ray on a Coral Island* as China's First Science Fiction Film," in *The Liverpool Companion to World Science Fiction Film*, ed. Sonja Fritzsche (Liverpool: Liverpool University Press, 2014), 39–55; Nathaniel Isaacson, "Media and Messages: Blurred Visions of Nation and State in Tong Enzheng's *Death Ray on a Coral Island*," in *Simultaneous Worlds: Global Science Fiction Cinema*, ed. Jennifer Feely and Sarah A. Wells (Minneapolis: University of Minnesota Press, 2015), 272–288.
16. Rudolf Wagner, "Lobby Literature: The Archaeology and Present Functions of Science Fiction in the People's Republic of China," in *After Mao: Chinese Literature and Society 1978–1981*, ed. Jeffrey Kinkley (Cambridge, MA: Harvard University Press, 1985), 17–62.
17. Li Hua, *Chinese Science Fiction During the Post-Mao Cultural Thaw* (Toronto: University of Toronto Press, 2021); Zhan Ling, *Dangdai Zhangguo kehuan zhuanxing yanjiu* (Beijing: Zongguo shehui kexue chubanshe, 2022).
18. Many of these new theories and scientific knowledge were introduced through a book series collectively titled *Zouxiang weilai* 走向未來 (edited by Jin Guantao 金觀濤 and Liu Qingfeng 劉青峰), which consists of seventy-four books about sciences, social sciences, and the humanities, published by Sichuan renmin chubanshe between 1984 and 1988.

4. A POETIC HEART IN THE DARK FOREST

1. Liu Cixin, *Death's End*, trans. Ken Liu (New York: Tor, 2016), 470–471.
2. Liu, *Death's End*, 474.
3. Kant's conceptualization of the sublime can be found in Immanuel Kant, *Critique of Judgment* (Indianapolis: Hackett, 1987); Kant, *Observations on the Feeling of the Beautiful and the Sublime* (Berkeley: University of California Press, 1991).
4. Han Song's words comparing Liu Cixin to Zhuangzi are found on the back cover of Liu's *Qiuzhuang shandian* (Chengdu: Sichuan kexue jishu chubanshe, 2004).

5. See C. T. Hsia, "Obsession with China: The Moral Burden of Modern Chinese Literature," in *A History of Modern Chinese Fiction* (Bloomington and Indianapolis: Indiana University Press, 1999), 533–554.
6. Liu, *Death's End*, 559.
7. Yan Feng, "Guangrong yu mengxiang," in Liu Cixin, *Liulang diqiu* (Wuhan: Changjiang wenyi chubanshe, 2008), 3.
8. Wang Xiaodong, "Zhongguo de gonyehua jiang jueding Zhongguo yu shijie de mingyun—jianlun 'Gongye dang' duijue 'Qinghua dang,' " *Lüye* 1 (2011); Lu Nanfeng and Wu Jing, "Lishi zhuanzhe zhong de hongda xushi: 'Gongyedang' wangluo sichao de zhengzhi fenxi," *Dongfang xuekan* 1 (2018); Yu Liang, "'Gongye dang' yishi, yizhong bei hushi de renwen jingshen," *Dongfang xuekan* 2 (2019).
9. Liu Cixin, "Weiguan jintou," in *Weijiyuan* (Shenyang: Shenyang chubanshe, 2010), 161–169; "Yuzhou tansuo," *Weijiyuan*, 171–182.
10. Liu Cixin, *Ball Lightning*, trans. Joel Martinsen (New York: Tor, 2018).
11. Liu Cixi, "Zhaowendao," in *Shiguang jintou* (Shijiazhuang: Huashan wenyi chubanshe, 2010), 12.
12. Liu Cixin, "Weishenme renlei hai zhide zhengjiu," in *Liu Cixin tan kehuan* (Wuhan: Hubei kexue jishu chubanshe, 2014), 34–42.
13. Liu, "Cong dahai jian yidishui," in *Liu Cixin tan kehuan* (Wuhan: Hubei kexue jishu chubanshe, 2014), 46.
14. Wu Yan and Fang Xiaoqing, "Liu Cixin yu xin gudian zhuyi kehuan," *Hunan keji xueyuan xuebao* 27, no. 2 (2006): 36–39.
15. Liu, "Cong dahai jian yidishui," 45.
16. Jia Liyuan, "Zhujiu women of weilai—90 niandai zhi jin Zhongguo kehuanxiao zhong de Zhongguo xingxiang" (master's thesis, Beijing Normal University, 2010).
17. Liu, *Death's End*, 518.
18. On the definition of the fictional "world system," see Franco Moretti, *Modern Epic: The World-System from Goethe to Garcia Marquez* (London: Verso, 1996).
19. On the definition and interpretation of "hard SF" in Western SF literature, see Kathryn Cramer, "Hard Science Fiction," in *The Cambridge Companion to Science Fiction*, ed. Edward James and Farah Mendlesohn (Cambridge: Cambridge University Press, 2003), 86–196. In actual SF writing, based on Cramer's observation, there is a great room for negotiations in the definition; "hard SF" does not always represent a "scientific" position and, on the contrary, often challenges such a position.
20. The story of Jia Baoyu taking a submarine is told in Wu Jianren, *Xin shitou ji* (Zhengzhou: Zhongzhou guji chubanshe, 1986).
21. Ye Yonglie, *Xiao Lingtong manyou weilai* (Beijing: Ertong wenxue chubanshe, 1978).
22. Jia, *Zhujiu women of weilai*, 6.
23. Fang Lizhi, "Keshi de he bukeshi de wuzhi," *Yuzhou de chuangsheng* (Hong Kong: Nanyue chubanshe, 1989), 79.
24. See Yan Feng, "Chuangshi yu jimie—Liu Cixin de yuzhou shixue" *Nanfang wentan* 5 (2011).
25. Liu, "Cong dahai jian yidishui," 277.

26. Liu, "SF jiao—lun kehuan xiaoshuo dui yuzhou de miaoxie," *Liu Cixin tan kehuan* (Wuhan: Hubei kexue jishu chubanshe, 2014), 86–89.
27. Liu Cixin, "The Village Schoolteacher," trans. Christopher Elford and Jiang Chenxin, in *The Reincarnated Giant: An Anthology of Twenty-First-Century Chinese Science Fiction*, ed. Mingwei Song and Theodore Huters (New York: Columbia University Press, 2018), 76.
28. Liu Cixin, "The Poetry Cloud," trans. Chi-yin Ip and Cheuk Wong, in *The Reincarnated Giant: An Anthology of Twenty-First-Century Chinese Science Fiction*, ed. Mingwei Song and Theodore Huters (New York: Columbia University Press, 2018), 143–173.
29. Here the judgment is exactly what Kant means, the "aesthetic judgment."
30. Liu, "Cong dahai jian yidishui," 47.
31. Liu, "The Poetry Cloud," 171–172.
32. Michel Foucault, "Language to Infinity," *Language, Counter-Memory, Practice* (Ithaca, NY: Cornell University Press, 1977), 65.
33. Foucault, "Language to Infinity," 56.
34. Li Miao, *Santi zhong de wulixue* (Chengdu: Sichuan kexue jishu chubanshe, 2015).
35. Liu, *Death's End*, 243.
36. Liu, "SF jiao," 88.
37. Arthur C. Clarke, *2001: A Space Odyssey* (New York: The New American Library, 1968), 191.
38. The three-body problem is about three mass points' positions, velocities, and motions based on Newton's laws of motion and universal gravitation. June Barrow-Green, "The Three-Body Problem," in *The Princeton Companion to Mathematics*, ed. Timothy Gowers, June Barrow-Green, and Imre Leader (Princeton, NJ: Princeton University Press, 2008), 726–728.
39. The novel's serialization in *SFW* began with the chapters about the Cultural Revolution, but when published in book form, the chapter order was rearranged, placing those chapters and the "Red Coast" chapters much later. The English translation restores the original chapter order.
40. Liu Cixin indeed refers to a famous piece of "scar literature," Zheng Yi's 鄭義 short story "Feng" 楓 (1979)."
41. For a comprehensive discussion on Mao's philosophy, see Fredrick Wakeman, *History and Will: Philosophical Perspectives of Mao Tse-Tung's Thought* (Berkeley: Center for Chinese Studies, UC Berkeley, 1973).
42. Mao Tse-tung, "On Protracted War," *Selected Works of Mao Tse-tung* (Beijing: Foreign Languages Press, 1967), II: 113–194.
43. Liu Cixin, *The Three-Body Problem*, trans. Ken Liu (New York: Tor, 2014), 272.
44. Li Xiaoming and Liao Shijun, "On the Stability of the Three Classes of Newtonian Three-Body Planar Periodic Orbits," *Science China Physics, Mechanics & Astronomy* 57, no. 11 (2014): 2121–2126.
45. The chapters depicting the contemporary scenes were moved to the beginning of the novel in the 2008 edition.
46. Liu Cixin, *The Dark Forest*, trans. Joel Martinsen (New York: Tor, 2015), 13.
47. Liu, *The Dark Forest*, 484.

48. Liu, *Death's End*, 132–133.
49. Yan Zuolei, "Santi zhong de pusu shehuizhuyi yu zuichu de ren," *Zhongguo xiandai wenxue yanjiu congkan* 6 (2020).
50. Li Guangyi and Chen Qi, eds., *Santi de X zhong dufa* (Beijing: Sanlian shudian, 2017).
51. Liu, *The Dark Forest*, 442.
52. See Huo We'ian, "Santi zhong de zhengzhixue," in *Santi de X zhong dufa*, ed. Li Guangyi and Chen Qi (Beijing: Sanlian shudian, 2017), 99–110. For Schmitt's political philosophy, see Carl Schmitt, *Political Theology: Four Chapters on the Concept of Sovereignty* (Chicago: University of Chicago Press, 2005).
53. Such grotesque cannibalism can be found in Han Song's novella "Meinü shoulie zhinan."
54. In a conversation with the historian of science, Jiang Xiaoyuan 江晓原, Liu Cixin directly challenges Jiang to answer the question whether they should eat the moderator of the conversation if they have to for survival. Jiang says absolutely no, but Liu says yes. See *Liu Cixin tan kehuan* (Wuhan: Hubei kexue jishu chubanshe, 2014), 42.
55. Liu Cixin, "Ren yu tunshizhe," *Shiguang jintou* (Shijiazhuang: Huashan wenyi chubanshe, 2010), 191–220.
56. Quoted from Liu, "The Worst of All Possible Universes and the Best of All Possible Earths: *Three-Body* and Chinese Science Fiction," in *Invisible Planets: An Anthology of Contemporary Chinese Science Fiction*, trans. and ed. Ken Liu (New York: Tor, 2016), 366.
57. The phrase appears in Voltaire's *Candide* in an ironic sense, as a critique of Leibniz. Voltaire, *Candide: A Norton Critical Edition* (New York: Norton, 1966), 2.
58. David Der-wei Wang, "The Panglossian Dream and Dark Consciousness: Modern Chinese Literature and Utopia," in *Utopia and Utopianism in the Contemporary Chinese Context*, ed. David Der-wei Wang, Angela Ki Che Leung, and Zhang Yinde (Hong Kong: Hong Kong University Press, 2020), 60–61.
59. Liu, *Death's End*, 253.
60. Liu, *Death's End*, 558.
61. Liu, *Death's End*, 559.
62. Liu, *Death's End*, 176.
63. Liu, *Death's End*, 590.
64. David Der-wei Wang, *Why Fiction Matters in Contemporary China* (Waltham, MA: Brandeis University Press, 2020), 19.
65. Liu, *Death's End*, 602.
66. In the unofficial sequel to the "Three-Body" trilogy, *The Redemption of Time*, Bao Shu gives the story a better interpretation: If the universe is rebuilt with the exact same amount of mass and materials, the next universe will repeat everything all over again, thus creating the eternal return; but exactly because Cheng Xin leaves behind her memory, it eventually changes how the next universe will become—it does collapse into zero, but all that happens after is no longer an eternal return. Bao Shu, *The Redemption of Time: A Three-Body Problem Novel* (New York: Tor, 2019).
67. Liu, *Death's End*, 369–370.

5. THE POWER OF DARKNESS IN HAN SONG

1. Han Song, *Ditie* (Shanghai: Shanghai renmin chubanshe, 2011), 187–188.
2. Han, *Ditie*, 170–171.
3. This scene appeared in an early chapter in *Subway*, with the green clothes suggesting the green military uniforms that Red Guards wore during the Cultural Revolution. Pushing nails into the foreheads of the kneeling elders suggests the torture of intellectuals. Han, *Ditie*, 39.
4. Han, *Ditie*, 197.
5. Han, *Ditie*, 199.
6. Ji Shaoting, "Yuzhou de guanchazhe Han Song," *Kehuan shijie* 3 (2009).
7. Jia Liyuan, "Han Song de 'guimei Zhongguo,'" in Han Song, *Yuzhou mubei* (Shanghai: Shanghai renmin chubanshe, 2014), 1–15.
8. H. P. Lovecraft, "The Call of Cthulhu," *Tales* (New York: Library of America, 2005), 167–196.
9. David Der-wei Wang, "Xuanxiang yu shensi: Lu Xun, Han Song yu weiwancheng de geming," *Zhongguo wenzhe yanjiu jikan* 57 (2020): 1–31.
10. Liu, "Weishenme renlei hai zhide zhengjiu," *Liu Cixin tan kehuan* (Wuhan: Hubei kexue jishu chubanshe, 2014), 34–42.
11. Han Song, *Huoxing zhaoyao Meiguo: 2066 nian zhi xixing manji* (Shanghai: Shanghai renmin chubanshe, 2011), 220–221.
12. Han, *Ditie*, 123.
13. Han Song, "Meinü shoulie zhinan," *Yuzhou mubei* (Shanghai: Shanghai renmin chubanshe, 2014), 370.
14. Han Song revealed to me that the inspiration for this story is *Jurassic Park*, because the dinosaurs are all "girls."
15. Han Song, *The Hospital*, trans. Michael Berry (Amazon Crossing, 2023), 170.
16. Istvan Csicsery-Ronay Jr., *The Seven Beauties of Science Fiction* (Middletown, CT: Wesleyan University Press, 2011), 182–185.
17. Mikhail M. Bakhtin, *Rabelais and His World* (Cambridge, MA: MIT Press, 1968), 335.
18. David Der-wei Wang, *Why Fiction Matters in Contemporary China* (Waltham, MA: Brandeis University Press, 2020), 166–167.
19. T. A. Hsia, "The Aspects of the Power of Darkness in Lu Hsün," in Hsia, *The Gate of Darkness: Studies on the Leftist Movement in China* (Seattle: University of Washington Press, 1968), 156.
20. Han Song began working on *Red Ocean* and *Mars Over America* around the same time. Both began as commissioned works, with suggested settings: a sea world for *Red Ocean* and the imaginary future of a real country for *Mars Over America*. This information was provided by Han Song.
21. Han Song, *Hongse haiyang* (Shanghai: Shanghai kexue puji chubanshe, 2004), 3.
22. Han, *Hongse haiyang*, 213.
23. Han, *Hongse haiyang*, 241–248.

24. Li Hua, "A Cautionary View of Rhetoric About China's Imagined Future in Liu Cixin's Alternate History 'The Western Ocean,'" *Frontier of Literary Studies in China* 10, no. 2 (2016): 184–203.
25. Han, *Hongse haiyang*, 459–531.
26. Lovecraft, "The Call of Cthulhu."
27. C. G. Jung, *Flying Saucers: A Modern Myth of Things Seen in the Skies* (Princeton, NJ: Princeton University Press, 1978).
28. Haraway, *Staying with the Trouble*, 81.
29. Haraway, *Staying with the Trouble*, 81.
30. Han, *Hongse haiyang*, 8.
31. Han, *Hongse haiyang*, 285.
32. Han, *Ditie*, 17.
33. Han, *Ditie*, 9 and 11.
34. Han, *Ditie*, 46, 138.
35. Han, *Ditie*, 90.
36. Han, *Ditie*, 293.
37. Han, *Ditie*, 16.
38. Han, *Ditie*, 16.
39. Han, *Ditie*, 18.
40. Han, *Ditie*, 27.
41. Han, *Ditie*, 107.
42. Han, *Ditie*, 135.
43. Han, *Ditie*, 93–94.
44. Han, *Ditie*, 154.
45. Han, *Ditie*, 94.
46. Han, *Ditie*, 128.
47. Han, *Ditie*, 190.
48. Han, *Ditie*, 198.
49. Lu Xun, "Shidiao de hao diyu," *Lu Xun quanji* (Beijing: Renmin wenxue chubanshe, 2005), 1: 437–443.
50. In addition to "A Madman's Diary," the short story "Medicine" represents the dual meanings of "medicine" as the enlightenment ideas and the body and blood of the revolutionaries.
51. Huang Ziping, *Bing de yinyu yu wenxue shengchan* (Beijing: Beijing daxue chubanshe, 2007).
52. The scene where the two women emerge is reminiscent of the sudden emergence from the mysterious gloom of a pair of horses in Kafka's "A Country Doctor," and Yang Wei's feeling struck in a conspiracy is similar to K's experience in *The Castle*.
53. Han, *Hospital*, 127–128.
54. Han, *Hospital*, 126.
55. Han, *Hospital*, 214.
56. Han Song, *Qumo*, 141. Translation is Michael Berry's (unpublished manuscript).
57. Han Song, *Qumo*, 263.

58. Han, *Wangling* (Shanghai: Shanghai wenyi chubanshe, 2018), 226–227.
59. Han, *Hospital*, 14–17.
60. Han, *Wangling*, 261.
61. Han, *Wangling*, 283.
62. Han, *Wangling*, 286.

6. VARIATIONS ON UTOPIA

1. Ban Wang, ed., *Chinese Visions of World Order: Tianxia, Culture, and World Politics* (Durham, NC: Duke University Press, 2017).
2. Lyman Tower Sargent, "Ideology and Utopia: Karl Mannheim and Paul Ricoeur," in *Utopia Horizons: Ideology, Politics, Literature*, ed. Zsolt Czigányik (Budapest, Hungary: Central European University Press, 2017), 31.
3. Nicole Pohl, "Utopianism After More: The Renaissance and Enlightenment," in *The Cambridge Companion to Utopian Literature*, ed. Gregory Claeys (Cambridge: Cambridge University Press, 2010), 51.
4. Fatima Vieira, "The Concept of Utopia," in *The Cambridge Companion to Utopian Literature*, ed. Gregory Claeys (Cambridge: Cambridge University Press, 2010), 4.
5. Paul K. Alkon, *Origins of Futuristic Fiction* (Athens: University of Georgia Press, 2010), 4.
6. Lyman Tower Sargent, *Utopianism* (Oxford: Oxford University Press, 2010), 25.
7. Edward Bellamy, *Looking Backward, 2000–1887* (New York: Oxford University Press, 2009).
8. Darko Suvin, *Metamorphoses of Science Fiction: On the Poetics and History of a Literary Genre* (New Haven, CT: Yale University Press, 1979), 37–62; Fredric Jameson, *Archaeologies of the Future: The Desire Called Utopia and Other Science Fictions* (London: Verso, 2005), 57–71.
9. Suvin, *Metamorphoses of Science Fiction*, 61.
10. Jameson, *Archaeologies of the Future*.
11. Suvin, *Metamorphoses of Science Fiction*, 61.
12. David Der-wei Wang, "The Panglossian Dream and Dark Consciousness: Modern Chinese Literature and Utopia," in *Utopia and Utopianism in the Contemporary Chinese Context*, ed. David Der-wei Wang, Angela Ki Che Leung, and Zhang Yinde (Hong Kong: Hong Kong University Press, 2020), 53–70.
13. Mill's speech in Parliament (1868), *House of Commons Hansard Archives.* Cf. *Oxford English Dictionary* (1989), oed.com/oed2/00071444 (accessed April 14, 2023).
14. Karl Mannheim, *Ideology and Utopia: An Introduction to the Sociology of Knowledge* (San Diego, CA: Harvest, 1985), 98.
15. The first version of Han Song's novel was published in 2000 by a provincial press in Heilongjiang.
16. Jeffrey N. Wasserstrom, *China in the 21st Century: What Everyone Needs to Know* (New York: Oxford University Press, 2010), 10.

17. Han Song, *Huoxing zhaoyao meiguo: 2066 nian zhi xixing manji* (Shanghai: Shanghai renmin chubanshe, 2011), 12.
18. Anindita Banerjee, *We Modern People: Science Fiction and the Making of Russian Modernity* (Middleton, CT: Wesleyan University Press, 2012), 81–85.
19. Banerjee, *We Modern People*, 56–58.
20. The novel *Journey to the West* is a fantasy narrative of the monk's travel to India, which is framed in traditional Chinese mythology and Buddhist religious imagery.
21. Han, *Huoxing zhaoyao meiguo*, 418.
22. Snow, *Red Star Over China: The Classic Account of the Birth of Chinese Communism* (New York: Grove Press, 1968), 35.
23. David Der-wei Wang, *Fin-de-Siècle Splendor: Repressed Modernities of Late Qing Fiction, 1849–1911* (Stanford, CA: Stanford University Press, 1997), 304.
24. Han, *Huoxing zhaoyao meiguo*, 201.
25. Han, *Huoxing zhaoyao meiguo*, 241.
26. Han, *Huoxing zhaoyao meiguo*, 10.
27. Han, *Huoxing zhaoyao meiguo*, 419.
28. Han Song, "The Passengers and the Creator," trans. Nathaniel Isaacson, in *The Reincarnated Giant: An Anthology of Twenty-First-Century Chinese Science Fiction*, ed. Mingwei Song and Theodore Huters (New York: Columbia University Press, 2018), 312.
29. For the intertextual reference to the American conspiracy to pack the entire Chinese population to tens of thousands of Boeing airplanes, see Han, *Ditie*, 126–128, 164.
30. Han Song, *Ditie* (Shanghai: Shanghai renmin chubanshe, 2011).
31. Li Hua, "The Political Imagination in Liu Cixin's Critical Utopia: *China 2185*," *Science Fiction Studies* 42, no. 3 (2015): 519–541.
32. Ye Yonglie published a series of unofficial biographies of the great leaders of China, including books on Mao and Deng Xiaoping, as well as on the key figures in the Gang of Four, during the 1990s.
33. In the published version, Mao's name disappeared from the text. Instead, the name of the leader is presented as three blank blocks. In the English translation, it is presented as XXX. Liu Cixin, *The Three-Body Problem*, trans. Ken Liu (New York: Tor, 2014), 165–173.
34. Liu, *The Three-Body Problem*, 390.
35. Wang Jinkang, *Yisheng* (Fuzhou: Fujian renmin chubanshe, 2007), 29.
36. Wang, *Yisheng*, 243.
37. Wang, *Yisheng*, 224.
38. Andrew Jones, *Developmental Fairy Tales: Evolutionary Thinking and Modern Chinese Culture* (Cambridge, MA: Harvard University Press, 2011), 4.
39. Wang Jinking, "The Reincarnated Giant," trans. Carlos Rojas, in *The Reincarnated Giant: An Anthology of Twenty-First-Century Chinese Science Fiction*, ed. Mingwei Song and Theodore Huters (New York: Columbia University Press, 2018), 313–353.
40. Han Song, "The Regenerated Bricks," trans. Theodore Huters. in *The Reincarnated Giant: An Anthology of Twenty-First-Century Chinese Science Fiction*, ed. Mingwei Song and Theodore Huters (New York: Columbia University Press, 2018), 3–44.

7. A TOPOLOGY OF HOPE

1. Chan Koonchung, *The Fat Years*, trans. Michael S. Duke (New York: Doubleday, 2011), 248.
2. Chan, *The Fat Years*, 249.
3. Han Song, *Huoxing zhaoyao meiguo: 2066 nian zhi xixing manji* (Shanghai: Shanghai renmin chubanshe, 2011), 11.
4. Han Song, "Dangxia Zhongguo kehuan de xianshi jiaolü," *Nanfang wentan* 6 (2010): 30.
5. Han Song, "Zhongtuobang: zhengge shijie dou hui biancheng yige Zhongguo," accessed August 11, 2020, http://blog.sina.com.cn/s/blog4757412101000081a.html.
6. Han Song, "Zhanzai xin qidian shang de 'Zhongtuobang,'" *Ershiyi shiji bimonthly* (December 2022): 10–13.
7. Michel Foucault, "Different Spaces," *Essential Works of Foucault 1954–1984 Volume 2: Aesthetics, Method and Epistemology*, ed. James D. Faubion (New York: The New Press, 1998), 185.
8. Chan Koonchung, *Living Out the Contradictions of Our Time* (Hong Kong: Jockey Club Design Institute for Social Innovation, 2016).
9. The novel was published in Taiwan and Hong Kong, but never printed in the PRC.
10. Charlotte Gao, "'A Community of Shared Future: One Short Phrase for UN, One Big Victory for China?" *The Diplomat*, November 5, 2017, https://thediplomat.com/2017/11/a-community-of-shared-future-one-short-phrase-for-un-one-big-victory-for-china/.
11. Chan, *The Fat Years*, 10.
12. Chan, *The Fat Years*, 123.
13. Old Chen recognizes in Fang Caodi and Little Xi "Idealism Chinese Style." Chan, *The Fat Years*, 199.
14. Bao Shu wrote a short story about this phenomenon, in which a person gave a negative answer to the question "Are you happy?" and later was treated with various virtual realities to enhance his feeling of happiness. Bao Shu, "Ni xingfu ma?" accessed November 2, 2020, http://www.wcsfa.com/scfbox-2433.html.
15. Wang Chaohua, "Dreamers and Nightmares: Political Novels by Wang Lixiong and Chan Koonchung," *China Perspective* 1 (2015): 23–31.
16. Lu Xun (as Suozi), "The Art of Creating Humanity," trans. Carlos Rojas, *Renditions* 77/78 (2012): 70–77.
17. Chan, *The Fat Years*, 286.
18. Dai Jinhua, "Rewriting the Red Classics," in *Rethinking Chinese Popular Culture: Cannibalizations of the Canon*, ed. Carlos Rojas and Eileen Cheng-yin Chow (London and New York: Routledge, 2009), 151–178.
19. Zhao Haihong, "1923: A Fantasy," trans. Nicky Harman and Pang Zhaoxia, in *The Reincarnated Giant: An Anthology of Twenty-First-Century Chinese Science Fiction*, ed. Mingwei Song and Theodore Huters (New York: Columbia University Press, 2018), 258–275.
20. La La, "The Radio Waves That Never Die," trans. Petula Parris-Huang, in *The Reincarnated Giant: An Anthology of Twenty-First-Century Chinese Science Fiction*, ed. Mingwei Song and Theodore Huters (New York: Columbia University Press, 2018), 227–257.
21. The star refers to Betelgeuse, the ninth brightest star in the night sky.

22. Bao Shu, *Gulao de diqiu zhi ge* (Beijing: Xinxing chubanshe, 2013), 126–162.
23. Bao Shu, "Songs of Ancient Earth," in *The Reincarnated Giant: An Anthology of Twenty-First-Century Chinese Science Fiction*, ed. Mingwei Song and Theodore Huters (New York: Columbia University Press, 2018), 375–409.
24. Bao Shu, "Songs of Ancient Earth," 408–409.
25. Bao Shu, "Yiqi qu kan nanhuchuan," unpublished manuscript, 2011.
26. The title is a quote from a poem by Pushkin, which is quoted in the text. Bao Shu, "What Has Passed Shall in Kinder Light Appear," in *Broken Stars: Contemporary Chinese Science Fiction in Translation*, trans. and ed. Ken Liu (New York: Tor, 2019), 160.
27. Bao Shu, "What Has Passed Shall in Kinder Light Appear," 204, 157.
28. David Der-wei Wang, *Why Fiction Matters in Contemporary China* (Waltham, MA: Brandeis University Press, 2020), 97.
29. In reality, Lao She committed suicide at the very beginning of the Cultural Revolution in 1966.
30. Ma Boyong, "The City of Silence," trans. Ken Liu, in *Invisible Planets: An Anthology of Contemporary Chinese Science Fiction* trans. and ed. Ken Liu (New York: Tor, 2016), 196.
31. Hao Jinfang, *Vagabonds*, trans. Ken Liu (New York: Sage, 2020), 4.
32. Hao Jinfang, "Folding Beijing," 230.
33. Hao, "Folding Beijing," trans. Ken Liu, in *Invisible Planets: An Anthology of Contemporary Chinese Science Fiction* trans. and ed. Ken Liu (New York: Tor, 2016), 255–256.
34. Hao Jinfang, "Invisible Planets," trans. Ken Liu, in *Invisible Planets: An Anthology of Contemporary Chinese Science Fiction* trans. and ed. Ken Liu (New York: Tor, 2016), 218. The italicization is the original.
35. Foucault, "Different Spaces."
36. This story was first published in *Hong Kong Literature Monthly* 香港文學, June 2019.
37. Dung Kai-cheung, *Atlas: The Archaeology of an Imagined City* (New York: Columbia University Press, 2012).
38. Ackbar Abbas, *Hong Kong: Culture and the Politics of Disappearance* (Minneapolis: University of Minnesota Press, 1997).
39. Dung Kai-cheung, *Shijian fanshi: yaci zhi guang*, vol. 2 (Taipei: Rye Field, 2007), 83–84.
40. Dung, *Shijian fanshi*, vol. 2, 426.
41. Lo Yi-chin, "Science Fiction," trans. Thomas Moran and Jingling Chen, in *The Reincarnated Giant: An Anthology of Twenty-First-Century Chinese Science Fiction*, ed. Mingwei Song and Theodore Huters (New York: Columbia University Press, 2018), 174–196.
42. Lo Yi-chin, *Kuang chaoren* (Taipei: Rye Field, 2018), 284.
43. Lo Yi-chin, *Mingchao* (Taipei: Jingwenxue, 2019).

8. CHINESE NEW WAVE GOES GLOBAL

1. The book was first released in English in the United States, then released in Chinese in Taiwan. The PRC version was not published until the next year, after going through censorship and some revisions.

2. Lee Kaifu and Chen Qiufan, *AI 2041: Ten Visions for Our Future* (New York: Currency, 2021), xxii–xxiii.
3. Adam Kirsch, *The Global Novel: Writing the World in the 21st Century* (New York: Columbia Global Reports, 2016).
4. Lee and Chen, *AI 2041*, 128.
5. Lee and Chen, *AI 2041*, 153.
6. Mikael Huss, "Hesitant Journey to the West: SF's Changing Fortunes in Mainland China," *Science Fiction Studies* 27, no. 1 (2000): 92.
7. Olivia Geng, "Chinese Sci-Fi Novel, 'The Three-Body Problem,' Touches Down in US,"*Wall Street Journal*, November 4, 2014.
8. Michiko Kakutani, "Obama's Secret to Surviving the White House: Books," *New York Times*, January 16, 2017.
9. Liu Cixin, "SF jiao—lun kehuan xiaoshuo dui yuzhou de miaoxie," *Liu Cixin tan kehuan* (Wuhan: Hubei kexue jishu chubanshe, 2014), 88.
10. David Damrosch, *What Is World Literature?* (Princeton, NJ: Princeton University Press, 2003), 5.
11. David Damrosch, "The Politics of Global English," *English Language and Literature* 6, no. 2 (2014): 193–209.
12. Emily Apter, *Against World Literature: On the Politics of Untranslatability* (London: Verso, 2013).
13. Damrosch, *What Is World Literature?* 117.
14. Liu Cixin, *Death's End*, trans. Ken Liu (New York: Tor, 2016), 502. The reference to a monument to the Earth civilization established on Pluto is similar to what the Jesuit found in the Vault on the surviving planet orbiting the remains of the supernova in Clarke's "Star."
15. Istvan Csicsery-Ronay Jr., "What Do We Mean When We Say 'Global Science Fiction?' Reflections on a New Nexus," *Science Fiction Studies* 39, no. 3 (2012): 488.
16. Susan Tyler Hitchcock, *Frankenstein: A Cultural History* (New York: Norton, 2007). Muriel Spark, *Child of Light: Mary Shelley* (New York: Welcome Rain, 1987); Alan Rauch, "The Monstrous Body of Knowledge in Mary Shelley's *Frankenstein*," *Studies in Romanticism* 34, no. 2 (1995): 227–253.
17. The 2007 print version, published by Chongqing Press, rearranges the chapter order by moving chapters about the preparations for the War with Trisolarans to the beginning.
18. Liu Cixin, *The Dark Forest*, trans. Joel Martinsen (New York: Tor, 2015), 412.
19. Liu, *Death's End*, 472.
20. Istvan Csicsery-Ronay Jr., "This Fractal, Alien World: SF in the Global Moment," presentation at Wellesley College, 2013.
21. Edward Said, *Humanism and Democratic Criticism* (New York: Columbia University Press, 2004).
22. Jessica Langer, *Postcolonialism and Science Fiction* (New York: Palgrave Macmillan, 2011).

23. These posthuman characters are depicted in Capek's play *Rossum Universal Robots* (1920), Lang's film *Metropolis* (1927), Belyaev's novel *Ariel* (1941), Tezuka's comic book *Atom Boy* (1952), Dick's *Do Androids Dream of Electric Sheep?* (1968), Kubrick's film *2001: A Space Odyssey* (1968), Spielberg's film *E.T. The Extra-Terrestrial* (1982), and Lundström's TV series *Real Humans* (2012).
24. David Mitchell, *Cloud Atlas* (New York: Random House, 2004), 509.
25. Mitchell, *Cloud Atlas*, 185.
26. Mary Shelley's *Frankenstein* includes an epigraph quoted from John Milton's *Paradise Lost* (Book X, lines 743–745), in which Adam asks God why he was made.
27. Chen Qiufan, *Waste Tide*, trans. Ken Liu (New York: Tor, 2019), 31–32.
28. Chen, *Waste Tide*, 33.
29. Chen, *Waste Tide*, 210.
30. Chen, *Waste Tide*, 286.
31. Chen, *Waste Tide*, 339.
32. Neil Badmington, "Introduction: Approaching Posthumanism," *Posthumanism*, ed. Neil Badmington (New York: Palgrave, 2000), 1–10.
33. Mo Yan, *Life and Death Are Wearing Me Out*, trans. Howard Goldblatt (New York: Arcade, 2008).
34. Yu Hua, *The Seventh Day*, trans. Allan H. Barr (New York: Anchor, 2016).
35. Chi Ta-wei, "Seqing wutuobang: kehuan, Taiwan, tongxinglian," *Chung Wai Literary Monthly* 35, no. 3 (2006): 17–48.
36. Chi Ta-wei, *Ganguan shijie* (Taipei: Lianhe wenxue, 2011), 193–234.
37. Chi Ta-wei, *The Membranes*, trans. Ari Larissa Heinrich (New York, NY: Columbia University Press, 2021).
38. Egoyan, *Shimengren* (Taipei: Lianhe wenxue, 2010), 238.
39. Egoyan, *Lingdu fenli* (Taipei: Ryefield, 2021), 42.
40. Chi Hui, "The Rainforest," trans. Jie Li, in *The Reincarnated Giant: An Anthology of Twenty-First-Century Chinese Science Fiction*, ed. Mingwei Song and Theodore Huters (New York: Columbia University Press, 2018), 354–363.
41. Rosi Braidotti, *The Posthuman* (Cambridge: Polity Press, 2013).
42. Donna J. Haraway, "A Cyborg Manifest," *Simians, Cyborgs, and Women: The Reinvention of Nature* (New York: Routledge, 1991), 149–182.
43. N. Katherine Hayles, *How We Became Posthuman: Virtual Bodies in Cybernetics, Literature, and Informatics* (Chicago: University of Chicago Press, 1999), 22.
44. Hayles, *How We Became Posthuman*, 6.
45. Cixin Liu, "The Robot Revolution Will be the Quietest One," *New York Times*, December 7, 2016.
46. Chan Koonchung, "Jishu qidian, jingji qidian, zhidu guaidian," *Wutuobang, etuobang, yituobang* (Taipei: Ryefield, 2018), 402–427.
47. Hayles, *How We Became Posthuman*, 5.
48. Ursula Le Guin, *The Left Hand of Darkness* (New York: ACE Books, 1969), 94.

EXCURSUS II. THE RISE OF SHE-SF: 2010-2022

1. N. Katherine Hayles, *How We Became Posthuman: Virtual Bodies in Cybernetics, Literature, and Informatics* (Chicago: University of Chicago Press, 1999), xii.

9. NEW WONDERS OF A NONBINARY UNIVERSE

1. Gu Shi, "Qianheti," in *Ta kehuan: jinshu de xinshi*, ed. Chen Qiufan (Beijing: Hangkong gongye chubanshe, 2021), 158.
2. Wu Yan, *Kehuan wenxue lungang* (Chongqing: Chongqing Press, 2011), 60.
3. Muriel Spark, *Child of Light: Mary Shelley* (New York: Welcome Rain, 1987).
4. John Milton, *Paradise Lost* (New York: Norton, 2005), Book X, lines 743–745, 250.
5. Adam Roberts, *Science Fiction* (London: Routledge, 2000), 48.
6. Roberts, *Science Fiction*, 56.
7. Murray Roston, *Milton and Baroque* (London: MacMillan, 1980).
8. Virginia Woolf, *The Diaries, Vol. 3: 1925–1930* (Boston: Mariner, 1980), 161.
9. Huang Yingying, "The Phantom Heroines and Gendered Worlds in Liu Cixin's Science Fiction," *Prism* 20, no. 2 (2023): forthcoming.
10. Huang, "The Phantom Heroines and Gendered Worlds in Liu Cixin's Science Fiction."
11. Chu T'ien-wen, "Fin de Siècle Splendor," in *The Columbia Anthology of Modern Chinese Literature*, ed. Joseph S.M. Lau and Howard Goldblatt (New York: Columbia University Press, 1995), 459.
12. Eileen Chang, "Speaking of Women," in *Written on Water*, trans. Andrew Jones (New York: Columbia University Press, 2007), 89 (translation with my modification).
13. Donna M. Haraway, *Staying with the Trouble: Making Kin in the Chthulhucene* (Durham, NC: Duke University Press, 2016).
14. Liu Cixin, *The Three-Body Problem*, trans. Ken Liu (New York: Tor, 2014), 27.
15. Liu Cixin, *Death's End*, trans. Ken Liu (New York: Tor, 2014), 467, 474.
16. Han Song, "Meinü shoulie zhinan," *Yuzhou mubei* (Shanghai: Shanghai renmin chubanshe, 2014), 306.
17. Justine Larbalestier, *The Battle of the Sexes in Science Fiction* (Middletown, CT: Wesleyan University Press, 2002).
18. Donna M. Haraway, "A Cyborg Manifesto," in *Simians, Cyborgs, and Women: The Reinvention of Nature* (New York: Routledge, 1991), 149–155.
19. Michel Foucault, *The History of Sexuality Vol. 2: The Use of Pleasure* (New York: Vintage, 1990).
20. Chen Qiufan, "G is for Goddess," trans. Thomas Moran, in *The Sound of Salt Forming*, ed. Geng Song and Yang Qingxiang (Honolulu: University of Hawaii Press, 2016), 101.
21. Chen, "G is for Goddess," 103.
22. Bao Shu, "Hai de nü'er," in *Shaonü de mingzi shi guaiwu* (Guangzhou: Huacheng chubanshe, 2020), 232.
23. Bao Shu, *Shaonü de mingzi shi guaiwu* (Guangzhou: Huacheng chubanshe, 2020), 363.

24. Zhao Haihong, "Bu kujie de quan," in *Ta kehuan: Xingchen de yanjing*, ed. Chen Qiufan (Beijing: Hangkong gongye chubanshe, 2021), 179.
25. Xia Jia, "Ni wufa dida de shijian," *Ni wufa dida de shijian* (Tianjin: Tianjin renmin chubanshe, 2017), 61.
26. Xia Jia, "Longma yexing," *Ni wufa dida de shijian* (Tianjin: Tianjin renmin chubanshe, 2017), 98.
27. Xia Jia, "Baigui yexingjie," *Ni wufa dida de shijian* (Tianjin: Tianjin renmin chubanshe, 2017), 206.
28. Both characters are originally from the ancient Chinese anthology of ghost stories *Liaozhai zhiyi*.
29. Xia, "Baigui yexingjie," 217. The translation is Ken Liu's. Xia Jia, "A Hundred Ghosts Parade Tonight," *Clarkesworld* 65 (February 2012).
30. Cheng Jingbo, "Ganzai xianluo zhiqian," in *Ta kehuan: Shijian de haizi*, ed. Chen Qiufan (Beijing: Hangkong gongye chubanshe, 2021)52.
31. Chi Hui, *2030: Zhongdianzhen* (Changsha: Hunan wenyi chubanshe, 2017).
32. Tang Fei, "Xiari zhi chan," *Kangjian jingyuzuo de ren* (Shanghai: Shanghai wenyi chubanshe, 2018), 247–256.
33. Tang Fei, "Call Girl," trans. Ken Liu, in *Invisible Planets: An Anthology of Contemporary Chinese Science Fiction*, ed. Ken Liu (New York: Tor, 2016), 274–275.
34. Tang Fei, "Baozi," *Aodesaibo* (Fuzhou: Haixia wenyi chubanshe/ Houlang chuban gongsi, 2021), 75. The English translation is Andy Dudak's. Tang Fei, "The Spore," *Clarkesworld* 176 (May 2021).
35. Tang, "Baozi," 81. The English translation is Andy Dudak's.
36. Lu Xun, "In Memoriam," in *The Real Story of Ah-Q and Other Tales of China: The Complete Fiction of Lu Xun*, trans. Julia Lovell (London: Penguin, 2009), 272.
37. Shuangchimu, *Sheli xuepai* (Beijing: Zuojia chubanshe, 2020), 1–2.
38. Refers to the golden record on *Voyager 1* and *Voyager 2*, two space probes launched by the United States into deep space in 1977.
39. Shuangchimu, *Sheli xuepai*, 50.
40. Peng Simeng, "Fenmi," *Fenmi* (Beijing: Zuojia chubanshe, 2020), 69.
41. Wang Kanyu, *Haixian fandian* (Beijing: Zuojia chubanshe, 2020), 17–18.
42. Gu Shi, "Mobiwusi shikong," in *Ta kehuan: Jinshu de xinshi*, ed. Chen Qiufan (Beijing: Hangkong gongye chubanshe, 2021), 72.

EPILOGUE: *THE WANDERING EARTH*, 2019

1. Shuo Fang, ed., *Liulang diqiu dianying zhizuo shouce* (Beijing: Renmin jiaotong chubanshe, 2019).
2. It was reported that 43 minutes of footage was cut from the film. See Sohu News, https://www.sohu.com/a/293834176_100080878, accessed October 12, 2020.
3. "Negative energy" 负能量 was a catchphrase in China's media censorship that discouraged news reports or literary writings about the negative effects of social problems

ranging from the prevailing social injustice to government officials' corruption. This term has been widely used in the Chinese government's censorship of the whistleblowing, investigative journalism, and public opinions during the COVID-19 pandemic since the spring of 2020.

4. Liu Cixin, *The Wandering Earth* (Beijing: Beijing Guomi Digital, 2013), 44.
5. Charlotte Gao, "'A Community of Shared Future': One Short Phrase for UN, One Big Victory for China?" *The Diplomat*, November 5, 2017, https://thediplomat.com/2017/11/a-community-of-shared-future-one-short-phrase-for-un-one-big-victory-for-china/.
6. Han Song, "Xinguan feiyan chenzhong daji le kehuan zixin," https://www.weibo.com/ttarticle/p/show?id=2309404467892325318746 (accessed October 14, 2020).
7. Han, "Xinguan feiyan chenzhong daji le kehuan zixin."
8. Jacques Derrida, "No Apocalypse, Not Now," *Diacritics* 14, no. 2 (1984): 20–31
9. Lu Xun, "Xiwang," *Lu Xun quanji* (Beijing: Renmin wenxue chubanshe, 2005), 2: 182.

BIBLIOGRAPHY

Abbas, Ackbar. *Hong Kong: Culture and the Politics of Disappearance.* Minneapolis: University of Minnesota Press, 1997.
Agamben, Giorgio. "What Is Contemporary?" *What Is an Apparatus?*, 39–54 Stanford, CA: Stanford University Press, 2009.
Aldiss, Brian W. *Billion Year Spree.* New York: Doubleday, 1974.
Alkon, Paul K. *Science Fiction Before 1900: Imagination Discovers Technology.* New York: Twayne, 1994.
——. *Origins of Futuristic Fiction.* Athens: University of Georgia Press, 2010.
Anderson, Marston. *The Limits of Realism: Chinese Fiction in the Revolutionary Period.* Berkeley: University of California Press, 1990.
Apter, Emily. *Against World Literature: On the Politics of Untranslatability.* London: Verso, 2013.
Asimov, Isaac. "The Last Question." *The Complete Stories: Volume One*, 415–429 London: Voyager, 1997.
Badmington, Neil. "Introduction: Approaching Posthumanism." *Posthumanism*, ed. Neil Badmington, 1–10. New York: Palgrave, 2000.
Baggott, Jim. *The Quantum Story.* Oxford: Oxford University Press, 2011.
Bakhtin, Mikhail M. *Rabelais and His World.* Cambridge, MA: MIT Press, 1968.
——. *Problems of Dostoevsky's Poetics.* Minneapolis: University of Minnesota Press, 1984.
Ball, Philip. *Invisible: The History of the Unseen from Plato to Particle Physics.* London: Vintage, 2015.
Banerjee, Anindita. *We Modern People: Science Fiction and the Making of Russian Modernity.* Middleton, CT: Wesleyan University Press, 2012.
Bao Shu 寶樹. *Santi X: Guanxiang zhizhou* 三體 X：觀想之宙. Chongqing: Chongqing chubanshe, 2011.

——. "Yiqi qu kan nanhuchuan" 一起去看南湖船. Unpublished manuscript, 2011.
——. *Gulao de diqiu zhi ge* 古老的地球之歌. Beijing: Xinxing chubanshe, 2013.
——. *Shijian zhi xu* 時間之墟. Wuhan: Changjiang wenyi chubanshe, 2013.
——. "Ni xingfu ma?" 你幸福嗎？ Accessed November 2, 2020. http://www.wcsfa.com/scfbox-2433.html.
——. "Hai de nü'er" 海的女兒. *Shaonü de mingzi shi guaiwu* 少女的名字是怪物. Guangzhou: Huacheng chubanshe, 2020.
——. "Shiguang de zhufu" 時光的祝福. In *2020 Zhongguo zuijia kehuan zuopin* 2020中國最佳科幻作品, ed. Yao Haijun 姚海軍, 28–57. Beijing: Renmin wenxue chubanshe, 2021.
Bao Shu. "Songs of Ancient Earth." In *The Reincarnated Giant: An Anthology of Twenty-First-Century Chinese Science Fiction*, ed. Mingwei Song and Theodore Huters, 375–409. New York: Columbia University Press, 2018.
——. *The Redemption of Time: A Three-Body Problem Novel*. New York: Tor, 2019.
——. "What Has Passed Shall in Kinder Light Appear." In *Broken Stars: Contemporary Chinese Science Fiction in Translation*, ed. and trans. Ken Liu, 151–222. New York: Tor, 2019.
Barrow-Green, June. "The Three-Body Problem." In *The Princeton Companion to Mathematics*, ed. Timothy Gowers, June Barrow-Green, and Imre Leader, 726–728. Princeton, NJ: Princeton University Press, 2008.
Baudrillard, Jean. *Simulation*. New York: Semiotext(e), 1983.
——. *America*. London: Verso, 1988.
Bellamy, Edward. *Looking Backward, 2000–1887*. New York: Oxford University Press, 2009.
Bloch, Ernst. *The Principle of Hope*, vol. 1. Cambridge, MA: MIT Press, 1995.
Borges, Jorge Luis. "The Library of Babel." *Collected Fictions*, 112–118 New York: Viking, 1998.
Braidotti, Rosi. *The Posthuman*. Cambridge: Polity Press, 2013.
Broderick, Damien. *Reading by Starlight: Postmodern Science Fiction*. London: Routledge, 1995.
——. "New Wave and Backwash: 1960–1980." In *The Cambridge Companion to Science Fiction*, ed. Edward James and Farah Mendlesohn, 48–63. Cambridge: Cambridge University Press, 2003.
Calabrese, Omar. *Neo-Baroque: A Sign of the Times*. Trans. Charles Lambert. Princeton, NJ: Princeton University Press, 1992.
Chan Koonchung 陳冠中. *Jianfeng Reign: xinzhongguo wuyoushi* 建豐二年: 新中國烏有史. Hong Kong: Oxford University Press, 2015.
——. "Jishu qidian, jingji qidian, zhidu guaidian" 技術奇點、經濟奇點、制度拐點. *Wutuobang, etuobang, yituobang* 烏托邦、惡托邦、異托邦, 402–427 Taipei: Ryefield, 2018.
Chan Koonchung. *The Fat Years*. Trans. Michael S. Duke. New York: Doubleday, 2011.
——. *Living Out the Contradictions of Our Time*. Hong Kong: Jockey Club Design Institute for Social Innovation, 2016.
Chang Eileen (Zhang Ailing). "Speaking of Women." *Written on Water*, trans. Andrew Jones, 81–90. New York: Columbia University Press, 2007.
Chang Hao 張灝. "Chaoyue yishi yu youhuan yishi: rujia neisheng waiwang sixiang zhizairen yu fanxing" 儒家內聖外王思想之再認與反. *You'an yishi yu minzhu chuantong* 幽暗意識與民主傳統, 23–43. Beijing: Xinxing chubanshe, 2006.

Chang, S. K. (Zhang Xiguo) 張系國. "Chaoren liezhuan" 超人列傳. *Di* 地, 85–148. Taipei: Hongfan shudian, 2002.
Chekhov, Anton. *Three Plays*. Trans. Constance Garrett. New York: Modern Library, 2001.
Chen Bochui 陳伯吹. "Rang ertongwenxue chashang kexue de chibang" 讓兒童文學插上科學的翅膀, *Renmin ribao* 人民日報, August 25, 1987.
Chen Mengxiong 陳夢熊. "Zhitang laoren tan 'Aichen,' 'Zaorenshu' de sanfengxin" 知堂老人談<哀尘>、<造人术>的三封信. In *Lu Xun yanjiu dongtai* 魯迅研究动态 1986:12.
Chen Qiufan 陳楸帆. *Huangchao* 荒潮. Wuhan: Changjiang wenyi chubanshe, 2013.
——. *Weilai bingshi* 未來病史. Wuhan: Changjiang wenyi chubanshe, 2015.
——. *Hou renlei shidai* 後人類時代. Beijing: Zuojia chubanshe, 2018.
——. "Chaozhenshishidai de wenxue chuangzuo" 超真實時代的文學創作. *Zhongguo xiandai wenxue* 中國現代文學 35 (June 2019): 51–64.
——. *Rensheng suanfa* 人生算法. Beiijng: Zhongxin chubanshe, 2019.
——. *Yihua yinqing* 異化引擎. Guangzhou: Huacheng chubanshe, 2020.
——. "Dui 'kehuan xianshizhuyi' de zaisikao" 對「科幻現實主義」的再思考. In *Zhongguo kehuan wenlun jingxuan*, ed. Wu Yan and Jiang Zhenyu, 266–269. Beijing: Beijing daxue chubanshe, 2021.
Chen Qiufan 陳楸帆. "G Is for Goddess." Trans. Thomas Moran. In *The Sound of Salt Forming*, ed. Geng Song and Yang Qingxian, 255–272. Honolulu: University of Hawaii Press, 2016.
——. *Waste Tide*. Trans. Ken Liu. New York: Tor, 2019.
——. "Contactless Love." In *AI 2041: Ten Visions for Our Future*, ed. Lee Kaifu and Chen Qifan, 123–153. New York: Currency, 2021.
——, ed. *Ta kehuan* 她科幻. 4 vols. Beijing: Hangkong gongye chubanshe, 2021.
Chen Sihe 陳思和. "Cong 'shaonian qinghua' dao 'zhongnian weiji'" 從「少年情懷」到「中年危機」. *Tansuo yu zhengming* 探索與爭鳴 1 (2010).
Chen Sihe. "'Rewriting Literary History' in the New Era of the Liberated Thought." Trans. Mingwei Song. In *A New Literary History of Modern China*, ed. David Der-wei Wang, 797–803. Cambridge, MA: Harvard University Press, 2017.
Cheng Jingbo 程婧波. "Ganzai xianluo zhiqian" 趕在陷落之前. In *Ta kehuan: Shijian de haizi* 她科幻：時間的孩子, ed. Chen Qiufan, 27–52. Beijing: Hangkong gongye chubanshe, 2021.
——, ed. *Ta: Zongguo nüxing kehuan zuojia jingdian zuopinji* 她：中國女性科幻作家經典作品集. vols. 1 and 2. Beijing: Zhongguo guangbo yingshi chubanshe, 2022.
Chi Hui 迟卉. "Yulin" 雨林. In *Zhongguo kehuan xiaoshuo xuan* 中國科幻小說選, ed. Liu Cixin, 1–9. Nanjing: Jiangsu wenyi chubanshe, 2007.
——. *2030: Zhongdianzhen* 2030：終點鎮. Changsha: Hunan wenyi chubanshe, 2017.
Chi Hui. "The Rainforest." Trans. Jie Li. In *The Reincarnated Giant: An Anthology of Twenty-First-Century Chinese Science Fiction*, ed. Mingwei Song and Theodore Huters, 354–363. New York: Columbia University Press, 2018.
Chi Ta-wei 紀大偉. "Seqing wutuobang: kehuan, Taiwan, tongxinglian" 色情烏托邦：科幻，台灣，同性戀. *Chung Wai Literary Monthly* 中外文學 35, no. 3 (2006): 17–48.
——. *Ganguan shijie* 感官世界. Taipei: Lianhe wenxue, 2011.

Chi Ta-wei. *The Membranes*. Trans. Ari Larissa Heinrich. New York: Columbia University Press, 2021.

Chiang, Ted. "The Story of Your Life." *Stories of Your Life and Others*, 91–146. Easthampton, MA: Small Beer Press, 2002.

Chu, Seo-young. *Do Metaphors Dream of Literal Sleep? A Science-Fictional Theory of Representation*. Cambridge, MA: Harvard University Press, 2010.

Chu T'ien-wen (Zhu Tianwen). "Fin de Siècle Splendor." In *The Columbia Anthology of Modern Chinese Literature*, ed. Joseph S.M. Lau and Howard Goldblatt, 444–459. New York: Columbia University Press, 1995.

Claeys, Gregory, ed. *The Cambridge Companion to Utopian Literature*. Cambridge: Cambridge University Press, 2010.

Clay, Diskin. *Lucian, True History*. Ed. James H. Brusuelas. Oxford: Oxford University Press, 2021.

Cramer, Kathryn. "Hard Science Fiction." In *The Cambridge Companion to Science Fiction*, ed. Edward James and Farah Mendlesohn, 86–196. Cambridge: Cambridge University Press, 2003.

Clarke, Arthur C. *2001: A Space Odyssey*. New York: New American Library, 1968.

——. "The Star." *The Collected Stories of Arthur C. Clarke*, 517–521. New York: Orb, 2000.

Csicsery-Ronay Jr., Istvan. *Seven Beauties of Science Fiction*. Middletown, CT: Wesleyan University Press, 2011.

——. "What Do We Mean When We Say 'Global Science Fiction'? Reflections on a New Nexus." *Science Fiction Studies* 39, no. 3 (2012): 478–493.

——. "This Fractal, Alien World: SF in the Global Moment." Presentation at Wellesley College, 2013.

Dai Jinhua. "Rewriting the Red Classics." In *Rethinking Chinese Popular Culture: Cannibalizations of the Canon*, ed. Carlos Rojas and Eileen Cheng-yin Chow, 151–178. London and New York: Routledge, 2009.

Damrosch, David. *What Is World Literature?* Princeton, NJ: Princeton University Press, 2003.

——. "The Politics of Global English." *English Language and Literature* 6, no. 2 (2014): 193–209.

——. *Around the World in 80 Books*. New York: Penguin, 2021.

Davis, Graeme, ed. *More Deadly Than the Male: Masterpieces from the Queens of Horror*. New York: Pegasus, 2019.

Davis, J. C. "Thomas More's *Utopia*: Sources, Legacy, and Interpretation." In *The Cambridge Companion to Utopian Literature*, ed. Gregory Claeys, 51–78. Cambridge: Cambridge University Press, 2010.

Deleuze, Gilles. *Foucault*. Trans. Sean Hand. Minneapolis: University of Minnesota Press, 1988.

——. *The Fold: Leibniz and the Baroque*. Trans. Tom Conley. Minneapolis: University of Minnesota Press, 1993.

Deng Tianyi 鄧天乙. "Lu Xun yi 'Zaorenshu' he Bao Tianxiao yi 'Zaorenshu'"魯迅譯〈造人術〉和包天笑譯〈造人術〉. *Changchun shifan xuebao* 長春師院學報（社科版）4 (1996): 26–30.

Denton, Kirk, ed. *Modern Chinese Literary Thought: Writings on Literature, 1893-1945* Stanford, CA: Stanford University Press, 1996.

Derrida, Jacques. "No Apocalypse, Not Now." *Diacritics* 14, no. 2 (1984): 20–31.
Deutsch, David. *The Fabric of Reality: The Science of Parallel Universe—and Its Implications*. New York: Penguin, 1997.
Donne, John. "An Anatomy of the World: The First Anniversary." In *John Donne's Poetry*, ed. Donald R. Dickson, 98–108. New York: Norton, 1992.
Drake, Stillman. *Galileo at Work: His Scientific Biography*. Chicago: University of Chicago Press, 1978.
Dung Kai-cheung 董啟章. *Shijian fanshi: yaci zhi guang* 時間繁史：啞瓷之光, vols. 1 and 2. Taipei: Ryefield, 2007.
——. *Atlas: The Archaeology of an Imagined City*. New York: Columbia University Press, 2012.
Egoyan 伊格言. *Shimengren* 噬夢人. Taipei: Lianhe wenxue, 2010.
——. *Lingdu fenli* 零度分離. Taipei: Ryefield, 2021.
Egoyan. *The Dream Devourer* (chapters 5–7). Trans. Cara Healey. In *The Reincarnated Giant: An Anthology of Twenty-First-Century Chinese Science Fiction*, ed. Mingwei Song and Theodore Huters, 111–129. New York: Columbia University Press, 2018.
Elman, Benjamin. *A Cultural History of Modern Science in China*. Cambridge, MA: Harvard University Press, 2006.
Fang Lizhi 方勵之 "Keshi de he bukeshi de wuzhi" 可視的和不可視的物質. *Yuzhou de chuangsheng* 宇宙的創生, 66–79. Hong Kong: Nanyue chubanshe, 1989.
Fei Dao 飛氘. "Jimo de fubing: xinshiji kehuan xiaoshuo zhong de Zhongguo xingxiang" 寂寞的伏兵：新世紀科幻小說中的中國形象. In *2010 niandu Zhongguo zuijia kehuan xiaoshuo ji*, ed. Wu Gan and Guo Kai, 313–317. Chengdu: Sichuan renmin chubanshe, 2011.
——. *Zhongguo kehuan dapian* 中國科幻大片. Beijing: Qinghua daxue chubanshe, 2013.
——. "Hewai youshang yizhong" 河外憂傷一種. *Hong Kong wenxue* 香港文學 (June 2019).
——. *Yinhe jianwen lu* 銀河見聞錄. Guangzhou: Huacheng chubanshe, 2020.
Foucault, Michel. "Language to Infinity." *Language, Counter-Memory, Practice*, 53–67. Ithaca, NY: Cornell University Press, 1977.
——. *The History of Sexuality Vol. 2: The Use of Pleasure*. New York: Vintage, 1990.
——. *The Birth of the Clinic: An Archaeology of Medical Perception*. New York: Vintage, 1994.
——. "Different Spaces." In *Essential Works of Foucault 1954–1984, Volume 2: Aesthetics, Method and Epistemology*, ed. James D. Faubion, 175–186. New York: The New Press, 1998.
Freedman, Carl. *Critical Theory and Science Fiction*. Middletown, CT: Wesleyan University Press, 2000.
Frye, Northrope. *Anatomy of Criticism*. Princeton, NJ: Princeton University Press, 1990.
Gao, Charlotte. "'A Community of Shared Future': One Short Phrase for UN, One Big Victory for China?" *The Diplomat*, November 5, 2017. https://thediplomat.com/2017/11/a-community-of-shared-future-one-short-phrase-for-un-one-big-victory-for-china/.
Geng, Olivia. "Chinese Sci-Fi Novel, 'The Three-Body Problem,' Touches Down in U.S." *Wall Street Journal*, November 4, 2014.
Gibson, William. "The Science in Science Fiction." *Talk of the Nation*, NPR. November 30, 1999.
Gu Junzheng 顧均正. *Heping de meng* 和平的夢. Shanghai: Wenhua shenghuo chubanshe, 1940.
Gu Shi 顧適. *Mobiwusi shikong* 莫比烏斯時空. Beijing: Xinxing chubanshe, 2019.

———. "Mobiwusi shikong." In *Ta kehuan: Shijian de haizi*, ed. Chen Qiufan, 69–83. Beijing: Hangkong gongye chubanshe, 2021.

———. "Qianheti" 嵌合體. In *Ta kehuan: jinshu de xinshi* 她科幻：金屬的心事 ed. Chen Qiufan, 152–209., Beijing: Hangkong gongye chubanshe, 2021.

Han Song 韩松. "Wo de zuguo buzuomeng" 我的祖國不做夢. Unpublished manuscript. 2002.

———. *Hongse haiyang* 紅色海洋. Shanghai: Shanghai kexue puji chubanshe, 2004.

———. "Zhongtuobang: zhengge shijie dou hui biancheng yige Zhongguo" 中托邦——整個世界都會成為一个中國. Accessed August 11, 2020. http://blog.sina.com.cn/s/blog4757412101000081a.html.

———. "Dangxia Zhongguo kehuan de xianshi jiaolü" 當下中國科幻的現實焦慮. *Nanfang wentan* 南方文壇. 6 (2010): 28–30.

———. "Zaisheng zhuan" 再生磚. *Wenyi fengshang* 文藝風賞1 (December 2010): 59–71.

———. *Ditie* 地鐵. Shanghai: Shanghai renmin chubanshe, 2011.

———. *Huoxing zhaoyao meiguo: 2066 nian zhi xixing manji* 火星照耀美國：2066年至西行漫記. Shanghai: Shanghai renmin chubanshe, 2011.

———. "Wei kehuan er huozhe: canjia xin shiji shinian wenxue guoji yantaohui" 為科幻而活著——參加"新世紀十年文學"國際研討會." In *2010 niandu Zhongguo zuijia kehuan xiaoshuo ji*, ed. Wu Gan and Guo Kai, 306–312. Chengdu: Sichuan renmin chubanshe, 2011.

———. *Kan de kongju* 看的恐懼. Beijing: Remin youdian chubanshe, 2012.

———. "Kan de kongju." *Kan de kongju*, 67–85.

———. *Gaotie* 高鐵. Beijing: Xinxing chubanshe, 2012.

———. *Yuzhou mubei* 宇宙墓碑. Shanghai: Shanghai renmin chubanshe, 2014.

———. "Meinü shoulie zhinan" 美女狩獵指南. *Yuzhou mubei*, 275–373.

———. "Xiehou keji shidai de wenxue" 邂逅科技時代的文學. *Yuzhou mubei*, 375–378.

———. *Yiyuan* 醫院. Shanghai: Shanghai wenyi chubanshe, 2016.

———. *Zaishengzhuan* 再生砖. Shanghai: Shanghai renmin chubanshe, 2016.

———. *Qumo* 驅魔. Shanghai: Shanghai wenyi chubanshe, 2017.

———. *Wangling* 亡靈. Shanghai: Shanghai wenyi chubanshe, 2018.

———. *Guidao* 軌道. Shanghai: Shanghai wenyi chubanshe, 2020.

———. "Xinguan feiyan chenzhong daji le kehuan zixin" 新冠肺炎沈重打擊了科幻自信. Accessed October 14, 2020. https://www.weibo.com/ttarticle/p/show?id=2309404467892325318746.

———. "Zichao de yishu" 自嘲的藝術. In *Zhongguo kehuan wenlun jingxuan*, ed. Wu Yan and Jiang Zhenyu, 260–265. Beijing: Beijing daxue chubanshe, 2021.

———. "Zhanzai xin qidian shang de 'Zhongtuobang'" 站在新起點上的「中托邦」. *Ershiyi shiji bimonthly* 二十一世紀 December (2022): 10–13.

Han Song. "The Passengers and the Creator." Trans. Nathaniel Isaacson. In *The Reincarnated Giant: An Anthology of Twenty-First-Century Chinese Science Fiction*, ed. Mingwei Song and Theodore Huters, 279–312. New York: Columbia University Press, 2018.

———. "The Regenerated Bricks." Trans. Theodore Huters. In *The Reincarnated Giant: An Anthology of Twenty-First-Century Chinese Science Fiction*, ed. Mingwei Song and Theodore Huters, 3–44. New York: Columbia University Press, 2018.

———. *A Primer to Han Song*. Wayne, IN: Dark Moon Books, 2020.

———. "Fear of Seeing." Trans. Nathaniel Isaacson. *A Primer to Han Song*, 81–103.

———. "My Country Does Not Dream." Trans. Nathaniel Isaacson. *A Primer to Han Song*, 107–145.
———. "Tombs of the Universe." Trans. Xueting Christine Ni. In *Sinopticon: A Celebration of Chinese Science Fiction*, ed. Xueting Christine Ni, 43–80. Oxford, UK: Solaris, 2021.
———. *The Hospital*. Trans. Michael Berry. Amazon Crossing, 2023.
Hanan, Patrick. "The 'New Novel' Before the Rise of the New Novel." In *A New Literary History of Modern China*, ed. David Der-wei Wang, 139–144. Cambridge, MA: Harvard University Press, 2017.
Hao Jingfang 郝景芳. *Gudu shenchu* 孤独深处. Nanjing: Jiangsu fenghuang wenyi chubanshe, 2016.
———. "Beijing zhedie" 北京折叠. *Gudu shenchu* 孤独深处, 1–40.
———. *Shengyu yijiubasi* 生於一九八四. Beijing: Dianzi gongye chubanshe, 2016.
———. *Liulang cangqiong* 流浪蒼穹. Nanjing: Jiangsu fenghuang wenyi chubanshe, 2016.
Hao Jingfang. "Folding Beijing." Trans. Ken Liu. In *Invisible Planets: An Anthology of Contemporary Chinese Science Fiction*, ed. and trans. Ken Liu, 219–262. New York: Tor, 2016.
———. "Invisible Planets." Trans. Ken Liu. In *Invisible Planets: An Anthology of Contemporary Chinese Science Fiction*, ed. and trans. Ken Liu, 201–218. New York: Tor, 2016.
———. *Vagabonds*. Trans. Ken Liu. New York: Sage, 2020.
Haraway, Donna J. *Simians, Cyborgs, and Women: The Reinvention of Nature*. New York: Routledge, 1991.
———. "A Cyborg Manifesto." *Simians, Cyborgs, and Women*, 149–182.
———. *Staying with the Trouble: Making Kin in the Chthulhucene*. Durham, NC: Duke University Press, 2016.
Hawking, Stephen. *A Brief History of Time*. New York: Bantam, 2001.
Hayles, H. Katherine. *How We Became Posthuman: Virtual Bodies in Cybernetics, Literature, and Informatics*. Chicago: University of Chicago Press, 1999.
Haynes, Roslynn D. *From Faust to Strangelove: Representations of the Scientist in Western Literature*. Baltimore: The Johns Hopkins University Press, 1994.
Healey, Cara. "Madmen and Iron Houses: Lu Xun, Information Degradation, and Generic Hybridity in Contemporary Chinese SF." *Science Fiction Studies* 46, no. 3 (2019): 511–524.
Heidegger, Martin. "Letter on Humanism." *Basic Writings*, 213–265. San Francisco: Harper San Francisco, 1993.
———. "The Origin of the Work of Art." *Basic Writings*, 143–212.
———. "Language." *Poetry, Language, Thought*, 185–208. New York: Perennial Classics, 2001.
Hill, Michael Gibbs. *Lin Shu, Inc.: Translation and the Making of Modern Chinese Culture*. New York: Oxford University Press, 2013.
Hitchcock, Susan Tyler. *Frankenstein: A Cultural History*. New York: Norton, 2007.
Hsia, C. T. *A History of Modern Chinese Fiction*. Bloomington and Indianapolis: Indiana University Press, 1999.
———. "Obsession with China: The Moral Burden of Modern Chinese Literature." *A History of Modern Chinese Fiction*, 533–554.
Hsia, T. A. *The Gate of Darkness*. Seattle: University of Washington Press, 1968.

Hsiao Kung-Chuan. *A Modern China and a New World: Kang Youwei, Reformer and Utopian, 1858–1927*. Seattle: University of Seattle Press, 1975.

Hu Shi. "Duanpian xiaoshuo" 短篇小說. *Xin qingnian* 新青年 4, no. 5 (1918).

Huang Ziping 黃子平. *Bing de yinyu yu wenxue shengchan* 病的隱喻與文學生產. Beijing: Beijing daxue chubanshe, 2007.

Huang, Yingying. "The Phantom Heroines and Gendered Worlds in Liu Cixin's Science Fiction." *Prism* 20, no. 2 (2023): forthcoming.

Huo Wei'an 霍偉岸. "Santi zhong de zhengzhixue" 《三体》中的政治学. In *Santi de X zhong dufa*, ed. Li Guangyi and Chen Qi, 99–110. Beijing: Sanlian shudian, 2017.

Huss, Mikael. "Hesitant Journey to the West: SF's Changing Fortunes in Mainland China." *Science Fiction Studies* 27, no. 1 (March 2000): 92–104.

Iovene, Paola. *Tales of Future Past: Anticipation and the End of Literature in Contemporary Chin.a* Stanford, CA: Stanford University Press, 2014.

Isaacson, Nathaniel. "Media and Messages: Blurred Visions of Nation and State in Tong Enzheng's *Death Ray on a Coral Island*." In *Simultaneous Worlds: Global Science Fiction Cinema*, ed. Jennifer Feely and Sarah A. Wells, 272–288. Minneapolis: University of Minnesota Press, 2015.

——. *Celestial Empire: The Emergence of Chinese Science Fiction*. Middletown, CT: Wesleyan University Press, 2017.

James, Edward and Farah Mendlesohn, eds. *The Cambridge Companion to Science Fiction*. Cambridge: Cambridge University Press, 2003.

Jameson, Fredric. "Third-World Literature in the Era of Multinational Capitalism." *Social Text* 15 (1986): 65–88.

——. *Archaeologies of the Future: The Desire Called Utopia and Other Science Fictions*. London: Verso, 2005.

——. *The Antinomies of Realism*. London: Verso, 2013.

Ji Shaoting 姬少亭. "Yuzhou de guanchazhe Han Song" 宇宙的觀察者韓松. *Kehuan shijie* 科幻世界 3 (2009).

Jia Liyuan 賈立元 (Fei Dao). "Zhujiu women of weilai—90 niandai zhi jin Zhongguo kehuanxiao zhong de Zhongguo xingxiiang" 筑就我们未来——90年代至今中国科幻小说中的中国形象. Master's thesis, Beijing Normal University, 2010.

——. "Han Song de 'guimei Zhongguo'" 韓松的「鬼魅中國」. In Han Song, *Yuzhou mubei*, 1–15. Shanghai: Shanghai renmin chubanshe, 2014.

——. "Guangrong Zhonghua: Liu Cixin kehuan xiaoshuo zhong de Zhongguo xingxiang" 光榮中華：劉慈欣科幻小說中的中國形象. In *Santi de X zhong dufa*, ed. Li Guangyi and Chen Qi, 119–135. Beijing: Sanlian shudian, 2017.

Jia Liyuan. "Gloomy China: China's Image in Han Song's Science Fiction." *Science Fiction Studies* 40, no. 1 (March 2013): 103–115.

Jiang, Jing. *Found in Translation: New People in Twentieth-Century Chinese Science Fiction*. New York: Association of Asian Studies, 2020.

Jiang Zhenyu 姜振宇. "Gongxian yu wuqu: Zheng Wenguang yu 'kehuan xianshi zhuyi'" 貢獻與誤區：鄭文光與科幻現實主義. *Zongguo xiandai wenxue yanjiu congkan* 中國現代文學研究叢刊 8 (2017): 78–92.

Jones, Andrew. *Developmental Fairy Tales: Evolutionary Thinking and Modern Chinese Culture.* Cambridge, MA: Harvard University Press, 2011.

Jung, C. G. *Flying Saucers: A Modern Myth of Things Seen in the Skies.* Princeton, NJ: Princeton University Press, 1978.

Kakutani, Michiko. "Obama's Secret to Surviving the White House: Books." *New York Times*, January 16, 2017.

Kant, Immanuel. *Critique of Judgment.* Indianapolis: Hackett, 1987.

——. *Observations on the Feeling of the Beautiful and the Sublime.* Berkeley: University of California Press, 1991.

Kirsch, Adam. *The Global Novel: Writing the World in the 21st Century.* New York: Columbia Global Reports, 2016.

Krell, David Farrell. "General Introduction: The Question of Being." In Martin Heidegger, *Basic Writings*, 1–35. San Francisco: Harper San Francisco, 1993.

Kunkun 困困. "Reng yo uren yangwang xingkong" 仍有人仰望星空. In *2011 niandu Zhongguo zuijia kehuan xiaoshuo ji*, ed. Wu Yan and Guo Kai, 397–412. Chengdu: Sichuan renmin chubanshe, 2012.

Kwok, D. W. Y. *Scientism in Chinese Thought 1900–1950.* New Haven, CT: Yale University Press, 1965.

La La. "The Radio Waves That Never Die." Trans. Petula Parris-Huang. In *The Reincarnated Giant: An Anthology of Twenty-First-Century Chinese Science Fiction*, ed. Mingwei Song and Theodore Huters, 227–257. New York: Columbia University Press, 2018.

Lacan, Jacques. "Seminar on 'The Purloined Letter.'" *Écrits*, 11–48. New York: Norton, 2002.

Langer, Jessica. *Postcolonialism and Science Fiction.* New York: Palgrave Macmillan, 2011.

Lao She. *Cat Country.* Trans. William A. Lyell. London and New York: Penguin, 2013.

Larbalestier, Justine. *The Battle of the Sexes in Science Fiction.* Middletown, CT: Wesleyan University Press, 2002.

Le Guin, Ursula. *The Left Hand of Darkness.* New York: ACE Books, 1969.

Lee, Kaifu and Chen Qiufan. *AI 2041: Ten Visions for Our Future.* New York: Currency, 2021.

Lee, Leo Ou-fan. *Voices from the Iron House: A Study of Lu Xun.* Bloomington: Indiana University Press, 1987.

Li Guangyi 李廣益 and Chen Qi 陳頎, eds. *Santi de X zhong dufa* 《三體》的 X 種讀法. Beijing: Sanlian shudian, 2017.

Li, Hua. "The Political Imagination in Liu Cixin's Critical Utopia: China 2185." *Science Fiction Studies* 42, no. 3 (2015): 519–541.

——. "A Cautionary View of Rhetoric About China's Imagined Future in Liu Cixin's Alternate History 'The Western Ocean.'" *Frontier of Literary Studies in China* 10, no. 2 (2016): 184–203.

——. *Chinese Science Fiction During the Post-Mao Cultural Thaw.* Toronto: University of Toronto Press, 2021.

Li Miao 李淼. *Santi zhong de wulixue*《三体》中的物理学. Chengdu: Sichuan kexue jishu chubanshe, 2015.

Li, Xiaoming and Liao Shijun. "On the Stability of the Three Classes of Newtonian Three-Body Planar Periodic Orbits." *Science China Physics, Mechanics & Astronomy* 57, no. 11 (2014): 2121–2126.

Liang Qichao. "On the Relationship Between Fiction and the Government of the People." Trans. Gek Nai Cheng. In *Modern Chinese Literary Thought: Writings on Literature, 1893-1945*, ed. Kirk Denton, 74–81. Stanford, CA: Stanford University Press, 1996.

Liang Qingsan 梁清散.*Xinxin ribao guan: jixie jueqi* 新新日報館：機器崛起. Changsha: Hunan wenyi chubanshe, 2017.

——. *Xin xinxin ribao guan: modu anying* 新新新日報館：魔都暗影. Beijing: Xinxing chubanshe, 2021.

Ling Chen 凌晨. "404 zhi jianlong zaitian" 404之見龍在天. In *Ta kehuan: Shijian de haizi*, ed. Chen Qiufan, 162–194. Beijing: Hangkong gongye chubanshe, 2021.

Liu Cixin 劉慈欣. *Zhongguo 2185* 中國2185. Accessed October 19, 2020. https://www.99csw.com/book/428/index.htm.

——. "Xiyang" 西洋. Accessed November 1, 2020. http://www.kehuan.net.cn/book/xiyang.html.

——. *Qiuzhuang shandian* 球狀閃電. Chengdu: Sichuan kexue jishu chubanshe, 2004.

——. "Daode de jintou jiushi kehuan de kaishi" 道德的盡頭就是科幻的開始. *Nanfang dushi bao* 南方都市報. August 31, 2008, B20.

——. *Hei'an senlin* 黑暗森林. Chongqing: Chongqing chubanshe, 2008.

——. *Liulang diqiu* 流浪地球. Wuhan: Changjiang wenyi chubanshe, 2008.

——. *Santi* 三體. Chongqing: Chongqing chubanshe, 2008.

——. *Chao xinxing jiyuan* 超新星紀元. Chongqing: Chongqing chubanshe, 2009.

——. *Weijiyuan* 微紀元. Shenyang: Shenyang chubanshe, 2010.

——. "Shan" 山. *Weijieyuan*, 225–258.

——. "Shiyun" 詩雲. *Weijiyuan*, 111–139.

——. "Weiguan jintou" 微观尽头. *Weijiyuan*, 161–169.

——. "Weijiyuan" 微紀元. *Weijieyuan*, 85–108.

——. "Yuzhou tasuo" 宇宙坍缩. *Weijiyuan*, 171–182.

——. *Shiguang jintou* 時光盡頭. Shijiazhuang: Huashan wenyi chubanshe, 2010.

——. "Dihuo" 地火. *Shiguang jintou*, 35–67.

——. "Huanle song" 歡樂頌. *Shiguang jintou*, 103–127.

——. "Ren yu tunshizhe" 人與吞食者. *Shiguang jintou*, 191–220.

——. "Zhaowendao" 朝聞道. *Shiguang jintou*, 9–33.

——. *Sishen yongsheng* 死神永生. Chongqing: Chongqing chubanshe, 2010.

——. *Liu Cixin tan kehuan* 劉慈欣談科幻. Wuhan: Hubei kexue jishu chubanshe, 2014.

——. "Cong dahai jian yidishui" 從大海見一滴水. *Liu Cixin tan kehuan*, 45–54.

——. "Diyidai kehuanmi de huiyi" 第一代科幻迷的回憶. *Liu Cixin tan kehuan*, 134–139.

——. "Sanwei de Han Song" 三維的韓松. *Liu Cixin tan kehuan*, 161–62.

——. "SF jiao—lun kehuan xiaoshuo dui yuzhou de miaoxie" SF 教—論科幻小說對宇宙的描寫. *Liu Cixin tan kehuan*, 86–89.

——. "Weishenme renlei hai zhide zhengjiu" 為什麼人類還值得拯救. *Liu Cixin tan kehuan*, 34–42.

Liu Cixin. *The Wandering Earth*. Beijing: Beijing Guomi Digital, 2013.

——. "Mountain." *The Wandering Earth*, 47–94.

——. *The Three-Body Problem*. Trans. Ken Liu. New York: Tor, 2014.

——. *The Dark Forest*. Trans. Joel Martinsen. New York: Tor, 2015.
——. *Death's End*. Trans. Ken Liu. New York: Tor, 2016.
——. "The Worst of All Possible Universes and the Best of All Possible Earths: *Three-Body* and Chinese Science Fiction." Trans. Ken Liu. In *Invisible Planets: An Anthology of Contemporary Chinese Science Fiction*, ed. and trans. Ken Liu, 361–367. New York: Tor, 2016.
——. "The Robot Revolution Will Be the Quietest One." *New York Times*, December 7, 2016.
——. *Ball Lightning*. Trans. Joel Martinsen. New York: Tor, 2018.
——. "The Poetry Cloud." Trans. Chi-yin Ip and Cheuk Wong. In *The Reincarnated Giant: An Anthology of Twenty-First-Century Chinese Science Fiction*, ed. Mingwei Song and Theodore Huters, 143–173. New York: Columbia University Press, 2018.
——. "The Village Schoolteacher." Trans. Christopher Elford and Jiang Chenxin. In *The Reincarnated Giant: An Anthology of Twenty-First-Century Chinese Science Fiction*, ed. Mingwei Song and Theodore Huters, 45–79. New York: Columbia University Press, 2018.
——. *Supernova Era*. Trans. Joel Martinsen. New York: Tor, 2019.
Liu, Ken, trans. and ed. *Invisible Planets: An Anthology of Contemporary Chinese Science Fiction*. New York: Tor, 2016.
——. *Broken Stars: Contemporary Chinese Science Fiction in Translation*. New York: Tor, 2019.
Liu, Lydia. *Translingual Practice: Literature, National Culture, and Translated Modernity, 1900–1937*. Stanford, CA: Stanford University Press, 1995.
——. "Life as Form: How Biomimesis Encounters Buddhism in Lu Xun." *The Journal of Asian Studies* 68, no. 1 (2009): 21–54.
Liu Na 劉納. "Shuo Bo, xin wulixue, zhongji: cong yige jiaodu tan Lu Xun jingshen yicha de duyixing he dangdai yiyi"〈說鉑〉，新物理學，終極——從一個角度談魯迅精神遺產的獨異性和當代意義. *Zhongshan daxue xuebao* 中山大學學報 46, no. 6 (2006): 39–48.
Lo Yi-chin 駱以軍. *Nü'er* 女兒. Taipei: Ink, 2014.
——. *Kuang chaoren* 匡超人. Taipei: Ryefield, 2018.
——. *Mingchao* 明朝. Taipei: Jingwenxue, 2019.
Lo Yi-chin. "Science Fiction" (a chapter of *Daughter*). Trans. Thomas Moran and Jingling Chen. In *The Reincarnated Giant: An Anthology of Twenty-First-Century Chinese Science Fiction*, ed. Mingwei Song and Theodore Huters, 174–196 (New York: Columbia University Press, 2018).
Lovecraft, H. P. "The Call of Cthulhu." *Tales*, 167–196. New York: Library of America, 2005.
Lu Nanfeng 卢南峰 and Wu Jing 吴静. "Lishi zhuanzhe zhong de hongda xushi: 'Gongyedang' wangluo sichao de zhengzhi fenxi" 历史转折中的宏大叙事："工业党"网络思潮的政治分析. *Dongfang xuekan* 东方学刊 1 (2018).
Lu Xun 鲁迅. *Yuejie lüxing* 月界旅行. *Lu Xun quanji* 鲁迅全集, 11: 7–119. Beijing: Renmin wenxue chubanshe, 1973.
——. "Bianyan" 弁言. *Lu Xun quanji* (1973), 11: 10.
——. *Didi lüxing* 地底旅行. *Lu Xun quanji* (1973), 11: 121–181.
——. "Mujiewen" 墓碣文. *Lu Xun quanji* 鲁迅全集, 1: 437–443. Beijing: Renmin wenxue chubanshe, 2005.
——. "Nahan zixu" 呐喊自序. *Lu Xun quanji* (2005), 2: 207–208..
——. "Po esheng lun" 破惡聲論. *Lu Xun quanji* (2005), 8: 25–40.

———. "Shangshi" 傷逝. *Lu Xun quanji* (2005), 2: 113–134.
———. "Shidiao de hao diyu" 失掉的好地獄. *Lu Xun quanji* (2005), 2: 204–205.
———. "Suoji" 瑣記. *Lu Xun quanji* (2005), 2: 301–312.
———. "Tengye xiansheng" 藤野先生. *Lu Xun quanji* (2005), 2: 313–320.
———. "340515 zhi Yang Jiyun" 340515致楊霽雲. *Lu Xun quanji* (2005), 13: 99–101.
———. "Xiwang" 希望. *Lu Xun quanji* (2005), 2: 181–184.
———. "Yao" 藥. *Lu Xun quanji* (2005), 1: 463–480.
———. "Ying de gaobie" 影的告別. *Lu Xun quanji* (2005), 2: 169–170.
———. "Zheyang de zhanshi" 這樣的戰士. *Lu Xun quanji* (2005), 2: 219–220.
———. "Zhongguo xin wenxue daxi xiaoshuo erji xu" 中國新文學大系小說二集序. *Lu Xun quanji* (2005), 6:, 246–274.
Lu Xun. "On the Power of Mara Poetry." Trans. Shu-ying Tsau and Donald Holoch. In *Modern Chinese Literary Thought: Writings on Literature, 1893–1945*, ed. Kirk Denton, 96–109. Stanford, CA: Stanford University Press, 1996.
———. *The Real Story of Ah-Q and Other Tales of China: The Complete Fiction of Lu Xun*. Trans. Julia Lovell. London: Penguin, 2009.
———. "Diary of a Madman." *The Real Story of Ah-Q*, 21–31.
———. "In Memoriam." *The Real Story of Ah-Q*, 253–272.
———. "New Year's Sacrifice." *The Real Story of Ah-Q*, 161–177.
———. "Lessons from the History of Science." Trans. Nathaniel Isaacson. *Renditions* 74 (2010): 80–99.
Lu Xun (as Suozi). "The Art of Creating Humanity." Trans. Carlos Rojas. *Renditions* 77/78 (2012): 70–77.
Ma Boyong. "The City of Silence." Trans. Ken Liu. In *Invisible Planets: An Anthology of Contemporary Chinese Science Fiction*, ed. and trans. Ken Liu, 153–196. New York: Tor, 2016.
Mao Tse-tung. "On Protracted War." *Selected Works of Mao Tse-tung*. Beijing: Foreign Languages Press, 1967, II: 113–194.
Mannheim, Karl. *Ideology and Utopia: An Introduction to the Sociology of Knowledge*. San Diego, CA: Harvest, 1985.
Mbembe, Achille. *Necropolitics*. Trans. Stephen Corcoran. Durham, NC: Duke University Press, 2019.
Merleau-Ponty, Maurice. *Signs*. Trans. Richard C. McCleary. Evanston, IL: Northwestern University Press, 1964.
———. *The Visible and the Invisible*. Ed. Claude Lefort. Trans. Alphonso Lingis. Evanston, IL: Northwestern University Press, 1968.
Milner, Andrew. "Science Fiction and the Literary Field." *Science Fiction Studies* 38, no 3 (November 2011): 393–411.
Milton, John. *Paradise Lost*. New York: Norton, 2005.
Ming, Feng-ying. "Baoyu in Wonderland: Technological Utopia in the Early Modern Chinese Science Fiction Novel." In *China in a Polycentric World: Essays in Chinese Comparative Literature*, ed. Yingjin Zhang, 152–172. Stanford, CA: Stanford University Press, 1998.
Mitchell, David. *Cloud Atlas*. New York: Random House, 2004.

Mo Yan. *Life and Death Are Wearing Me Out*. Trans. Howard Goldblatt. New York: Arcade, 2008.
More, Thomas. *Utopia: A Norton Critical Edition*. New York: Norton, 2011.
Moretti, Franco. *Modern Epic: The World-System from Goethe to Garcia Marquez*. London: Verso, 1996.
Ni, Xueting Christine, ed. *Sinopticon: A Celebration of Chinese Science Fiction*. Oxford, UK: Solaris, 2021.
Peng Simeng 彭思萌. *Fenmi* 分泌. Beijing: Zuojia chubanshe, 2020.
——. "Chenzhou ji" 沉舟記. *Fenmi*, 141–199.
——. "Fenmi" 分泌. *Fenmi*, 1–69.
——. "Yeshou quanji" 野獸拳擊. *Fenmi*, 70–127.
Penley, Constance. *NASA/TREK: Popular Science and Sex in America*. London and New York: Verso, 1997.
Pohl, Nicole. "Utopianism After More: The Renaissance and Enlightenment." In *The Cambridge Companion to Utopian Literature*, ed. Gregory Claeys, 51–78. Cambridge: Cambridge University Press, 2010.
Pusey, James Reeve. *Lu Xun and Evolution*. Albany: State University of New York Press, 1998.
Rauch, Alan. "The Monstrous Body of Knowledge in Mary Shelley's *Frankenstein*." *Studies in Romanticism* 34, no. 2 (1995): 227–253.
Roberts, Adam. *Science Fiction*. London: Routledge, 2000.
——. *The History of Science Fiction*. London: Palgrave MacMillan, 2005.
Rojas, Carlos. "Introduction: 'The Germ of Life.'" *Modern Chinese Literature and Culture* 23, no. 1 (2011): 1–16.
——. "Of Canons and Cannibalism: A Psycho-Immunological Reading of 'Diary of a Madman.'" *Modern Chinese Literature and Culture* 23, no. 1 (2011): 47–76.
Roston, Murray. *Milton and the Baroque*. London: MacMillan, 1980.
Ruiz, Ruiz. *Poetics of Cinema*. Paris: Editions Dis Voir, 2005.
——. *Poetics of Cinema, 2*. Paris: Editions Dis Voir, 2007.
Said, Edward. *Humanism and Democratic Criticism*. New York: Columbia University Press, 2004.
Sargent, Lyman Tower. *Utopianism*. Oxford: Oxford University Press, 2010.
——. "Ideology and Utopia: Karl Mannheim and Paul Ricoeur." In *Utopia Horizons: Ideology, Politics, Literature*, ed. Zsolt Czigányik, 19–40. Budapest, Hungary: Central European University Press, 2017.
Schmitt, Carl. *Political Theology: Four Chapters on the Concept of Sovereignty*. Chicago: University of Chicago Press, 2005.
Scholes, Robert. *Structural Fabulation*. Notre Dame: Indiana University Press, 1975.
Scholes, Robert and Eric S. Rabkin. *Science Fiction: History, Science, Vision*. Oxford: Oxford University Press, 1977.
Schwarcz, Vera. *The Chinese Enlightenment: Intellectuals and the Legacy of the May Fourth Movement of 1919*. Berkeley: University of California Press, 1986.
Schwartz, Benjamin. *In Search of Wealth and Power: Yen Fu and the West*. Cambridge, MA: Harvard University Press, 1964.

Shelley, Mary. *Frankenstein: Norton Critical Edition*. New York: Norton, 2012.
Shuangchimu 雙翅目. *Sheli xuepai* 猞猁學派. Beijing: Zuojia chubanshe, 2020.
——. "Sheli xuepai" 猞猁學派. *Sheli xuepai*, 5–16.
——. "Taiyangxi pianchang" 太陽系：片場. *Sheli xuepai*, 51–85.
——. "Women bixu tubu chuanyue taiyangxi" 我們必須徒步穿越太陽系. *Sheli xuepai*, 17–50.
Shuo Fang 朔方, ed. *Liulang diqiu dianying zhizuo shouce* 流浪地球電影製作手冊. Beijing: Renmin jiaotong chubanshe, 2019.
Snow, Edgar. *Red Star Over China: The Classic Account of the Birth of Chinese Communism*. New York: Grove Press, 1968.
Soh, Yoojin 徐维辰. "Cong kexue dao chiren: Lu Xun 'Zaorenshu' fanyi yu yeman de qianzai shuxie" 从科学到吃人：鲁迅"造人术"翻译与野蛮的潜在书写. *Wenxue* 文學 (Spring/Summer 2017): 67–83.
Song, Mingwei. *Young China: National Rejuvenation and the Bildungsroman, 1900–1959*. Cambridge, MA: Harvard University Asia Center, 2015.
——, ed. "Chinese Science Fiction: Late Qing and the Contemporary." *Renditions* 77/78 (November 2012).
Song, Mingwei 宋明煒. "Tanxingzhe yu mianbizhe: Liu Cixin de kehuan shijie" 彈星者與面壁者：劉慈欣的科幻世界. *Shanghai wenhua* 上海文化 [Shanghai culture] 3 (2011): 17–30.
——. "Zhongguo kehuan de xinlangchao" 中國科幻的新浪潮. *Wenxue* 文學 1. no. 1 (Spring/Summer 2013): 3–16.
——. "Huoxing etuobang: *Maocheng ji* yu Lao She de gushi 火星上的惡托邦：《貓城記》與老舍的故事. *Shucheng* 書城 137 (October 2017): 44–50.
Song, Mingwei and Theodore Huters, ed. *The Reincarnated Giant: An Anthology of Twenty-First-Century Chinese Science Fiction*. New York: Columbia University Press, 2018.
Spark, Muriel. *Child of Light: Mary Shelley*. New York: Welcome Rain, 1987.
Strong, Louise J. "An Unscientific Story." *The Cosmopolitan* 34, no. 2 (February 1903): 411–417.
Suvin, Darko. *Metamorphoses of Science Fiction: On the Poetics and History of a Literary Genre*. New Haven, CT: Yale University Press, 1979.
Tan Sitong. *An Exposition of Benevolence: The "Jen-hsüeh" of T'an Ssu-t'ung*. Trans. Chan Sin-wai. Hong Kong: The Chinese University Press, 1984.
Tang Fei 糖匪. *Kangjian jingyuzuo de ren* 看見鯨魚座的人. Shanghai: Shanghai wenyi chubanshe, 2018.
——. "Bowuguan zhi xin" 博物館之心. *Kangjian jingyuzuo de ren*, 29–50.
——. "Huangse gushi" 黃色故事. *Kangjian jingyuzuo de ren*, 117–128.
——. "Sui xingxing" 碎星星. *Kangjian jingyuzuo de ren*, 1–28.
——. "Xiari zhi chan" 夏日之蟬. *Kangjian jingyuzuo de ren*, 247–256.
——. *Aodesaibo* 奧德賽博. Fuzhou: Haixia wenyi chubanshe/ Houlang chuban gongsi, 2021.
——. "Baozi" 孢子. *Aodesaibo*, 63–83.
Tang Fei. "Call Girl." Trans. Ken Liu. In *Invisible Planets: An Anthology of Contemporary Chinese Science Fiction*, ed. and trans. Ken Liu, 265–275. New York: Tor, 2016.
——. "The Spore." Trans. Andy Dudak. *Clarkesworld* 176 (May 2021).
Tarumoto Teruo 樽本照雄. "Lu Xun 'Zaorenshu' de yuanzuo, buyi" 鲁迅〈造人术〉的原作·补遗. Trans. Xu Changfu 许昌福. Ed. Beijing Lu Xun Museum. *Lu Xun fanyi yanjiu lunwenji* 鲁迅翻译研究论文集), 186–187. Shenyang: Chufeng wenyi chubanshe, 2013.

Tong, Enzheng. "Death Ray on a Coral Island." In *Science Fiction from China*, ed. Wu Dingbo and Patrick Murphy, 97–122. New York: Praeger, 1989.

Tsu, Jing. "Why Sci-Fi Could be the Secret Weapon in China's Soft-Power Arsenal." *Financial Times*, May 29, 2020.

Tu, Hang. "Long Live Chairman Mao! Death, Resurrection, and the (un)Making of a Revolutionary Relic." *Journal of Asian Studies* 81, no. 3 (2022): 507–522.

Tweedie, James. *The Age of New Waves: Art Cinema and the Staging of Globalization*. New York: Oxford University Press, 2013.

Verne, Jules. *From the Earth to the Moon, and a Trip Around It*. New York: Scribner, Armstrong & Company, 1874.

Vieira, Fatima. "The Concept of Utopia." In *The Cambridge Companion to Utopian Literature*, ed. Gregory Claeys, 3–27. Cambridge: Cambridge University Press, 2010.

Volland, Nicholai. *Socialist Cosmopolitanism: The Chinese Literary Universe, 1945–1965*. New York: Columbia University Press, 2017.

Voltaire. *Candide: A Norton Critical Edition*. New York: Norton, 1966.

Wagner, Rudolf. "Lobby Literature: The Archaeology and Present Functions of Science Fiction in the People's Republic of China." In *After Mao: Chinese Literature and Society 1978–1981*, ed. Jeffrey Kinkley, 17–62. Cambridge, MA: Harvard University Press, 1985.

Wakeman, Fredrick. *History and Will: Philosophical Perspectives of Mao Tse-Tung's Thought*. Berkeley: Center for Chinese Studies, UC Berkeley, 1973.

Wang Anyi 王安憶. *Niming* 匿名. Beijing: Renmin wenxue chubanshe, 2016.

Wang, Ban, ed. *Chinese Visions of World Order: Tianxia, Culture, and World Politics*. Durham, NC: Duke University Press, 2017.

Wang, Chaohua. "Dreamers and Nightmares: Political Novels by Wang Lixiong and Chan Koonchung." *China Perspective* 1 (2015): 23–31.

Wang, David Der-wei. *Fin-de-Siècle Splendor: Repressed Modernities of Late Qing Fiction, 1849–1911*. Stanford, CA: Stanford University Press, 1997.

——, ed. *A New Literary History of Modern China*. Cambridge, MA: Harvard University Press, 2017.

——. "The Panglossian Dream and Dark Consciousness: Modern Chinese Literature and Utopia." In *Utopia and Utopianism in the Contemporary Chinese Context*, ed. David Der-wei Wang, Angela Ki Che Leung, and Zhang Yinde, 53–70. Hong Kong: Hong Kong University Press, 2020.

——. *Why Fiction Matters in Contemporary China*. Waltham, MA: Brandeis University Press, 2020.

Wang, David Der-wei 王德威. "Wutuobang, etuobang, yituobang" 烏托邦，惡托邦，異托邦. *Xiandangdai wenxue xinlun: yili, lunli, dili* 現當代文學新論：義理，倫理，地理), 247–276. Beijing: Sanlian shudian, 2014.

——. "Xuanxiang yu shensi: Lu Xun, Han Song yu weiwancheng de geming"「懸想」與「神思」—魯迅、韓松與未完的文學革命. *Zhongguo wenzhe yanjiu jikan* 中國文哲研究集刊 57 (2020): 1–31.

Wang Hui. "Lu Xun and Tombstones." Trans. Michael G. Hill. In *A New Literary History of Modern China*, ed. David Der-wei Wang, 306–311. Cambridge, MA: Harvard University Press, 2017.

Wang Jinkang 王晋康. *Yisheng* 蚁生. Fuzhou: Fujian renmin chubanshe, 2007.

Wang Jinkang. "The Reincarnated Giant." Trans. Carlos Rojas. In *The Reincarnated Giant: An Anthology of Twenty-First-Century Chinese Science Fiction*, ed. Mingwei Song and Theodore Huters, 313–353 (New York: Columbia University Press, 2018).

Wang Kanyu 王侃瑜. *Yunwu 2.2* 雲霧2.2. Shanghai: Shanghai wenyi chubanshe, 2018.

——. "Haixian fandian" 海鲜饭店. *Haixian fandian*, 1–18. Beijing: Zuojia chubanshe, 2020.

Wang Quangen 王泉根. *Xiandai Zhongguo kehuan wenxue zhuchao* 现代中國科幻文學主潮, 141–142. Chongqing: Chongqing chubanshe, 2011.

Wang Xiaodong 王小东. "Zhongguo de gongyehua jiang jueding Zhongguo yu shijie de mingyun—jianlun 'Gongye dang' duijue 'Qinghua dang' 中国的工业化将决定中国与世界的命运——兼论"工业党"对决"情怀党". *Lüye* 綠葉 1 (2011).

Wasserstrom, Jeffrey N. *China in the 21st Century: What Everyone Needs to Know*. New York: Oxford University Press, 2010.

Williams, James. "Event." In *Gilles Deleuze: Key Concepts*, ed. Charles J. Stivale, 80–90. New York: Routledge, 2011.

Woolf, Virginia. *The Diaries of Virginia Woolf, Vol. 3: 1925–1930*. Boston: Mariner, 1980.

——. *Orlando: A Biography*. New York: Harvest, 1992.

Wu Dingbo and Patrick D. Murphy, eds. *Science Fiction from China*. New York: Praeger, 1989.

Wu Jianren 吳趼人. *Xin shitou ji* 新石頭記. Zhengzhou: Zhongzhou guji chubanshe, 1986.

Wu Jike 武际可. *Jindai lixue zai Zhongguo de chuanbo yu fazhan* 近代力学在中国的传播与发展. Beijing: Gaodeng jiaoyu chubanshe, 2006.

Wu Ming-yi. *The Man with the Compound Eyes*. Trans. Darryl Sterk. New York: Random House, 2014.

Wu Yan 吴岩. *Kehuan wenxue lungang* 科幻文學論綱. Chongqing: Chongqing Press, 2011.

Wu Yan 吴岩 and Fang Xiaoqing 方晓庆. "Liu Cixin yu xin gudian zhuyi kehuan" 刘慈欣与新古典主义科幻小说. *Hunan keji xueyuan xuebao* 湖南科技学院学报 27, no. 2 (2006): 36–39.

Wu Yan 吴岩 and Guo Kai 郭凯, eds. *2010 niandu Zhongguo zuijia kehuan xiaoshuo ji* 2010年度中國最佳科幻小說集. Chengdu: Sichuan renmin chubanshe, 2011.

——. *2011 niandu Zhongguo zuijia kehuan xiaoshuo ji* 2011年度中國最佳科幻小說集. Chengdu: Sichuan renmin chubanshe, 2012.

Wu Yan 吴岩 and Jiang Zhenyu 姜振宇, eds. *Zhongguo kehuan wenlun jingxuan* 中國科幻論文精選. Beijing: Beijing daxue chubanshe, 2021.

Xia Jia 夏笳. "Baigui yexingjie" 百鬼夜行街. *Ni wufa dida de shijian*, 204–217. Tianjin: Tianjin renmin chubanshe, 2017.

——. "Longma yexing" 龍馬夜行. *Ni wufa dida de shijian*, 94–108.

——. "Ni wufa dida de shijian" 你無法抵達的時間. *Ni wufa dida de shijian*, 1–62.

Xia Jia. "The Demon-Enslaving Flask." Trans. Linda Rui Feng. In *The Reincarnated Giant: An Anthology of Twenty-First-Century Chinese Science Fiction*, ed. Mingwei Song and Theodore Huters, 130–139. New York: Columbia University Press, 2018.

——. "A Hundred Ghosts Parade Tonight." Trans. Ken Liu. *Clarkesworld* 65 (February 2012).

——. *A Summer Beyond Your Reach*. Stirling, NJ: Clarkesworld Books, 2020.

——. "A Time Beyond Your Reach." *A Summer Beyond Your Reach*, 93–153.

Xiong Rong 熊融. "Lu Xun zuizao de liang pian yiwen—'Aichen' he 'Zaoren shu'" 魯迅最早的兩篇譯文—〈哀塵〉和〈造人術〉. *Wenxue pinglun* 文學評論 3 (1963).

Xue Shaohui 薛紹徽 and Chen Shoupeng 陳壽彭. *Bashiri huanyouji* 八十日環遊記. Shanghai: Jingshi wenshe, 1900.

Yasuo Nagayama 長山靖生. *Riben kehuan xiaoshuo shihua: cong mufumoqi dao zhanhou* 日本科幻小說史話——從幕府末期到戰後. Nanjing: Nanjing daxue chubanshe, 2012. Original title: 日本SF精神史 幕末・明治から戦後まで.

Yan Feng 严锋. "Guangrong yu mengxiang" 光榮與夢想. In Liu Cixin, *Liulang diqiu*, 1–6. Wuhan: Changjiang wenyi chubanshe, 2008.

——. "Chuangshi yu jimie—Liu Cixin de yuzhou shixue" 创世与寂灭—刘慈欣的宇宙诗学. *Nanfang wentan* 南方文坛 5 (2011).

Yan Fu 嚴復 and Xia Zengyou 夏曾佑. "Benguan fuyin shuobu yuanqi" 本館附印說部緣起, *Guowenbao* 國聞報, November 10, 13, December 8, 11, 1897.

Yan Lianke. *Discovering Fiction*. Trans. Carlos Rojas. Durham, NC: Duke University Press, 2022.

Yan Zuolei 閻作雷. "Santi zhong de pusu shehuizhuyi yu zuichu de ren" 《三体》中的"朴素主义社会"与"最初的人." *Zhongguo xiandai wenxue yanjiu congkan* 中國現代文學研究叢刊 6 (2020).

Yang Qiong. "A Writer's Dilemma: Gu Junzheng and a Turning Point of Chinese Science Fiction." Master's thesis, The Ohio State University, 2010.

Ye Yonglie 葉永烈. *Xiao Lingtong manyou weilai* 小灵童漫游未来. Beijing: Ertong wenxue chubanshe, 1978.

——. *Shishi feifei huiguniang* 是是非非灰姑娘. Fuzhou: Fujian renmin chubanshe, 2000.

Yu Chen and Regina Kanyu Wang, eds. *The Way Spring Arrives and Other Stories*. New York: Tor, 2022.

Yu Hua. *The Seventh Day*. Trans. Allan H. Barr. New York: Anchor, 2016.

Yu Liang 余亮. "'Gongye dang' yishi, yizhong bei hushi de renwen jingshen." "工业党"意识，一种被忽视的人文精神. *Dongfang xuekan* 东方学刊 2 (2019).

Zamora, Lois Parkinson. *The Inordinate Eye: New World Baroques and Late American Fiction*. Chicago: University of Chicago Press, 2006.

Zamora, Lois Parkinson and Monika Kaup, eds. *Baroque New Worlds: Representation, Transculturation, Counterconquest*. Durham, NC: Duke University Press, 2010.

Zhan Ling 詹玲. *Dangdai Zhongguo kehuan xiaoshuo zhuanxing yanjiu* 當代中國科幻小說轉型研究. Beijing: Zongguo shehui kexue chubanshe, 2022.

Zhang, Jie. "*Death Ray on a Coral Island* as China's First Science Fiction Film." In *The Liverpool Companion to World Science Fiction Film*, ed. Sonja Fritzsche, 39–55. Liverpool: Liverpool University Press, 2014.

Zhang Zhi 張治, ed. *Huitoukan jilue* 回頭看紀略. In *Zhongguo kehuan wenxue daxi: wanqing juan* 中國科幻文學大系：晚清卷, ed. Li Guangyi, *Bianyi yiji* 編譯一集. Chongqing: Chongqing daxue chubanshe, 2020.

Zhao Haihong 趙海虹. "Bu kujie de quan" 不枯竭的泉. In *Ta kehuan: Xingchen de yanjing* 她科幻：星辰的眼睛, ed. Chen Qiufan, 175–193. Beijing: Hangkong gongye chubanshe, 2021.

Zhao Haihong. "1923: A Fantasy." Trans. Nicky Harman and Pang Zhaoxia. In *The Reincarnated Giant: An Anthology of Twenty-First-Century Chinese Science Fiction*, ed. Mingwei Song and Theodore Huters, 258–275. New York: Columbia University Press, 2018.

Zheng Bijian. *China's Peaceful Rise*. Washington, DC: Brookings Institution Press, 2005.

Zheng Wenguang 郑文光. "Zai wenxue chuangzuo zuotanhui shang guanyu kehuan xiaoshuo de fayan" 在文学创作座谈会上关于科幻小说的发言. *Kehuan xiaoshuo chuangzuo cankao ziliao* 科幻小说创作参考资料 4 (May 1982).

Zhengzhiquan 政知圈. "Li Yuanchao daizhe Santi yu Liu Cixin zuotan" 李源潮帶著《三體》與劉慈欣座談, *Takunpao* 大公報, September 16, 2015. http://news.takungpao.com/mainland/focus/2015-09/3167721.html.

Zhou Zuoren 周作人. "Zhenshi de gushi" 真實的故事. *Zhou Zuoren yiwen quanji* 周作人譯文全集, 5: 559–616. Shanghai: Shanghai renmin chubanshe, 2012.

Zhou Zuoren. "Humane Literature." In *Modern Chinese Literary Thought: Writings on Literature, 1893–1945*, ed. Kirk Denton, 228–232. Stanford, CA: Stanford University Press, 1996.

Zhu Weizheng 朱維錚, ed. *Kang Youwei Datongshu erzhong* 康有為大同書二種. Beijing: Sanlian shudian, 1998.

INDEX

"A lonely hidden army," 2, 7–9
A Que, 10
Adichie, Chimamanda, 70
Adventures of Huckleberry Finn, The, 210
aestheticism, 217, 270, 312
Agamben, Giorgio, 310; bare life, 310
Age of Discovery, 50–51
Age of the Baroque, 51–53
algorithm, 12, 16, 23, 28, 39, 60, 125–126, 162, 164, 167, 171, 188, 191, 193, 195–196, 212, 224, 296, 310
alien/alien intelligence, 3, 5, 11, 18, 46–47, 57, 83, 103, 110, 112, 117–118, 128, 130–133, 135–136, 139–142, 148, 150, 157, 190, 213, 235–236, 254, 267, 269, 302–303
Alkon, Paul K., 47
alternative history, 33, 176
anachronism, 27, 34, 237
anarchism, 258, 285; anarchy, 171, 227
anatomical aesthetics, 163, 165, 167, 169; detail, 150, 164–168, 171, 184
anatomy of evil, 187, 197–198
Andersen, Hans Christian, 291
Anderson, Marston, 59
androgyne, 279

Anglo-American empiricism, 273
Anglo-American missionaries, 87
Anthropocene, 12, 150, 178
anthropocentric sexual experience, 291
anti-utopianism, 205
Arendt, Hannah, 155
Aristotle, 49
artificial human, 283
artificial intelligence, 10, 22, 39, 45, 114, 164, 192–193, 197, 204, 207, 230, 237, 248–249, 252, 265–266, 274, 278, 282, 301, 310
Asimov, Isaac, 45, 53, 112, 255, 259; *Foundation,* 54; *Foundation* series, 259; "The Last Question," 45
Associated Southwestern University, 93
Atom Boy, 112, 262
Atwood, Margaret, 53, 55, 260, 284, 309; *The Handmaid's Tale,* 260
augmented reality, 63, 264
avant-garde, 2, 4, 54, 67, 77, 95, 114–115, 128, 164, 184, 186, 284; aesthetics, 164; experimentalism, 128; spirit of the 1980s, 115; avant-gardism, 14, 91, 115, 308; avant-gardist, 4

Ba Jin, 98; *Family*, 98
Bacigalupi, Paolo, 257
Baconian optimism, 83
Bakhtin, Mikhail, 49, 168–169; cosmic terror, 15, 168–170, 251
Bao Shu, 4, 104, 112, 228, 236–241, 256, 266, 290–293; "Blessings of the Time," 104; "Let's Go to See the Boat on the South Lake," 238; *Redemption of Time*, 239, 266; *Ruins of Time*, 239; "Songs of Ancient Earth" (also known as "Star Songs"), 236–238, 256; *The Girl's Name Is Monster*, 291; "The Great Times" (also known as "What Has Passed Shall in Kinder Light Appear"), 239–240, 256, "The Little Mermaid," 291–293
Baroque, 19, 45–47, 49–53, 55, 66–67, 74, 134, 165, 280, 284–285, 287, 291, 295, 299–300, 309
Barth, John, 284
Baudrillard, Jean, 60, 265
Beethoven, 90
Bellamy, Edward, 204–205; Bellamy effect, 204; *Looking Backward: 2000–1887 A.D.*, 204
Belle Époque, 204
Belyaev, Alexander, 262
big data, 10, 34, 40, 241
big data analytics, 21
"Big Three," 214, 217, 276–277
biguan suoguo (closing doors to the world), 201
binary gender politics, 287
biopolitics, 82, 219
black hole, 63, 73, 119, 151, 161, 199, 247, 250
Bloch, Ernst, 204; *The Principle of Hope*, 204
Bodhisattva (Guanyin), 166, 196
Bogdanov, Alexander, 209; *Red Star*, 209
Bohr, Niels, 92; Bohr-Einstein debate, 91
Bolaño, Roberto, 284,
Borges, Jorge Luis, 45, 53, 134, 245; "The Library of Babel," 45; "The Secret Miracle," 134

Bo Xilai, 236
Bradbury, Ray, 53
Braidotti, Rosi, 272–273; decentering of "Man," 272
Brecht, Bertolt, 55
Broderick, Damien, 56
Buddhism, 79, 171, 183, 191, 195, 197, 199–200, 209
Butler, Octavia, 282

Cai Yuanpei, 93
Calabrese, Omar, 66, 67
cannibalism, 6, 75, 84–86, 92, 95, 97–101, 103, 150, 164, 172–174, 176, 179, 194, 212; "eating people," 75, 84, 173, 176
Čapek, Karel, 53, 261; *R.U.R.*, 261
Carson, Rachel, 289; *Silent Spring*, 289
censorship, 2, 203, 232, 256, 307
centralism, 229
Chan Koonchung, 13, 225, 228–234, 240, 256, 274, 309; *Beijing Zero Kilometer*, 233, 309; *The Fat Years*, 225, 229–231, 233, 256; collective amnesia, 230–232; Fang Caodi, 230–231; "high lite-lite," or small-small high, 230–232; "Idealism Chinese Style," 231; Little Xi, 230; MDNA-Ecstasy, 232; Old Chen, 230–233; *The Second Year of the Jianfeng Reign: A Uchronia of New China*, 240; Formosa Incident (1979), 240
Chang, Eileen (Zhang Ailing), 288
Chang Hao, 28
Chang Jia, 4
Chang, S. K., 111; "Biography of a Superman," 111
chaos theory, 113
Chekhov, Anton, 70–74; play-within-a-play, 71–72; *The Seagull*, 70–71, 73
Chen Chuncheng, 41
Chen Duxiu, 93, 98,
Chen Qiufan, 4, 12, 59, 60, 112–113, 252–254, 257, 263, 265, 267, 272, 278, 290, 309; *AI 2041: Ten Visions for Our Future*,

252, 254; "Contactless Love," 253; "G Is for Goddess," 290–291; *Waste Tide,* 253, 256–257, 263, 265–267, 272; Chen Kaizong, 266; first notable cyborg in Chinese SF, 265; *guiyu,* 263; Mimi, or Xiaomi, 265–266; waste people, 257, 263–264, 266
Chen Shoupeng, 106
Chen Xi, 4, 276
Cheng Jingbo, 4, 276, 278, 295; "Before the City Falls," 295–296
Chi Hui, 4, 272, 276–277, 296; *2030: Terminal Town,* 296; "The Rainforest," 272; trans-species protagonist, 272
Chi Shuchang, 221; "Elephants with Their Trunks Removed," 221
Chi Ta-wei, 13, 254, 269–270, 272; "Beneath His Eyes, in Your Palm, a Red Rose Is About to Bloom," 270; *The Membranes,* 270
Chiang, Ted, 45, 240; "Story of Your Life," 45
chimera, 11, 12, 68, 71, 73, 278–285, 289–292, 294–295, 300, 312
Chinese dream, 14, 37, 39, 40, 121, 186, 193, 198, 202, 207, 226–227, 229
Chinese enlightenment, 76, 208
Chinese new wave science fiction (SF), 11, 13, 15–16, 42, 45–46, 65, 77, 103, 108, 249, 252, 254, 267, 270, 286
Chinese Science Fiction Conference, 308
Chinese University of Science and Technology, 127
Chinese Writers Association, 308
chronotope, 227, 234, 236, 246
chthonic abyss, 199
chthonic aesthetics, 13, 200, 254
chthonic deep, 198
Chu T'ien-wen, 269, 288; "Fin-de-Siècle Splendor," 269; *Notes of a Desolate Man,* 269
Chu, Seo-Young, 56, 60
Chuwo (Ding Zuyin), 82

Clarke, Arthur C., 45, 54, 112, 136–137, 255, 257, 259; Space Odyssey series, 259; "The Star," 45, 257; *2001: A Space Odyssey,* 47, 136–137
cognitive estrangement, 10, 55–57, 181
Columbus, Christopher, 43, 50–52, 175–176, 258
Commercial Press, 78, 80
conformism, 231
Confucianism, 78, 83, 85, 89, 92–93, 95–97, 105, 107, 211–212, 229
contemplative literature, 59
continental philosophy, 238, 273
Copernican Revolution, 50
Copernicus, Nicolaus, 22, 43, 50–52, 135
Cosmopolitan, The (magazine), 80
COVID/COVID-19, 240–241, 253, 278, 308, 311
cross-species sexuality, 302
cryptic knowledge of SF, 158
Csicsery-Ronay Jr., Istvan, 41, 56, 60, 168–169, 258, 260; seven beauties, 56
cthulhu, 164, 177–179, 302,
Cultural Revolution, 38, 59, 109, 120, 141–142, 146, 181–185, 188, 194, 206, 214, 216–217, 219, 225–226, 231, 239, 256
cyber politics, 33
cyber surveillance, 40
cyberism, 122
cybernetics, 14, 21, 34, 113, 257, 265, 273; cybernetic subjectivity, 31; cybernetic totalitarianism, 33; democratic cybernetics, 34
cyberpunk, 34, 114; political, 34
cyberspace, 31–34, 57, 104, 311
cyborg, 68, 71, 83, 115, 165–166, 183, 189, 192, 214, 235–236, 248–249, 261–262, 265–267, 270–272, 279, 289–290, 295, 300; cyborgian constrcutions, 12
cynicism, 27, 121, 124, 231

Damrosch, David, 256–257
dark consciousness, 17, 23, 28–29, 48, 170, 205, 290, 312

dark forest, 16, 31, 44, 89, 116, 119–124, 139, 141, 143–147, 149, 151, 153–156, 199, 216, 226, 228, 239, 278, 286–289; dark forest deadlock, 151; dark forest theory, 147, 153, 155; "hide well and cleanse all," 117, 120, 141

Darwinian jungle, 144

Darwinism, 87–89, 145–146, 288

Daudet, Alphonse, 94

debate on science and metaphysics, 82

de Bergerac, Cyrano, 49; *Voyage dans la lune*, 49

deep surveillance, 34

degendering, 288

Deleuze, Gilles, 66–67, 265

de Maupassant, Guy, 94

Deng Xiaoping, 220, 223

Density, 165, 167, 191, 270

Derrida, Jacques, 309

determinism, 32, 40, 47, 114, 127–129, 139, 146, 152, 171, 177; historical, 32, 40, 112, 146, 177; political, 171; scientific, 127; technological, 171

Dick, Philip K., 54, 164, 257, 260, 262; *The Man in the High Castle*, 260,

Donne, John, 51; "An Anatomy of the World," 51

dreamscape, 39, 100, 164, 172, 174, 189, 193, 217, 233, 271, 297; dream narrative, 270–271

Duan Ziqi, 12, 277, 296

Duncan, Isadora, 92

Dung Kai-cheung, 13, 41, 228, 247, 249, 284, 309; *A Posthuman Comedy*, 248–249, 309; *Atlas*, 247; *Beloved Wife*, 248; *Histories of Time*, 228, 247; "Natural History" Trilogy, 247

Dushu (magazine), 160

dystopia, 13, 20–21, 23–24, 34, 40, 49, 67, 83, 103, 109, 111, 120–121, 123, 132, 147, 202–203, 205–207, 214–216, 223–225, 227–229, 232–233, 241–243, 252, 259–260, 274, 277, 301, 309, 311; dystopian fiction, 13, 49, 206, 277, 309; dystopian gaze, 23, 232–233; dystopian variations, 123, 203, 206, 214–215, 233; Orwellian authoritarianism, 206; Orwellian dictatorship, 208

ecological crisis, 257, 260

Einstein, Albert, 22, 91–93, 160; theory of relativity, 87, 91, 93, 128

Enlightenment, 75–76, 83–85, 95–97, 115, 130, 170, 173, 176, 178, 183, 187–188, 196–197, 199–200, 208, 258, 261, 267, 284, 291; intellectuals, 173, 208

environmentalism, 278

escapism, 6, 24, 64

espionage SF, 109

estrangement, 55–57, 77, 94, 99–100, 143, 181, 192, 207, 244

eternal return, 161, 163, 171, 184, 194–197, 199, 215, 224, 239, 245

événement, 10

experimentalist surrealism, 297

Extraordinary Voyages, 53

extremism, 70

Fang Lizhi, 93, 127–128

fascism, 70

fear of seeing, 11, 16–17, 21, 38, 44, 64, 74–75, 85, 99–100, 103, 123, 137, 161–162, 167, 170, 212, 290, 296

Fei Dao, 2, 4–9, 76, 85, 104, 113, 228, 245–247, 305, 308; "Chinese sci-fi blockbusters," 76; *Cube*, 76, 104; "One Kind of Melancholia Outside the Galaxy," 246–247

feminism, 258, 273, 285

fin de siècle, 53, 288

fin du monde, 53, 288

fold, 66–67, 74, 84, 124, 129, 134, 158, 180, 224, 229, 233, 248, 253, 270, 284, 298, 300, 303–304; in thinking, 84, 124; Foucauldian, 66; Leibnizian, 66; linguistic, 270

formalism, 55
Foucault, Michel, 19–20, 23, 28, 64, 134, 227, 245, 291; fold, 66; gaze, 197; heterotopia, 227; invisible visibility, 19, 64; language to infinity, 134
Freedman, Carl, 56
Frontier (magazine), 277
Frye, Northrop, 49
Fryer, John, 79
Fudan University, 1, 302
Fukuyama, Francis, 146; "Last Man," 146
futurology, 8, 113

Galileo Galilei, 22, 50–51, 299, 300
gaze as a technology, 10, 16, 19–20, 23, 76, 162, 165–167, 170, 191, 194, 197–199, 215, 230, 232–233, 238, 258, 299, 300; anatomic gaze, 19; fearless gaze, 16, 167; gaze back, 162, 166–167, 170, 198–199; gaze of power, 19, 167, 170, 191, 197
gender binary, 290
gender essentialism, 290
genre/gender convention, 282
Gernsback, Hugo, 47
gewu, 96; *kexue* (science), 96; investigation of things and the extension of knowledge, 96
Gibson, William, 21, 54
global English, 256
global SF, 108, 253–255, 258–259, 261, 263
Godwin, William, 259, 262
Goethe, Johann Wolfgang von, 259, 283; *Faust*, 283
Golden Age of SF, 14, 54, 106, 108, 113, 276; in late Qing, 113
"good China stories"/"telling the good China story," 163–164, 193, 233, 245
Great Famine, 221
Great Firewall, 34, 241
Great Revolution, 53
Greek *silloi*, 49
Gu Junzheng, 109; "A Dream of Peace," 109; "Under the North Pole," 109

Gu Shi, 12, 277, 280, 282, 296, 303, 312; "Chimera," 280; "Möbius Continuum," 303–304
Guo Fan, 305; *The Wandering Earth* (film), 305–307

Han Song, 2–7, 9–12, 16, 20–21, 23–24, 26–30, 35–40, 48, 59–60, 62–63, 70, 74–75, 93, 103–104, 112–113, 115, 119, 121, 150, 160–200, 201, 203, 207–216, 223–228, 232–234, 244–245, 248–249, 254, 257, 267–268, 272, 276, 278, 290, 296, 298, 305, 307–309, 311–312; "Fear of Seeing," 35–36, 38; "Guidebook to Hunting Beautiful Women," 166, 299; *High Speed Rail*, 187
—"Hospital" trilogy, 16, 74, 168, 187–188, 193, 216, 224, 244, 245; "Age of Medicine," 188; Ai Lao, 194; Bai Dai, 189–193; *Dead Souls*, 163, 188, 191, 193, 215; death machine (Death), 196; "Empire of Medicine," 188, 194; *Exorcism*, 163, 188, 192–193, 245; *Hospital*, 16, 62, 74, 187–199, 207, 216, 224, 233, 244, 307; infernal pool of dead souls, 194; Life Control, 23, 191–193, 196, 208; medical punk, 167–168, 190–191; "Medicinal War," 188, 192; "ocean of bitterness," 191; *Pax Hospitium*, 190; "possessor," 191; Professor Eternal, 192–193, 198; "The good hospital story," 192–193, 198; "The Other Shore of the Sea," 195; Xia Quan, 193–194; Yang Wei, 189–196; Zifeiyu, 194; Zi Ye, 192–193
—*Mars Over America*, 24, 163, 165, 172, 201, 203, 207, 209–211, 213, 225, 227; "Amanduo Dream Society," 207–208; fudi, or land of happiness, 213; Newman, 165; Tang Long, 210, 212; "2066 nian zhi xixing manji," 207
—"My Fatherland Does Not Dream," 36, 38–39, 48, 223, 307; Darkness Committee, 37, 39; *mengyou* (dream walking), 36
power of darkness, 11, 102, 163, 170

Han Song (continued)
—*Red Ocean*, 61, 163, 172–180, 194, 199; cannibalism, 172–174, 176, 179; fundamental ethics of being human, 174; huaite ren, 174, 176; Sea Star, 172–176, 180; Zheng He, 175–177, 179
  "Regenerated Bricks," 223–224, 268; sleepwalking, 36–39, 103, 160, 183–184, 215
—*Subway*, 10, 38, 60, 160, 162–163, 166, 181–183, 185–187, 207, 223, 268, 307; "cosmo-transformation," 182; "Paradise," 182; "Ruins," 183; S city, 185; "Symbols," 182, 184, 186; "The Last Train," 182–183; "The Passengers and the Creator," 213–214, 223; "Thrilling Mutation," 182; "Tombs of the Universe," 24, 26, 28–29, 48, 163; *Tracks*, 163, 186, 223; truth investigation, 20; truth investigator, 38, 75, 97, 161, 298; Xiao Wu, 160–161, 184–186
Hanan, Patrick, 79
Hao Jingfang, 4, 22, 228, 241–244, 267, 276–277; *Born in Nineteen Eighty-Four*, 242; "Folding Beijing," 242–243, 267, 277; "Invisible Planets," 244; *Vagabonds*, 242
Hara Hôitsu-an, 80
Haraway, Donna J., 178–179, 195, 272–273, 288–290, 302; Capitalocene, 178; Chthulhucene, 178–180; "staying with the trouble," 23, 178, 289; sympoiesis, 12, 68, 289; sympoietic relationship with nature, 179; tentacular thinking, 289, 302
hard science fiction (hard SF), 126–129
"harmonious society," 187, 208, 212, 230
Harrison, Mark, 225–227; futures of China, 225
Harvest (magazine), 277
hauntology, 199, 204, 227
Hawking, Stephen, 22, 39, 128; *A Brief History of Time*, 128

Hayles, N. Katherine, 272–274, 278; *How We Became Posthuman*, 278; information/materiality separation, 273
He Xi, 4, 114
hedonism, 121, 231; hedonistic indulgence, 232
Hegelian dualism, 179
Heidegger, Martin, 18
Heinlein, Robert A., 54
Heisenberg, Werner, 22, 72, 92, 95, 99; Uncertainty Principle, 99
Herbert, Frank, 54; *Dune*, 54
hermeneutics, 78, 104, 157, 187, 190, 197, 199
heterochronia, 8
hetero-chronotope, 227, 234, 236, 246
heterotopia, 8, 13, 21–24, 60–61, 63, 68, 70, 163, 197, 203, 214, 227–229, 236, 241, 243–251, 269, 274, 310, 311
Hiroyuki, Kato, 106
Ho Ching-pin, 13
Hopkinson, Nalo, 257
Hsia, T. A., 170; *Gate of Darkness*, 170
Hu Shi, 94–95, 98, 101; "Short Story," 94
Huacheng (magazine), 277
Hugo Award, 10, 242, 247, 255, 277
humane literature, 98
humanist ideals of the 1980s, 33
Hundred Days' Reform, 79
Hung Ling, 13
Husserl, Edmund, 18
Huxley, Aldous, 49, 53, 109, 208, 309; *Brave New World*, 49, 109
Huxley, Thomas, 87, 205; *Evolution and Ethics*, 87, 205
hyperdimensionality, 68

identity politics, 256
ideology, 40, 67–68, 110–111, 114–115, 122, 129, 170, 187, 194, 197, 202–203, 207, 214, 216, 229, 231–232, 236, 290
inclusive otherness, 269
informatics, 113–114, 273

intuitive/counterintuitive knowledge, 8, 43–45, 52, 63–64
investigative journalism, 36
invisible visibility, 19, 64

Jameson, Fredric, 64–65, 202, 205; *The Antinomies of Realism*, 64
Jiang Bo, 4
Jiang Yunsheng, 111
Jiao Juyin, 71
Jin Yong (Louis Cha Leung-yung), 121
Jobs, Steve, 39
Journey to the West, 209; Xuanzhuang, 209
Joyce, James, 92
Jung, Carl, 178; collective subconscious, 178

Kafka, Franz, 92; Kafkaesque, 36, 164, 189
Kang Youwei, 205
Kant, Immanuel, 90, 118, 131, 137, 249; feeling of the sublime, 118; judgment, 131; *mysterium tremendum et fascinans*, 118; transcendentalism, 137; tradition, 137
karma, 171, 196
Kirsch, Adam, 252–253
Klein bottle, 38, 303
Kōbō, Abe, 53,
Komatsu, Sakyo, 112
Kubrick, Stanley, 262

La La, 228, 234–236; "The Radio Waves That Never Die," 234–235
Lacan, Jacques, 17–18; the Real, 17; "purloined letter," 17
Lang, Fritz, 261
Lao She, 109, 206, 240, 309; *Cat Country*, 109, 206
Larbalestier, Justine, 290; battle of the sexes, 290
late Qing Shanghai, 105
Le Guin, Ursula, 242, 274–275, 282, 284; *The Dispossessed*, 242; *The Left Hand of Darkness*, 274

Lee Kai-Fu, 252–253
Lee, Tsung-Dao, 93
Leibniz, Gottfried Wilhelm, 66, 299–300
Lem, Stanisław, 53
Li Hongwei, 41; *The King and Lyric Poetry*, 41
Li Yuanchao, 307
Liang Qichao, 32, 78–79, 105–106, 205, 211–212, 225, 229; *Future of New China*, 32, 211, 225; *kexue xiaoshuo*, literally "scientific fiction," 106; new fiction, 51, 106
Liang Qingsan, 105; *From The New Daily News: Mechanical Wonders*, 105; *From The New New News: Metropolitan Phantoms*, 105; The Lone Fisherman on a Cold River (Huangjiang Diaosou), 105
Liao Shubo, 277
Liao Weitang, 41
Lin Shu, 79
Ling Chen, 4, 112, 276, 293
literal/literalness, 45, 61–64, 95, 97, 100, 126, 132, 137, 138, 142, 158, 166, 175, 183, 232
Liu Cixin, 3–7, 9–10, 12, 15–16, 21–22, 29–35, 41, 44, 47–48, 51, 60–61, 70, 74, 88–89, 93, 102–104, 112–115, 116–159, 164–165, 168–170, 175, 182, 191, 199–200, 202, 214–217, 228, 234, 239, 247, 249–251, 254, 255, 257, 259–260, 266–268, 272, 274, 276, 278, 286–290, 306–308, 310, 312; *Ball Lightning*, 123
—*China 2185*, 29–34, 122, 124, 215, 217, 307; Huaxia Republic, 31–33; Da Liu, 121; Ding Yi, 124, 260; "Hearing the Right Way in the Morning," 124; "Man and Devourers," 150; macro detail, 132–134, 137–138, 152, 156, 158–159, 164–165, 168–169; "Mountain," 43, 45–46, 48, 50–51, 74, 132, 139–140, 254; poetic heart, 118, 132, 156, 159, 199, 269, 288, 295

Liu Cixin (*continued*)
—"Poetry Cloud," 118, 131, 134, 139–140, 202; Li Bo, 131, 133

Remembrance of the Earth's Past, 118, 132, 139, 155–156, 159; *Supernova Era*, 30, 139; "The Collapse of the Cosmos," 123; "The End of the Microscopic," 123, 126; "The Micro Era," 120–121, 135, 140, 120; "The Sun of China," 216

—The "Three-Body" trilogy, 3, 5, 9, 16, 44–46, 88, 103, 116, 121–123, 135, 139, 147, 158, 168, 215, 217, 239, 250, 254–255, 286–287, 308, 310; Alpha Centauri, 117, 142; amoral universe, 119, 140, 144, 154, 216, 288; Battle of Darkness, 149; Cheng Xin, 153–156, 159, 269, 287–288; cosmic sociology, 144; *Death's End*, 3, 9, 46, 116, 122, 125, 132, 139, 145, 217, 255, 257, 259, 288–289; dual-vector foil, 117; Doomsday Battle, 148–149; droplet, 89, 148, 260; "First Man," 146; Guan Yifan, 136, 151, 154; Luo Ji, 144–147, 149, 151, 153–154, 216, 286, 288; Singer, 116–120, 132, 137, 141, 151–152, 260, 269, 288–289; Sophons, 135–136; Star-Plucker, 116–121, 142, 260; Starship Earth, 103, 147–151, 202; Starship Earth civilization, 148; Swordholder, 145–146, 153–154, 287; Swordholder Deterrence, 151; *The Dark Forest*, 3, 139, 144, 255–256, 286, 289; *The Three-Body Problem*, 3, 10, 43, 102, 139–141, 143, 150, 255–256, 259, 278; three-body movement, 139; technological explosion, 144, 147; Trisolarans, 102, 117, 135, 140–143, 145, 148, 153, 157, 216, 259, 286; Trisolaran civilization, 139, 142, 156; Trisolaris, 143, 153, 155; two-dimensionalization, 137–138, 148, 289; Wallfacer, 120–122, 141, 145–146, 148, 216, 286, 288; Ye Wenjie, 117, 141–144, 154, 216, 287, 289; Yun Tianming, 156–159, 228; Zhang Beihai, 148–151, 154; Zhuang Yan, 286–287

—"The Village Schoolteacher," 130–131, 139; cosmic divine comedy, 130

"The Wandering Earth," 126, 139–140, 306–307; "The Western Ocean," 175; "To Joy," 118, 132, 139

Liu Wenyang, 4

Liu Xingshi, 111

Liu Yang, 12

Liu, Ken, 10, 239, 255–256, 297

Lo Yi-chin, 13, 41, 228, 249–251, 284, 310; *Daughter*, 249; hole, 252; *Mingchao*, 228, 249–251; Ming Dynasty, 175, 250–251; *Superman Kuang*, 228, 249; surface world, 251; tomorrow, 237, 251

Lovecraft, H. P., 164, 177–179, 302; Cthulhuian mythological world-building, 166; "The Call of Cthulhu," 177

Lu Shi'e, 229; *New China*, 229

Lu Xun, 6, 10–11, 26–29, 37, 47–48, 62, 74–104, 109, 120–121, 130–131, 150, 161, 163, 164, 169–173, 175–176, 179, 185, 187–190, 199–200, 213–214, 230, 232, 283, 286, 298, 309; "Adventures at the North Pole," 80; "A Madman's Diary," 47–48, 75, 77–78, 84–86, 90–91, 94–96, 98–103, 130, 161, 171, 173, 175–176, 187, 199, 283, 286; divine thought, 91; "In Memoriam," 298; "Inscriptions on the Tomb," 26, 179; iron house, 6, 85, 104, 120, 130, 171–172, 187, 189, 192, 198, 214; "Kong Yiji," 101; "Lessons from the History of Science," 90; literary legacy, 6; Lu Xunsque, 11, 62, 109, 170; Mr. Fujino, 89–90

—"New Year's Sacrifice," 102, 104; Xianglin's Wife, 102, 104

"Old Chinese Tales Retold," 76; "On Radium," 92; "On the Power of Mara Poetry," 91; Sendai Medical Academy, 89; Suozi (penname), 76, 80; "The Art of Creating Humanity," 76, 80, 84; *The Grave*, 27; "The History of Man," 90; translation, 6, 76, 78–84, 91; *Wild*

Grass, 101, 170–171; Zhijiang Suozi (pen name), 76; Zhou Shuren, known as, 76, 96–97
literary legacy, 6; translation, 6, 76, 78–84, 91
Lucian of Samosata, 47; "A True History," 47–48
Lundström, Lars, 262

Ma Boyong, 4, 241, 256; "The City of Silence," 241, 256
Machiavellianism, 146
Mannheim, Karl, 202, 206
Mao Dun, 58, 109
Mao Zedong, 31–34, 93, 109–111, 119–120, 127, 141–143, 145, 147, 188, 194, 202, 205–206, 208–211, 214–221, 223, 225–226, 234, 236–240; specter of, 34, 220; vision of permanent revolution, 32, 141, 147, 208
Martin, George R.R., 255
Martinsen, Joel, 255
Matrix, The, 44, 307
Maxwell, James Clerk, 293
May Fourth Movement, 98; literary tradition, 58, 78
McEwan, Ian, 55
megatext, 45–46, 73, 254
melancholia, 28–29, 73, 192, 246
Menippean satires, 49, 52, 54
Mercier, Louis-Sébastien, 204; *L'An 2440*, 204
Merleau-Ponty, Maurice, 18; Chiasm, 18, 26, 42, 77, 135, 165; *The Visible and the Invisible*, 18
metafiction, 9, 54–55, 60, 158, 198, 248
metaphor/metaphorical, 56, 60–64, 84–86, 91, 97–98, 114, 119–120, 126, 130, 134, 150, 157–158, 166, 170–172, 183–185, 187–188, 191, 198, 213–214, 232, 247, 249–250, 262, 270, 295, 298, 300
metaphysical fluidity of ideas, 126
metatext, 35, 38, 45–46, 48, 157, 254

metaverse, 10, 19, 68
metonym, 56, 60, 243–244
Middle Kingdom (China), 5, 109, 208, 231, 255, 265
Miéville, China, 257
Mill, John Stuart, 206
Milton, John, 259, 263, 283–285; *Paradise Lost*, 283–285
mimesis, 11, 42, 44, 48–49, 52, 57–58, 60, 67, 102; high-intensity, 57, 60; mimetic mode of representation, 114
Mitchell, David, 64–65, 253, 257, 262; *Cloud Atlas*, 64–65, 253, 262, 307
Mo Yan, 1, 2, 4, 267–268; *Life and Death Are Wearing Me Out*, 267
Möbius time-space, 12
Monster Hunt, 273
More, Thomas, 49, 50, 202, 204, 226, 258; *Utopia*, 49, 50
Mu Ming, 12, 277, 296
multiverse, 19, 22, 68, 115, 128
Murakami, Haruki, 284
mythology, 54, 82, 94, 107, 162–163, 169, 172–174, 176–178, 180–181, 199; of the chthonic, 160, 162–163, 180; Cthulhu, 178

Nebula Award, 223
Neo-Baroque, 17, 46, 65–68, 70–71, 251, 253, 262, 270, 282, 296, 300, 310; aesthetics, 67, 300
neoclassicist, 124
neonationalism, 40, 70; "Industrial Party," 122; neoauthoritarianism, 40
netizen communities, 9
New China, 23, 32, 204, 212, 225, 238, 240
New Culture Movement, 77, 98; New Culturalists, 85, 93
New Left/New Leftist, 149, 201
new physics, 22, 87, 92–93, 102
Newton, Isaac, 21, 50–51, 66, 87, 90–92, 128, 130–131, 135, 160; Newtonian mechanics, 91; Newtonian universe, 21, 87, 91–92

New Wave, 1–2, 6, 8–17, 19–21, 23–24, 26, 28–30, 35–36, 38–42, 45–46, 54, 58–61, 64–68, 70, 76–77, 101–104, 108–109, 112, 113–115, 121, 139, 151, 163, 170, 186, 202–203, 206, 211, 214–215, 221, 226, 233–234, 249, 252–275, 276, 282, 284, 286, 293, 303, 308, 310; allusion to Lu Xun's images, 6, 29; Anglo-American new wave, 10, 284; Chinese new wave SF, 11, 15–16, 45, 65, 77, 103, 249, 254, 286; experimental metafiction, 54; French New Wave (nouvelle vague), 15
New World, 50
New Youth, 85, 87, 94, 99
Ni Kuang, 110; Wei Sili, 110
nihilism, 171
nirvana, 191, 194, 196
nonbinary, 12, 17, 21, 23, 46–47, 58, 68, 70–72, 74, 77, 101, 169, 195, 227, 269, 272–274, 277–279, 280–304, 309, 312; nonbinary coexistence, 169; nonbinary posthuman universe, 12
nostalgia, 65, 102, 234, 237, 246–247, 254
nothingness, 26–27, 29, 102, 152, 167, 181, 183, 186, 191, 199, 291
nova, novum, 8, 24, 45, 56, 57, 95, 107, 231, 235, 252, 297

Obama, Barack, 255, 308
"obsession with China" (C. T. Hsia), 119
Olympic Games (Beijing, 2008), 226, 229, 231, 239
Orwell, George, 49, 53, 142, 147, 206, 208, 232, 241–242; *Nineteen Eighty-Four*, 49, 208, 241,
other/otherness, 23, 227–228, 243–244, 251, 261, 269, 273, 275, 310
Ouyang Jianghe, 41
Ozaki, Yukio, 106

pandemic, 12, 17, 53, 70, 104, 226, 244, 260, 271, 278, 309–312
Pan Haitian, 4

Panglossianism, 29, 203, 205; dream, 29, 151; optimism, 162
Peking University, 10, 93, 293
Peng Simeng, 12, 277, 296, 301, 309, 312; "Beast Boxing," 301; "Chronicle of the Sinking Boat," 301; "Secretion," 301, 309
Penley, Constance, 3
Penrose, Roger, 22
People's Literature, 10
People's Republic, 12, 93, 109, 220–221
Petöfi, Sándor, 309,
phenomenological seeing, 18
Picasso, Pablo, 92
Ping Lu, 269; "Taiwan Miracle," 269
Planck, Max, 91–93, 103; black-body radiation, 92
planetary consciousness, 67, 226, 278; novel, 55
Plutarch, 47
poetics of the invisible, 7–8, 13, 14–42, 74–75, 164; invisible truth, 11, 28, 44, 72, 100, 124, 128, 230, 312
point of difference, 107, 211
popular science, 21, 127, 308
post-anthropocentrism, 23, 254, 272, 289, 310; attitude of, 23
postcolonial/postcolonialism, 55, 175, 261–262, 273
postgender, 290
posthuman, 12–13, 16–18, 23, 27, 29–30, 32–33, 39, 53, 55, 60, 65, 68, 103, 114–115, 120–121, 148, 150, 152, 159, 161–162, 165, 171–172, 175–176, 179, 182, 188, 192, 199, 202, 206, 234, 236–237, 247–249, 252–254, 257–258, 262–263, 265–274, 278–279, 283, 288, 291, 293, 295–296, 299, 309–311; apocalypse, 268; estrangement, 33; identity, 266; image, 53, 177, 254, 267–269; narrative, 13, 273, 283; predicament, 253; revelation, 266; revolution, 266; subversion, 13; universe, 12, 152, 159
postmodernism, 54, 56, 64, 66, 247, 273
pragmaticism, 231

Proust, Maucel, 18, 92, 118
Ptolemaic system, 50, 299
Pynchon, Thomas, 53–54, 284

Qi Yue, 4
Qian Lifang, 4, 276
Qian Xuantong, 85, 94
Qian Xuesen, 59
Qing Dynasty, 8
quantum theory, 87, 93; quantum aesthetics, 46; quantum computing, 22, 281
queerness, 284
"quest for reality," 206

realism, 2, 6, 10, 13, 16, 18, 21, 42, 44, 46, 52–55, 57–61, 64–65, 67, 74, 77, 88–90, 94–95, 98–102, 104, 109, 113, 119, 124–125, 129, 132, 197, 203, 284, 297; canonical, 99; classical literary, 42; conventional, 21, 57, 60–61, 125; critical, 58, 101; fictional, 6, 58; hyperrealism, 60, 63; literary, 2, 18, 42, 46, 53, 58–59, 61, 77, 95, 98, 100–102, 104, 109; mimetic, 10, 13, 16, 21, 42, 46, 61, 64–65, 67, 94, 100; naturalistic, 109; neorealism, 124; objective reality, 42, 65; SF reality, 60–61; science fictional realism (SF realism), 58–61, 197; scientific, 88–90; Tolstoian realism, 124
Red Classics, 234–235, 237
Red Guards, 38, 141, 183, 215
"Red Songs," 236–237
Reform Era (of the 1980s), 2, 8, 93, 110–112, 115, 181, 222–223, 234; China's early Reform Era, 8, 111–112
regendering, 288
Renaissance, 51, 55, 153, 262
Republican Revolution, 97
Revolution in Fiction, 78–79, 106
Rhapsody of the Ming Tombs Reservoir, 110
Ricoeur, Paul, 202
Roberts, Adam, 47–48, 52, 284
Robinson, Kim Stanley, 255
robotics, 21, 257,

Romanticism, 83, 102, 258, 288, 291
Roston, Murray, 51; *Milton and the Baroque*, 51
Rousseau, Jean-Jacques, 160, 258
Ruiz, Raúl, 66–67
Russ, Joanna, 282
Russian school of formalism, 55

Said, Edward, 261; democratic version of humanism, 261
Saramago, José, 284
scar literature, 59, 141
Schmitt, Carl, 149, 310; state of exception, 149, 310, 311
Scholes, Robert, 45, 56
Schrödinger's cat, 72
Schwartz, Benjamin, 88
science fiction: grotesque, 168; in Hong Kong, 13, 41, 110, 228, 247–249; inversion of the sublime, 168; as a method, 46, 74, 303; soft, 127, 129, 156, 276, 293; in Taiwan, 13, 41, 111, 228, 249–251, 257, 269–272; wonder, 35, 168
science fiction under socialist regime, 108, 110; *kexue huanxiang xiaoshuo*, 110
science fictionality, 41–42, 56, 60–61, 78, 84, 134, 158, 198, 248
Science Fiction Studies, 255
Science Fiction World (SFW), 24, 277
Science Literature, 112
scientific discourse, 21, 40, 59, 61, 63, 91, 104, 126
scientific modernity, 82
scientific optimism, 81, 127
Scientific Revolution, 43, 51–53, 87, 114,
scientific romance, 47, 53
scientific speculation, 49, 91, 94, 125–126, 129, 199
scientism, 40, 82, 124, 127, 131, 164, 169; relationship to humanism, 131
sentimental romanticism, 291
separationism, 70
Shanghai Literature, 277

368 INDEX

Shanhaijing, 107
Shelley, Mary, 47, 53, 83, 258–259, 262, 283–285; *Frankenstein*, 47, 53, 83, 258–259, 261–264, 283–285, 292; *The Last Man*, 53
shengshi or Pax Sinica, 224, 229–233, 239
She-SF, 46, 71, 275, 276–279, 293, 300, 303
Shuangchimu (Feng Yuan), 12, 70–72, 74, 277, 296, 299–300, 309, 312; "On Foot I Had to Walk Through the Solar Systems," 299–300, 309; "The School of Lynx," 299; "The Solar Studio: Seagull," 68–74, 299–300, 309
simulacrum, 131, 188, 265
singularity, 3, 5, 28, 45, 199, 234, 250, 262, 266, 274, 301
Sinophone, 13, 228, 245–251, 267–268, 278, 284, 296
Sinotopia, 11, 39, 60, 164, 197–198, 208, 225–229, 237, 240–241, 245, 251, 268, 278
Snow, Edgar, 209–211; *Red Star Over China*, 209; *Xixing manji*, 209
social Darwinism, 88–89, 145–146, 288
Södergran, Edith, 299
soft science fiction (soft SF), 127, 129, 156, 276, 293
Solvay Conference (1927), 91
space opera, 114, 124, 255, 259; space saga, 5, 88, 114, 124, 134, 138, 141, 217, 242, 286
spaceships, 12, 126, 136, 195, 236–237, 280–282, 299, 305, 308
speculative literature, 11, 14, 18–19, 21–22, 44, 48, 50, 55–56, 65, 99–101, 118, 122, 126, 128, 134, 138, 140, 143, 164, 202, 251, 283, 294, 310, 312; fiction, 11, 55
Spencer, Herbert, 88, 120
Spielberg, Stephen, 262; *E.T.*, 47, 262; *Jurassic Park*, 47, 290
spiritual pollution, 6, 112, 114, 215; anti-Spiritual Pollution Campaign, 215
Star Trek, 54
Star Wars, 47, 54, 112
steampunk, 105, 235, 294
Stravinsky, Igor, 92

Strong, Louise Jackson, 80; "An Unscientific Story," 80, 82–86
structural fabulation, 45, 56
Su Tong, 2
sublime aesthetics, 251; astronomical detail, 170; cosmic sublime, 119–120, 122, 138, 165, 216–217, 224; Kantian sublime, 137; Maoist sublime, 217; sublime cosmos, 132, 147, 156, 191, 199, 254, 288; sublime invisible, 138
subversion, 4, 12–14, 24, 39, 54, 99, 109, 166, 168, 197, 202, 205, 272, 312
subversive force of SF, 10, 113
Sun Yat-sen, 205
superstring multiverse, 22, 115; superstring theory, 128, 135
survivalism, 120
Suvin, Darko, 55–58, 205; *The Metamorphosis of Science Fiction*, 55
Swift, Jonathan, 49; *Gulliver's Travels*, 49

Tales of the Moon Colony, 105
Tan Sitong, 105; *ren* (benevolence), 105
Tang Fei, 12, 277, 296–298, 309, 312; "Broken Stars," 297; *Odyssey(cy)ber*, 296–297, 309; "Spore," 297–298, 312; "Summer Cicada," 297; "The Heart of the Museum," 297; "Yellow Story" (a.k.a. "Call Girl"), 297
trans-species kinship, 12; in Shuangchimu, 299–300
technocracy, 120, 122, 129, 202–203, 211; technocratic society, 149
technological optimism, 106, 202
technological singularity, 274
technologism, 27, 122, 288
teleology, 40, 65–66, 110, 177, 191, 273; of historical narrative, 177
textual labyrinth, 184; labyrinthine narrative, 168, 186, 196, 228, 249; textual inferno, 196
Tezuka, Osamu, 262
Tiananmen Incident, 24; student protest in Tiananmen Square, 30, 113
tianxia, 201

INDEX 369

Tides of Zhejiang (magazine), 76
Tolstoy, Alexei, 209; *Aelita: Queen of Mars*, 209
Tolstoy, Leo, 124; *War and Peace*, 124
Tong Enzheng, 110–111; "Death Ray on a Coral Island," 111
trans-anthropocentric posthumanism, 33
transgression, 23, 67, 174, 228, 249, 269, 273, 291
translatability, 256–257
translations as rewritings, 79
transnational configuration, 259
Travels of Marco Polo, 212
truth-claiming discourse/storytelling/speculation, 11, 13, 16, 20, 22, 24, 35–36, 38–40, 42, 44–46, 48–52, 62, 64–65, 87, 91–92, 94, 95–96, 100–104, 109, 117–118, 123, 125–126, 128–129, 132, 134, 155, 157–159, 164, 169–170, 172, 174, 177, 185, 187–200, 228, 232–233, 241, 244–245, 248–249, 251, 273–274, 286, 304, 306, 309–310, 312
Turing, Alan, 22
Turing Test, 278

uchronia, 204–205, 240
utopia, 19, 31, 23, 24, 32–34, 39–40, 49–50, 55, 67, 79, 103, 105–107, 114–115, 117, 119–120, 123, 131–132, 141, 147, 151, 161, 163, 180, 187, 194, 201–224, 226–236, 238–243, 255, 258, 260–262, 269, 284, 309, 311; utopianism, 21, 23, 34, 40, 83, 106, 114, 120, 123, 151, 201–206, 208, 215, 217, 219, 226, 234, 260; humanism versus totalitarianism, 147; one-state utopia, 234; political utopianism, 106, 202; utopian impulse, 23, 117, 205, 218–220, 227, 234, 241, 260–261, 309; *wutuobang*, 205
utopia/dystopia dualism, 229
utopian/dystopian variations, 21, 23, 123, 203, 206, 214–215, 232–233

Valéry, Paul, 18
Verne, Jules, 6, 53, 76, 79, 83, 106–107, 259, 261, 284; *A Journey to the Center of the Earth*, 76; *Around the World in 80 Days*, 106; *From the Earth to the Moon*, 76
VFX, 305
virtual/virtuality, 8, 11, 17, 20, 23, 31–34, 54, 60, 63–64, 68, 73–74, 76, 85, 101–102, 117, 125, 126, 131, 134–135, 138, 152, 156–159, 161–163, 167, 174, 180, 188, 192–193, 195, 197–198, 207, 212, 232–234, 240, 244, 246–248, 250–251, 264–266, 287, 303, 304, 311; virtual form of storytelling, 159
virtual reality (VR), 10, 17, 22, 31, 54, 63, 76, 101–102, 135, 192, 301
visible invisibility, 21, 23, 28, 135–138
Voltaire, 50, 205; *Candide*, 205; *Micromégas*, 50
Vonnegut, Kurt, Jr., 54

Wagner, Rudolf, 112; Chinese SF as lobby literature, 112
Wall Street Journal, 255
Wang Anyi, 2, 41; *Anonymity*, 41
Wang Ao, 41
Wang, David Der-wei, 10, 28, 59, 77, 91, 151, 155, 169, 205, 240; "From Lu Xun to Liu Cixin," 10; repressed modernities, 77
Wang Jinkang, 4, 7, 9, 114, 214, 217–222, 228, 234, 267–268, 276, 278
—*Ant Life*, 217–221; altruistic element, 218; Yan Zhe, 218–220
Escaping the Mother Universe, 217; *Father Heaven and Mother Earth*, 217; *The Crystal Egg of the Universe*, 217
—"The Reincarnated Giant," 221, 268; Jinbei Wuyan, or Imagai Nashihiko, 222; *zengzhang* (growth), 222
"To Live" trilogy, 217–218
Wang Kanyu, 12, 277, 296, 301–303, 309, 312; *Cloud Mist*, 302; "Seafood Restaurant," 302–303; *Seafood Restaurant*, 301, 309
Wang Nuonuo, 277
Wang Weilian, 41
Wasserstrom, Jeffrey, 208
wave-particle duality, 72–73, 290

Way Spring Arrives and Other Stories, The, 278
Wei Yahua, 111–112; "Conjugal Happiness in the Arms of Morpheus," 112
Wells, H. G., 20, 53, 71, 83, 104, 259–260, 284; *The Invisible Man*, 83; *The Island of Dr. Moreau*, 83; *The Time Machine*, 71, 83; *War of the Worlds*, 259–260
Westworld, 44, 262
white hole, 199
Women's World (magazine), 80–81
Woolf, Virginia, 92, 280, 285; *Orlando*, 280, 285
world-building, 6, 15, 18, 22, 24, 31, 33–34, 44–46, 49–50, 64, 74, 100, 102, 118, 122–123, 128, 133–134, 140–141, 143, 162, 164–165, 170, 171, 179, 198, 202, 204, 234, 249, 270, 288, 294, 300; mimetic reflections of reality, 128; speculative possibilities, 128
World Expo (Shanghai, 2010), 226, 229, 231
world literature, 46, 86, 254–259, 307, 310
world science fiction/world SF, 54, 83, 147, 255, 261, 308
World War II, 54, 192–193
worlding, 18–19, 73–74, 125, 128, 306
Wu Jianren, 106–107, 229; Civilized Realm, 107; Jia Baoyu, 107, 127; Lao Shaonian, 107; *New Story of the Stone*, 107, 229
Wu Ming-yi, 13, 257, 272; *Land with Little Rain*, 272; *The Man with the Compound Eyes*, 272
Wu Shuang, 277
Wu Ta-You, 93
Wu Yan, 4, 112, 282–283, 286

Xi Jinping, 193, 245
Xia Jia, 4, 276–277, 293–296
—"A Hundred Ghosts Parade Tonight," 295; Ning Caichen, 295; Nie Xiaoqian, 295
A Summer Beyond Your Reach, 294; "A Time Beyond Your Reach," 294; "Night Journey of the Dragon-Horse," 294–295;

porridge science fiction (porridge SF), 293; "The Demon-Enslaving Flask," 293–294
Xia Yuanli, 93; "Quantum Theory," 93; "Theory of Relativity," 93
Xia Zengyou, 78, 93
Xiao Jianheng, 111
Xing He, 4
Xinhua News Agency, 11, 164
Xu Nianci, 106
Xue Shaohui, 106

Yan Feng 3, 5
Yan Fu, 78, 87–89, 93, 205; *Tianyanlun*, 87–89, 205
Yan Lianke, 65, 267, 268; mythorealism, 65
Yang, Chen-Ning, 93
Ye Yonglie, 110–111, 215; *Little Smartie Travels to the Future*, 111
Yeats, W. B., 92
Youth Literature, 297
Yu Chen, 278
Yu Hua, 2, 4, 267–268; *The Seventh Day*, 268

Zamyatin, Yvegeny, 53
Zhai Yongming, 41
Zhang Ran, 4
Zhao Haihong, 4, 228, 234–236, 276, 293; "1923: A Fantasy," 234–235; "The Undying Spring," 293
Zheng, Egoyan, 13, 254, 270–272, 309; "Say I Love You Once More," 271; *The Dream Devourers*, 270; *Zero Degree of Separation*, 271, 309
Zheng Wenguang, 58–59, 110–112; "The Mirror Image of the Earth," 112
Zhou Wen, 277
Zhou Zuoren, 47, 80–81, 98; "Humane Literature," 98; Lady Pingyun (pen name), 81
Zhuangzi, 107, 119, 174, 180, 183, 194
Žižek, Slavoj, 265

GPSR Authorized Representative: Easy Access System Europe, Mustamäe tee 50, 10621 Tallinn, Estonia, gpsr.requests@easproject.com

www.ingramcontent.com/pod-product-compliance
Lightning Source LLC
Chambersburg PA
CBHW031230290426
44109CB00012B/232